INTERSUBJECTIVE EXISTENCE

Intersubjective Existence

A Critical Reflection on the Theory and Practice of Selfhood

OLIVA BLANCHETTE

Edited by Cathal Doherty

The Catholic University of America Press
Washington, D.C.

The paper used in this publication
meets the minimum requirements of
American National Standards for Information Science—
Permanence of Paper for Printed Library Materials, ANSI Z39.48-1984

Cataloging in Publication Data is available from the Library of Congress
ISBN: 978-0-8132-3467-0 | eISBN: 978-0-8132-3468-7

Printed in the United States

Book design by Burt&Burt
Interior set with Minion Pro and Meta Pro

Contents

PART I

Critical Reflection on Theory of Selfhood

Introduction

Our aim in this essay is to develop and articulate a certain wisdom about human life, a theory of selfhood, so to speak, based on a systematic inquiry into what we call human existence, to be followed by a reflection on what is called for in the practice of human existence in keeping with its ethical exigencies.

Etymologically, the term *philosophy* suggests an idea of love of wisdom. Apart from other considerations, such as academic course requirements, it is a love, or a desire for wisdom, that brings us to philosophy, and in some sense, every human being has a love or a desire of this sort. Everyone wants to know what human life is all about. Hopefully, it is from such a personal desire in each and every one of us that this essay begins, a desire to know more about ourselves and about what we desire as human beings, so that we may live more fully in this world as human beings. More is at issue here than simply fulfilling an academic requirement.

Wisdom, however, is a special kind of knowledge in that it tries to understand things as a whole. Thus, *wisdom about human life* will have to be understood as a kind of knowledge about *human life as a whole*. This is what will distinguish our philosophy of human existence from other kinds of knowledge about human life, such as biology, psychology, or economics.

Most of the sciences pursued in a university can be said to deal with human life in some way. But most of them deal with life or some aspect of it in a particular way and according to a particular discipline or method, not with the whole of it according to the whole. One thing that distinguishes philosophy from other disciplines is its attempt to deal with the whole of things as a whole. For us here, this means we will try to deal with the whole of human life as a whole.

This peculiarity of philosophy is what makes it especially difficult as a scientific discipline, but we shall try to meet the difficulty head on in a disciplined way, as every science tries to do.

But before we try to say how we shall proceed in this discipline, let us try to make sure we are clear about how the philosophy of life as a whole relates to the other sciences about living things and nonliving things, not to mention more specifically about rational animals and nonrational animals.

First, philosophy is *not separate* from those other more particular sciences, nor is it about a life other than the one in relation to the human being. It is about one and the same life, which they study just as we do, the one we experience as human beings in this world. In some way philosophy presupposes some acquaintance or some knowledge of these other more particular sciences. It is not a substitute for them. It has to integrate them into its understanding of the whole, though we may not have the time here to see how this is done in any great detail. Thus, whatever knowledge we may already have about human life from any of the particular sciences has to serve us well in our philosophy of human existence.

Second, philosophy is a necessary *complement* to the other sciences in the study of human life, to the extent that it tries to deal with the whole as a whole, while the other sciences can only deal with a part or deal with the whole in a partial way. Actually, there is a tendency in sciences like psychology, sociology, or economics to do as if they were dealing with the whole of human reality as a whole, as if they had an explanation for everything in human existence. They sometimes talk as if there were a psychological explanation, or a sociological explanation, or an economic explanation for everything in human life. To the extent that they try to do this, it is as if they were trying to take the place of philosophy or to ignore it, as if it were not a science in its own right as a whole. In other words, they cease to be particular sciences and become philosophies with a tendency to reduce the whole of human existence to their particular dimension, whether it be psychological, sociological, or economic. If they do this, they cease being good sciences, without becoming good philosophy, since they do not, as particular sciences, have a properly philosophical method, which is to deal with the whole precisely as a whole. We shall refer to this tendency in particular sciences as a kind of *reductionism* of the whole to a part; the part is studied in the particular science without consideration of any other part and much less of the whole.

This reductionist tendency in most of the particular sciences having to do with human life is indeed an indication of the need for a philosophical consideration of human existence. Even if it turns out that it is one of the particular sciences that gives us the ultimate understanding of human existence, the wisdom about human life as a whole, that will still have to be established philosophically, and that science will by that very fact become the philosophy of human existence. We sometimes find claims such as this in behaviorism, for example, or in Freudianism and Marxism, but such claims are usually not well established scientifically, as we shall have occasion to see.

The particular natural or social sciences are based on different considerations of different natural or social human activities. Psychology, for example, might focus on learning or copying activities, while biology focuses on life functions. Sociology might focus on different kinds of social relation, while economics focuses on the production and exchange of goods. There is a certain amount of overlapping between them, even though each has a method of its own, and all have something to say about human existence. Inasmuch as the philosophy of human existence also has to start from natural human activity, there is bound to be a connection between what we have to do in this philosophical science and any one or all of these particular natural and social sciences.

Here, however, we shall not start from any one of these particular sciences. This is why this essay should be thought of as a philosophy of human existence. We shall start from human existence as we come to know it spontaneously, as we experience it historically, and as we exercise it and bring it to life ourselves. We already know something about human existence as a whole. We have learned about it both personally and vicariously. Our aim here is not to call this knowledge into doubt. We wish only to develop it more precisely and more rigorously. We wish to extend it and make it more comprehensive, if need be, so that it will become more truly a wisdom about human life as a whole.

Our method will involve starting from the phenomenon of human life as a whole, as we experience it, and trying to formulate some of the principles on the basis of which we can come to our own critical conclusions and judgments in the theory and practice of selfhood or of human existence as a whole.

THE PHENOMENON OF HUMAN LIFE AS A WHOLE

GIVEN THE COMPLEXITY OF HUMAN EXISTENCE, it would seem useful to formulate some preliminary determinations of the phenomenon by what is called, in phenomenology, a sort of reduction of human life as a whole to some of its essential or dialectical structures.

This reduction can be done by trying to consider the phenomenon itself as a whole, independently of any particular content it may have at any given moment or in any given place. This sort of phenomenological reduction seeks to uncover or disclose the essence of human experience as such, whatever the content of any particular experience may be. It prescinds from any particular object in order to arrive at the intentional structure that makes any object an object of experience or of consciousness.

Such a reduction brings out a number of polarities in tension with one another within the phenomenon of human life as a whole:

A. The phenomenon of human life presents two *sides* or a twofold aspect:

- an outside, or *external*, aspect: human life is an adaptation to a global environment through experience. This aspect can be studied by observation. It is the expression of
- an inside, or *internal*, aspect: human life as a consciousness that makes experience possible as experience; for example, as in learning or in willing. This is something intentional that tends to realize itself through expression in an exterior and through a sort of assumption of what has been exteriorized back into the internal.

Note that everything about this polarization is real as well as ideal and not just ideal on one side, the interior, and real on the other side, the exterior, as many are inclined to say in their reductionist assessment of human consciousness, favoring only one side of consciousness at the expense of the other.

As an example of this polarity in tension, think of the connections between thinking and language, or of external actions as a test of sincerity in our intentions or in our respect for others. What we do in reality is an indication of where we stand with our ideas.

B. The phenomenon of human life entails two *poles* in dynamic interaction:

- a *subjective* pole: a conscious subject reacting to something other than itself, whether that something be another subject, an object, or the subject itself considered as another, as when I make myself the object of my observation;
- an *objective* pole: the-other-than-the-subject that can be viewed as the ensemble of stimulants that constitute a situation for the subject, or as the world of the subject with many different things in it and many inclinations corresponding to these stimulants.

Note that the consciousness of the subject somehow *encompasses* its world of objects as a whole at the same time as the world *contains* the consciousness. The two poles are somehow inclusive of one another and yet are irreducible to one another. There is an intentional or dialectical tension between the two. I am myself, a subject, only with reference to my world, which envelops me and is at the same time the world that also envelops other subjects such as myself.

Note also that this intentional tension is rooted in a *primordial unity*, the unity of "my world" or myself-in-this-world. This unity is primordial in the sense that it comes before any distinction of objects apart from one another and apart from the subject in the world and before the distinction of the subject from the objects of its experience as such, and in the sense that it remains immanent to all such distinctions. Consciousness is always "consciousness of ..." in a world of objects along with other subjects that have caught my attention. This is what philosophers have in mind when they speak of the intentionality of consciousness. As we enter this intentionality of consciousness, objects are always taken as objects *of* consciousness.

For example, think of your effort to pay attention to something, an object. The thing or the object of your attention has to be a part of your world, which implies an antecedent unity between the world and you. It has to be present for you to see it, but you wouldn't see it if you were not attentive to it or aware of it as you are aware of a friend in the world.

Think of your effort to form a habit as a performer in some human endeavor. In forming a habitual way of doing or performing certain kinds of acts, such as playing the piano or doing math, I am forming myself as a subject, but I am also running the risk of losing myself as a subject in this performance by falling into a rut of mindlessness about everything else in my life as a human being. My conscious effort leads to a kind of loss of consciousness, as when I act unthinkingly or without paying attention to what I have come to do only routinely. I can recuperate that act as *mine* but never effortlessly possess it as I do objects I acquire without any requirement of performance.

C. The phenomenon of human life has two interrelated *dimensions*:

- an *individual* dimension: myself as this-here and yourself as this-there, each an object of recognition and respect for one another, and for others as well, each a center of interests and initiatives;

- a *communal* dimension: the relatedness of myself and yourself to each other and to other selves through the things of the world, a relatedness proper only to selves, you, me, and other selves.

It is important to note how each of these two dimensions is found on either side of the two polarities already mentioned. It is not just the individual who has an inside and an outside. The communal does as well. A community has a spirit shared by more than one individual, and the individual who shares in that spirit internally is also recognized externally by others in the community. Nor does a community of subjects exist as purely spiritual, but it exists in a world of objects where the subjects figure prominently for one another as centers of attention and principles of order in a communal life.

D. The phenomenon of human life further distinguishes itself into two *levels of existence*:

- a *natural* level: myself and yourself, or the human community in general, who exist as given or as produced by the processes of nature, with all our natural endowment, which includes intelligence and will along with our senses and our emotions or affections.
- a *historical* level: myself and yourself, or our community, who exist as achieved or as produced by human culture through the initiative of human subjects exercising their intelligence and will creatively above and beyond the merely given of nature.

This fourth polarity includes a *temporal* dimension. Whatever is given to us by nature is given at a certain point in an evolutionary process. Whatever we initiate as cultivated and cultivating human beings appears as something original and revolutionary within this evolutionary process.

But such a temporal dimension was already implicit in the tension between the internal and the external and in the relation between the subjective and the objective aspects of human life. These two polarities, between the internal and the external and between the subjective and the objective, have to be understood as part of a sort of historical tension within human subjects and among them, or within communities.

Moreover, the distinction between the historical and the natural grows out of the distinction between the individual and the social since it is the social that enables us to speak of history as a whole, even though historical initiative does not take place except as individual.

This distinction between the historical and the natural further presupposes a certain freedom and transcendence in human action over merely natural processes, a freedom and transcendence that integrates the natural processes into its own higher unity as historically constituted in cultures.

But this is something we shall have to work out in our reflection on human existence as a whole, which is at once both historical and natural as well as social and individual, objective and subjective, external and internal. It is enough for the moment to have suggested something of these polarities in the phenomenon of human life as an indication of what the science of the phenomenon of human life as a whole has to contend with.

Keep in mind that when we speak of polarities here, we do not have in mind two extremes opposed to one another. Rather, we are thinking of two orders distinct from one another but interweaving with one another in the whole of one's human experience, complementing one another in our striving, not just for survival but for our own perfection as existing human beings.

THE SCIENCE OF THE PHENOMENON OF HUMAN LIFE AS A WHOLE

The sciences we spoke of earlier as particular can also be thought of as empirical in the sense that they proceed from observation of objects in experience to inferences about these particular objects. Philosophical science differs from these sciences not only in the sense that it is more universal, or about the whole as a whole, but also in the sense that its method is more reflective upon itself as an activity of the subject or, better still, an activity of the subjects in a community ready to discuss what it takes to bring human existence to perfection. As such philosophical science is not separate from any empirical science of the subject. On the contrary, it assumes what we come to know objectively in our empirical knowledge, but it treats this information in a more global human perspective that brings us back to what we are in our subjectivity.

If we think of this subjectivity as the soul, we can then think of this science of human life as a psychology, as Aristotle did. In Greek, the word for soul is *psyche* so that, etymologically speaking, "psychology" means discourse about soul. We are accustomed to thinking of psychology as empirical, but here we are trying to introduce the idea of psychology, or of science of the soul, as a more philosophical type of discourse; that is, as one more comprehensive and more reflective on the soul itself.

Thus, we can speak of our philosophical science as a science of the soul where, again in the language of Aristotle, the soul (or the psyche) is understood as *the principle of life in a body having life in potency.*[1] We shall have a lot more to say about this idea of soul as principle of life for a human being later on, but note how the definition as given could apply to any science of living things as living. However, since we shall be doing a philosophy only of human life or existence, we shall be developing a science only of the human soul and not of other souls as found in other animals or in plants. This will be an important distinction to keep in mind when we come to speak of the human soul later on.

Following Aristotle further, we could also define life as capacity for immanent operation, where immanent operation means an operation that remains in the being from which it proceeds as its perfection. Learning is such an operation, as

1 This is in reference to the beginning of Book II of the treatise *On the Soul (De Anima)*, where Aristotle is setting up the language he will use for his science of the soul, including that of the human being.

is acquiring a habit or a skill, both of which are internal to the human subject. We shall have a lot more to say about this later on.

For the moment, let us note that all definitions from the philosopher remain rather formal or abstract. How can they be made more concrete so that they can be made to serve as a method for developing our own science of the soul or of human life as a whole? It will be noted that *life* is spoken of as a capacity for operation or for activity, and *soul* is understood as principle of life and therefore of a certain kind of activity. To understand life we must therefore understand soul, the principle of life. But how do we come to know the soul? Do we have an immediate intuition of it, independently of its activity, or do we come to know it only through reflection on its activity?

There have been philosophers, such as Descartes, who claimed to have some sort of immediate purely internal intuition into their soul. But we make no such claim here. In fact, we shall argue that there is no such immediate intuition into what the soul is. The only claim we will make is that the soul can be known through its activity. Hence we shall proceed in a way similar to that of all the other sciences of human life: starting from the activities of life itself, not just by observation and inference but by internal reflection on our own intelligence and free will as well, and through these activities we shall reflect back into their principle, the soul, even as the form of its body.

Ours will not be a method of merely external observation and inference, as in a purely empirical science, although surely there will be a good deal of observation and inference. Nor will it be one of mere introspection, which is only another form of observation, turned inward, where a subject endeavors to observe itself, as one would an object, and record observations as would any other objective observer. Ours will be a method of reflection on one's very own proper activity as a human self. It will depend on how we experience ourselves when we experience other selves and other things in the world.

Every being has a proper activity of its own through which it can be known in its essence, whether it is conscious or not. But as a self-conscious being, the human being gives rise to an activity that includes a reflection upon itself. For example, when I think, I am conscious, not only of an object, which I am thinking about, but also of what it is to think. When I will something, I am conscious, not only of what I will, but also of what it is to will. Our method will be to insist upon this reflective knowing always at work in properly human activity in order to arrive at a better understanding of *what* the human being is as a whole.

There will be two parts to this philosophical science. The first will try to get at the human being in *what* it is in itself, or at how it is constituted in its essence, as the human being given in our experience. This will be the *theoretical*, or speculative, part of this science of human existence based on our own reflection of our immanent operation or proper activity as human beings. It will be followed by a second *practical* part whereby we consider *how* the human being has to act in the world of nature and of other human beings. This will be the more ethical part of our science in which we endeavor to be more prospective about what we are to do with our lives rather than just reflective on what we have already done.

In the theoretical part of our science we shall focus on what the human being is as what is revealed through its activity as found in our own experience, and then we will focus more on the activity itself as it proceeds from our being and brings it to a certain kind of fulfillment or to a second perfection of its own.

Here, in the theoretical part, our method will be circular in fashion, but the circle will not be vicious. It will be progressive and forward looking. It will be similar to the circle in any science, empirical as well as philosophical, which proceeds first by examining the activity of any being in order to know *what* it is and then develops its understanding of the activity itself on the basis of what the being has been discovered to be. In other words, we shall focus first on the nature of the soul for what it is as we reflect on its activity, and then we will examine this activity itself as it flows from the soul in its historical existence, or in its going out of itself into community and the world.

We shall make every attempt not only to clarify but also to justify our method along the way. But as we begin we should note that our attitude will be one of *exacting confidence* in the knowledge we already have of our being and in the desire for wisdom, or for a better knowledge of ourselves, as referred to previously, as a desire for wisdom about human life or existence as a whole—*confidence*, because we do not start by calling into doubt whatever truth we may have concerning the soul but by becoming conscious of the confusion of our ideas about the soul, its capacities, its durability, or whatever else we may think about it.

At the outset we acknowledge the reality of the life that ties us to one another in the world, as we saw in our preliminary determination of the phenomenon of human life as a whole, and we propose simply to attempt to clarify our understanding of this reality by trying to comprehend it in a systematic fashion or in the fashion of some scientific wisdom. Concretely, such an attitude comes down to paying careful attention to the life we are already actually leading. We may have to discuss and contend with one another about what this life really means, but the point will not be to gain the upper hand over anybody but, rather, to get whatever help we can in understanding for ourselves what human existence amounts to, even if it be from those who do not have the right idea of human existence.

We have to be exacting as well, because it is not easy to pay attention to the soul in an exact sense or in a scientific way. We can easily be distracted from the essential point of understanding human life as a whole into tangents that can confuse the part for the whole. It is also easy to jump to conclusions carelessly without proper understanding or without watching whether we have erred along the way, or to jump to practical applications before our theoretical understanding has been sufficiently elaborated.

It would be helpful to know something about how our wisdom about human life has been developed in the past in a long tradition going all the way back to the Greeks, to the Bible, and even to more primitive times, but we will not have time to explore any of this history of philosophical psychology in any detail.

Let it simply be noted in passing that a lot of our understanding and a lot of the language we use will be indebted to different parts of this tradition and the wise people who have furthered it along. We try to acknowledge some of this debt as we go along.

More specifically, our method consists of focusing on a series of headings designed to help us get at a closer scientific approximation of the various aspects of what it is to be human and what it is to act as human beings or as rational animals. The headings will be stated categorically, but they are not meant to be definitive. They are meant more as approximations to be discussed and to be modified if necessary as the investigation proceeds.

Ideally the discussion involves the participation of everyone ready to join in, either explicitly or implicitly, whether in silence or by jumping in, because it is for each one of us to develop our own wisdom about life as well as we can.

1

The Primordial Fact of Human Existence

We start our inquiry from the primordial fact of human existence in all its amplitude. It is in this fact that we find ourselves as human beings. We do not start from nothing or from an absence of human being as in beings that are nonliving, beings that are living but nonsentient, or beings that are sentient but nonrational. We start from beings we take to be human, which is to be the subject matter of our investigation, and we try to specify more precisely what it is that we are inquiring into. We all know what a human being is, but have we thought precisely enough about what makes such a being human, or a self, in a strict sense of the term?

In this question as to what a human being is, our attention is first brought to bear on ourselves, or on selfhood, which is at the core of what it is to exist for each one of us as a human being or as the center of interest for our science or our philosophy. Without some initial reflection on selfhood, there cannot be any science or philosophy of human existence as a whole.

This does not mean that we must take selfhood as isolated from everything else in experience, or from other selves that are also part or factors of our primordial experience of human existence as selves. The fact is that there is always some communion with other selves present in anyone's self-consciousness. And we must inquire as to how essential or necessary that communion is in the emergence and development of any self in its self-consciousness.

In *Phenomenology of Spirit*, as Georg Wilhelm Friedrich Hegel begins to think of spirit in human experience, he makes the point that there is no self-consciousness except in the presence of another self-consciousness.[1] Is this a necessary or essential factor in the primordial fact of human existence, along with the factor of self-consciousness itself, or is it just an incidental factor like so many others that may or may not come into play in the way one comes to one's self-consciousness

1 See the last paragraph of the Introduction to Hegel's long chapter 4 on self-consciousness, where he is very careful in lining up the problem that will occupy him for hundreds of pages more to get to the true spiritual meaning of human existence in religion.

in one part of the world or another? Could one come to human self-consciousness without ever encountering another self?

Finally, there is the factor of the world, or *a* world, for self-consciousness or for the plurality of self-consciousnesses in the presence of one another. Is that something we should take into account in exploring the primordial fact of human existence? If so, how is it a factor essential for understanding, not just self-consciousness, but any consciousness in lesser beings whether reflective or not, as in animals with merely sense consciousness and without rational consciousness?

Our purpose in opening this question of the primordial fact of human existence as a fact is not to explore all the presuppositions of this global fact of human being, nor to develop all its implications. Hopefully we will do more of that as we proceed with the further notions that we will draw from this fact. Our purpose here is only to focus on the global fact of human existence as clearly as we can and to formulate our comprehension of it in a general but inclusive way as the subject matter of our inquiry into human existence as a whole.

We start from more than just a bare statement of fact. We start with a reflection on what we take to be essential and necessary factors in the primordial fact of human existence and self-consciousness that will yield a better conception of what we have to deal with in this theory of selfhood.

Thus, there are three essential points to be called to our attention reflectively in this primordial fact of human existence: (1) the *self* as the center or the core of what it is to be a human being, (2) *communion* among selves from within this center or this core of selfhood, and (3) the *world* as the framework within which a self-consciousness comes to be in this communion of selves.

1.1 THE IDEA OR THE CONSCIOUSNESS OF SELFHOOD IN HUMAN EXISTENCE

1.1.1 We speak of ourselves as human beings to distinguish ourselves from the many other kinds of being we find in our experience of the world. This human being is to be the subject of our investigation. We do not include all human beings in our consideration, but we do include those who are at hand: you, me, and others around us whom we are conscious of as human beings. This is the kind of being to be understood here in our discourse, the specific kind of being designated as human.

What we take to be most specific about this being is that it is a self, what one refers to when one speaks of *oneself*. This self has also been referred to as the *I* or the *ego*, as the origin of my activity or my enduring, as when I say: I think, I feel, I wish, I will, I am hungry, I have a headache, et cetera.

With regard to acting and enduring, we speak of the self as a *subject* acting or taking action of one kind or another, or just enduring, and remaining the same in its identity as itself despite the dispersion of many sorts of action in time and space. We also speak of the self as a *person* finding and forming itself, becoming responsible for its actions and so on from childhood to adulthood.

Not every individual human being may be a fully developed self, but here we wish to focus on the human being as a self-conscious individual with at least some sense of identity of one's own and some experience of thinking and willing as we shall insist in the later part of our reflection. Other individuals with a less developed selfhood or very little sense of identity of their own, but who may still be of human nature, can be better understood starting from the more fully developed type or essence of the human being.

1.1.2 We shall see later why we start from selfhood in our critical reflection on what it is to be human. For the moment let us consider reflectively or be mindful of the evidence for thinking of the human being as first and foremost a self in its enduring identity in all the variety and diversity of its experiences and activities.

The evidence for this central factor of selfhood in our human consciousness is already at hand in the consciousness each one of us has of our own activity as our own and of our own being as our own. Each one of us has a self-consciousness of one sort or another, and the argument for affirming this factor of selfhood present in our experience as human beings exists in paying attention to or being mindful of the consciousness of ourselves that has been waxing and waning as part of our experience for some time and which we now have to attend to critically as real in the initiative we are taking to philosophize about selfhood.

There is no other way of discovering the self or oneself except through the reflective self-consciousness we must now attend to or be mindful of, not in someone else's experience, nor in some past experience still vivid in our mind or memory, but in the actual experience we are entertaining as we enter into this inquiry. What we are inquiring into is the actual exercise of this inquiring here and now, of which you or I cannot but be conscious as we begin this inquiry into selfhood.

This kind of paying attention, not to other things but to our own selves, can be called the act of reflection. Such an act of mindfulness is already implicit in such human activities as learning or loving, but the point here is to bring that act to the fore of our attention and to reflect not on things as given in experience, nor even on the self as a thing given in experience as psychologists usually do, but rather to reflect on the reflective act itself that constitutes the self as self-consciousness, as knowing itself in its acts.

At first this reflection may seem like a sort of bending of our attention from objects back inward into our own individual self, but that is not quite what it is. That would still be discovering myself only as an object or a thing given in experience, whereas in a proper act of self-conscious reflection I discover myself as a *subject*, as one who is active and self-conscious in the very act of discovering itself. I discover *myself* as the one who is discovering in the discovering.

This is not a discovering that takes place once and for all in one's life. It is a discovering that has its ups and downs in our experience, its highs and lows. Just to follow that discovering taking place in your life or in mine would take volumes. Novelists and dramatists are good at describing such moments of self-discovery or self-disclosure in their characters. But our task now is not to reconstruct any of these moments of self-discovery, fictitious or real-life, though we shall do some of that later. It is, rather, to begin with, to take cognizance of, not just the fact but the act in that fact, into which we must inquire, not in abstraction from your present experience of beginning to do a philosophy of human existence but with all the complexity of other factors that come into play for each one of us in this act at this moment.

What counts most for you here is how you become self-conscious in what you do or fail to do at this moment of beginning our inquiry, without prejudging what might be the outcome on the basis of any particular experiences or any of the particular sciences.

1.2 COMMUNION AS AN ESSENTIAL ELEMENT FOR ACTUAL SELF-CONSCIOUSNESS

In *Phenomenology of Spirit*, as we mentioned earlier, Hegel makes the point that there is no self-consciousness except in the presence of another self-consciousness. Is this just a matter of fact in human experience or is it a necessary or essential factor in the primordial fact of human existence, along with the factor of self-consciousness itself, so that if there were no communion, there would be no self-consciousness?

Is communion just an incidental factor like so many others that may or may not come into play in the way different selves come to their self-consciousness in one part of the world or another, or is it something essential in the very self-consciousness we are starting from, something necessary for there to be self-consciousness in any human being? Could there be a factor of self-consciousness in the primordial fact of human existence without a factor of communion among selves in that very fact of self-consciousness?

There are two ways of viewing this relation between self-consciousness and communion: first, as a simple matter of fact for any kind of human self-consciousness we know of and, second, as a matter of necessity for there to be authentically human self-consciousness of any kind.

1.2.1 Let us begin by reflecting on the evidence for the immediate communion among selves (or for intersubjectivity) as a matter of *fact* that can be found in our current experience by noticing the presence of others in the reflective activity of each and every one of us here and now as we begin this inquiry into human selfhood. Concretely, in this essay, we have been developing the notion of selfhood together. You have been present in my reflection and I have been present in your reflection. Each one of us has been attending to our own self-consciousness in the presence of one another in a way that we would not have done otherwise. The self-consciousness we are taking to be the matter of fact for us in this text is not some other self-consciousness we could otherwise imagine independently of this discussion, as when we read René Descartes's discourse on method. It is the self-consciousness that has been raised as a result of our coming together for this book, which is, de facto, a communion with one another.

Of course, this is not the first time any one of us has come to the kind of reflective self-consciousness we are referring to. There have been many other selves who have influenced us in our reflective selfhood and whom we have influenced in their reflective selfhood. But that has always taken place in the same way as we are influencing one another now in our reflective self-consciousness, either explicitly, as we are doing in this discussion, or implicitly in the way we are aroused to our self-consciousness by other self-consciousnesses, in our family life, in our schooling, in our enthusiasm for sports, in our memberships of all sorts. There is no human being of any age we know of who has come to some actual self-consciousness in isolation from other self-consciousnesses.

The kind of mutual influence and interdependence we are speaking of as communion begins long before we are even conscious of ourselves and never ceases even after we achieve a first-degree self-consciousness. In fact, the communion itself even affects the self-consciousness as such, since coming to self-consciousness in the presence of another self-consciousness includes an act of mutual recognition wherein I see the other precisely as other than myself and myself as other than the other self, and wherein the other self the other self sees itself no less as itself and other than myself and myself as other than itself.

Much of the communion we speak of as a simple matter of fact in our lives can be seen as casual, in contrast to moments when the communion with another is much more intense and formative for our own self-consciousness. But even casual communion remains as a factor affecting and effecting our self-consciousness, as we affect and effect the self-consciousness of others when they pay attention to us as selves.

1.2.2 Now, granting this pervasive fact of communion among human beings in their very self-consciousness, we are brought to the question of whether there must be communion for there to be self-consciousness as we know it reflectively. This question can be formulated in one of two ways.

First, is this interdependence constitutive of selves necessary in such a way that a human being would be inconceivable in its essence, except as in communion with other human beings, or is it merely incidental to human existence or to the essence of reflective self-consciousness, so that an individual could be self-consciously human in the absence of any other self-conscious individual, even though we know of no such case of self-consciousness in total isolation from any other?

Second, the question can be formulated in the terms we have just been using in our first point. Is the reflection into self possible without a prior act of mutual recognition with another self? Does one become oneself only in the presence of another who is also becoming themself, or can one become a self without ever encountering another self?

There are many ways in which human beings are tied to one another physically, biologically, psychologically, or economically, as demonstrated in the natural and social sciences. But the necessity of such ties among human beings is not the same as the necessity of communion we are reflecting on. Such ties are a necessity external to the self in its internal self-consciousness, to be taken into consideration in a philosophy of human existence, but not the one we are now inquiring into regarding the internal fact of human self-consciousness or the fact of internal human self-consciousness.

Either formulation of the question we are raising takes us far beyond the fact of biological, psychological, and economic necessity or interdependence that ties individual human beings together in nature and society. The fact of external interdependence is indisputable at all these levels of human experience. The human being is the neediest of animals. But the question remains for us: is human being communal merely as animal or is it communal precisely as human—that is, as rational, as free, as self-conscious?

We cannot fully answer this question without a fuller elaboration of the concept of selfhood, which we shall get to later, but we could look at some indications that would point to the idea that the communal dimension of selfhood is strictly necessary for the constitution of a human being on the internal level of self-consciousness as well as any other external level of human existence.

Let us think, for example, of the way an ancient poet speaks of a child coming to the consciousness of its mother and itself by a smile:

> Incipe, parve puer, risu cognoscere matrem:
> Matri longa decem tulerunt fastidia menses.
> Incipe, parve puer, cui non risere parentes,
> Nec Deus hunc mensa, Dea nec dignata cubili est.[2]

The poet speaks of ten months of long toil borne by the mother. He says also that if the parents had not smiled to the child, it would not have come to this divine state of partaking at the table and fitting into a social nest. On the other hand, we should note that the perception of a smile or the actual smile itself is something peculiarly human. Other animals do not smile, nor do they perceive smiles as such, whereas there is something divine or spiritual about the human smile.

Research has shown that cats, which have a vision six or seven times better than human vision, do not see human faces or cannot differentiate between them. At first, when human parents are beginning to smile at their newborn, the infant may still be like the cat, unable to differentiate the smiling face as such. But gradually, as the parents persist in smiling, the infant begins to perceive the difference and enter into it as something quite new and original, something divine, the poet suggests, by smiling in return. It begins to know its mother and communicate with her by a smile (*risu*), an act that characterizes it as human for the first time.

At the heart of this primordial human experience, the awakening of the child begins by a smile, there is a first smile of mutual recognition for both the child and the mother with one another. The question for us, as we reflect on this phenomenon of an infant coming to its first act of human self-consciousness, one that differentiates it from any other kind of animal, such as the cat, is: Whose smile? Is it that of the mother by herself, which has been there for so long, though unrecognized by the infant? Is it that of the child by itself, which is there now for the first time but

2 Virgil, *Bucolica*, Ecloga IV, ll. 60–63. The Loeb Classical Library has this translation:

Begin, baby boy, to know thy mother with a smile / to thy mother ten months have brought the weariness of travail. / Begin, baby boy! Him on whom his parents have not smiled, / no god honours with his table, no goddess with her bed!" Translated by H. Rushton Fairclough. Revised by G. P. Goold. Loeb Classical Library 63. Cambridge, Mass.: Harvard University Press, 1916.

which would have to be supposed as coming from nothing, no smile, in this first moment of recognition?

How could this incipient smile be that of the mother, if it has been there for so long before being recognized by the infant? How could it be that of the infant, if it has taken so long to recognize and to respond to the mother, by smiling back? What is there in this moment that makes the difference for these two individual self-consciousnesses so that they recognize one another in a way they have never done before? What is happening to make the world of difference there is between a smiling mother and her smiling infant that a cat will never see? Is it not the smile of both at the same time recognizing one another, wherein the child comes to consciousness of *itself* in the recognition of another self for the first time and in which the mother comes to new recognition of her infant as another self?

Think also of experience of feral children found in the wild, nurtured by wolves or other animals and apparently deprived, not only of human nurturing but even of smiling, from a very early age. Why is it so difficult for them to learn to communicate with other humans even though they have the organs of communication within them? What sort of consciousness do they come to, of themselves or of other selves? Is it ever a fully human consciousness, as for children who do not lose contact with human beings at a young age?

Think of the difficulty that comes from being deaf from birth and being closed off from all means of communication, of not being able to get beyond the smile of recognition because one cannot access the rest of the communication taking place through sound and the spoken word.

What happens to human consciousness then? What if there is no signing of any kind or only the most primitive kind of signing, apart from smiling? Is bare human contact enough to come to a full self-consciousness? Why did the family of Helen Keller think that she was perhaps intellectually disabled until some form of verbal communication was finally established with her with the intervention of Annie Sullivan?[3]

All of this points to some kind of necessity for communion with other selves to become fully a self in one's own self-consciousness, a necessity that is perhaps more fundamental than even reflection in the constitution of a self, a necessity without which there would not be any reflection into self.

We return to this question later, when we ask what makes communion among selves possible. For the moment it should be clear that communion with other

3 We refer here to the renowned drama of *The Miracle Worker*, which after playing on Broadway was made into a movie and a video widely available in libraries. Helen was both blind and deaf from early infancy and unable to understand or use language of any kind until she was in her teens, when Annie Sullivan was hired to care for her and teach her some language.

The play portrays the problem and the strategies used in the confrontation between Annie and Helen very vividly on how to make intelligent human contact possible, until it finally happened unexpectedly—like a miracle. We refer to this confrontation again and again as we proceed, to show how much human self-consciousness depends on mutual recognition between selves, as both Helen and Annie learned from their experience together.

selves is a fundamental trait of human historical existence, whether as only a matter of fact or also as a matter of necessity for effective self-consciousness.

1.3 THE WORLD AS A NECESSARY FACTOR TO BE TAKEN INTO ACCOUNT IN RELATION TO SELF-CONSCIOUSNESS IN HUMAN EXISTENCE

We have attended thus far to selfhood and to communion as essential factors in the basic fact of human existence. These are factors to be thought of as pertaining to the internal aspect of human experience as distinct from the external, or to the subjective pole as distinct from the objective. Our reflection begins by turning within ourselves in our consciousness of intelligence taking place, and sorting out different aspects of our experience and of our willing as we choose diverse ways of taking action in response to those with whom we are in communion.

All this suggests an approach to human existence that goes from the inside out, from the subjective to the objective, and not the reverse as is usually done in the particular sciences we call empirical, natural, or social. These normally proceed from the outside in, from what has come to existence to what has brought it to existence as we know it, as the smile of mutual recognition and human communion take hold in the rational and historical experience of selves.

Going from the inside out or from the subjective to the objective does not make the external factor or the objective pole of experience any less real or necessary from the standpoint of human existence. In fact, it enables us to see how much the internal side of human experience is wrapped up in the external side or how much the subjective pole of selfhood is caught up in the objective, so much so that we do not come to any consciousness of our selves as selves except by starting from our consciousness of the external world in which we literally find ourselves. The fact is that even our presence to ourselves, which is our philosophical starting point, can never be purely immediate within ourselves in total isolation as the Cartesian dictum, "I think, therefore I am," would have it, without reference to something or someone already other than ourselves. One does not begin to think in a vacuum or isolated as in an oven, as we shall find in reflecting on those who become isolated or remain isolated from any other self, due to handicaps, such as Helen's, or due to becoming isolated from other human beings.

We become present to ourselves always only in an act of *reflection* on an activity that has begun spontaneously outside the inner core of our reflective self-consciousness. The same thing can be said even of the smile of recognition, not just in the infant who has the externals of a smile even before there is recognition but also in the adult, whose spontaneous smile predisposes one to recognize the other as a self responding to one's own smile as a self.

We start off being outside of ourselves, as it were, like mere cats, for example, and always have to recuperate ourselves from this being in the world as animals. Consciousness is always consciousness of a world from which we turn back into ourselves. Our *re*flection and our mutual *re*cognition start in an activity that is always caught up in a world, a home, a school, a town for each self, an activity that has to be assumed as a means of communication with other selves. Hence the importance of bodies, language, social structures, and so on for human selfhood as such. Part of our essential task here is to inquire how and why this is so for human life as a whole in the world.

1.4 INADEQUATE VIEWS OF THE FACT OF HUMAN EXISTENCE IN THE WORLD

Our reflective survey of all that is given or taken for granted in the basic fact of self-conscious human existence has ranged far and wide, both interiorly and exteriorly, from the standpoint of both subject and object, including not just reflection into self but communion with other selves in an ever-expanding conception of the world in which we find our selves through communion as we penetrate ever more deeply into ourselves and into others as selves.

There are innumerable ways in which one could take issue with all that we have included in what we take to be this basic fact of human existence, some common sense, some scientific, and some philosophical. To sharpen our conception of how ample the basic fact of self-conscious human existence can be or has to be to equal the fullness of its basic factual content, let us examine some alternative views of the basic fact of human existence to see how they fall short of the existential fact to be examined. These are views that cut philosophy short of much that is to be examined in the basic fact of human existence and leave us with a stunted view of selfhood to work with. It is important for our philosophy of human existence to take these views into account and to see in what respect they fall short of the phenomenon we start from in our inquiry.

We examine three of these shortsighted views that have been prevalent in much of modern philosophy and that are especially significant for a philosophy of human existence that wants to be equal to the task of developing a science of human life as a whole.

1.4.1 First, there is the purely external view of the self or of selfhood. Such a view is usually due to an approach to reality and human existence that is purely extrinsic, mechanical, or nominalistic with regard to this I here and I now, and that ignores what is known from intelligence and will in the reflective act of self-consciousness.

David Hume, for example, reduces knowledge to a matter of vivid impressions and treats the subject or the self as no more than a bundle of impressions in which the I was especially prominent, singled out as vivid, and later gathered together with other vivid impressions of the same kind. If there is anything like a substantial unity for oneself, there is no knowledge of it except by some association of vague impressions we speak of as an idea of oneself.

Behaviorism, by limiting its study of human behavior to what is knowable through an objectified scheme of stimulus-response, tends to see the self only in terms of a mechanical response to a mechanical stimulus. Ultimately it tends to deny not only selfhood as such but also the freedom and dignity we usually attach to it, not to mention the originality we associate with each reflective self in what it does or accomplishes as a self.

Then there are those who think of consciousness as no more than a matter of neurology in physical brain waves and synapses within the skull that function in varying degrees of coordination affecting an individual's disposition of well-being or discomfort.

Note that in taking exception to such restrictive views of the self, we do not deny the truth that may be in them. The *being-in-the-world*, which we refer to in the third moment of our reflection, surely entails aspects of vivid impression and mechanical response to stimuli as well as some electrical functioning of the organ we call brain.

What we assert is that there is more to the self that we know reflectively than is known by these methods that look only to what is externally observable about the self as this or that vivid impression, or as this *response* to that *stimulus*, or as coordinated to some functions in the brain.

1.4.2 Then there is the view of the self as primordially constituted in itself *in isolation* from any other self. This is a characteristically modern view that tries to think of the human self as completely constituted in its selfhood in isolation and as entering into contact with others only as a matter of physical, biological, psychological, or economic necessity, or as one of competition for scarce external goods, or as a matter of both.

Think, for example, of Thomas Hobbes's idea of "man in the state of pure nature," of Jean-Jacques Rousseau's notion of "the noble savage . . . born free," of John Rawls's view of man as establishing his conception of justice from an "original position" of mutual disinterest, or of Jean-Paul Sartre's conception of the self as *pour soi* (for itself) in such a way that the other inevitably appears as an intruder or as an assault on oneself. The other is for me hell, as Sartre would say.

Views such as this give rise to the presence of "other minds" in the world as a problem that is unanswerable in purely analytical philosophy. And they inevitably lead to an understanding of human relations in terms of domination or violence and ultimately of competition for scarce goods. They make it impossible to conceive the relation between selves on a basis of genuine equality or community and true intersubjectivity.

While we do not deny any aspect of conflict and competition in human relations, we maintain that the aspect of communion is more fundamental for self-consciousness in the act of recognition constitutive of human selfhood than any of these other types of interdependence and mutual influence that arise through merely external contact.

1.4.3 Finally there is the view of the self as *separate* from the world. This is the view of certain kinds of philosophy that try to think of the self as something apart from the world, or other-worldly, a view that goes all the way back to Plato and comes all the way down to Martin Heidegger.

Descartes, for example, tries to think of the self purely as a "thinking thing" (*res cogitans*) apart from any and every "extended thing" (*res extensa*), even apart from his imagination and body.

Plato tends to think of the mind as functioning apart from the senses and as intent on knowing forms separate from the world of the senses.

Kant tries to think of the self as a purely cognitive function in his *Critique of Pure Reason*, or else as an object of experience like any other animal in the world of nature. In the *Critique of Practical Reason*, he tries to think of the moral self as completely separate from his inclinations or his emotions, a pure idea of freedom with only its law to guide it.

While recognizing that there is a transcendent aspect to the self that begins to emerge in the very act of smiling, in a clear and distinct act of reflective self-consciousness, we insist that this transcendent aspect cannot be grasped apart from the inclinations and emotions in which we are tied to the world. Our reflection into self not only starts from the world. It cannot maintain itself except in relation to this world in our imagination.

Our thinking starts from sense experience and maintains itself in relation to the senses even though it is not reducible to the senses. Our willing starts from the sense inclinations and maintains itself through these sense inclinations even though it cannot be reduced to a mere sense inclination. Even our self-consciousness starts in the presence of other self-consciousnesses *in* the world.

We shall see more on all these points as we proceed and examine more closely the self communing with other selves in the world.

2

The Human Self as a Substance Existing in Historical Tension with Itself and with Other Human Selves

We have begun to focus on the self as the center of our attention in trying to formulate *what* a human being is. As a human being you refer to yourself as a self. As a human being I refer to myself as a self. And we refer to one another as selves and as human beings. What kind of thing is this self as a human being? How is it a thing constituted in its selfhood as a human being? How is it thought of as existing in the world in the presence of other selves and other objects?

We take the human self as the subject for this inquiry. Not the self taken as an ideal self-consciousness in isolation from other selves and from the world, but the self communing with others and with the natural world of other beings: sentient or animal, living or plant, and even nonliving or mineral. For us as philosophers, the self is the subject matter of our inquiry or the formal object we are inquiring about, and at the same time the subject doing the inquiring about itself and about other selves as well as about nonselves in the world. But it is not such a subject without there being objects to which it relates in its scientific consciousness, including not just things that are nonliving, nonsentient, or nonrational but also things that are rational and self-conscious, such as other selves or even itself as object of its own consciousness and its self-consciousness.

We think of each self as individual and singular, this one here and now, or that one there and then, myself and yourself. And yet we think of each one as a self, something, an identity we all have or share in common as selves, in the same way as we think of cats as something, an identity they all have or share in common as cats. What can be said of this common characteristic of selfhood in all those we think of as human selves? How is it one characteristic in each self and how does it remain the same in each self even as each self changes and pursues its own human interests?

Our description of the primordial fact of self-consciousness, the self-consciousness we start from in our inquiry, has been extensive and wide-ranging, referring not just to selfhood and communion among selves but also to all sorts of lesser things we find in the world of human selfhood, objects that are not subjects as well as objects that are in fact selves in the way they present themselves to one another, at least for anyone who has come to an authentic self-consciousness of one's own.

Given this wide complexity of selves and nonselves in this primordial fact of human self-conscious existence, the question arises as to where precisely or where ontologically a human being stands in what we think of as the real or as beings. Is it a part of the real world or is it apart from the real world? If it is a part of the real world, how is it to be conceived? Should it be conceived as substantial part in itself, or as something accidental or adventitious, standing in something else, as in a substance with its own standing? Or should it be conceived, as Dutch philosopher Baruch Spinoza would have it, as a mode alongside another mode of the one absolute substance, when he speaks of thought and thinghood as modes of the one and only absolute substance? When we speak of selves communing with one another in self-consciousness, are we allowing for individual selves standing in themselves or are we combining all of them into one spiritual identity, as Georg Wilhelm Friedrich Hegel seems to do when he speaks of the community of selves as the substance or as the substantial spirit of selfhood?

We also think of the self as the consciousness that takes shape in an activity as it launches this activity. The self is discovered in its action, in what I do and in what you do, in what I think and feel and in what you think and feel. It is discovered in the actual communication we have with each other, in this inquiry here and now, or in other interactions with other people, in much the same way the infant does in responding to its mother as a mothering self and thereby becomes conscious of its mother as a self and of itself as a self, as the mother becomes conscious of her infant as a child recognizing her as a mothering self; or again as a student does in responding to the words of a teacher, whether at home or in school, and thereby becoming further conscious of oneself and of one's teacher, as the teacher becomes more conscious of a student recognizing the teacher as a teaching self. How is the self related to this activity in its existing? Is the activity something necessary for it, or can we think of the self without any activity whatsoever? How does the activity itself relate to the self? Does it add anything to selfhood as such, and if so, what?

The idea of action is intimately tied to the idea of substance in the self and in other lesser beings we find in the world, those without self-consciousness, or those without sense consciousness at all, or even those without life. But we must not let this close relationship deceive us into thinking that "substance" and "action" mean one and the same thing in each kind of being. There is no action without a substance, as we shall see quite clearly. And there is no substance without its proper action by which we identify it for what it is. One way to maintain the distinction between substance and action is to think of the substance as something real in itself, and of action as something real, not in itself but in another, namely in a substance, as an ontological accident in an ontological substance.

If a self is discovered only in its action, can it exist without this action? Is there existence for the self apart from its taking action? Is there an action so proper to a self that we can define the self as existing in this action?

The word *self* is quite simple, but our understanding of it cannot be quite as simple. The term *action* is also simple, but it covers a wide diversity of activities, not just of a self or of a plurality of selves but also of lesser beings who are known by what they do, which may be less ontologically than what selves do. It is by observing what things do in their action that we come to know what they are in their substance. This is especially true of selves in their substance, but it is also true of anything else in the world we identify as a substance.

Our first inquiry, then, starting from the complex fact of selfhood, must be into the basic, essential components of this complex fact of the human self, without which there is no self to reflect on or to begin with.

2.1 THE HUMAN SELF AS PERDURING SUBSTANCE

We begin our inquiry through reflection on the ground we have just laid out as the primordial fact of our experience as human selves in our own self-consciousness. If we do not know ourselves in our selfhood, we do not know anything else, because knowing anything else presupposes that we know what knowing is and that there is knowing of knowing only where there is self-consciousness. In other words, we are inquiring into the absolute beginning of knowing for any self-consciousness.

That is our starting point in this critical reflection on what it is to be a human self. Note that this beginning, the human self we are actually reflecting on as actually experienced, is not a fixed point, which we leave behind as we go forward. It is a whole rather than a point, and it cannot be fixated in the framework of any particular aspect of its being that can be studied in any particular science. It is a beginning in motion that will be part of the self-understanding we are seeking. Self-understanding is part of the self's own identity and being as a whole.

To speak of this self as human may seem redundant since it could be said that the only self we acknowledge at this point is human. We could conceive of other "selves" analogous to the human self, but we do not wish to include any other such selves at this point in our reflection, lesser selves, so to speak (such as cats and dogs, for example), or higher selves, separate from matter (such as angels or pure spirits).

All that we wish to include in our strictly scientific investigation are human selves as both an identity and a whole in communion with other selves, as we find them in our primordial experience of ourselves, of other selves, and of the world.

To speak of this self as a substance may sound confusing at this point of our investigation because of the many different and often reductionist ways the term *substance* has been used in the history of western philosophy and science, not to mention in ordinary and legalistic language, as when we speak of illegal substances.

Many speak of "substance" exclusively as something material, without reference to anything living or conscious, not even in living things, and much less in conscious things, such as animals or human selves. And there are philosophers, such as Plato, or Spinoza, or Hegel, who speak of substance or essence as something separate from matter pertaining only to a realm of ideas and not to the realm of empirical reality.

Because of this general misunderstanding, some, like Whiteheadians, advise simply abandoning the language of substance altogether in favor of what they call *process*, as if there could be no substances in a world where process is taking place. Others are in favor of using the term *substance* or *substantial* only in the realm of subjectivity, as if there were no factor of objectivity in the consciousness or the self-consciousness of selves.

Instead of abandoning the language of substance, which has a strong backing in the history of philosophy going all the way back to Aristotle and which proffers an important advantage for understanding the nature of the self in its permanent or perduring identity relative to the wide and changing diversity of activities in which it engages, we need to reemphasize it in order to maintain the integrity of a self in its identity, even as it undergoes radical change through its own activity and the influence from the activity of other selves and other things of the world that are not selves.

To absolutize "process" instead of self-consciousness as the beginning of our inquiry is to lose sight of the self in its actuality as given in experience and in its activity as distinct from its substantial identity. To insist only on pure subjectivity, without reference to intersubjective interaction in the objective world of nature, is to ignore how the self has come to its current perfection as an enterprising self-consciousness in communion or in contention with other selves.

The question is not one of whether to abandon all these other factors that come into play when self-consciousness as substance seeks its ulterior perfection, whether through a natural process working toward its first perfection or through taking action of its own initiative working toward a second perfection. Rather, it is one of how to see self-consciousness take its stand as a perduring self, an identity, in search of its ultimate second perfection.

The question is how to adopt a strategy of rectifying the understanding of substance and reintroducing into it the dynamic aspect that at least some of the ancients such as Aristotle gave it, in the way substance relates to its proper activity in going from its first or given perfection to its second or acquired perfection. Without the concept of substance, there is no way of maintaining the identity of each self as it engages with other selves in the world with its own project.

We should note that we are using the term *perfection* here in its etymological and ontological sense more than in its moral sense, although the latter sense is not excluded. Something is said to be perfect when it has come to a certain degree of completion or when it has been perfected.

Moreover, there is a double sense in which a thing can be said to be perfected, first as a substance that has been empowered with all its natural abilities, and second as a substance that has used the abilities it has been endowed with to bring itself to a perfection in keeping with the proper exercise of those abilities or powers.

We shall speak of the first as the first perfection of a thing or of a self in its substance, and of the second as the second perfection, to be actualized through the exercise of a thing's or a self's proper activity. We speak of things generally here only by analogy with what we discover to be the double sense of perfection for a self, which is the first thing we have to talk about in both its substance and its proper activity.

Before proceeding along those lines, we must consider the self under another aspect than that of its substance, the aspect of its existence in seeking its own fulfillment through its own activity.

2.2 THE SELF AS EXISTING THROUGH ITS OWN PROPER ACTIVITIES

THE TERM *EXISTENCE* HAS BEEN USED IN MANY WAYS, especially since the rise of Existentialism in philosophy after World War II in the mid-twentieth century. In ordinary language it is usually taken as a variant for the verb *is*, referring to some matter of fact or other as given empirically. We say there exist trees just as we say there are trees in the backyard. Whatever is as a substance is said to be or to exist like any other substance. The notion of existence remains flat and lifeless, much as the notion of substance does, when we ignore the different ways in which different beings or substances act and interact among themselves. But that is not the way we wish to take the notion of existence here, not just with regard to the self but with regard to any kind of substance as well, each with a proper activity of its own.

The human self we are inquiring into is not something merely given for us to observe passively, such as a rock or some object outside ourselves. The self we are reflecting on is our own self, in the act of transcending ourselves as given here and now, by nature and by our past experiences. In reflecting upon myself in my self-consciousness, I am finding myself as already active in all sorts of ways, including the actual ongoing activity in which we find ourselves reflecting. When we think of ourselves simply as being, we are not yet thinking of ourselves as existing. It is in its activity that the self exists in the proper sense of this term, as we are going to use it here.

We do not know that we are, even in our self-consciousness, without knowing that we are active in our selfhood. We discover ourselves as always already active, even if it is only in the activity of reflecting itself. That is why we give priority to existence over being or essence, as every existentialist does, in our thinking about ourselves and about other selves.

What we are in our self-consciousness is what we have made ourselves, and we come to know what we are by reflecting on the activity, or the existence, by which we have made ourselves what we are. I know I am a skier, for example, by reflecting on what I have done as a skier. And I know I am in my essence as a rational animal by reflecting on the rational activity that has made me what I am as a junior or a senior in college, or as a professor of philosophy.

All of this insistence on activity as proper to a substance is said primarily of the self-conscious human being, but it can also be said analogously of other beings that are not self-conscious and that do not reflect on their own activity as we do. We know that there are other substances such as nonrational animals studied in zoology, like cats, and dogs, and elephants, and we come to know what they are in their substance by what we see them do. They have an activity of their own in which they exist in their own way and which defines them for us, even though they do not reflect on that activity for themselves as we do on our own activity for ourselves.

Similarly, we know that there are nonsentient living things or substances, such as trees and flowers, studied in biology, that have an activity of their own that defines them for us, even though they do not appear to have any consciousness of that activity as their own. And we know that there are nonliving things or substances, such as stones and minerals, studied in physics or geology, that show no signs of life, let alone of consciousness, but have an activity of their own in which they exist in their own way and which defines them for us in our physical sciences.

Everything we think of as being, we think of as active, as existing, and as defining itself through its activity in the world, starting from human beings as the first kind of substance we know of. Existential philosophy has made this point primarily about human beings in their self-consciousness, but the point can be extended to all kinds of lesser beings, active in lesser ways, with regard to their existence as well as their being. All the natural sciences follow the course of the different activities of different beings as they inquire into what those beings are.

To speak of existence as we do here implies a distinction between what a thing is in its substance and what it does in its activity, even though that activity is proper to it in its substance. In fact, we come to know what a thing is in its substance only by reflection on what we take to be its proper activity. In this sense we can also speak of a distinction between existence and essence in the human being primarily, and in other beings by analogy, wherein a certain priority is given to existence over essence, even though essence is what a being is in its substance.

In existentialist reflection we turn first to what a thing does in its existence in order to arrive at what it is in its essence, even when we think of essence as given prior to what it does in its proper activity. But we think of its essence as given prior to existence or in abstraction from existence still only on the basis of some proper activity for the self as rational and animal. Essence, especially the human essence, is not given as something fixed abstractly in a particular state once and for all. Here, we take it as existentially something that still has essentially to actualize itself in accordance with what it is as a self-conscious rational animal or that essentially still has to perfect itself in a second perfection, starting from a first perfection it has arrived at as a rational self-consciousness reflecting upon itself. This is not an easy notion to get a hold of without coming to it by reflection on what we take to be our proper activity as rational substances, namely the activities of intelligence and will.

The essence of the self, as given at any moment of its existence, has to be thought of as still only its first perfection, given to it only in view of striving for an ulterior perfection, which we can speak of here generally as its second perfection, to be actualized through the whole of the self's own proper activity.

The essence of the human self as given here and now at any moment of its existence can thus be thought of as relating to a future and to a past. As relating to a future, essence has to be taken as something oriented to its self-actualization or its second perfection. In this relation, existence has priority over essence. But as relating to the past, whether it be that given by nature, out of which the self emerges, or that constituted by the self itself in its own past historical initiative of self-actualization, essence has priority over existence, in the sense that what I can make of myself in the future depends on what I have already become in my nature and what I have already made myself in the past.

The existentialist has to take the human essence into account no less than the essentialist. In giving priority to existence over essence, the existentialist is only saying that what the essence is is what the self-conscious human self has made of itself in some second perfection. This is no less a one-sided view of the human essence than that of the essentialist, who is taking the human essence only in its first perfection, as if it were already in its final perfection and did not have to actualize itself further through its proper activity. We shall try to counteract the one-sidedness of existentialism without falling into the one-sidedness of essentialism by speaking of substance as the essence of the self and as distinct from its activity in its very existing.

2.3 THE SELF IN ITS HISTORICAL TENSION WITH ITSELF AND WITH OTHER SELVES

THERE IS TENSION IN EVERY HUMAN BEING, and by analogy, in every being we take to have a proper activity of its own as distinct from its substance. The general distinction between accidents and substance as it has come down to us from Aristotle, when understood concretely, implies such a tension. Accidents can be taken as distinct from substance, but not as in themselves, separate from substance. Accidents, as accidents, are real only as in something else than themselves, namely in substances. They are thought of as being in another.

Substance, on the other hand, has to be understood as being in itself and as the underlying principle for its accidents or for its proper activity as emanating from itself. In the world as we know it, there are no substances without accidents of one kind or another and, more significantly for us here, without some proper activity, which, while being necessary for the second perfection of a being or of beings in general, are nevertheless accidents with respect to the substances from which they have their being, as accidents.

This does not mean that accidents of or in substances are purely accidental in the sense of incidental, without any necessary connection with what a substance is in itself. Some accidents are necessary for the fulfillment or the second perfection of substances, especially in the human substance. The proper activities we have been referring to are such necessary accidents in and for selves and for other substances, all of which are taken to have a proper activity of their own. It is from the power or powers to engage in proper activities, as both accidental and necessary, in selves and in other substances, that we get what we can call an *ontological tension* in any substance in relation to its proper activities, and this most properly in the human substance.

It should be noted here that when we speak of a distinction between essence and existence, or of what a thing is in its substance and what a thing is in its proper activity, we do not mean to say that these are two separate things, much less two separate selves, within one and the same thing or one and the same self. The term *distinction* tends to suggest an interrelation between the two poles of the distinction, as we saw in reflecting on the four sets of distinct poles in the phenomenon of human life, so that neither pole can be understood without its relation to the other, much less as a thing separate from the other. Even selves in communicative interaction with one another are not separate in this absolute sense.

But the self in its substance and the self in its proper activity are not two separate selves. They are only one self in its substance with a plurality and a diversity of proper activities, each of which is in view of the second perfection of that same identical self. Each self, even in a community, is only one thing or one being, within which the activities or the relations with other selves are distinct from the substance, however proper they may be to this being in its substance.

The grounding for making this distinction within the self between substance and proper activities comes from the fact that, for each self in its substance, there are many proper activities to be reckoned with. If we take thinking and willing to be proper activities of one and the same self, for example, we have to distinguish not only each one from the other but also both of them from the substance, all of them intricately or infinitely interwoven with one another. And so also of the many other proper activities a self might initiate for itself in working toward its second perfection.

I think of many different things in many different ways, but it is always the same self that thinks in these activities. I will many different things and in many different ways, but it is always the same self that wills. If we take thinking and willing as real activities of one and the same self, we have to think of them not only as distinct from one another but also as distinct from the self in its substance, or from the substance of the self that is perfected by these activities. Needless to say, we have to think of them as also distinct from the real activities of reciprocity in any communicative interaction, since real activities, even of thinking and willing, are essentially real activities of individual substances. Moreover, there are many sorts of proper activity that come into consideration, each one of them proper to a self in the sense that each one flows from a self in its substance and is attributable only to the self from which it flows. When I think of how to reflect on my own self-consciousness, it is I who thinks, and when I will to take some action, it is I who wills. When you think about anything, it is you doing the thinking, not me, and when you will, it is you doing the willing, not me.

What allows us to say all this is a distinction between a substance and its accidents, in a dialectical relation between the two that results in what we can call an *ontological tension* on two levels for the human being in its self-consciousness, one on the level of nature and one on the level of what we have been referring to as the historical. We hear a lot about tension on the level of nature regarding matters of health, of economic well-being, or of ecology, but that is not the tension we wish to insist on in our existential reflection on the proper activity of human selves.

The human self is a substance of a very special kind. As a matter of fact, it is what we first come to understand as substance, as one self in confrontation with another self, even as we think of each self/substance as existing through its own proper activity.

When we speak of the self as a substance, we refer to it as a being, as that which is in the most fundamental sense of being and from which properties or actions are understood as emanating. Substance means a whole that has a unity perduring as the same identity in the development of the being. Here the term refers to the self in its permanence and initial completion or in its first perfection.

Although a substance changes in any change, even so-called accidental change, it does not change substantially; that is, it does not lose its identity as a whole according to what it is, this or that self. I am always myself, this human being, in whatever I become, as you are always yourself in whatever you become, that human being born on such and such a date and so on. It is this substantiality of the self that we are concerned with here. The tension we wish to speak of is that between what a self is as given by nature and by its past action, and what it still has to make itself in its relation with other selves.

As it exists, the self is not just a thing of nature, a mere given. In initiating its own activity in the past, it has surpassed or transcended itself on what, in our introductory reflection on the phenomenon of human life, we have already distinguished as a historical level of existence. This is the level that emerges, historically, as selves exercise their intelligence and will creatively in cultures that surpass the merely given in nature. The self is a maker of history, its own and that of its community, in what we shall refer to as *cultures.*

The self is a being that has to achieve itself through its own activity; it is in tension with itself as a historical being, which is in itself only by going out of itself, by existing, as given by nature, by actualizing itself through its own action. This it does with other selves. The historical tension we speak of is not just within each self individually, between its substance and its activity, but also among selves recognizing one another and interacting with one another *historically* in families and in communities. This has to be a communicative interaction among selves, not just as a matter of reciprocal influences determined by nature or by established social structures; it also has to be a matter of mutual understanding and recognition among selves leading to free cooperation in the historical self-actualizing of communities and of their cultures.

2.4 THE SELF IN ITS DIVERSE PROPER ACTIVITIES

What we distinguish from the substance within one and the same historical self in tension with itself and with other selves are activities we take to be proper to that self. It is through such activities that every self actualizes itself.

The self maintains itself as an identity in its substance, which perdures in different states and in its different activities. This identity, however, is not a simple, fixed identity. It is an identity taking action in its historical tension with itself and with other selves.

We use the term *distinct* here, as indicated earlier, to bring out a complexity within the self, which is not reducible to a simple identity, such as a point or self-enclosed quantum, but we do not mean to say that a self is two separate things, much less two separate selves. When two things or two selves are taken as separate from one another, they are isolated from one another as things, or as selves. They remain connected with one another in some way through communicative interaction in a world of interaction, both subjective and objective. This interaction may be essential or ontologically necessary for them but would still be accidental to each one of them as a substance in itself separate from other substances. Each self is only one thing or one being, but within each being the activities or the relations to other selves are distinct from the substance, even though the activities or the relations are proper to each individual being in its substance.

The reason for making this distinction within the self between a substance and its proper activities, as we have already indicated, comes from the fact that for each self in its substance, there are many proper activities to be reckoned with. If we take thinking and willing to be proper activities of one and the same self, for example, we have to distinguish not only each activity from the other but also both of them from the substance, as well as of the many other proper activities a self initiates or might initiate.

I think in many different ways and about many different things, but it is always the same self that thinks. I will in many different ways and regarding many different things, but it is always the same self that wills. If we think of thinking and willing as real activities of one and the same self, we have to think of them not only as distinct from one another but also as distinct from the self in its substance, or from the substance of the self. Needless to say, we have to think of them as distinct from the real activities of other selves as well, in any communicative interaction, since real activities are essentially real activities of individual substances.

There are many sorts of proper activity that should be taken into consideration in our reflection on selfhood. They are proper to a self in the sense that each one flows from the self in its substance and is attributable only to the self from which it flows. When I think, it is I who thinks, and when I will, it is I who wills. When you think, it is you who thinks, not I, and when you will, it is you who wills.

Activity, as attributable to a substance, is spoken of as an accident in the sense that it accedes to the substance taken as the perduring identity of a particular being, just as color and size accede to any substance such as a rock, a tree, or a cat. Accident here can refer to anything that is real in the being as a whole relating to the substance, such as quantity, quality, or location, which is not part of the substance. Any particular activity or any distinct kind of activity, such as thinking and willing for a self, emanating from a substance is an accident in this sense of the term. Even if it passes over into something else, it remains nevertheless the activity of the substance from which it emanates. Accidents, as we speak of them here can also be thought of as *inhering* in their substance. They have being but not in the same sense that substances have being. Substance is being-in-itself. Accident is being-in-another, namely being-in-the-substance.

Though we speak of proper activity as accidental to the substance, we do not mean that it is accidental or incidental for the self as a whole to have its proper activity. As we saw in speaking of existence, it is essential for every self, and in fact for any substance, to have or to exercise some activity of its own as a way of coming to its own second perfection or actualization in the world. For selves, this exercise of proper activity can take many directions in relation to many things and to other selves, but there are two categories of proper activity that should be distinguished, one proper to the self in the initiatives it has taken as an individual, and one proper to the self as typically or specifically human in the way these initiatives have been taken.

There are activities of human beings, for example, such as skiing and stamp collecting, that are ways of coming to a second perfection for a self but that we would not say are required for every human being in its existence as a self. There are many particular ways of coming to one's second perfection as a self, and each way that is chosen by a self is proper to itself as an individual, or as a member of a club, but not proper to being human or a self as such.

What is proper to being human or a self as such are activities such as thinking, willing, seeing, feeling, and a host of others that we exercise for the sake of being human selves and that find their way into all the particular activities we initiate as selves. One does not have to engage in all these particular activities to arrive at one's second perfection as a self, but one does have to engage in some of them in a way that is thoughtful of others as well as of oneself and with a feeling that is consonant with being human.

We take activities like thinking and willing or making judgments and making decisions to be more properly human, in the sense that every human engages in them in order to make itself a self in a complete way or in its second perfection. Such judgments and decisions are still accidental to the substance of the self, especially as to what concerns their content: what I judge or what I decide at any given moment can still be incidental to what I am in my substance. For example, I may judge the price of a car to be too high and decide not to buy it. These activities of thinking and willing are also accidental in the sense that I can engage in them in varying degrees of intensity at different times.

But thinking and willing as proper activities of a self are not incidental to what I am as a self or to what I have to make myself. They are what I do most properly as a self, no matter what I may be judging or deciding about at any given time. Even if such activity remains accidental to or distinct from the substance of the self, as we shall argue, it is necessarily part of the self as it exists or actualizes itself. No human substance or self can be utterly devoid of such activity, which is why we refer to the activity when we define what a self is in its substance as a rational animal.

When we include animal in the definition of the self in its substance, we do so on the basis of other proper activities of the self, those of sensation and feeling, in which we are like other nonrational animals, albeit in a way that relates our animality to reason and will. In fact, we should even include the functions of nutrition and reproduction as somehow proper to the self, insofar as the self is a living thing as well as a rational and a sentient thing. All these activities, or dimensions of activity, are necessary parts of the self and relate as proper accidents to what it is in its substance. I cannot be myself or a self without sensation and feeling and without such vital functions as nutrition and reproduction, which can be engaged in in original ways, depending on what reason and will might devise.

Indeed, the way we engage in eating and reproducing as well as in sensing and feeling may be characteristically or properly human in that it is informed by reason, as in the case of gourmet cooking or marriage, or in the way we see things and react to them. But even apart from the rational dimension in human activity, the dimensions of sensation, feeling, and of physical life itself remain integral to a self's proper activity.

Our point here will not be to explore these different dimensions of the self's proper activity. We will do more of that later, at least with regard to knowing and willing, after we have tried to lay out more of what the self is in its substance. Our point now is to arrive at the notion of proper activity in its relation to the substance of the self. In doing so, however, it is important to keep in mind that what we refer to as the proper activity of the self is something quite complex, with dimensions of thought, willing, sensation, feeling, and vital functions.

2.5 THE HISTORICAL ORDER OF SELFHOOD AS DISTINCT FROM ITS NATURAL ORDER

It is not enough to distinguish the proper activities of selfhood from its substance. We must also distinguish two realms of proper activity for the self, that of nature and that of history. The realm of nature is the one we share with other living and sentient things as animals, and the realm of history is the one we share with other selves as rational. We emerge and we begin to exist from nature as infants without speech or recognition of other selves, and we continue to depend on nature for our survival and for our power of knowing and willing, the power through which we become makers of our own history, both personally and communally.

This is an important distinction to keep in mind in our philosophy of human existence. We do not exist simply, like other animals that are nonrational, with little or no conception of different ways of seeking their second perfection other than the one nature has given them and which determines whether they survive or not in their given habitat. We exist as recreators of the world in which we find ourselves, not just barely to survive like nonrational animals but, rather, to remake ourselves and our habitat so as to survive and to live more perfectly in almost any habitat in the world, thanks to the exercise of our own intelligence and will.

We have already spoken of this historical level of existence as distinct from the natural level from the beginning in describing the phenomenon of human life. Now we have to reflect on how it distinguishes itself from the merely natural level of existence in ourselves through the activity proper to rational animals exercising their powers of intelligence and will in striving for a higher second perfection than just surviving, not just as individuals but also among selves recognizing one another and interacting with one another historically as families and as diverse communities.

The interaction among selves is not just a matter of reciprocal influences determined by nature or by established social structures. It is also a matter of mutual understanding, recognition, and agreement among selves leading to free cooperation in the formation of self-actualizing communities, not just adapting to given natural conditions of existence in nature but also reshaping nature for the betterment of communities and for new projects they envision for themselves in their second perfection as cultures.

We continue to use the term *perfection* here in its etymological sense more than in its moral sense. Something that is perfect is something that has been brought to completion, or is perfected. But we distinguish between two levels of perfection in a being or in the self, the level it has reached when it has completed itself through its activity and the level it has reached in its completion as a substance empowered to act on its own. We refer to the former as the second perfection of the being or the self, or as its final perfection, and we distinguish this from a first perfection of a substance given in an act, with a first perfection already accomplished and ready to act on its own for its own second or ulterior perfection.

Thus we can speak of two degrees of act and two levels of perfection within the self. We can speak of the substance as being in first act or having its first perfection insofar as it has reached a certain completion in itself as a self, say the completion of a child, or a 13-year old, or a 40-year old. At any age I am already or actually myself in my substance. Just being human is already a perfection given by my nature and by what I have made of myself through intelligence and will. But I am myself in this first perfection only in a way that has yet to be completed through a second act, or what I refer to as my proper activity as a human being in the act of perfecting myself. This activity has to be referred to as its second perfection, whatever form it might take. It is in the nature of the self as first act or first perfection to be ordered to some second act or second perfection. We discover it to be so in reflecting on our own proper activity, which is already a second perfection of sorts in our selves.

This second or ulterior perfection is something to which the self is ordered by its very nature, not as animal but as rational or as empowered with intelligence and will. Even in its first or substantial perfection as intelligent and willful, the self has not reached its ultimate perfection. Though it is already actualized in its identity as a self at whatever age, it still has to actualize itself further through its activity as both animal and rational.

2.6 EXPLORING THE SELF IN ITS DISTINCTION AS SUBSTANCE WITH PROPER ACTIVITIES OF INTELLIGENCE AND WILL

PART OF THE DIFFICULTY WITH THE DISTINCTION we are making stems from the static understanding of "substance," which has prevailed in most of modern thought since Descartes and Locke, an understanding that is found as much in those who reject the idea of substance as in those who have defended it. In view of this general misunderstanding of the idea, it might seem advisable simply to abandon the language of substance in favor of some other language, like that of process, as Whiteheadians do, or that of subjectivity, as some post-moderns have done, or that of ontology, which is still in common use.

But in doing so we might also be losing an important advantage in understanding the nature of the self in its permanent identity and in its relation to its activity as distinct from its substantial identity, a relation that is collapsed and lost sight of in the term *subjectivity* or that is ignored in the term *process*, which has more to do with how a thing comes to be in its first perfection as a substance than with self-actualization through one's own proper activity of thinking and willing.

It would seem better, therefore, to adopt a strategy of rectifying the understanding of "substance" and reintroducing into it the dynamic aspect that at least some of the ancients such as Aristotle gave it as it relates to its proper activity. Hence our insistence on existence as actualization, but only as the existing or the proper activity of a substance by which such an actualization is initiated. Moreover, the term *substance* focuses our attention much more concretely on the being of what we are talking about than the more abstract modern term *ontology*.

Our exploration, therefore, will proceed in two stages: first we shall try to clarify our understanding of the substance/accident distinction as it relates to the proper activity of the self in its substance, so as to clear the ground of any misunderstanding that has prevailed regarding substance as static and fixed in modern philosophy and to open the way for a proper understanding of the relation between the substance of the self and its proper activity as striving for some necessary second perfection. Then we shall try to show more positively how one's proper understanding takes hold in relation to the experience we have of our selves or to our existence over and above what we are given by nature in our substance.

2.6.1 Let us begin by considering how we first come to know the self. In our discussion of the primordial experience of self communing with other selves in the world, we insisted on reflection as the proper way of knowing the self as we have to think of it here in a philosophy of human existence. Reflection is the act in which we are conscious of ourselves in any one of our activities. It is the act wherein we become conscious of our self as subject or as the originator of the activity, in which I recognize that it is I who am learning, I who am playing, I who am loving, I who am deciding, even I who am distracted from my task of reflection at the moment. In doing something as a self-conscious self, I am conscious not only of doing it myself but also simultaneously of myself doing it.

Through reflection upon what I take to be my proper activity as rational self-consciousness, I not only discover myself as an inescapable fact but also what I have become as a self and what it is to be a self as this substance identifiable as human. This is not just an abstract concept of substance, applicable to all sorts of things, human as well as nonhuman, indiscriminately or in static fashion. It is a concept of substance in concrete experience as applied or discovered with reference to me or to other selves, all in our substance as selves.

In all of this reflecting upon my activity, it is not only my self that I am discovering but also what I am in my essence as a self, in myself as a substance. We have said that other things such as water, rocks, trees, and cats can also be thought of as substances. But none of those is the first instance of what we mean by substance here. The first instance of what we mean by substance here is the self as known through reflection on the self's proper activity; that is, as self-conscious. In fact, the self may be the very first instance of the idea of substance we know of, so that all other instances of substance, including rocks, trees, and cats, and even cells or subatomic particles, may be known as substances in a way that is derivative from or analogous to the self in its substance as first instance or as the primary analogate of substance. We do not have to go into this broader metaphysics of analogy here. Suffice it to focus primarily on the self as a substance with its proper activities of thinking and willing.

What is important for us to note in a philosophy of human existence is that the idea of substance we arrive at through this reflection is anything but fixed or static. It is a very dynamic concept that is associated with activity, even though what it represents may have to be distinguished from the activity. The self, we said earlier, is not a fixed point we leave behind or add on to, as if by juxtaposition of another self, as we go forward. The same can be said of the self as substance. It is not a fixed point that we leave behind as we move forward reflecting on our own self-conscious activity. The activity we are focusing on can only be real as the activity of a self in its substance.

Nor is the substantial self an unchanging substratum of change upon which we build superstructures. In its substance it is a moving and acting thing that, in its present completion or first perfection, is the outcome of a natural process and its own past activity but at the same time, even in its given completion, is still incomplete and still has to complete itself in a continuing historical self-actualization. The self is a substance that is subject and a subject that is substance; a substance/subject that has to constitute itself in its own final actualization through its own activity.

This is the way existence takes precedence over essence in human experience, as existentialists say. Without existing through its activity, the self is not truly itself in accordance with its essence or its substance. It is the substance or the essence of the self as subject that requires this. The existence of the self does not obliterate its substantiality but, rather, presupposes it and promotes it so that through existence we do not go from being one self to being another self but instead develop an identity of one and the same self.

When we speak of human substance, we have in mind this identity of the self that implies a certain permanence of the self or of the changing subject, which may be accidental but also perfects the self in one way or another. I am still substantially the same self I was when I first left home many years ago, even though I have changed a lot from the boy I was then and have made myself in a way that I did not imagine then. I have come to exist more truly as a self through all that I have accomplished as a self at different stages of my self-actualization. One can appreciate this about existing in true selfhood, not only as one approaches the end of life but also at every stage along the way.

Moderns and postmoderns prefer to speak of the self only in terms of subjectivity rather than substance. But in doing so they collapse the distinction we are trying to maintain between the substance of the self and its proper activity. They speak of subjectivity, as though there were no substance or permanent identity in the subject as distinct from the plurality and the diversity of its activities. Or else they speak of process as if nothing, no substance, came of it. Existence, as we understand it here, begins with a substance from which it issues forth as act or as activity, and it does not obliterate substance but, rather, keeps on presupposing it as initiator of the activity.

We insist on the notion of substance as referring to something distinct from the activity in the subject or in the process in order to uphold an essential identity in selfhood that perdures in whatever it does even as it changes. The point of the moderns about activity as constitutive of the self is well taken, as we shall see later on when we attend more to the activities themselves of intelligence and willing, but for the moment we have to insist on the point that in its activity the self is still an identity that is developing and is all the more substantial by reason of its subjectivity. This is something that is overlooked or denied in many philosophies of subjectivity.

Moreover, by insisting on this substantial identity of the self as distinct from its activity, we are better able to understand the historical tension that characterizes the human self in its existence. At any given moment in its existence, the self can be seen as at once a point of achievement in its identity and a point of departure for further achievement in the same identity.

We are led to distinguish between the substance of the self and its activity only because of the wide diversity and the great multiplicity of the activity through which the self maintains or, better still, achieves its identity. If there were no diversity in the activity of the self, we would not have to make such a distinction, and every self would end up perfecting itself in exactly the same way as every other self, as we see happens in nonrational species of animals and in lesser beings as well. But given the diversity of what different selves do in actualizing themselves, we cannot but maintain, as we shall argue, a distinction between what a self is in its substantial identity or essence as a self and what it does or makes itself through its different activities.

At the same time, however, we must maintain, with the moderns and postmoderns, that these many and diverse activities one finds in modern civilizations are still proper to individual substantial selves and that through them each self constitutes itself in its identity as we come to know it. Without its proper activity the substantial self could not be what it is or has become, nor could we know it for what it is in its essence or its substance. It may be free to act one way or another, but it is not free not to act. It is constituted in such a way that it must act and so bring its identity to achievement. It must have some activity that is proper to it in its very substantiality or according to what it is as intelligent and free. Young people often say that they are different or that they want to make a difference. This comes from their consciousness of themselves as active in their substantial or essential identity, or as substances, to recall what was said earlier about a substance in its identity.

Thus, the idea of the self as substance is anything but static. It is a dynamic concept that focuses on the identity of the self as this self advances from its first perfection to its ulterior or second perfection, the form of which it is free to choose but which it is not free not to choose given the necessity for any finite substance to take action, especially the human substance, as we shall see presently. Substance is the identity that binds second perfection to the first perfection of the self as self.

2.6.2 Let us turn again, then, to the experience we have of ourselves, to see how we come to conceive of the self as substance and how we come to conceive of this substance as distinct from its activity even though substance is seen as necessarily giving rise to this activity. Once we have seen this distinction, we shall be in a better position to see how the activity comes as a second perfection for the substance itself.

In a sense in returning to experience in this way we are returning to the essential core of our method of reflection. We are not merely trying to observe ourselves as objects as empirical or behavioral psychology might do, although there is an element of that in what we are doing. Nor are we trying to proceed from some preestablished concept of substance into which the self has to be fitted. On the contrary, we are discovering the concept of substance as the essence of the self in its existence through its activity.

We do not claim to know the self first in its substance and only thereafter in its activity. In fact, we know the self first in its activity and only then, through reflection, in its substance as that which is active in its self-consciousness. The idea of the self thus entails a kind of circularity between activity and substance. The self as we understand it can be known in its substance only through reflection upon the self's own activity. We have no pure intuition of our essence or substance as self. Thus, in order to know what we are in our essence or substance or how we are constituted, we have to reflect on our activity. However, through this reflection on our activity we do come to a proper knowledge of what we are and how we are constituted in our essential perfection as actual selves here and now and thus can account for why our activity has to be what it is.

This is the way every science has to work. If we do not have any direct intuition into what we are ourselves, we have much less direct intuition into what other things or other selves are in their substance. We know what these others are, as rational or nonrational, as sentient or nonsentient, as living or nonliving, a fortiori only through what they do in their proper activity. It is through observation of what things do that empirical sciences arrive at saying something of what things are. They too are proceeding from a certain kind of reflection on what has to be thought of as a proper activity of their subject matter, whatever kind of substance that may be.

But empirical sciences do not and cannot come to a method of total reflection, as we do for our knowledge of the self. Just as there is a certain element of observation in our method, so also there is an element of reflection in their method, in that they go by a certain circularity between what things do and what they are or between their activity and their substance if they allow for this kind of language in speaking of their subject matter, as they should. But they do not push this reflection all the way back to the question of substance, as we are doing here with regard to the self. They only make the same supposition as we do in terms of some proper activity of some substance. Here we are trying to explore this supposition critically with regard to the self in order to show how the self can be known for what it is through what it does in its proper activity.

We should not ignore the circularity of this or any other scientific method. It represents a hermeneutic circle or a circle of discovery and disclosure. The supposition is simply that every being has an activity of its own, its proper activity, and that it can be known in its substance or for what it is in its essence through this proper activity. As we have noted from the beginning, in the introduction to this philosophical science of the self or of human life as a whole, we do not question whether we can know ourselves. Now the point is to see more exactly that we come to know what we are through reflection on our proper activity in our self-consciousness.

This is a supposition we do not question. To question it would be to make an even more difficult supposition to sustain. We would have to suppose that we have a direct intuition into what we are in our substance, and we would have to describe in what this intuition consists independently of all activity, something that no one can do given the way we come to know anything, our own selves included. Even Descartes had to use his methodical doubt, which was an activity, to get to what he thought of as his innate idea of the soul as thinking.

In fact, it would be impossible to really question our supposition since the only way of answering any question about any being is by looking at its activity; that is, by looking at what it does and how it does it. This is the only way of coming to know what a thing is in its substance.

The real question for us is how the substance of the self comes to be distinguished from its activity and how its activity comes to be seen as distinct from it as substance. It should be clear that we are not trying to do as if the substance could be separated from the activity or the activity from the substance. This is why we speak of the self as positively existing. As a substance, it cannot be except with its proper activity through which it actualizes itself or exists. Nor can the proper activity be except as the activity of this substance, which produces it in its existing. That is the point of referring to the activity as *proper*. It is proper to the substance of which it is the activity in such a way that it can be used dialectically to identify the substance to say what it is in itself.

The reason for proposing a distinction between the substance of the self and its proper activity or activities is that the activities are diverse while the substance is one. For example, in one and the same self there is the activity of intelligence and the activity of will, both proper to the same substance. To will is not the same as to understand, yet both to will and to understand are acts of the same self.

In fact, there is even a diversity of intellectual acts and willful acts, different judgments and different decisions made, all of which are acts of the same self. I decide to do different things at different times and I follow different intellectual pursuits, as I constitute myself in my existence. If in this sort of diversity of acts and activities the self is and remains an identity in itself, what we call a substance, then it follows that the activity has to be distinct from its substance or the substance from its activity.

I make this kind of distinction when I speak of my activity, not as myself, but as *mine*. My activity cannot be except as mine; that is, unless I produce it. Nor can I be fully myself without producing my activity. But when I produce this activity,

I produce it as something that is an "accident" to my self; that is, which accedes or inheres in me as in a substance even though I do not exist as a substance except with and through such an actualization or an "accident." I actualize myself or *what* I am substantially through my activity.

2.6.3 Granting this distinction between activity and substance, then, how is the relation between the activity and its substance to be understood in human existence as we understand it here? Substantial being already entails a certain degree of completion or perfection, what we have referred to as its first perfection. At whatever stage of my development I may be as a self, I am already conscious of myself as something or someone with an identity of my own and with a certain degree of completion or perfection. But this perfection, which I have as a substance, is only a first perfection, which calls for a further or second perfection.

I discover myself, not just as already having arrived at a certain completion through my activity but also as still having to always complete myself further, as having to act in one way or another, in order to bring my being to its second or ulterior perfection in a process of self-actualization.

This relation between a first and a second perfection is something essential to the existence of the self. Action is a way of perfection for the self, and it is a necessary way as long as the self remains somehow imperfect or still to be perfected in the historical tension of its human life.

Moreover, this second perfection cannot come to the self except through its own activity, which remains in it as its perfection. I become what I do to the extent that what I do remains in me as my perfection. And I cannot not do; I require this second perfection for myself. This is what makes me exist as the self that I am and want to be.

How long this goes on, of course, depends on the life of the self, which has its highs and lows. It is not restricted to just a first moment of substantial existence for the self, whenever that would be. At any moment of its substantial development, the self still has this exigency for further perfection. It is as though every achievement of second perfection passed into the realm or became part of the self's first perfection, calling for still further or second perfection, for the substance of the self is never something static or closed in on itself. It is ever in communicative interaction with other selves, shaping and reshaping the world and itself, in taking its own historical initiative. What is called for in the perfecting of self differs at different stages of life, but something is always called for at every stage of life in accordance with what the self wants of itself and of others in the world. This is why we have to speak of existence as having a certain priority over essence for the self. It is a historical priority oriented toward a future second perfection of self as communing with others in the world, stemming from an essence already constituted in a perfection as given or as actualized in the present.

Finally, all this is true, not only of myself but of every self in the world. We have spoken of the self as communing with others in the world. In seeking its own perfection through activity, each self encounters other selves also seeking their own perfection in the world. Such encounters open the way to mutual recognition, which is also historically constitutive of selfhood as we shall see when more is said later about communicative interaction on the level of rational self-consciousness.

But in the very idea of encounter between selves, each seeking its ulterior perfection, it is already possible to see how a world is constituted for selves in communicative interaction. Each self, seeking its own second perfection in its existing, meets other selves seeking their own second perfection in their existing, and through this intersection of projects a new perfection is constituted, that of a community reshaping the world or of a universe intimately bound up with the perfection of selves.

There is more to explore about this ulterior or second perfection of the universe in what will be discussed as culture when we have seen more about the activity of the selves in the world. For the moment it is enough to have seen how the universe itself is not just something given by nature but also something historically constituted in its second perfection through human activity.

2.7 ALTERNATIVE VIEWS

Apart from the general difficulty that many have with the idea of substance as representing something distinct from activity or process and that we tried to deal with directly in our discussion, two views in particular seem especially worth mentioning in connection with our view here, that of David Hume and Immanuel Kant.

Hume rejects not only the idea of the self but also the very idea of substance as anything more than a bundle of impressions in one's consciousness. In this he may have had too fixed an idea of substance and too narrow an idea of impression.

We do not deny that coming to know the self is a matter of impressions. We only insist that it is also a matter of reflection and self-consciousness that unifies impressions and mindfulness into an identity of substance or a substantial identity.

Kant took issue with Hume and, through a reflection on the activity of knowing and of willing, arrived at a knowledge of the self as I (*Ich*) or as ego, but he denied that this ego could be known as substance or in its substantiality. He too may have had too fixed an idea of substance, but his insistence on transcendental reflection to arrive at a knowledge of the knowing subject was well taken.

Kant rejected any idea of a direct intuition on our part into the nature or the substance of the self. In this we agree with him. But he supposed that only such a direct intuition can give us a knowledge of the self in its substance. We claim that reflection gives us knowledge of the self in its substance as distinct but not separate from its activity. In what follows we inquire further into what the self is in its substance and in its properly human activity as intelligent and willful.

3

The Substance of Human Selfhood as Union of Body and Soul Understood as Composite of Matter and Form

Having distinguished selfhood in its substance from its activities as existing in its historical as well as its natural tension, we now turn to examine more precisely *what* it is in its substance. What immediately occurs in this regard is that this has to do with how we refer to ourselves sometimes as bodies and sometimes as souls alternatively, as bodies or as souls or as both at once, not as two substances but as one substance, or again as two substances, each with an identity of its own as a whole.

This has been labeled as the "mind/body problem" in modern philosophy, even though the problem arose long before modern philosophy, in ancient philosophy with Plato and Aristotle.

We think of the self as being or as having a body through which it is in the world. But the body of a self is not just any body. It is a living body with consciousness and with a mind.

We also think of the self as having a soul or a mind in communion with other selves in a way that distinguishes it from any other living or sentient bodies in the world. How is all this to be understood with regard to *what* the self is in its substance?

In what sense do we say that we are or have a body? In what sense do we say that we are or have a soul? If we say that the self has an identity of its own, how can we say that the self is both body and soul? If we say that it is or has both body and soul, can we still say that it is one substance in its identity? How are the two one in the identity of a self? How is this union between the two to be understood?

Moreover, if there is a union of body and soul, which of the two most properly gives the self its identity as a self—the body or the soul? Is it enough just to be a body or even a living body in order to be a self? Or is a soul or mind also required and even a higher kind of soul than that of nonrational animals?

If it is the soul that more properly gives the self its identity as a self, how is the body part of this identity? Is the body essential to the identity, or is it only an appendage to the soul, something accidental or incidental to what it is in its substance as a mind or as a soul? Could the soul be the soul of a self without being the soul of its body? How does the body of a self enter into the identity of a self so that the self is not like any other body in the world?

The self finds itself in the world as a material being among other material beings and acts as a material thing even though it thinks of itself as something more than just material, such as a rock, a tree, or even a cat. The self also depends on the material world, uses it, expresses itself in it, and transforms it in the very activity of being itself as something historical as well as natural.

The self also transcends the merely material or natural world, as we have already seen in the primordial fact of human existence. It transforms the world by elevating its own human body to a higher degree of perfection in being without ceasing to be material and natural.

3.1 FRAMING THE MIND/BODY PROBLEM REGARDING HOW WE CONCEIVE THE SELF IN ITS SUBSTANCE EXISTING IN HISTORICAL AND NATURAL TENSION

WE HAVE COME TO A DISTINCTION OF A SELF in its substance from itself as existing in its many and diverse proper activities using illustrations of activities of many kinds, some in the order of nature alone, some in the order of historical cultures, and many in the order of both as combined in our rational consciousness without distinguishing whether they were activities of the mind or activities of the body, whether they were mental or bodily, mindful or physical, or both at the same time. The mind/body problem arises when we start distinguishing proper activities from one another and then start considering one or the other as more indicative of what the self is in its substance, sometimes even to the point of excluding any other as indicative of what the self is in its substance.

If we take the position of Descartes, for example, we find that he has taken thinking as the sole activity indicating what the self is in its substance. "I think, therefore I am," he says, and this is for him in his reflective self-consciousness a clear and distinct idea of what he is in his substance, a *res cogitans*—a thinking thing.

He is not unaware that that there are other things that have their own proper activity as *res extensa*, or as extended thing, which have their own proper activities, including some that may also have the proper activity of thinking like he does. But that does not pertain to anything in his substance as a thinking thing. He even excludes his own imagination from the clear and distinct idea of what he is in his substance, though he is left with the problem of what to think of his body existing with proper activities of its own in a world of many bodies weighing and pressing on his body.

Thus, we see in what sense the position of Descartes regarding the self in its substance is branded as idealist or mentalist. But not everyone goes along with Descartes when it comes to saying what the self is in its substance. In fact, there are many more who take a position directly opposite of Descartes's, saying that the self in its substance is no more than a body. And they have many reasons for saying that in the proper activities that indicate interaction among the many bodily parts, from the most minute parts of the brain all the way to biggest muscles and the toughest bones of head and body, not to mention the nerves.

When we see all that as proper to a self, it is indicative of how the self is a body in its substance. This is often dubbed the realist position in opposition to the idealist position of Descartes and of many others in modern philosophy, whence comes the mind/body problem in indicating what the self is in its substance. Which of the two, mind or body, is truly indicative of what the self is in its substance, or at least more indicative than the other? Or again, can we have one without the other in some union that we can call substantial?

This is the mind/body problem reduced to its simplest form. Is the self in its substance a mind or is it a body? There are reasons for saying yes on either side: It is a mind, actually exercising intelligence and will in their reflective consciousness. We have adopted some of this reasoning to show that the self is a substance in its identity as a reflective self-consciousness. Others who have also followed this sort of reasoning starting from reflective self-consciousness in the self speak of a first-person ontology as distinct *from a third-person ontology* in referring to things that do not speak in the first person and are only spoken of in the third person.

Even when the distinction is made between activities of the mind on the one hand and activities only of the body on the other hand, apart from mind, the mind/body problem remains, calling for a theoretical resolution. There are very strong reasons for saying that the self is a mind in its substance or ontology. But there are also very strong reasons for saying that the self is a body in its substance, as has long been shown in the physical, the biological, and now in the neurological sciences, where states of consciousness can be closely mapped out in different parts of the physical brain.

Philosophers looking at both sides of this question find it difficult to go with either side. To go with only one side alone would be to reduce the other side to nothing. To go with the side of the body would be to reduce to nothing the very side on which the problem has arisen for us as philosophers, that of reflective self-consciousness. To go with the side of the mind alone would give us the idea that the self is pure idea in its substance having nothing to do with the body.

Among those who consider this mind/body in terms of these two alternatives, mind or body, and who give serious thought to each alternative in their reflective self-consciousness, the inclination usually goes to the side of the body or to the side of the third-person ontology rather than to the side of the mind or of the first-person ontology even though they want to give the mind its due as something substantial for the self in its self-consciousness. But there is another way of giving both the mind and the body their due with regard to the self in its substance than remaining caught in this interplay of either one or the other in opposition to one another. That way is going with both one and the other, both mind and body, as we have seen in reflecting on our human existence or our proper activities that indicate what the self in its identity as mindful in engaging in the most physical activities.

3.2 THE CONCEPT OF SELF AS UNION OF BODY AND SOUL IN ITS SUBSTANCE

We have seen how we come to a distinction of the self in its substance as representing its identity in all the diversity of its proper activities and in the development and the plurality of those proper activities coming after one another in a tension that is both natural and historical.

We have also seen how the human soul, which includes mind or mindfulness, is the principle of life in a body having life only in potency; that is, as being in tension toward life. This presupposes that the soul is something in the substance or in the body as identity in the making for the self through activities proper to the self in its existing.

Now when we speak of life with regard to the self, we do not mean just bare life, as in plant life, nor just sentient life, as in animals, but *rational* life as in human selves. And we have seen how that includes a diversity of activities: activities of the soul or the mind, such as those of intelligence and will on the level of reasoning, judging, and willing, or those of the body, such as physical exercise or other bodily functions, or those of the two combining as one in activities of rational consciousness as we find in the rise of many different cultures, each one a distinct mode of communion for selves in the order of historical consciousness.

To conceive the idea of a substantial union of body and soul for the self in its substance in the context of a distinction not a separation between the two, it is especially important to focus on this third, or combinatory, kind of proper activity in the existence of the self, which as self is in tension toward a first perfection that is both natural and historical, or as cultural, according to both natural and historical nurturing. It is there that we see clearly and distinctly, to use the expression of Descartes, how closely interweaving body and soul are in the proper activity of the self as one identity in the making as it moves toward its first perfection as a substance.

But it is not only there that this union is to be found. It is also to be found in activities of the self that come before the emergence of reflective consciousness and mindful communion and are in preparation for that emergence, both naturally and historically in human communities, in the way elders care for emerging identities in their communities, again both naturally and historically or culturally.

And it is to be found in all the proper activities of a self who has come to its first degree of perfection as a self in its self-consciousness, as is evidenced in the way our thinking is influenced by and depends on what we see and what we hear and in the way our free will is influenced by and depends on our natural inclinations. We shall see more about this later on when we come to reflect more directly on intelligence and free choice in our reflective self-consciousness. But it is enough for now to acknowledge this influence and this dependence on sensation and on natural inclinations in our reflective self-consciousness generally, as has long been pointed out to us not just by psychologists and sociologists but also more recently and increasingly by neuroscientists.

What they have to say that is true and important for selfhood in its substance is not that the powers of reasoning and willing are reducible to merely natural functions as seen in the particular sciences of psychology, sociology, or neurology but that these powers of reasoning and willing in reflective self-consciousness can act only in unison with a mature healthy body, perceptive senses, and strong natural inclinations.

What we demonstrated above, by reflection on proper activities that combine reason with sense perception and free will with natural affections or tension, is that reasoning and willing freely, even in their highest degree of first perfection, still are influenced by and depend on for the whole of our lives the functions of sense perception in consciousness and of natural inclinations in free willing.

3.3 THE UNDERSTANDING OF SELF AS A COMPOSITE OF MATTER AND OF RATIONAL SOUL AS FORM

It should be noted that we have shifted from speaking of mind and body to speaking of soul and body. This is to adjust the formulation of the problem as not just a mind/body problem primarily as one of body with which the idea of substance is more usually associated.

We speak of soul as the principle of life, or more explicitly of proper activities, both natural and historical. As only a principle, soul is not of itself a substance or a body. It is only one of two principles that constitute a material substance or a body, the other principle of which we speak as *matter*, to be understood not as a body but as a principle constitutive of a material substance or of a body. The other coprinciple with matter we speak of as constitutive of a living material substance or living body, we speak of as soul or as form for any body or three-dimensional object, living or nonliving, *form* being the generic name for the principle that determines matter as one kind of body or another, living or nonliving, sentient or nonsentient, rational or nonrational.

In other words, *matter* and *form* are conceived as two distinct principles implicated with one another in the constitution of a body or of a material substance of any kind, while soul is the specific kind of form of living bodies or material substances at the three levels of living we distinguish in our experience, the rational, the sentient, and the plant. The question then is: how do we show that this is the truth concerning the reflective self-consciousness of the self in its substance?

As we have seen, there are many approaches to the mind/body problem with regard to the self in its substance, some from the standpoint of the mind and some from the standpoint of the body. Those who start from the standpoint of the body, of a third-person ontology, or of a three-dimensional object in the world, as in physicalism, suppose that the self is first and foremost something physical with its own set of physical functions or neurons wired together in the head of a self. They presuppose that the human substance is a body and have difficulty conceiving of mind or self-consciousness as anything more than a body or three-dimensional object, even as living.

Those who start from the standpoint of the mind, of a first-person ontology, or of subjectivity in self-consciousness, as we have done here and as many existential philosophers do, suppose that the self is first and foremost a consciousness in its substance. They presuppose that the human substance is a mind or a soul and have difficulty including any body under that, as Descartes did when he spoke of himself as a thinking thing apart even from his own body as an extended thing.

We have already argued that the human substance has to be understood first and foremost as something actively and reflectively self-conscious; that is, something having to do with mind or soul as distinct from any bodily function as such or any third-person ontology as such. It is from this side that we must approach the mind/body problem, which is perhaps the only way to arrive at a philosophically satisfying solution to the problem.

Coming at the problem from the other side, which presupposes that the human body can be considered as a complete substance in itself without mind or without soul not only creates the problem of having to think of the mind as something other than the body but also makes it impossible to unite body and soul in one substance once a gap has been opened up between soul and body. If one assumes that the human body is a complete substance in itself, one is left with the problem of whether or how there can be mind in the human being as such and, if the existence of such a thing as mind or reflective self-consciousness is admitted, whether it can be substantially one with the body and not just an epiphenomenon or some abstract idea separate from the body.

From the standpoint that we have taken from the beginning of our reflection on human existence, the self in its substance is understood more readily in terms of the mind or the soul. When I reflect on my self-conscious activity, I find myself more in my soul than in my body. In fact, it might even be thought that from this perspective the body should be excluded from the substantiality of the self, taking the soul as a complete substance in itself, as Descartes did in his exercise of methodical doubt.

We shall argue that neither the soul nor the body of a self can be taken as a complete substance in itself, but the problem for us will be to show how the body cannot be excluded from the substantiality of the self even from the standpoint of the human mind or the rational soul.

3.3.1 Our task therefore is to show how the body is essential to the human substance in such a way that the substantial soul would not be what it is essentially, even in its own subsistence, without its body. For this task let us pick up our reflection from where we left off in the third part of our discussion on the primordial fact of human existence, when we were speaking of the self as *in the world*, by reflecting now particularly on the necessity of coming to know ourselves in our selfhood only by way of a reflection on an activity that starts in our body as a three-dimensional object in the world.

What we showed as part of the fact we begin with in our reflective self-consciousness is that this reflection takes place always in some ongoing activity that starts off as physical and organic in our body and that remains bodily even as it becomes part of our sense consciousness in our reflective self-consciousness, the reflection that takes place in the presence of other self-consciousnesses, not just by looking into other selves objectively as in a mirror to discover ourselves but by a sort of recuperation of our self-consciousness in communicative interaction with other selves in the world through physiological, psychological, and economic contacts of all sorts.

Other selves have to be understood as substances in their own selfhood no less than our own selves, even as three-dimensional objects facing us as three-dimensional objects in mutual recognition. But there are also other objects or substances to be considered that are not selves in the full sense that we are thinking of when we think of a self-conscious self, substances or three-dimensional objects like cats, trees, and stones. These too can be considered as substances in that they are seen as having an identity of their own, albeit in a lesser sense than a self. They too are bodies, like the self, but of different kinds, some living and therefore with a soul, whether sentient or just vegetative, and some not living and therefore with a form that is not a soul. Soul in its diverse forms is the form for living things, as Aristotle explains, but there are also things that can be identified as things even if they are not living.

Having surveyed all these different things that can be identified as substances in the world, I now have to come back to myself to think about how my body is a part of me in my substance; that is, in a substantial union with my soul. To do this I must understand how it is necessary that reflection into my self-consciousness always begins for me as a kind of recuperation in an ongoing activity in which the initiative has not been entirely from me in my self-consciousness. It is through an action that is already external to my self-consciousness that I come to discover myself even interiorly.

To be sure, this reflective activity is mine in that it flows from me in my substance. It is important to keep this in mind. But at the same time it is important to recognize that the activity did not begin only from me in my self-consciousness. The question for us is: how can it be mine prior to my being self-conscious? Or how can it be mine even as something physiological?

If we tried to think of what a pure self-consciousness would be in act, we would have to say that it begins only from itself as self-consciousness, purely out of its own initiative as act. It would be a pure transparency to itself, without any density from an exterior ongoing activity on which it would have to reflect. It would be pure certainty of itself without any doubt about its identity, a pure Cartesian cogitation or a pure Kantian intuition into self, which we say are not true acts of reflective self-consciousness such as the ones we start from in our human consciousness.

We are not such pure self-consciousnesses. We are a kind of consciousness that has to reflect into itself from an activity that is external to it, even in a physical sense as well as a psychological sense. Now this activity, as external and physical, can be associated with the wide diversity of objects in the world we surveyed briefly earlier, all of them impressing themselves upon me as bodily things. It is only as a bodily thing that I am receptive of them as bodily things, even as I receive recognition from other self-consciousnesses through seeing, hearing, and feeling other selves in their caring for myself.

We can also associate this external activity with the self-consciousness of other selves by whom we are illuminated and enlightened in our own self-consciousness in acts of mutual recognition such as smiling and speaking. But in thinking of the soul/body problem, we have to associate this external activity more immediately with our own body, for that is where the external activity we have to reflect on comes to existence. Reflection into my own self-consciousness begins always from an activity I have to think of as my own and at the same time as external to my self-consciousness as such.

What gives rise to my reflective self-consciousness most immediately is an activity that I see as more intimate to myself than any other activity that is external to me in my self-consciousness, an activity that is emanating from me rather than from any other self or any other three-dimensional object in the world. This activity that I think of as mine or proper to myself is still somehow external to me in my self-consciousness, insofar as it is already ongoing as I become self-conscious in it. Yet I also think of it as mine or of myself as performing it. As I come to think of it as mine, as something that flows from me as a substance, I come to think of myself as a body as well as a self-consciousness, that is, as a union of body and soul, even as a three-dimensional object surrounded by other three-dimensional objects.

3.3.2 To see all this more clearly and to understand how body and soul compose with one another as one substance constituted of matter and form, we have to reflect more particularly in a phenomenology of activities of the self that more precisely represent the kind of composition that we are trying to define, activities such as those of sensation and feeling.

3.3.2.1 Let us begin with a phenomenology of sense perception. I see, I hear, and I touch things in the world, three of our most basic sense activities as human beings. I find myself as one seeing, hearing, and touching within a whole world of things seen, heard, and touched. But I see only by opening my eyes to see. I hear only by listening. I touch only by reaching out to take in. In other words, I discover myself in the tension of one already opening my eyes to see, listening in order to hear, and reaching out in order to touch.

What is involved here is not just some passivity with regard to external things impressing themselves as objects upon my senses but also an activity on my part using external organs, such as eyes, ears, and touch as receptive senses. These are activities in which I am conscious of myself seeing, hearing, and touching; activities that are composites of an external bodily organ and an internal act of sensation giving form to an external act such as vision of color, hearing of sound, touch of texture. I can think of these three different kinds of sensation as three different forms or acts, each with its own external physical organ. Sense consciousness is thus a composite activity requiring both a bodily organ and an internal form or act of consciousness that emerges through various bodily functions.

Now these are activities that I consider proper to myself as a human substance and hence as expressive of a composition that is characteristic of me in my substance. Thus I infer from the composition in this, *my* sense activity, which I consider integral or proper to myself as a self, a similar composition of matter and of substantial form, understanding matter as a principle that is perfected by a form, as it is in the organs of vision, hearing, and touching. From this I conclude not only to a union of body and soul in my substance but also to a composition of matter and form necessary even for the existence of the rational soul, just as eyes are necessary for the act of seeing, ears necessary for the act of hearing, and touch necessary for the act of touching.

3.3.2.2 A similar argument can be constructed reflectively from a phenomenology of feelings and emotions in our rational consciousness. These too are composite activities in which I come to know myself as a human substance in my rational consciousness. I find myself affected by moods, not just by things seen, heard, or touched but also by physiological movements within myself as a body. These moods or emotions are not just passively received in my consciousness but also are actively taken over in my subjectivity or in my existence as a rational consciousness. I make them my own, I make them my very own so to speak, and I feel depressed or elated. But I also know that these moods can come and go through changes in my physical makeup and that I can control them by taking different physical means, such as chemicals and physical exercise or by just talking about them with someone in psychiatric therapy.

Through psychoanalysis I may try to account for these moods of mine through events that took place in my past, but in all of this I am still discovering only that, no matter what the level of my self-consciousness, I am a body in the world affected in different ways, not only by what I see, hear, and touch with regard to external objects in the world but also by traces of past experiences going back even to the womb, as well as by chemicals I may be ingesting. I am changing not only in my consciousness but also in the way my consciousness depends on my body, as functions of sense existence depend on organs or as feelings depend on emotions in my subconscious. The composition of my changing moods as different forms of my consciousness affected by changes in my physical makeup is a sure indication of the composition of my soul as form with its matter in my substance.

3.3.2.3 Hence, in conclusion, to speak of my body is to think of what is most properly mine in the world that I face in consciousness. We have spoken of only one or two of the composite activities of what Maurice Merleau-Ponty speaks of as my own or my proper body (*mon corps propre*), those that seem to touch most immediately on consciousness and lend themselves more readily to some reflection in rational consciousness. There are other activities of the body, such as digestion and reproduction, that are also composite activities of the composite but that do not relate so immediately to selfhood in its reflective self-consciousness.

We do not have to go into these here. All that needs to be said is that all are activities of the self as a living thing or substance, composite activities from which we infer a union of body and soul or a composition of form and matter that is peculiar to the rational species of being or substance in a first-person ontology.

It is for other, more particular sciences, such as psychology, biology, or neurology, to explore the ins and outs of these diverse activities and functions on which the existence of rational self-consciousnesses depends in the exercise of all its sense and emotional activities.

All that needs to be said here in our philosophical inquiry is that if the reflective activity of the self depends on its activity as a composite, then, it can only be because the soul, which is the principle of perfection in relation to matter as that which is to be perfected in the composite as well as the principle of its own reflective activity, is the substantial form of the composite requiring its own matter or the form of a composite having self-conscious life in potency, to hearken back to Aristotle's definition of soul. For this reason, any deficiency in the material order of the body can seriously affect the very level of one's self-consciousness, as in the case of a migraine headache or severe hunger.

My body, then, is precisely this thing in the world in which I always already find myself. It is a momentum in tension for me individually, and it is also what weighs me down and requires me to labor in everything I undertake to make myself.

All my activities of knowing and willing begin in sensation, imagination, and sensitivity, as we shall see more clearly later on, activities that are an integral part of the self's bodily existence. Every internal act of mine always has an irreducible exteriority to it so that I can never say that I am myself except in my body and through my body. Even my freedom can only start from the interplay of emotions in my body, as we shall also see more clearly later, again activities that are an integral part of my body. This necessity of always starting and having to start from the body is proof that matter is an essential constituent of the self in its substance and that the rational soul is its substantial form in the first-person ontology of the self in its reflective consciousness.

3.4 THE DYNAMIC OF MATTER AS BEING IN POTENCY IN THE THIRD-PERSON ONTOLOGIES RISING UP TO THE FIRST- AND SECOND-PERSON ONTOLOGIES OF SELVES

With this understanding of the rational soul as substantial form of its body in composition with its perfectible matter in potency to that form, we can show further or demonstrate that there are not just two ontologies—one, the first- and second-person ontology and the other, the third-person ontology—but at least three, if not more, ontologies in what is referred to as the third-person ontology—that is, ontologies that do not include a rational soul, or a reflective self-consciousness in the first or second person, as their substantial form if we include communion or the I/thou relation among selves as part of the first- and second-person ontology.

It is the diversity of these ontologies that gives rise to the diversity of the particular sciences within the phenomenon of human life and communion in the world. We have spoken repeatedly of three such ontologies in their substance: the sentient, the plant, and the nonliving. Each one represents a composite of a different kind due to its substantial form, as sentient soul, as plant soul, or as substantial form that is not a principle of life. And to each of these ontologies we have assigned different particular sciences such as psychology and sociology for the sentient level of ontology, biology and zoology for the living level of ontology, and physics and chemistry for the nonliving level.

This we have spoken of from the standpoint of a philosophy of human life as a whole or of the philosophy of a self's human existence in communion with other selves in the world. Now, from the same standpoint, with the understanding of the rational soul as the substantial form of its body in composition with its perfectible matter in potency to that form, we can also show how the self in its first- and second-person ontology does not simply drop or leave behind all third-person ontologies but, rather, integrates them into its first- and second-person ontology as necessary conditions for its own proper emergence as rational and communal.

For in the understanding of matter and form as principles of any corporeal thing, including the self as a corporeal thing, we have to take the form as the principle of perfection and matter as that which is perfectible or in potency to the perfection, of which the form is the principle. This holds for the human or rational form as well as any of the lower levels of ontology. This is where we get the idea of a first perfection for any substance, at whatever level of ontology we can think of: rational or nonrational, sentient or nonsentient, living or nonliving.

But we do not get this idea of first perfection for a substance without the idea of something perfectible or in potency to that perfection, whence the idea of matter as a principle at every level of composite ontology. Matter has to be thought of as the principle of individuation for all bodies that come under diverse substantial forms in their first perfection. Such a principle, namely matter as being in potency and as principle of individuation, cannot be understood except by analogy to the form of which it is being in potency.

In other words, we have to think of matter as a kind of disposition toward a substantial form that can take some time to develop in an individual substance, especially in a self whose form of consciousness requires so many functions to come together, both physical and psychological, and that can also wax and wane according to different conditions of age and of psychological health or pathology. Matter as found in any composite is first and foremost in potency to its form in a substance as long as that substance perdures. But there is more to potency in matter than just the potency to a particular substantial form. There is also potency to other forms. That is why material substances are subject to corruption, where matter is not annihilated but becomes substrate for another form, as in the case of death for a self when its matter becomes substrate for a corpse, rather than continuing as the matter of a living, rational human being.

It is interesting to note that the ancients thought of the heavenly bodies as incorruptible. Aristotle accounted for that in his cosmology by saying that the substantial form of the heavenly bodies exhausted the potency of their matter. But this did not prevent him from seeing that there was also in the matter of lower or sublunar bodies a potency to the substantial form of higher bodies whence came a certain theory of evolution of species in the universe that we have alluded to and that we can now show or demonstrate to be true in the universe that we know in experience.

Starting from basic elements or from nonliving substances we observe in the universe, we can say that their matter is in potency, not just to their substantial form as principle of their first perfection but also to the next higher form of first perfection in substances we also observe in the universe, which we call living and includes a wide variety of plants. From this idea of potency in matter we conclude that matter is not left behind but integrated into a higher species of substantial form, which we call living.

Then, starting from the level of living substances with their higher level of first perfection as substances, we can say the same thing again regarding the potency of their matter. It is in potency, not just to its substantial form as its living first perfection but also to the next higher form of first perfection in substances we observe in the universe, namely the sentient, which again does not leave the living form behind but integrates it as a condition for this higher species of substantial form, the sentient.

And finally, starting from the level of living sentient substances, we can say the same regarding the potency of their matter. It is in potency not just to its substantial form as living sentient but also to the next higher form of first perfection in substances we observe in the universe, namely the rational self-consciousness, which again does not leave the sentient, the living, and the nonliving behind but integrates it all as a necessary condition for this higher species of substantial form to be in composition with matter.

There are no higher forms of first perfection in substances to turn to in our reflective self-consciousness than this, the one of rational consciousness, from which we started our entire inquiry into the substance of the self. What the understanding of the composition of the rational soul as substantial form of its body demonstrates is that mind or soul and the body are one substance in its first- and second-person ontology or its first perfection as substance and that the higher consciousness of the self is not higher without integrating the lower degrees of first perfection in substances and without depending on such integration for its own first perfection as substance and for its own proper activity as rational.

Thus the entire process of an evolution of species in nature, from the lower to the higher third-person ontologies all the way to the first-person ontology of selves who are still enmeshed with the potency of their matter, can be understood in relation to matter as being in potency even in a substance whose substantial form is at the same time spirit that is one and simple, struggling for its own second perfection as intelligent and free; that is, transcending this realm of the material principle in its substance.

It remains for us to inquire more deeply into the first- and second-person ontology of selves in communion with one another on the level of intelligence and will, where the body gives way to a higher degree of first perfection for the self purely in its reflective self-consciousness.

4

The Human Soul as Truly, but Not Purely, Spiritual in Its Subsistence

It is relatively easy to conceive of the self as a composite of matter and form in its substance and of the rational soul as form of its body in the natural order we share with other animals, which have their own sense consciousness and their own sense appetites or emotions. But is it enough to account for every aspect of the rational soul in its reflective self-consciousness, with its own intelligence and its own free will in creating its own original communal historical order out of the natural order for its own second perfection as rational, intelligent, and free?

Resolving the mind/body problem as we have done, with the notion of a substantial union of body and soul, or the concept of a substance composed of matter and a rational soul as substantial form, does not answer this further question. It only brings us to this question, which does not even occur to many or to most who deal with the mind/body problem but which must occur to us here in our inquiry, as the question of a reflective self-consciousness in its own first- and second-person ontology, not found in any third-person ontology, where there is no reflective self-consciousness to be found, not even in the sphere of nonrational animals

There is more to the first- and second-person ontology of selves in their reflective self-consciousness than just being the substantial form of some matter in a composite. There is something that pertains to this form in its first perfection, not just as being rational or reflectively self-conscious but also as entering into communion with other rational and reflectively self-conscious selves so that this higher ontological dimension of selfhood has to be seen as proper, not just to highly developed intelligences and wills but also to all selves in their reflective self-consciousness at whatever level of culture they may find themselves in their second perfection.

We shall identify this higher ontological dimension as something properly *spiritual*, that is, as something that is often thought of as separate from matter, which is something hardly in keeping with the idea of the human soul as the substantial form of a composite that is principle of life in a body that has life in potency. Such a substantial form can hardly be thought of as separate from matter since it is a constitutive principle of a material thing along with its matter.

Hence there is a paradox in speaking of the human soul as spiritual along with its being substantial form of a material composite. But it is a paradox we cannot avoid if we are going to account for every aspect of human existence we find in our experience of the primordial fact we start from in our methodical scientific reflection, including the aspect of a first- and second-person ontology, or mindfulness, that is so often overlooked or minimized in solving the mind/body problem.

To insist on mindfulness in a first- and second-person ontology in resolving the mind/body problem, without denying the essential givenness of the body in a third-person ontology, is to open up a whole new dimension for inquiry, which is not exhausted by any account of second perfection in the physical order, the biological order, the psychological order, or the economic order of proper activities, a dimension that is first seen in any reflective self-consciousness but that rises to higher degrees of second perfection for human beings through the exercise of intelligence and will.

It is to this higher degree of second perfection for selves in their reflective self-consciousness that we must now turn in our inquiry, to examine the paradox of a soul that is at once substantial form of its matter but whose life is oriented to higher, more spiritual ends or second perfection, both personally and communally.

This is the ontological dimension of selfhood we shall name *spirit*, over and above the soul's being merely rational, in relation to our animal senses and our natural emotions. It is the ontological dimension of selfhood we have to explore in terms of intelligence and will as distinct from human senses and human emotions. It is the dimension in which, far from being isolated from one another, we find ourselves most in communion with other selves as we shall see when we come to examine the practice of selfhood in the historical order as a whole.

4.1 THE REFLECTIVE SELF-CONSCIOUSNESS OF THE HUMAN SOUL AS TRULY, BUT NOT PURELY, SPIRITUAL IN ITS COMMUNION WITH OTHER SELVES

THERE IS MORE TO THE HUMAN SOUL than just being the substantial form of its matter in a composite, like the soul of any animal. There is something that raises the human composite to a higher degree of first perfection or of ontology in its substance than that attained by lower, merely sentient animals, something that gives rise to a higher kind of proper activity that we call rational, as it lends a higher dignity and respect for all that human beings or selves are and do in communicative interaction with one another.

We know this implicitly in our reflective self-consciousness as human beings, but we do not always think of it explicitly. Nor do we ordinarily try to specify more accurately what this something more is in our substance or what it may be about in our soul, something we have not yet examined in our philosophy of human existence. This is something that pertains primarily to the rational soul but that also pertains to the composite as a whole, inasmuch as the human soul is nevertheless the form of its body in that composite, lending its dignity to the whole substance in its identity. It is something that we have yet to name and to consider in the simple identity of the self.

What is this higher dignity of the soul and of the entire self in its reflective self-consciousness, and how is it to be conceived as pertaining to the self in its individual essence and in its communion with other selves?

We speak of the human soul, as we have come to understand it here, as substantial form in composition with its matter, but now we say that, as spirit, it subsists as something with its own identity in all the diversity of its proper activities and in the matter that it informs as form of a composite substance.

This idea of spiritual subsistence is not to be confused with the idea of substance we have already mentioned regarding its perduring identity as it develops in its first perfection. Nor is it to be confused with the idea of existence through proper activities discussed in chapter 2 as leading to one's second perfection. We tell of the subsistence of the soul in order to highlight its own proper ontology as spiritual, which underlies all the first- and second-person ontologies in every human self but which we have not mentioned yet, an ontology that marks the human soul as something higher in dignity than any composite of matter and form and that paradoxically elevates the entire human composite to something spiritual in both its substance and its existence, an elevation that makes it all the more difficult to peg as only a composite, such as any other composite of matter and form.

With the term *subsists* we refer to an ontological identity that is proper to each and every self. This subsistence, which we say is not tied directly to any physical organ or function of the composite, like the sentient and the emotional form is in the composite, takes precedence over the self as composite substance and elevates the sentient and emotional composite to the higher dignity of selfhood as rational.

Thus, we are using the term *subsists* to get at the most fundamental ontology of rational selfhood. We could in fact speak of any material composite, whether sentient, living, or nonliving, as subsisting as a whole, but that would not be enough to speak of any self in terms of its first-person ontology as *spirit*. To speak of the self as a body or as a composite material substance is still to speak of it in terms of a third-person ontology relevant to any material thing whether sentient, living, or nonliving. To speak of the human soul as subsistent in itself is to speak of it in its first-person ontology as a simple identity, not as a composite.

This is not to say that the soul subsists in itself independently of its being the substantial form of its matter. On the contrary, we shall see that the human soul does not subsist independently of its being the form of its body. This is part of its being rational in the way we exercise our proper activities of intelligence and will, which are not directly tied to any sense or emotional organs as are the powers of sensation and of emotion. The human soul does not and cannot function in its own proper activities of intelligence and will without some prior sense and emotional activity on which to reflect in its coming to its own self-consciousness as rational and deliberative.

We are only saying that the rational soul subsists as transcending its proper activities as activities of the composite and that, as transcending, it subsists in itself as spirit even though it does not do so without some extrinsic but still essential dependence on the direct experience of a sensible and emotional composite. This is the only way of doing justice to everything the human soul is in itself and in the substantial composite we have been speaking of.

To speak of the human soul as substantial form is still to speak of it as principle of specification for the material composite and as principle of its own proper activities as the form of its matter. To speak of the human soul as spiritual in itself is to speak of it as something irreducible to its being just the form of a composite, both as principle of specification for the material composite and as principle of the activities proper to the composite. It is to speak of the human soul as *spirit*: the name we give to what we think of as subsisting in a way that transcends material substance as such, even though this spirit, as the substantial form of a composite, depends on the composite and on the proper activities of the composite in the exercise of its own proper activities of intelligence and will, as we shall see later in terms of intelligence and of willing as the proper activities of the truly spiritual soul.

The term *spirit* is used in many ways in ordinary language. But here we will try to specify what it means for us in terms of what we shall call the properly spiritual or intentional activities of the self; namely those of intelligence and will. But there is one way of speaking we do want to include here in what we have in mind when we speak of spirit in a community or, more precisely, the spirit *of* a community. To speak of a spirit in each and every self in a community is to speak at the same time of these many selves in communion with one another on a level of intelligence and free will in *mutual recognition*, even if they are separate from one another as composite substances with matter as substantial principle of individuation for each one in its substance.

Georg Wilhelm Friedrich Hegel speaks of the spirit of a people as somehow embodied in a common substance for all, a people or a nation, or as the substance for all the individuals that make up a people or a nation. We do not wish to speak of any material or worldly substance that way, as if it were not substantially individuated in a composite of matter and form. But we do want to keep in mind that there is no individual self-consciousness or spirit except in the presence of other self-consciousnesses or in mutual recognition with other self-consciousnesses.

Spirit, as we want to speak of it here, even as a simple identity, is always at once personal and communal, as we have seen from the beginning regarding self-consciousness, without reducing individual selves to being mere parts of only one substance or collectivity. Even when we speak of purely spiritual or immaterial substances, we cannot speak of them in this way, much less than when we speak of spiritual substances that are also substantial forms of individualized material composites, as in the case of human composite substances.

We shall see all this more clearly when we come to define the different kinds of spiritual forms we can think of, some that are immaterial as well as some that are material, and the one that we are now speaking of paradoxically as at once immaterial in its subsistence and as substantial form in composition with some individuating matter.

Moreover, in order to think of the human soul as one in its subsistence prior to its being substantial form of a composite, we also have to think of it as truly, but not purely, simple in its identity as a self. It is this simple identity of the soul as spirit that explains how the self perdures in its substance even as it develops toward its second perfection through its proper activities of intelligence and free will. Spirit has to be thought of as simple in its identity relative to the identity of the composite as a whole constituted of both form and matter so that the identity of the composite self as material substance has to be thought of as derivative from this simple identity of its form as spiritual, and therefore as integrated into the dignity of its form as spirit. That is why the whole of a human being, body and soul, has to be treated as a matter of inalienable rights and duties.

It is in this sense that we have to speak of the spiritual soul as informing its body and of the human body as embodying a spiritual soul. Though we do want to speak of the human soul as truly spiritual and truly simple, we do not mean to say that it is purely spiritual and purely simple as a purely immaterial spirit or substantial form would be. The truly spiritual form that we are speaking of in the case of the human soul in its identity is at the same time essentially or ontologically one that is substantial form of its body. It is still one that is in historical tension with other selves through its body, as we will see more clearly when we reflect closely on the properly human activities of rational knowing and willing as these relate to or depend on the activities of sensation and emotion.

In seeking its own second perfection, taken as subsisting in itself or in its simple identity as spiritual soul, the human soul has to be taken as principle of its own proper activity as spiritual soul, like any other substantial form, whether in a composite or not, in the pursuit of its second perfection as a spiritual soul through the reflectively self-conscious activities of intelligence and free will. Pure spirits might do this in an instant, but the human spirit that is at once substantial form of its body in its development takes a lifetime to do it.

4.2 THE CONCEPTION OF INTELLIGENCE AND FREE WILL AS SPIRITUAL POWERS OF THE HUMAN SOUL CONTENDING WITH SENSE AND EMOTIONAL CONSCIOUSNESS IN REFLECTIVE SELF-CONSCIOUSNESS

How we are to conceive this second perfection for the spiritual soul remains a question for us at this time, as long as we have not reflected further on what the proper activities of the soul as spiritual lead to, both within history, as culture, or even beyond history, as religion. We shall do more of this reflection when we come to reflect more directly on these proper activities of the human spirit as such. Before we can do that, however, we must inquire more deeply into how the proper activities of the soul as spiritual come into play for the self in relation to the other activities of the soul we have already discussed as proper to the soul as substantial form of a material composite, namely those of sensation and emotion.

As substantial form, the soul is principle, not just of specification for a human being but also of its own proper activities as animal or as form of a composite, as we have shown. Now we are raising the question of another aspect of the human soul as principle of a proper activity not reducible to the composite activity of the sentient and emotional soul, from which we can infer a better idea of its subsistence as a spiritual soul, albeit not purely such.

We use the term *rational* to specify the human soul as different from the souls of other animals that are sentient and emotional but not rational, as qualifying both intelligence and will in the proper activities of the soul as spiritual, not just to name the specific difference of the human being in relation to the lower species in the genus of animal life but also to indicate what would be the degree of intelligence and will in an order of more purely spiritual or immaterial forms or substances that would not be ontologically in composition with matter as the human soul is.

The idea would be that if there are substances with higher degrees of intelligence and will separate from matter, the human soul would be the lowest degree of such spiritual substances, truly spiritual, having to exercise itself in a way that is discursive and deliberative with regard to its consciousness as sensible and emotional or as animal.

When we speak of rationality we refer to discursive forms of intelligence and deliberative forms of will that are tied to the activities of the soul as the form of its matter or to its composite activities of sense and emotion, as we shall try to show more clearly.

If we try to suppose that there are higher kinds of spiritual beings, not ontologically tied to any composition with matter, we have to think of their intelligence and will not only as higher but also as nondiscursive and nondeliberative even though we do not know precisely what that would be in itself. Our intelligence and will, of which we have no direct intuition but come to know only by reflective self-consciousness, are discursive by reason of being tied in natural tension with the sense and the emotional activity of self as a composite of form and matter. We have to labor and struggle to come to some spiritual understanding of what we are as intelligent and free. Indeed it is in such labor and struggle that we come to know reflectively that we are intelligent and free responsible spirits if we act in accordance with our powers of intelligence and free will.

Here we have to reflect on what we have already achieved of our second perfection as rational selves in this labor and in this struggle for understanding and freedom in our lives and on how we have achieved this second perfection through a proper activity that is specifically intellectual and willful and not just sentient and emotional, even though we are always starting from a sentient and emotional consciousness in order to rise above mere sense and emotion in our reflective self-consciousness.

We distinguish intelligence and free will as the two proper activities of the human soul, as spirit, by which it passes from its first perfection as spiritual and simple to its second perfection in much the same way as we distinguish between the sense powers of perception and the emotional powers of attraction and repulsion in the rational soul as substantial form of the animal composite. Intelligence is the counterpart of the senses in the human spirit, while the will, traditionally referred to as the rational appetite, is the spiritual counterpart of the emotions or of the sense appetites, as they are also called, with reasoning coming into play on both sides of the distinction to mediate between sense and intelligence on the one hand and between the emotions and free will on the other hand.

For, on the one hand, human intelligence does not proceed from pure insight into essences or what things are in themselves, not even in relation to itself or to other selves in mutual recognition. It proceeds discursively, or rationally, in answers to questions it raises with regard to things as given in experience or as perceived by the senses, including with regard to itself and to other selves with whom it is in communion, not just as a matter of primordial fact but also as a matter to be inquired into or to wonder about.

On the other hand, human willing does not proceed from sheer freedom formally, apart from any thought of natural inclinations, as it is represented in Immanuel Kant's *Critique of Practical Reason*, as if the emotions or the natural inclinations in a human psyche had nothing to do with the exercise of free will. Human willing proceeds from deliberation, or again rationally, amid the flow of a plurality of motives for taking action, choosing from among them the ones it deems more conducive to its own second perfection as spirit and to that of other selves with whom it is in communion, and struggling against the ones that would keep us from arriving at the second perfection of our choice.

All this bespeaks of a certain necessity of inquiry and puzzlement in order to learn what things are and what we and other selves are in our essence or substance, as well as a certain necessity of labor and struggle with material conditions of the world and of ourselves, in working toward a second perfection of our own, in making something of ourselves as communities, necessities that are part of our nature as composites of matter and form and that we have to adjust to in making whatever we can of ourselves. But we should keep in mind that they are necessities incumbent upon spirits empowered to deal with them as self-promoting intelligences eager to learn and as powers capable of bringing our many particular emotions or reasons for taking action in the world under the control of our free will.

There is a lot more to be said about intelligence and will as spiritual powers of the human soul that we shall come to later in discussing how each of the two powers develops. But what we have said of each of the two here as rational, at the juncture of spirit and matter or nature in the self's reflective consciousness, is enough to bring out the necessity of affirming the spiritual dimension of the first- and second-person ontology of selves, not only as uppermost in this ontology that takes in the world as a whole but also as most indicative of what the self is in its substance as a composite as well as in its subsistence as spirit.

We should also keep in mind that these activities of intelligence and free will not only are the ones that are most proper to the self as self or as spirit in its simple identity but also are not found de facto except where there is communion among selves, as we have seen from the beginning of our reflection on selfhood in the world in the primordial fact of human existence.

We advert to this communion among selves here only as a matter of fact still pertaining to the human soul as spiritual and simple in its subsistence, in the labor of its intelligence and the struggle of its will from age to age, communally at the same time as personally. We have adverted to this fact from the beginning of our reflection in saying with Hegel that there is no self-consciousness except in the presence of another self-consciousness. We shall see more of the necessity for selfhood as such implied in this fact of communion among selves when we come to focus more on the necessity of mutual recognition for a reflective self-consciousness. Here we have only to keep it in mind as not excluded by the thought of the human soul as spiritual and simple but, rather, as all the more crucial for the subjectivity of selfhood or, more exactly, for the intersubjectivity of the human spirit as such.

4.3 HOW WE COME TO KNOW THE HUMAN SOUL AS SUBSISTENT IN ITSELF AND AS ESSENTIALLY SPIRITUAL IN ITS SIMPLE IDENTITY IN THE SPECULATIVE EXERCISE OF OUR INTELLIGENCE AND IN THE PRACTICAL EXERCISE OF OUR FREE WILL IN THE HISTORICAL ORDER

4.3.1 Regarding the speculative exercise of our intelligence, we should note first that it is what we take to be a proper activity of the human soul as spirit. In other words, our discussion of this first point concerning speculative intelligence hinges on the activity we wish to speak of as proper to the human soul as subsisting in itself or in its simple identity, the activity we take note of in our self-consciousness and upon which we have to reflect in our reflective self-consciousness. This is how we come to know ourselves as spirits and not by any direct intuition into what we are as spirits, as idealist philosophers like Descartes would have it.

We begin to do this by distinguishing any act of reflective self-consciousness as such from what we have already mentioned as acts of the human being as composite of form and matter, such as acts of seeing, hearing, touching, feeling, and so on, where there is no act or form except in some composition with a physical organ or function as component of the experience as a whole.

To illustrate this sort of composite activity, we have made mention mainly of the external senses, such as that of sight, or hearing, or touching, where we are conscious of the organs as distinctly external, as parts of the body. We also referred to neurological functions that we know are firing in the physical makeup of the brain and of the nervous system in conjunction with the external senses of which we are directly conscious in our reflective self-consciousness. We are not directly conscious of these neurological functions in our bodily experience, but recent studies have shown how much they are a part of the composite activity of which we are conscious and how they affect us in our consciousness for ill or for good. What we know of them is further evidence of how much we are composites of form and matter in the complexity of our substance as rational animals. But it is not evidence for what we know of the inquiring mind or intelligence at work in these data given to us in our sense consciousness in seeking to know *what* things are in their essence as well as in their existence.

There are also internal senses that we should take into consideration as components of the composite activity proper to the self as a composite of matter and form. These include the imagination, memory, and what used to be referred to as the common sense, the sense that coordinates our disparate external senses as the perception of one and the same object, from the perspective of our different external senses.

There is a whole phenomenology of perception that could be brought to bear here along with memory and imagination, which would bring out more of the composition of form and matter characteristic of the self in its substance. The thing to keep in mind in all this, however, would be to understand that the aforementioned memory, imagination, and common sense, as internal as they may be to human consciousness, are still in the order of what we have termed composite proper activities of the self, not strictly activities of intelligence as such in one's reflective self-consciousness.

There is memory to be found in sentient nonrational animals, along with some imagination and common sense, though surely not with as much scope as in rational animals. But even with their broader scope in the rational animal, thanks to their being ordered to reason, as we shall see, these internal senses do not reach the level of understanding in consciousness. They do support understanding and open the way for it, as we shall also see later on, but they are no substitute for it, as any scientist or epistemologist will tell us and as we all find out when we realize that no measure of memory or imagination will get us through a rigorous scientific inquiry, or through writing a truly reflective paper on something we have learned about things or about ourselves, or through translating a difficult poetic or philosophical text from one language into another.

To get at the activity proper to the human soul as subsistent spirit in its simple identity, we have to distinguish what we shall call *intellectual consciousness* from what we have been speaking of as sentient or composite consciousness. In every form of consciousness there is some kind of reflection, which always presupposes some prior activity in which reflection has taken place, whether it be intellectual or sentient. Sentient activity has to be conceived as stemming from the human being in its substance as composite, giving rise to the sentient or composite kind of activity in human consciousness. It has its beginning or its principle in the material substance as composite.

But what about reflection itself as an act of reflective self-consciousness or as the critical act of intellectual consciousness in coming to some judgment regarding the essence of something given in sense experience? Is it just another act of the composite such as we find in some sensation or in some emotion? Or is it an act that transcends the material conditions of the composite or of sensation and emotion? If so, how is that transcendence to be understood in relation to what it transcends?

As forms of consciousness, sensation and emotion entail some kind of reflection in that I see that I see and I feel that I feel. When we speak of any kind of consciousness, we always presuppose some kind of reflection in an activity. But is the act of reflection itself reducible to this kind of sense consciousness, which depends intrinsically on a physical organ in good order? Does this act not presuppose a more reflective kind of critical consciousness that is more complete and self-contained, without depending intrinsically or directly on a physical organ, a consciousness that is more perfect and total in its self-consciousness, in a way that sense or phenomenological consciousness alone cannot achieve?

Let us reflect for a moment on how far sense or phenomenological consciousness can go in returning upon itself. It can return to the act in which I say I see or I feel. I can see that I see and I can feel that I feel. This is all part of my complex sense or phenomenological consciousness in which I distinguish not just various things before me in the world as well as in my own consciousness but also my own activities in relation to these things, such as looking, listening, reaching out, feeling, and so on. But in this consciousness have I yet reflected on the act of consciousness itself? For example, can I see *what* it is to see? Or can I feel *what* it is to feel? This is something that mere sense or phenomenological consciousness cannot do in the same way that intellectual consciousness can and does.

In intellectual consciousness we have acts that totally reflect on themselves, that is, return into their own self-consciousness in such a way that they are conscious not only that they know but also of *what* it is to know, not only that they choose freely but also of *what* it is to choose freely. When I understand, for example, I understand not only that I understand but also *what* it is to understand, as well as what it is that I understand, so that in intellectual consciousness I come to know, without direct reference to or without intrinsic dependence on any sense organ or physical function as in the case of any sense or emotional consciousness, not only that I act but also *what* is the nature of this act in which I come to know myself as a self-consciousness in relation to other self-consciousnesses and to other things in the world.

If we ask what it is to understand, as distinct from what it is that we understand, we find that we are no longer referring to an object as a composite of form and matter, which is to be understood, or even to ourselves as similar composite objects with sentient and emotional activities of our own, also to be understood. We find that we are referring to an act of our self-consciousness trying to come to some understanding discursively and to exercise some judgment of our own concerning what things are in their *essence*, including ourselves as things or as bodies, and what we can do as rational beings with all these things or selves other than ourselves.

Having that act in mind is not just an act of remembering or imagining. It is an act of reflective self-consciousness implicit in the act of understanding itself, or in the exercise of judgment as such, an act that can be made explicit in terms of that act of understanding alone or that exercise of judgment as a critical act of their own. It is an ongoing act that gives rise to another kind of reflection than the one we find implicit in the discursive exercise of judgment we start from in the senses.

When I exercise judgment about things I find directly in experience, such as other selves and myself, for example, or like less than animate objects, such as sticks and stones, I am conscious not only of the things themselves I am exercising judgment about but also of my being conscious of them and of my exercising judgment about them. And I can at any time in that direct exercise of judgment, whether it be about individuals or about particular sciences such as discussed at the beginning of this science of the self as a whole, turn my attention to the actual exercise of judgment itself in an indirect exercise of judgment concerning the direct exercise of judgment in which I was inquiring about what a particular object is in its essence or about the subject of a particular science such as physics or psychology.

Let us suppose, for example, that a physicist were to begin reflecting on his own act of doing or understanding physics, which he can do only as a philosopher of his science, as we are doing here, and not as merely a physicist exercising the particular critical judgment about physical objects as physical and not as biological or psychological or economic. Or let us suppose that a psychologist were to begin reflecting on what he is doing as a psychologist studying the consciousness of the human subject as distinct from the consciousness of other nonrational animals and not as a zoologist or as a sociologist might. The psychologist in that instant would no longer be exercising judgment as a psychologist directly on the subject of psychology but, rather, on the act of doing psychology scientifically; that is, on the act of exercising judgment in his particular science. He would be discovering himself as one exercising judgment in the sphere of psychology.

To illustrate the case in point more concretely here and in more formal terms as philosophers, we could come to the judgment or the conclusion that a human being (S) is one capable of exercising critical judgment (P): S is P. As one reflects on this direct judgment, S is P, arrived at upon reflection on what human beings do by nature, one can turn to an indirect kind of judgment or conclusion about the act itself or the exercise of judgment itself (S2), where S2, or the point of reference, is now the act or the exercise of judgment, whether regarding common sense about things or regarding the exercise of direct judgment in particular sciences about objects formally defined. One then judges or concludes that this act or exercise of judgment (S2) is itself an act of a certain kind, P2, in which P2, or S is P, is predicated of the act, S2, in which I say S2 is P2 or S is P.

What we refer to then is no longer just a thing or an object for one's consciousness but an act wherein the thing or the object is contained in our consciousness as a predicate for some particular subject, whether it be a judgment about this or that in particular or about the subject of a particular science. That is one way of saying not only that we know and understand something but also that we know and understand what it is to know and what it is to understand.

The formal statement of the indirect reflective judgment on the act of judgment itself, or S2, is an act in which one predicates S is P of S2 or the act in which such predication takes place, gets complicated, but that statement is possible or justified only on the basis of the implicit reflection that takes place within the actual exercise of direct judgment as such, of which we are reflectively self-conscious as our own when we exercise it, as physicists, psychologists, or people of common sense. The direct exercise of judgment is not something rare among intelligent human beings.

What the statement of the indirect reflective judgment brings out is a certain simplicity in the reflective act of intellectual self-consciousness, one that is not in composition with any sense organ. It brings out the transcendental unity of an activity that finds its way into any particular exercise of judgment, whether it be that of individuals in particular circumstances or that of particular sciences exploring what different things are in their composite essences. As we consider that this intellectual activity as such is proper to the self, not as a sentient composite but as a soul or as an intelligence in an identity of its own, we infer that this soul as principle of this activity truly subsists in itself as spirit and not just as form of a composite. It is the principle of a life that is spiritual as well as rational. We shall see more of what that implies when we come to speak more directly of human intelligence as proper to the human soul in its subsistence.

To speak of the spiritual in the activity and in the subsistence of intellectual consciousness, as complicated as it may be for us, in the context of the soul as substantial form of an animal, is not to speak of something rare or extraordinary in the experience or in the exercise of judgment coming from the human soul of the rational animal. Any human experience in which there is some intelligent or critical exercise of judgment has to be deemed spiritual, even that of the positive scientist or that of a materialist who ignores this spiritual dimension of total reflection in his exercise of judgment as a scientist or a person of good sense.

One follows common sense or does one's particular science only in one's reflective self-consciousness. Every scientist, as rational and intelligent, has to understand not only what his science is about but also what it is to do science or to exercise judgment in science. That is a spiritual activity stemming from what one is in one's subsistence as spirit. Without some critical reflection of what one is doing as a scientist as well as in common sense, there is no science in the proper sense of the term. Similarly, there is no common sense for a rational animal without some learning from a critical exercise of intelligence in one's life.

The same has to be said of religious experience in which there is also a component of intelligence, whether of reason or of faith in communion with other selves, over and above the component or the composite of sense and of feeling. Religion without this critical intelligent component is not properly human. Nor is it properly religion as transcending the realm of composite things. It is only superstition reducing selfhood or critical reflective self-consciousness to nothing but idolatry regarding things or to autolatry regarding oneself as a composite of matter and form.

This is not to say that there are not varying degrees of spiritual intelligence in religion, from the most ordinary in religious communities that form around some cult of the divine, to the most extraordinary experiences of mystics who stand out in such communities intellectually as well as spiritually. But it is to say that without the activation of spiritual intelligence of one kind or another there is no authentic religion in any human soul in the same way as there is no authentic science in anyone's soul without the activation of the same sort of spiritual intelligence in the soul of the scientist. This is to say that there has to be spiritual activation of intelligence on both sides of that dichotomy between science and religion in human self-consciousness, an activation that has to be understood as flowing from the human spiritual soul as subsistent in itself no less than in relation to other selves and even to other lesser things in one's experience.

4.3.2 The same sort of induction into the spiritual ontology of the human soul can be made starting from the act or the exercise of free will, which is also a proper activity of the self as spirit, along with the exercise of our intelligence. Willing is an exercise in decision-making that takes place amid a plurality of particular emotions and particular interests that come spontaneously and directly to our attention in our consciousness as rational animals, a plurality of motives and occasions for action among which we constantly have to choose after deliberation in what we speak of as our self-actualization or our self-determination, which is supposedly free, but which starts from the determinism of a plurality of particular emotions agitating each for their own fulfillment in our rational consciousness in competition with one another at any moment when some choice has to be made.

Nonrational animals do not have such freedom for the actualization of what they are in their essence or according to their nature. They are determined to one thing or one way of acting in which they can either fail or succeed in surviving as individuals or as species in the world as a whole.

The power of willing that comes with reason, however, opens the way for many emotions and many interests to emerge at once in one's rational self-consciousness, each emotion or motive for taking action a determination unto itself and in competition with other emotional determinations within one and the same self-consciousness, thus giving rise to the need for taking counsel with ourselves and other selves as to which one is to be actualized by a self at a given moment in time and the need for a decision by the will as to which determinations will be cut off and which ones will become the determination of self at any particular moment of its activity.

Emotions, as we have seen, or natural inclinations or passions are movements that arise spontaneously in our rational consciousness, not by choice but by a certain necessity in our composite animal nature. Each emotion identifies itself, so to speak, as an object or as a motive for taking a particular action in contrast to and in contention with other objects or motives for taking other particular actions, each with its own natural tension for taking a particular action, all within one and the same consciousness. And when we do make our choice for what particular emotion or set of emotions we shall follow in striving for our second perfection, we find ourselves having to struggle against or overcome the emotions we have decided against in choosing as we have. Rational choices always require discipline in the emotional life of our self-consciousness.

The reason we give ourselves or those with whom we are in communion for taking any particular course of action is in the good or the satisfaction we expect to find in pursuing the course itself. One pursues a particular course of action only if it can be seen as adding to one's second perfection. But the particular reason we find or give for pursuing a particular course of action at any time is not the only reason there is for pursuing any particular course of action. There is also the reason that comes with the will itself in the act of willing, the will exercising its own power as rational appetite over all the particular sense appetites, striving for a higher, more transcendent second perfection, a more perfect freedom to be all that one wants to be in communion with other selves.

The motions and the emotions that are studied in the particular sciences such as biology, psychology, medicine, or marketing, along with the determinisms that give rise to them in our neurological and our social systems have to be to recognized by rational agents and by philosophers of human existence as necessary preludes for the exercise of deliberation in free choice. But we do not have to examine them here in all their details. What we also have to recognize is that all of these finite and particular motives and occasions are brought to a halt by reason in moments of deliberation when one has to make a decision as to which of these particular motives will be realized in one's life and which will be cut off, because not all can be realized at any given time and not all are in keeping with the requirements of the self's second perfection as an intelligent and free self-consciousness.

We shall see more about how all of this gets coordinated in the exercise of one's own willing as the proper activity of oneself in its self-determination later, when we come to examine how the human will follows from the emotions. Here, however, we have to examine how we come to know this complex situation in our human existence as agents of free will, by reflection on the exercise of any particular act of decision.

Nonrational animals do not have to make decisions about their life the way we do. Nor do they have the capacity to do so since they are nonrational. They are driven by whatever dominant emotion floods into their consciousness at any particular time. In making any particular decision at a particular moment in my life as a rational animal, I have to attend to the particular emotions and interests that come into play in my consciousness at this particular moment in my life as a self. These are the things that I have to deliberate about in terms of what I will to be or will to make of myself in my second perfection as a self. And I make my decision more or less freely or deliberately as to what I will to be in liberating myself from certain predeterminations in my soul or in my psyche as manifested in certain emotions.

That is how I become conscious of what I am deciding in particular and what it is to decide in the act of willing or the exercise of my will amid the plurality of inclinations moving me in my consciousness at any given time. But in the consciousness of this act there is also the consciousness of what it is to decide on a course of action, or what is the act of deciding. I am conscious that it is I myself deciding and coming to a self-determination of my own in my second perfection.

This too is an act of reflective self-consciousness in the exercise of willing, like the act of reflective self-consciousness such as we found earlier in the intellectual exercise of judgment. What we are concerned with *directly* in the deliberation that precedes the act or the actual exercise of our free will are the particular emotions and particular interests that are in contention in our consciousness at a time certain.

But what we are also conscious of reflectively or *indirectly* is the act that must come of that deliberation, the necessity of exercising one's free will in choosing from among many determinations the determination we will to be our own. What we deliberate about directly may be emotions or particular interests, in contention with one another, matters or affairs in the realm of composites of matter and form such as health, pleasure, learning, art, or technology, but what is to come of this act becomes part of what we are to be in our ultimate self-determination.

Here too we could speak of religious experience as we did in connection with the component of intelligence in our reflective self-consciousness. The exercise of free will is a component of the self's spiritual activity no less than the intelligent exercise of judgment. It takes the shape of hope and confidence as we deliberate over the particular options that have opened up in our consciousness and in the one option that we choose to follow, hope and confidence in something divine as well as in the communal life we share with other selves.

As rational selves, we have to decide which of the particular emotions or inclinations in our consciousness we will choose to follow and which we shall let go of or set aside for ourselves. But the act of deciding or choosing itself, in its identity as the act of a self, transcends the particularity of any of the emotions or inclinations one may choose to follow, especially in its communal form where we share hope in a communal good as the second perfection of many selves.

This too is a truly spiritual act stemming from a spiritual soul subsisting in itself throughout its discursive activity as a reflective self-consciousness. In the case of willing, our reflective self-consciousness depends on having already exercised willing of some kind or another and on one's continuing to actually will, but ontologically it is rooted in a soul that actually subsists in itself, which is another way we come to know that the rational soul does subsist in itself as *spirit*.

4.4 HOW THE SPIRITUAL SUBSISTENCE AND EXISTENCE OF THE SELF RELATES TO WHAT WE ALREADY KNOW OF THE HUMAN SOUL AS THE SUBSTANTIAL FORM OF ITS MATTER IN THE COMPOSITE OF MATTER AND FORM

We have reasoned that the human soul is truly spiritual and simple in its subsistence and its identity as the soul of a rational self on the basis of its proper activities as intelligent and willful, in contradistinction from its proper activities as a sentient and emotional composite on the basis of which we had reasoned that the selfsame soul is the substantial form of its matter in that composite. The question comes up, then, as to how these two affirmations about the rational soul are not just compatible but even necessary concerning one and the same soul in a human existence, especially in a context of ontological dualism where soul or mind and body are seen by many as two separate substances.

We have been at pains to demonstrate that the human soul subsists in itself as spirit in its simple identity as a self-consciousness. How or why do we still have to maintain that this self-same soul is the substantial form of some matter in a composite? And in what sense do we have to maintain that it is the substantial form of such a composite, even as having a subsistence of its own in its spiritual self-consciousness? What sort of strange ontology is this for ourselves as the thing we know best in human experience?

Let us begin with the idea of subsistence, which we attribute to the soul prior to attributing anything to the composite of substantial form and matter. We have not touched on any subsistence for the composite or for the human body up to now, other than the subsistence of the soul in itself as spirit. To speak of the human body as having a subsistence of its own other than that of its soul would be once again to separate the body from the soul or to break up the substantial union of body and soul in the human being as we have already alluded to and to make the ontology of selfhood either purely third person or purely first person rather than both at the same time as we have maintained up to now.

We cannot think of two separate subsistences for one and the same thing or substance, even though we can say that there is a subsistence for any substance we take to be real or to be subsisting in itself in its perduring identity as a substance. If we want to speak of a subsistence for the human body or composite, as animal as it may be, we have to say it is a subsistence that comes from the human soul subsisting as spirit, thus specifying the ontology of the human being as uniquely but not purely first and second person in its very existence as a self.

This is an important thing to have established for the human being. It is the basis for all the special consideration we have to give for every individual we take or recognize to be a human being, in health care, in business transactions, in politics, or in any other kind of interaction where there has to be *mutual recognition* among selves.

We shall see more about this and about human dignity and human rights when we come to speak of the practice of selfhood in human social interactions. Before that, however, we must understand how we come to posit this identity of subsistence for the human soul as both spiritually subsistent in itself and as substantial form of its matter in a union of soul and body. Why is it necessary to posit such a substantial union of body and soul for a soul that is thought of as subsisting in itself, as a spirit in its simple identity as a self or in its first- and second-person ontology, and how do we come to know this in our reflective self-consciousness?

What we know to start with is that we are selves subsisting in our own identity as spirits. But we do not know that by some sort of intuition into our identity as subsisting or by resolving some doubt as to our existence as a self in saying merely, I think, therefore I am. We know it by reflecting on proper activities of intelligence and will that we know to be simple relative to other proper activities, such as the sentient and the emotional, which we know to be composite. We know that we are composites by reflecting on our activities that are of the composite. We know that we subsist in our simple identity as spirits by reflecting on our relatively simple acts of intelligence and will, which are not directly tied to any sense organs or physical conditions. But knowing these two aspects of one and the same fact, the fact or the subsistence of selfhood in human experience, in our reflective self-consciousness is not like knowing two things separate from one another. It is knowing them as relative to one another in one and the same fact and subsistence of a self, namely the subsistence and the existence of the rational soul in its twofold act of intelligence and will, each relating respectively to movements of sense and of emotion in its nature as a composite.

Moreover, knowing these two aspects of the soul reflectively as relative to one another in one's human experience is to know them as necessarily or essentially linked to one another in one subsistence, that of the soul subsisting in itself as spirit.

We have insisted from the beginning that we come to know what we are in our substance, and now in our subsistence, only by reflection upon an ongoing activity that is bodily, even physical, as well as sentient and emotional. This is a matter of direct experience for us that we cannot forget or let go of in our reflective self-consciousness. It is not just a matter of past experience. It is a matter of constant experience, even for the rational consciousness as well as for the sentient and emotional consciousness. Our intelligence and our will remain discursive or tied to the material conditions of our sensations and our emotions even when they have come to some total reflection in themselves.

We shall see more about how this is when we come to reflect more on how these rational activities always relate back to sense and emotional activities as a beginning for them, as something they begin from and depend on, as that upon which they have to reflect in coming to self-consciousness. For the moment it is enough to recognize this fact of discursivity in rational consciousness as an indication of some constant dependence on sense consciousness, even if it be just memory and imagination and not direct observation of things and of feelings.

Furthermore, we have discussed the exercise of judgment in total reflection as an *indirect* exercise of judgment and of the exercise of the will in decision making as an indirect exercise of will concerning what we will most fundamentally in making any particular choice. We made mention of the exercise of these rational activities as indirect only because we had to presuppose other activities more directly associated with the senses and the emotions to reflect on as also proper to the rational self.

Total reflection in rational consciousness as we know it does not totally close in on itself. It does not exclude sense consciousness or emotional consciousness. In fact, it includes these two kinds of consciousness as a precondition for its own total reflection as intelligence and will in the indirect exercise of judgment and free will. And in so doing it raises these sentient and emotional powers into a higher sphere of reflection than we see in nonrational animals, a degree of higher ontology.

Human sensation and imagination share in some of the versatility of intelligence through being one with intelligence in the self. Human emotion shares in some of the freedom of the will through being one with willing in the self. Human sensation and human emotion remain directly united to the physical organs and functions in the body as they are stretched upward into the rational soul, so to speak. And conversely, the rational soul as transcending the material conditions of its body, or as intellectual and free, is only indirectly related to the body through the senses and the emotions, which require properly functioning physical organs.

The rational soul as such does not require any physical organ or function of its own, other than the organs and functions required for the senses and emotions, for the exercise of either of its twofold activities of intelligence and will in total reflection, though it does depend on a proper disposition of those organs and functions for its own self-actualization as rational spirit. Severe pain or illness, or malfunctioning of the senses or emotions or of their underlying neurological conditions, can and do interfere with one's use of both intelligence and will and even make it impossible at times, but that takes nothing away from the subsistence of soul in itself, which we come to know through reflective self-consciousness in one's use of intelligence and will, whatever shape it may take in one's experience.

Self-consciousness does not begin absolutely from itself. Its beginning is relative to its body as it emerges from the ongoing activity of the composite. We experience total reflection in ourselves as always already tied essentially to sensation and emotions. If it were not so tied, intellectual consciousness would come much more easily for us without any need for effort or reflective concentration on our acts of intelligence and free will. Nor would there be any need for making decisions to come to our self-determination. We would be much more immediately transparent to ourselves in our self-consciousness and much more instantaneous in choosing all that we want to be. We would not have to labor and to struggle with our emotions and our perceptions. But that is not the kind of spirit we are.

What this means is that while the human soul is truly spiritual in its simple identity, it is not purely spiritual or purely one, as the form of its matter in a composite. In the total reflection of its properly intellectual and voluntary activity and in its very subsistence, the human soul is still essentially a form of its body. This brings up another question pertaining to death and immortality of the self: can the soul subsist separated from its body, or does it cease to be as its body decomposes in death? This is the question we must now turn to before inquiring further into the complexity of the proper activities of the soul as intelligence and free will.

4.5 TERMINOLOGY PERTAINING TO THE FIRST- AND SECOND-PERSON ONTOLOGY OF SELFHOOD AS SURPASSING THIRD-PERSON ONTOLOGY IN ITS COMMUNICATIVE REFLECTION

In conclusion of this long consideration of the self in its first- and second-person ontology, let us lay out the systematic or scientific language we have been using to sum up the different kinds of ontology we have had to attend to in our reflection on what the self is in its essence.

Reflection in general: a characteristic of life and activity we find wherever there is some consciousness that returns upon itself.

Total reflection: the conscious return upon itself in act or in the actual exercise of the rational self's own intellectual or voluntary activity, with a knowledge of what the nature of that activity is. Note that this total reflection turns on the actual exercise of an act or an activity and not just some objectified or remembered representation of the activity, no matter how vivid it would have to be for David Hume. As actual, it has more to do with the present, or a now, than an activity objectified as remembered from the past or as projected in the future.

Such reflection goes beyond mere introspection, which considers specific acts of consciousness as objects, beyond mere phenomenological reduction (Maurice Merleau-Ponty) and beyond a merely transcendental analysis (Kant), which ignores the actual content of the act of total reflection as such.

Note also that such total reflection is not exclusive of other selves as is sometimes supposed in certain theories of justice or of human rights. It is inclusive of other selves with whom a self is in communion through mutual recognition. That is why we speak of a first- and second-person ontology and not just of a first-person ontology.

Total reflection in communion with other selves is implicit in every act of intelligence; it is exercised properly in any judgment; it is exercised most properly in the reflective or critical judgments where the act of judging itself becomes transparent to itself as the subject or the act being reflected on. Similarly, total reflection is implicit in every act of the will; it is exercised properly in any act of deliberation; it is exercised most properly in the deliberate decision where the act of willing becomes transparent to itself as the objective or the resolve to take some action of one's own for a good that is common to many.

***Material substance*:** A substance in a third-person ontology of which matter is a constitutive principle along with its form. Such a substance is generally referred to as a body. Inasmuch as the self is a body, or inasmuch as matter is a constitutive principle of its substance, the self is a material substance on a par with other selves as material substances in a third-person ontology that encompasses material substances with lesser degrees of first perfection or of substantial form, that is, nonrational, nonsentient, nonliving, all the way from nonrational animal and nonsentient plant down to the nonliving.

***Prime matter*:** matter considered as co-constitutive principle of material things or substances. Prime matter is not a thing, does not exist as such, and has never existed, not even in the form of some original chaotic matter or primordial soup or magma from which higher forms of material beings have evolved. Such original or primordial matter already had a form, though one that is far less articulated than the form we now find, say, in the matter of diverse material substances, including that of a human being. What exists and has existed from the beginning is some composite of matter and form caught up in a cosmic flux of matter in generation rising from primordial forms to higher forms and then passing away into lower forms again in corruption.

As a principle of material things, prime matter is a principle of change and of coming to be and ceasing to be. Inasmuch as it is individuals who come to be and cease to be, prime matter is the *principle of individuation*. It is not the principle of bodies in general but of this body and that. As such it can be called *signate matter*, or matter designated as this or that, inasmuch as it can only be signaled or pointed to as this or that individual without specification of *what* it is or has come to be, which is given through form in matter.

Insofar as many individuals of one and the same species, such as the human, come to be, prime matter is the *principle of multiplicity* in one and the same species. It has to be thought of as *dynamic* or *potential*, as open or in potency to different possibilities and different forms. As distinct from form in material things, it is indeterminate and passive, merely receptive of form, though ontologically oriented to form in one way or another and not to nothingness. It is pure potency for becoming something determinate through a form.

Substantial form: the principle constitutive of a material substance along with matter and really distinct from matter as principle. The form is not strictly distinct from the body as such or as a determinate whole since it is the form of the body, its first wholeness, so to speak, or its first perfection. Hence, strictly speaking, the human soul, which is the form of its matter or of the body of the self, is not distinct from the body but, rather, from the material principle in union with which it constitutes the body. Matter as such, or as principle, is not a body because a body is a composite of matter with its form. The soul is substantial form to a signate matter, which the form determines as a specific kind of body with an ontology of its own, such as the human body.

Form is thus *principle of determination* in *what* comes to be. It determines specificity of an individual body. It is principle of identity according to what kind of being a substance is. It is also principle of unity of the composite and of its activity, whence the idea of a proper activity that flows from a composite substance.

Subsistent substantial form: a substantial form that has a subsistence of its own communicated to the prime matter that it informs.

This is the kind of form we have argued the human soul to be; for all we know, human souls are the only forms of the sort.

To help clarify the peculiarity of the human soul as form, it might be helpful to distinguish it from two other kinds of substantial form we can think of:

- *material substantial form*: a form that has no subsistence of its own and subsists only by reason of the composite of which it is a constituent principle. Such a form is said to be *intrinsically* dependent on matter.
- *pure form:* a form that is not in composition with matter and that exists apart from matter, inasmuch as such a form has a subsistence of its own. Such a form would have to be thought of as a substance unto itself, without matter, and therefore as subsistent apart from any composition with matter, as an immaterial substance, or as a separate substance in a purely first-person ontology, as only one of the kind.

According to what we have argued, the human soul is neither just a material substantial form, nor just a pure subsistent form, but both at the same time. It is subsistent but simultaneously a form of its body. It is subsistent intrinsically to itself to the extent that it transcends merely material conditions. But at the same time it is essentially united to matter in that its subsistence is one that is embodied. Thus the human soul can be said to be essentially but extrinsically dependent on matter, though intrinsically subsistent.

Substantial union: the union of principles constitutive of one and the same substance. Note that we do not start our consideration from principles as things separated from one another, which then have to be put together, such as pieces of a puzzle. Principles are not things or pieces of a puzzle. We start from things that we call or refer to as *substances*, and we are led to distinguish principles within the unity of a substance in order to account for what it is in its substance. We do not bring principles together, nor do we have to. We find them together in the unity of a substance, both as distinct from its proper activities as a composite and as the origin of those activities as a composite of matter and form.

The question then is more one of understanding how soul and body can be distinguished and in what sense the soul can be thought of as separate from the body or, conversely, how the soul can still constitute one substance with the body if it is only extrinsically related to matter. We have to say that the soul, though it has a subsistence of its own, still is not a complete substance without a body, as a pure form is in its separation from matter.

This is the only way of taking into account every aspect of our experience without falling into the oversimplifications of materialism and idealism, or of animalism and angelism. The human soul is neither a merely material substantial form nor a pure form. It is a material form that has a subsistence of its own even as part of a composite, or conversely it is a subsistent form that is at the same time ontologically the form of a composite.

As in any substantial union, the soul is immediately united to the matter of which it is the form without the mediation of intermediate specific or substantial forms, and it determines that matter to be the kind of being it is; that is, a reflectively self-conscious human being.

Also, as for any substantial form in composition with matter, the soul is multiplied for each individual self and is unique in each so that there cannot be one soul for many individuals, even though there is no self-consciousness except in the active presence of other self-consciousnesses, each in communion with the others at the same time as each is individualized by its being a material substance. Each individual self has full dignity of a human being conferred on it by having—or better still by being—a human soul in reflective consciousness of itself, which is not without some communion with other selves on the level of reflective self-consciousness. Both of these aspects of selfhood, the reflective and the communicative, have to be taken together to understand what is meant by calling the human soul spiritual.

***Spirit*:** a substantial form subsisting in itself in a first- and second-person ontology without intrinsic dependence on matter or without any composition with matter whatsoever and principle of its own proper activity through intelligence and will in reflective self-consciousness.

We discover the existence of such a subsistent substantial form through the *total reflection* in the simple and transparent identity of our self-consciousness as we came to conceive it in our discussion of the human soul as truly spiritual in its first- and second-person ontology, though not as purely spiritual because of its extrinsic yet essential dependence on matter by reason of taking that same identical form to be the soul or the principle of life in a body having life in potency, as we have noted previously.

Starting from that discussion, we can also conceive of a substantial form without any essential or ontological dependence on matter or on physical organs of any kind; that is, as purely simple and purely one in the simple identity of its self-consciousness exercising intelligence and will. But such is not the case for ourselves as rational self-consciousnesses, having to discourse and to deliberate about ourselves and about things given in experience as matters of fact to start from in our inquiries and our deliberations as rational animals. We are truly spiritual and truly one in our reflective self-consciousness as we strive toward our second perfection as spiritual selves communing with one another, but we are not purely such. Hence the necessity of discursive intelligence for us to learn truths about ourselves in the world and the necessity of deliberation and decision in the pursuit of our second perfection as spirits in communion with one another.

5

The Elevation of Human Selfhood in Its Communal Existence into a Spiritual Existence in Its First- and Second-Person Ontology through the Empowerment of Intelligence and Free Will

We have been exploring what the self is in its substance as composite of soul and matter and in its identity as spirit subsisting in itself, starting always from our reflective self-consciousness in what we take to be our proper activities as selves in both sense and intellectual consciousness. In doing so, we have come to a better understanding of what the self is in its first perfection as a rational animal, still working toward its second perfection as both animal and rational through the very activities we have been reflecting on.

We have been looking back from our given communal existence, or from the proper activities we reflect on as proper to us as selves, to get to a better understanding of *what* we are in our essence or substance as selves or as rational animals. But that is not all there is to communal existence as proper activity of selfhood, enabling us to look back into our essence. The communal existence we actually find in the exercise of sense and intellectual consciousness is better understood as looking forward toward what we have been referring to generally as second perfection for human beings but as something that has to be achieved by selves in their communal existence as selves.

This exercise of our critical intelligence and our free will is something we have been taking to be part of the primordial fact of human existence from the beginning but which we have not yet explored as a necessary factor in the primordial fact of human existence or of human life as whole. It is the factor that not only gives us access to a better understanding of what we are in our substance, as we have been proceeding up to now in our critical understanding of what we are in our nature or in our substance but that also gives rise to some striving for a second perfection of our own in what we call a *culture* or a wide diversity of cultures in the historical order of human existence, all of them the result of some critical exercise of intelligence and of free will in diverse communal existences about the world.

Hence the need in our philosophy of human existence to explore more critically how reflective self-consciousness is constituted communally in properly human activities and how this communal self-consciousness gives rise to not just an intersubjective philosophy of human existence but also a diversity of such intersubjective philosophies or cultures in the world historical order of humankind, not to mention the possibility or the necessity of a higher spiritual consciousness in a religious self-consciousness proportionate to the fullness that transcends the very historical order of human existence and of human perfectibility in the world as we know it now.

We mention this higher order transcending even human existence only in passing as a possibility or a necessity for the second perfection of human selves in a communion of saints, so to speak, but not with the intention of exploring it even as a hypothesis in this philosophy of historical human existence. That would be the subject for another inquiry into all that the philosophy of human existence could include in keeping with the immortality of the human soul even as the form of its matter in the natural composite. The second perfection we have to include here is that of communities operating intelligently and willingly according to their endowments in the historical order of human achievement in the world as we know it.

We shall begin by having a second look at how human self-consciousness is constituted only communally in a dialectic of mutual recognition. Then, we shall indicate how this dialectic takes place only through two distinct powers—intelligence and willing in the human soul irreducible to merely brain functions. Third, we will show how the exercise of these two powers in human consciousness rises from and above the exercise of the sense and emotional powers of the human soul, all of which builds up to culture and to a diversity of cultures in the world-historical order.

5.1 HOW THE HUMAN SELF IS CONSTITUTED IN ITS SELF-CONSCIOUS EXISTENCE THROUGH A DIALECTIC OF MUTUAL RECOGNITION WITH OTHER SELVES

WE HAVE BEEN REFLECTING ON *WHAT* THE HUMAN SELF CONSISTS IN, in its identity as both spirit and matter, in its simplicity, and in its composition with matter, starting from the activities we take to be proper to selves in their historical existence. This has taken us back into the essence of selfhood and of the rational soul in its consistency as a first perfection from which the self takes off in search of a second perfection that can only come from its own initiative and its proper activities as historically self-conscious.

We must now reflect more precisely and more deeply on how this initiative takes place, starting from the essence of selfhood in the first perfection of its ontology and going into how the self is in fact constituted through its activity. What does all this activity lead up to in the life and in the historical consciousness of people and of peoples?

In relation to the simplicity of the soul, we discussed an identity that is not purely individual but that is already intersubjective in its very objectivity. The self's dependence on matter is at the same time an interdependence with other selves. This could be viewed merely as a matter of fact or as a matter of necessity for the individual self, as we saw in our initial elaboration of the primordial fact of human existence. A fully developed human being could not come to be, develop, or even survive in the world as a self except in dependence on other human beings. But is this all there is to the interdependence of human selves? Is it just a matter of biological, psychological, or economic necessity? Or does that interdependence enter more deeply into the very constitution of human selfhood, in its very self-consciousness as spiritual and as simple?

We also previously mentioned communion with other selves as a matter of necessity for the self in such a way that without the presence of another self an individual human self-consciousness would be unthinkable precisely as a self-conscious human being. Since then we have considered and reflected at some length on the kind of reflective activity that is constitutive of the self as such. Now we can ask more precisely whether that reflective activity can be constitutive of a self by itself alone as a reflective self-consciousness or whether it does not itself presuppose a more profound activity of mutual recognition between one self and another.

The question arises with regard to the ontological self we have been reflecting on in its essential consistency as an identity. This self is not just a moving ground for its proper activity as a self. It is not just a given nature, a fait accompli; it is itself a self in the making through its own proper activity, a self in the act of actualizing itself in the world, for itself at least, if not for other selves as well.

We referred earlier to *matter* and *form* as constitutive components of the self in its substance but in a relatively abstract way, as if they were separate from one another and only juxtaposed to one another. We did not refer to the way in which these two principles actually come together in an activity that joins them to one another in the identity of one self and opens them up to the wider world of rational consciousness where other things and other selves are also present and active and where the question of one's self-consciousness and other self-consciousnesses arises on the level of communion with other selves in a first- and second-person ontology.

There are many ways of conceiving this factor of communion or interdependence in the primordial fact of human existence as a matter of necessity in the particular sciences, whether it be in physics, biology, psychology, or economics. Each one of these sciences has its own particular way of conceiving the necessity, both natural and historical, of having human beings together with other human beings, but none of these particular kinds of necessity for social interaction is in question here, except insofar as it is something to be managed through human initiative and ingenuity, the kind of thing we do day in and day out in organizing our lives or the lives of our communities.

What we rather wish to bring into question is the constitution of self-consciousness as such in its very reflection into itself or into selfhood. Such reflection is often represented as purely individual, fixed in an opposition to the reflection of other individuals, equally fixed in their opposition, each seeking from its own perspective only its own interests and none other. Such a fixation or absolutization of individuals in isolation from one another is called into question, but not with the idea of a totalitarian collectivity that would be nothing more than a counterpart of the fixation and absolutization of individuals in isolation from one another. What we wish to call into question is abstract absolutization of any kind, individualist or collectivist, with the idea of a *mutual recognition* as constitutive of reflective self-consciousness itself at the core of rational consciousness as such.

Absolute collectivism is no more acceptable for an intersubjective philosophy of human existence than absolute individualism in the constitution of a reflective self-consciousness. Each self must be seen in its own identity as other than any other self, even where there is a tension or an opposition in the interests of the one and the other, with an irreducible polarization between the two.

Both poles or all the poles that come into play as part of communion in the primordial fact of human existence must be taken into consideration as distinct from one another but not as isolated from one another, much in opposition to one another, in ignorance of one another in their respective reflective self-consciousness. What we must find at the root of our question in this inquiry is the idea of a relation between irreducible poles or extremes in relation with each other as selves actually relating to one another in what we shall call a *dialectic of mutual recognition*, where each pole somehow contains the other pole and is in turn contained by the other pole.

Such a relation can be represented as an interaction between two subjects, for example, as in the dialectic of the play *The Miracle Worker*, with each subject, Helen Keller and Annie Sullivan, having to be thought of as distinct but in a distinction that is immediately overcome in the awakening of a dialectical relationship through a language that both become conscious of in their communion with one another.

What we shall find or demonstrate is that such a language starts from a dialectic of mutual recognition between two or more selves, whereby one recognizes the other and in doing so comes to its own self-consciousness even as the other recognizes the first and thus similarly comes to its own self-consciousness.

One self becomes present to itself in the presence of another, even as the other self becomes present to itself in the presence of the first. Mutual recognition is a *presencing* wherein two or more selves become conscious both of self and of the other as another self in one and the same act. It is in this kind of presencing that the idea of dialectical relation can best be understood existentially.

Moreover, we shall find that such a dialectic of mutual recognition is found and can only be found among selves in their first- and second-person ontology, each with its own intelligence and free will and consequently with its own rights in the presence of other self-consciousnesses, based on a mutual recognition that is reciprocal through and through.

There can be a kind of recognition also of lesser beings than selves, as we have been thinking about selves up to now; for example, of lesser animals or of lower natures as such. We speak of animal rights or of ecological rights in nature on the basis of some recognition that animals and things in nature have a reality of their own that should be respected. But this recognition of nonrational animals by humans is not fully mutual as it is among selves. Nor is it reciprocal in that nonrational animals and lesser things of nature lack the kind of self-consciousness with intelligence and free will that is presupposed in a dialectic of mutual recognition.

Note that in social relations it is rights that derive from mutual recognition and not mutual recognition that derives from rights. Mutual recognition is the ground of personal rights even though in established social relations the idea of rights may be used to determine what kind of recognition is owed to an individual in one social context or another.

Our focus here in the discussion of mutual recognition as constitutive of reflective self-consciousness must be on the internal act of self-consciousness and not just on the external aspects of the self where interdependence is already evident on many levels—biological, psychological, and sociological or economic.

We are not questioning the necessity of interdependence on these different levels of human collectivity. Our question is about the necessity of interdependence among selves on the level of reflective self-consciousness as an *internal* act of selfhood. How is such an internal act to be conceived, and how can it be thought of as communal prior to any idea of its being independent of other selves in any way? Can this internal act of our self be thought of as constituted in isolation from any other self without any communicative interaction or communion whatsoever with other selves?

5.1.1 Let us begin by trying to suppose that the internal act of reflective self-consciousness can be thought of in isolation from other selves, as in most modern versions of social contract theory. Such a self would have to be thought of as existing in its own self-consciousness by itself and to have come to such self-consciousness all by itself in isolation from any other, indifferent as to whether there are other selves or not. This is the position of many in modern philosophy who take their lead from René Descartes and Thomas Hobbes and who are left with the problem of proving that there are other selves than oneself and of saying what to do with or against them, especially in social contract theory.

They begin with asserting the fact of reflective self-consciousness as if it were the only factor in the primordial fact of human existence while ignoring the factors of communion among selves and of the world in that same primordial fact. Having done so, they are left with the unsolvable problem of proving that there are other selves who are also interior to themselves and with whom they have to contend. For if a self is a self only by its internal act of self-consciousness in isolation from any other self, how can it know that there is another self with its own internal act of self-consciousness? How could any such self come to discover the existence of another self, no less interior to itself or hidden from it than the other is to itself?

To do so, a self would have to proceed from its own self-consciousness either empirically or reflectively. If it proceeded empirically, it would have to begin by using itself as a model for selfhood in the world and then, by a process of induction, establish whether anything else in the world given by nature corresponds to such a model. If it found something that did fit the model, another self similarly constituted in its self-consciousness in isolation from any other, it would then find itself locked out from the internal aspect of the other and be forced only to guess as to what that might be through purely external criteria. It would still know nothing of another self.

It is interesting to note in passing that this is a problem that all those who proceed only empirically in their inquiry into the self run into. They start from only an external structure taken for granted as selfhood, whether that be biological, neurological, psychological, or political, even for what they are in themselves, thus reducing their own selfhood to something purely given by nature, a phenomenon given objectively in the world without any aspect of active subjectivity where reflective self-consciousness is to be found. And if any thought is given to it, it is relegated to the realm of what has been called mystereanism with which rational inquiry has nothing to do, so that for such a theory of selfhood the problem of other selves does not even arise.

Where the problem does arise in a purely empirical approach to the nature of selfhood, it remains an unsolvable problem of the "existence of other selves." Indeed, when it does arise, it only shows that selfhood has been misconceived; it does not know even its own internal self for which the problem arises, since that itself cannot be reduced to or represented by a model, external to reflective self-consciousness. It can only be known reflectively.

If, on the other hand, the supposedly isolated self proceeds reflectively, it would have to withdraw deeper and deeper into itself until it came to its very core as a self, as Descartes was when he came to the clear and distinct idea of himself as a thinking thing. Once there, however, the self would have to suppose that it is the only one of its kind and that everything else is at the periphery of its core, or external to it. It could not think of another self without abandoning itself as the core of selfhood, for another self like itself would have to be at least another core and, as some existentialists end up maintaining, another self hostile to oneself. The other self would be hell for me, as Jean-Paul Sartre has maintained. But then the question would become: how could such a self-centered consciousness even know of another core of self-consciousness unless that other core were already at the core of its own reflection into self?

The supposed experience of an absolutely isolated self thus cannot seem to make sense as an experience of reflective self-consciousness. Either it is an experience that simply evacuates selfhood into a purely external model and so loses sight of the self in its *internal* dimension, or it simply presupposes the existence of another self as a matter of empirical fact, not knowing exactly how it is to relate to the supposedly isolated self except as a threat to oneself, another absolute core of selfhood standing over against itself as an absolute core in a state of war with the other, as Hobbes would have put it.

5.1.2 The only way out of such an impossible supposition for selfhood to emerge is perhaps to deny the supposition on which it is built, namely that a self is constituted in isolation from any other self and to totally reverse the perspective—that is, recognize that the self is not constituted in isolation but only in a relation or a dialectic of mutual recognition with another self. The point, however, is for us to see that this reversal of perspective is not only a counterposition to the first but is rather what happens to be really the case with human self-consciousness in its need and its infinite desire for encountering other selves.

Concretely, as we have seen from the beginning, reflective self-consciousness starts not from an isolation but from a communicative interaction among selves, which takes place not only through the smile or the gaze but also emerges more fully through language. Earlier, we spoke mainly of the smile as the primordial mode of communicative interaction, or of the gaze into one another's face, something that is lacking in the newborn infant or deficient in feral children who have been too long deprived of properly human communication in their development, or even in children who have been deprived of properly human attention or respect while growing up in collectivities that have no regard for them as budding reflective self-consciousnesses.

The more profound mode of communicative interaction among humans is language, something that emerges for the infant after the smile and enables the child, who is now more than just an infant—literally, "one incapable of speaking"—to enter more deeply into the phenomenon of human confrontation and communion with others. Even zoologists in their observation have remarked on this emergence of language for children as a trait that characterizes the human animal, a trait or a phenomenon we must now reflect on to enter more deeply into the question of communicative interaction or mutual recognition as constitutive of self-consciousness.

The question we now have to raise, if language is that which ties us together as human beings at the same time as it distinguishes us from one another, is this: can there be any self-consciousness without language, and can there be any *language* in the full human sense of the word except as a communication between selves?

The Miracle Worker dramatizes this crucial mediation of language in the constitution of two selves, that of Helen and that of Annie. At the outset only one seems to have language and to be fully self-conscious, while the other is lacking both language and an adequate sense of herself. The one who knows language tries to teach the other but can only go so far from the exterior. The breakthrough for the one who does not know, or lacks self-consciousness—that is, Helen—has to come from the interior, but it is not known how to reach that interior or even whether there is an interior—enough intelligence, for example—to be reached as long as there has not been a breakthrough in language.

For a time Helen knows something of language: she has signs for certain things such as her mother or her favorite cake; she even learns to spell words, but she does not know what *language* is. She can sign, but she does not know what it is to sign. Her use of words is limited to only a very limited scope of particular desires and needs on the animal side of her nature. She remains enclosed within the darkness of those particular desires, fixated on the one that is most prominent in her consciousness at any particular time. She has access neither to her act of consciousness—much less to that of another self—nor to the broader world of objects. Left to herself she would have remained locked in this darkness, like a feral child unable to enter into more human communion with other selves.

It is Annie who finally reaches her by confronting her, challenging her, and teaching her obedience, discipline, and a new means of communicating—a sign language—even before Helen knows what communicating means or that she wants to communicate.

But all that sign language by itself does not seem to be enough as long as Annie is still holding back in her own willingness to communicate with Helen. She too is somehow trapped in a darkness of her own by her voices from the past, by her resistance to loving again, as she had loved her deceased brother. As long as this reserve on the part of Annie exists, she cannot reach or confront Helen in her selfhood, even though she is very anxious for Helen to learn, more perhaps than Helen's parents, who cannot stand to be separated from Helen even though this separation might be for Helen's good. Once this last barrier is overcome, however, once Annie shows affection as well as the will to discipline, Helen is finally able to respond and "the miracle" takes place.

But it is important to understand what precisely this "miracle" consists in. It is not precisely in the awakening of consciousness or self-consciousness as such. Every human being has to go through such an awakening, or even many such awakenings, in order to become fully human as a self-conscious articulate self. There is a lot of learning to be done, through "millions of words," as Annie says at one point, or perhaps relatively few words, before a child comes to some mature self-consciousness in a language of his or her own.

This normally takes place through conversation in the context of family life, which can be viewed as a social womb that is required for the newborn infant to reach its final human form through mutual recognition. The etymology of the term *conversation* speaks for itself in the ordinary practice of mutual recognition, a going back and forth among individuals in communion with one another.

However, not every human being has the external handicaps Helen had in her interaction with her parents and other members of her family. Annie was the "miracle worker" precisely in having found the way around those handicaps for Helen so that Helen could finally enter into conversation with other human beings in a human way—that is, through language. But in doing so Annie was also finding a way around her own handicaps, her inability to let go of her past and enter into a new relation with a self other than her brother. Both had to be unlocked from their individual isolation.

In a sense, therefore, Annie too was being confronted and challenged, as Helen's half-brother says to Annie at the climax of Helen's resistance to Annie's disciplining. Annie had to be confronted, not just by her situation and her job but by Helen as another self to be loved as well as to be disciplined. The confrontation was thus mutual even though it seemed only one-sided for a time, and when it became completely reciprocal on both sides, the breakthrough happened on both sides. It was a "miracle" for both Helen and Annie.

In the play the first moment of recognition seems to come at first only on the side of Helen. And it seems to be only something going on in the mind of Helen. She gets the idea of water and comes to know, through a total reflection in her own act of understanding, that the name "water" is an expression of that idea, and she starts looking for all sorts of other ideas about things for which she asks to know the name. She comes to understand what it is to understand and to have names for things.

But that is only one side of what was going on for her. There was also another side in which Helen was beginning to realize something about herself and about other selves—her parents and most importantly Annie—on a new level of confrontation and recognition that is now truly spiritual. After asking for the names of things like water, earth, and tree, she turns to the "things" that had long since become more special to her—her mother and father—and eventually the one who is most special in this moment of her coming to self-consciousness—her teacher. It is at this point that the moment of recognition reaches its completion, when Annie also comes into her own self with Helen, even as Helen comes into herself with Annie. Both Annie and Hellen are liberated, each in herself, in this moment of mutual recognition and reconciliation.

What is happening in this moment of mutual recognition is not just a new sense of awareness taking place in each soul individually but, rather and more profoundly, a simple response of two selves to one another. It is impossible to speak of this simple response simply, even if we leave out of consideration the other individuals who are part of the scene and concentrate only on Helen and Annie. Each one is recognizing herself in a dialectical relation to the other—that is, each one in being recognized by the other is at the same time recognizing herself in the other by setting herself off from the other and by letting the other go free, even as she sets herself free—and each one does this from her own side precisely insofar as the other is doing the same from her side since the recognition is mutual.

The language or the words that come into play are a sign or an expression of this very mutuality in the simple response of two selves to one another. Language cannot be just a game that an individual can play any way she wants. As long as it is only that for Helen, she does not know what language is. It is only a game she tries to teach her dog with her hands. Nor can it be just a discipline to be imposed on oneself or another. As long as it is only that for Annie, she cannot get Helen going.

Language is most fundamentally communication between selves, and it is in an effort to communicate that Helen gets her first idea, even if it is just the idea of water. The idea becomes a "name" for Helen—that is, the expression of an idea—only in her recognition that it is already a name for Annie and that it is a name for both of them at the same time. The word as word cannot be just from Annie alone or from Helen alone; it has to be from both. As long as it is only from one side or the other, either as a game (for Helen) or as a discipline (for Annie), Helen and even Annie are at a loss for words in their self-consciousness.

Language may not be the only form of basic intersubjective communication. The smile, for example, could be another on a less articulate level, or music on a more articulate level. But language is the act that offers the widest scope because of its direct relation to ideas and to understanding, and to what it is to understand. It is the highest external form of communication as well as the medium for the most basic level of spiritual confrontation and communion among selves. Without it, not only would we be unable to develop the slightest degree of culture and/or technology through labor, but we would not even be able to emerge as selves since that seems to require the kind of mutual recognition that only language can provide.

Hence, in a framework of evolution where we have to suppose the existence of human individuals in nature before there was any properly human consciousness and hence before there was any language, one has to wonder how the first moment of mutual recognition could have taken place. Wouldn't it have to be between two beings like Helen, or beings perhaps even more primitive than that, unable to teach one another, and with no one else to teach either one of them? How would the spark of recognition come to be ignited between them, the spark that lights up the way for everything after that?

Regardless of how we try to think of recognition through language, whether as a long, slow process with a gradual ignition at the end or as a sudden explosion touched off by a sudden confrontation, it would have to be thought of as a radically new beginning, which nothing could completely account for in what had gone on previously because the emergence of reflective self-consciousness represents something completely original in the course of the world or of what we have been referring to as a first- and second-person ontology.

To the extent that the "miracle" of Helen Keller and Annie Sullivan is only an exceptional case of the kind of awakening to self-consciousness that every human being has to come to, we can say, in conclusion, that the dialectic that we see at play in this miracle is also at play in the constitution of any self-consciousness. It is only because it takes place less dramatically and more gradually that it is more difficult to trace in the case of more normal individuals who are not deprived either of any of their senses or of human attention as they are growing up; that is, the attention of other selves confronting them in a loving struggle of recognition.

5.1.3 Concerning the priority of mutual recognition or communicative interaction in the constitution of reflective self-consciousness, there are two alternative views we could mention in order to flesh out the position more clearly.

One is the modern view to which we took exception in our discussion, the one that characterizes the self as radically individual in its constitution, as "born free" by nature, so to speak, and as entering into social relations only after it is constituted in its self-consciousness and not in the very constitution of the self's existence as a self. This view, some elements of which we referred to in our discussion of the problem of the existence of other selves, goes back to Hobbes and runs through John Locke, Jean-Jacques Rousseau, David Hume, Immanuel Kant, and down to Jean-Paul Sartre and John Rawls in our day.

In opposition to this view, we maintain that rational self-consciousness and freedom are not given by nature but, rather, are constituted or achieved through the reflective activity of selves and that they are achieved not in isolation but in a communion, namely, of mutual recognition with other selves.

The second view we take exception to is the postmodern view, which agrees that the self is constituted through a dialectic of mutual recognition but thinks of this dialectic as beginning in a confrontation unto death and as having to go through a master–slave relationship where labor, not language, has the primordial role of mediation. This is a view laid out by Georg Wilhelm Friedrich Hegel early in his *Phenomenology of Spirit* and taken up by Karl Marx in his conception of the class struggle on a social level of culture, where spirit is found alienated from itself.

In opposition to this view, we maintain that language, not labor, is the primordial concern of historical consciousness and that the primordial confrontation among selves is one of loving struggle through language and communicative interaction and not one of confrontation unto death through labor for oneself and competition for dominance.

To illustrate this primacy of communicative interaction in the constitution of reflective self-consciousness even further, we could reflect on the case of someone who was even more deprived of human consciousness than Helen Keller was initially and yet came to be recognized as having some reflective consciousness without any words of her own in response to the attempts of others to communicate with her, through a language of music alone, without words.

The case was presented in an op-ed piece by a professor of neurology and neurophysiology, Dr. S. Allen Counter, for the *Boston Globe* that appeared on March 25, 2005, at a time when the subject of human and even spiritual consciousness was being brought into question regarding neurologically impaired individuals who were thought to be living in a purely vegetative state without consciousness of any kind, whether of sense or of intelligence.

It was the case of a thirty-two-year old woman in a condition of hydranencephaly, with only water in her cranium instead of a full complement of brain—a condition that is usually fatal prenatally or in infancy. She had survived thanks to good custodial care, including being fed pureed foods by a caretaker all her life, not without doctors who had monitored all the care she needed and who were now bringing this patient to be evaluated by the expert in neurology and neurophysiology.

What the expert found was that her eyes were open wide, she could move her head from side to side, and she could make groaning sounds. She was a quadriplegic, bedridden or strapped to a wheelchair, weighing seventy-seven pounds and four-and-half-feet tall, able to swallow and breathe on her own. The neurological examination revealed that the woman failed to blink in response to objects rapidly approaching her eye and had no clear sensitivity to touch. A bright light shone on her cranium revealed only a bright red fluid-filled cranium. The subsequent MRI revealed the absence of cerebral hemispheres, with only small remains of cerebral tissue and a small brain stem.

The conclusion by the attending physicians had been that this woman was unresponsive to sensory stimuli, devoid of any intellectual function, and in a persistent vegetative state. They were now seeking confirmation of these conclusions through a further evaluation of the brain's electrical activity and her response to sensory stimulation, including sound, sight, and touch. What the neurologist found was that although her eyes were open and moving from side to side, there was no brain response to visual input. Similarly, mild electrical stimulation in the fingers and toes traveled up the spinal cord to the brain stem, but no farther in the absence of cerebral hemispheres.

The case thus seemed open and shut with regard to not just brain function but also any intellectual function until something else supervened in this evaluation that astounded the evaluator as coming from the one being evaluated: "When I turned on a child's music box in the room, I observed that this hydranencephalic patient turned toward the music device and began to smile and make sounds, as if she were enjoying the experience."

Further observations proved this to be a consistent response to sound stimulation. And further neurological tests showed that the patient had normal hearing, which enabled her to be aware, at some level, of the sounds people make in her environment and to respond to these sounds with the appearance of joyfulness, not unlike the infant smiling back at its caretaker or Helen finding new joy in her ability to use language as communicative of ideas with Annie and her own family.

What results from this examination of the thirty-two-year-old hydranencephalic woman is much more than what could be expected by the neurologist and the attending physicians who were consulting him. It is an elation for both neurologist and physicians who come to discover the woman they were dealing with was not just a chunk of flesh or a brain "in a vegetative state" but a person with a degree of reflective self-consciousness in a soul with a minimal degree of intellectual function.

We are told that upon seeing the patient's face light up, the neurologist "immediately brought her other doctors back into the room, where they began to interact with her in a totally different manner, in some cases holding her hand and trying to speak with her, and treating her like a normally functioning human being." For himself, the neurologist "was so emotionally moved by her struggle for human attention through the single modality of hearing that I went down to a local electronics shop and bought her an audio cassette player, and some modern and classical music."

Having remarked on this phenomenon of human consciousness and communicative interaction between doctors and a patient toward the end of a long and careful neurological evaluation, a phenomenon which he characterized as astounding from a neurological point of view and in which he expressed admiration, or "was emotionally moved by her struggle for human attention through the single modality of hearing," the neurologist then returned to his talk about brain functions without asking whether brain functions are enough to account for the phenomenon of human self-consciousness and interaction that he describes, admires, and takes pleasure in as joyful. Were the neurologist and the attending physicians sufficiently aware of the human side of their intervention with this patient in addition to their expertise in neurology?

If we ask that question, as we must in a philosophy of human existence, we have to say no. Talk of brain functions alone cannot account for the phenomenon of human, if not totally rational, consciousness they finally recognized. We have to distinguish the intellectual function of the human soul from its brain function, even in sense consciousness. And we have to recognize the exercise of such a spiritual function in the exercise of properly human activity, even if it is only in conjunction with hearing, as the neurologist and the other attending physicians came to recognize at the end of their evaluation of that thirty-two-year-old hydranencephalic patient, which became a phenomenon of mutual recognition among selves, including themselves and their patient.

For in that recognition there was indeed an intellectual function at play in the perception of music and in the reaction to music on both sides—that of the patient and that of the attendants. In the rational animal there is a sense of music that is found nowhere else in nature or in the animal kingdom. Music is a sort of extension of the smile we find in the infant when it first recognizes its mother, as we may infer from what the neurologist says when he first notices a smile on the face of his patient. Music is discursive, even without words, and it takes a rational animal to appreciate and enjoy it. That is why it can be used so effectively both to pacify and to inspire human activity, at least for those who can hear and listen. It is a tool that Annie could not avail herself of in her efforts to elicit an intellectual consciousness from Helen, whereas Mozart symphonies have been used to stimulate intelligence prior to taking IQ tests.

For the neurologist and the attending physicians the final conclusion was not just a final recognition of intelligence in the patient but also a mutual recognition from which both sides, patient and doctor, learned about being human and about what is to be done with one's selfhood or humanity. In this regard we could say that the neurologist learned something about being human and courageous from a patient who was not even conscious of what she was offering as a self.

What remains for us to do in this theory of selfhood based on mutual recognition is to examine how the power of intelligence, which we have just brought out as part of mutual recognition, and the power of free will, which comes into play as rational appetite as a consequence of intelligence, both function in a human existence and what they add to rational subjectivity as well as to the world as given de facto by nature.

5.2 HOW THE ACTIVITIES OF INTELLIGENCE AND FREE WILL ARISE FROM TWO DISTINCT POWERS IN THE SPIRITUAL SOUL AT WORK IN MUTUAL RECOGNITION AMONG SELVES IN THE HISTORICAL ORDER

What results from mutual recognition among selves is a self, or a plurality of selves in their first perfection as subsistent substantial form. This is the self, or selfhood, that discloses itself in our primordial experience as human beings in some reflective self-consciousness. It is the self in its first identity as a substance that we distinguish from its proper activities, as both animal and rational, the self that at any moment of its existence in history still has to actualize itself and perfect itself through its own proper activities, starting not just from brain functions but also from powers of the human soul that transcend brain powers and that the brain cannot account for, even though we have to presuppose a proper disposition in the brain functions as a condition for the proper exercise of intelligence and free will in human activities.

We first discussed intelligence and free will as proper activities of the self in order to bring out the identity of the self in its substance as distinct from either one of these activities, which we take to be distinct from one another even though they are both proper to one and the same self. There are many and diverse activities that come into play in mutual recognition and communicative interaction among selves whose substantial form in its first perfection is oriented to some second perfection, both personal and communal, activities that transform us in our identity as well as the world in which we find ourselves, through an intentional effort and labor that takes place historically in the world.

Since then, we have dwelled on some sense and emotional activities of the human soul as form of its body, or of the composite, in which we find a strong correlation with dispositions or powers in the brain functions of the human being as animal. But now we turn more to the self's spiritual activities of knowing and willing, which are rational activities of the human soul as distinct from its sense and emotional activities and that are proper to the self as rational and as spiritual, as we have demonstrated in establishing that the human soul is truly, though not purely, spiritual in its subsistence. As activities that are proper to the soul as spiritual, intelligence and will flow from powers proper to the soul as *spiritual* and not just from powers of the composite, such as the powers of sense perception and the powers of emotion in reaction to sense perceptions.

The question for us then is how these two activities, knowing and willing, differ from one another while being proper to one and the same self and in what sense we are to distinguish them from one another without tearing human existence apart by separating them from one another and from the self. How do they come together in one and the same self, seeking its own second perfection, and how do they remain distinct from one another without being reduced one into the other?

Activity is at the core of human existence as superadded to what is given by nature and by past performance in a human essence. Spiritual existence of the self is given and known through reflective self-consciousness as what is superadded to mere nature in its self-consciousness through the exercise of human intelligence and human willing. We do not know ourselves reflectively in our subjectivity except in the activity through which we come to our own second perfection by bringing ourselves to completion as the accomplishment of our nature and our lives.

We distinguish two such activities on the level of our first- and second-person ontology as specifically different within the self but as coordinated, not separated, in human activity as a whole. We recognize a plurality of acts in each kind, whether of knowing or of willing, but we find activities of one kind irreducible to activities of the other kind, each with its own object in reality as distinct from the object of the other; *truth* in the case of knowing and *goodness* in the case of willing.

For knowing, the object is *truth* concerning what we find given in reality. This entails an intentional grasp of reality, as when I understand that I am a rational animal and that other selves I encounter are rational animals as well, even with their individuating circumstances, such as color, location, or size. For lesser beings in a third-person ontology, the intentional grasp does not include rationality, but it does include appreciating intelligently *what* the thing is in our world, as when

Helen first came to know what water is and not just the name "water," which she already knew how to spell with her hands.

Knowing of reality inside ourselves as well as outside in all its diversity and plurality includes many acts and many levels of both sense and intelligent consciousness. It starts with simple identification of selves and of things for what they are, and it expands into ever more complex understandings of what selves and what things are in a universe that is quite diverse, giving rise to a wide variety of particular sciences or of intentional grasps of the physical, biological, psychological, economic, and political, each with a science of its own as its culture. What all these acts and all these sciences have in common is some truth in the intentional grasping of reality. Critically established truth, and nothing but the truth, is their object.

Willing, on the other hand, is another activity of selfhood that distinguishes itself from knowing in relating to reality, not as intentional grasping and understanding, but as appetite for what is good. For willing, the object is not *truth* in the intellect with reference to reality but the *good* in reality, or reality itself as good or as object of appetite. There are many appetites in the rational animal, each a power to generate some activity in a self, sense appetites, often in contention with one another as objectives to be actualized. But among them there is one that rules over them all, or at least should—namely the will or the rational appetite with its power to choose what good or what objective it will pursue as we come to discover in deliberation and in the exercise of free choice.

For in that exercise, we do not start from some idea of the good, which we then decide to pursue. We start from a reflective self-consciousness in which we find ourselves desiring things we have to think of as good, at least for our rational appetite. In other words, we come to the idea of the good as correlative to our appetite, as we become conscious of our appetite for something—namely the good as the object of our appetite. The good is what we desire when we don't have it, and what we acquiesce in when we do have it. Both ideas, of appetite and of good, are discovered in their relation to one another.

This holds for the many acts and the many levels of emotion or appetite in which we find ourselves deliberating, deciding, and choosing, as the way to self-determination in our second perfection or in the good of selfhood, as that in which we can acquiesce as rational selves.

Given this distinction between the *true* and the *good* as objects in the proper activities of reflective self-consciousness, we are led to distinguish not just between two aspects in this activity itself but also two *powers* in the soul from which these higher-level activities flow, one which we refer to as intelligence and the other as free will. This is the question we must now endeavor to answer: is this distinction of two powers in the soul something called for not just by our understanding of human activity as distinct from merely animal activity but also by the *reality of the self itself* as constituted in its reflective self-consciousness?

Again, we have to keep in mind that when we speak of a distinction here, we are not thinking of a separation such as can be conceived when we think of different parts of the brain as the location required for different kinds of conscious operation. We are not talking about brain powers as such. We are talking about principles of activity, such as inquiry for understanding or deliberation for choosing, that are part of the soul as given by nature and as amplified in historical consciousness through mutual recognition among selves.

These powers are "accidents," so to speak, in the soul as form of the substance of the self, but accidents necessary for the self to take action as a rational animal in search of its second perfection as rational. But even as accidents, they are necessary powers in the constitution of the self in its substance as *given by nature* and as *enhanced by culture* in historical consciousness. These powers are not things in themselves, but they are real and really distinct from one another as well as from the substantial soul in which they occur, known for *what* it is by the activities that emanate from it, which cannot be accounted for by any part of the brain.

We can only think of them as *powers*—the *power* of intelligence and the *power* of free will—and we have to think of them as real, in the spiritual soul, since it is through them that the soul exercises its most proper activities as *spirit*. Intelligence is the *power* of knowing critically on the level of *spirit*, while *will* is the *power* of willing freely on the same level of *spirit*, though not without some dependence on the powers of sense life, either as powers of sense perception or as sense appetites in correlation with powers in the brain.

Two basic points are to be made clear here: how the activities of intelligent knowing and free willing are distinct from one another even though they are both part of the proper activity of one and the same self, and what sort of distinction this implies for the internal constitution of the self in its historical existence or self-consciousness.

5.2.1 We have already distinguished between the substance of the self and its diverse activities through which it perfects itself. We now have to further distinguish between the substance of the self and the diverse powers through which it exercises these diverse activities of knowing and willing. This distinction of powers, however, cannot be seen through a mere inspection of the self in its essence, apart from its activities, as if they were located in one part of ourselves as composite substances, such as the brain or the muscles in our arms. We can understand the distinction of powers only through reflection on the different activities that emanate from them and through the different objects they aim at as appetites of a self, which is more than what they are geared for, so to speak, in the fabric of the brain.

Let us begin therefore by reflecting on how different activities of one and the same self are distinguished from one another as human endeavors in the world on the basis of different objects we aim at and acquiesce in.

Think of the way two crafts or two different types of activity are distinguished from one another. It is easy to think of each as distinct when each is found in a different person. The craft of carpentry is not the same as that of surgery. And we see that most clearly when we find the craft of carpentry in one person who is a carpenter and not a surgeon, or the craft of surgery in another person who is a surgeon and not a carpenter.

But what if one and the same person is in possession of both crafts? Are the crafts still distinct or are they the same? One and the same person can be both a carpenter and a surgeon, though not in one and the same activity. One is not a carpenter insofar as one is a surgeon, nor is one a surgeon insofar as one is a carpenter. Yet, each one of these two crafts or activities can be found in one and the same self.

Each of these crafts aims at a different object and so remains distinct from the other even when both are found in the same person, as anyone who is a master of two crafts is well aware when exercising one craft and careful not to let the other craft interfere with the craft currently being attended to. One craft aims at building. The other aims at healing. For this reason one person can be good at one activity and not good at the other. I may be a good carpenter but a poor surgeon, or a good surgeon but a poor carpenter, depending on how much of each craft I command. I can improve in one and not in the other, and so on, depending on how well I can achieve the aim or the object of each craft or type of activity.

Knowing and willing, which are both proper activities of the same self, also have to be distinguished in the same way by what they aim at, or by their respective objects. To put it in the simplest terms, knowing aims at obtaining *truth*, which pertains to intelligence, and willing aims at the *good* in things, which pertains to things themselves as objects of appetites. Just as truth and goodness differ as objects of human activity, so also knowing and willing differ as activities. One and the same person may be proficient at knowing the truth, say of a craft, but not at seeking the good the craft aims at. For example, I may have excellent skill as a carpenter but not care much about doing a good job on a cabinet. Or conversely, one may be proficient at seeking the good or wanting to do a good job but not at knowing the truth or how to do the job rightly.

In certain kinds of activity, such as doing scientific research, the two distinct kinds of activity can be seen as including one another in a kind of *circumincession*. Truth can be seen as the good we seek in the critical exercise of our intelligence, while good can be seen as the truth we seek for the same intelligence in search of the truth.

5.2.1.1 Let us try to think first of how the two activities are distinct from one another before trying to think of how they mutually include one another. The distinction can be illustrated in terms of any particular craft, which always involves both knowing and willing. In carpentry, for example, there is the art, the skill, or the discipline, which is a knowing, aiming at the truth of the craft or knowing how things work according to this craft. But there is also the ambition or the desire or the care, which is a willing to do good work or produce some good, a good result we can acquiesce in.

The same can be said of surgery, teaching, piloting, and so on. In each craft or activity, which we refer to alternatively as a discipline to be learned or as taking care to obtain a good result, there is both intellectual discipline and affective caring. But the two remain distinct as knowing and willing, insofar as one can have the discipline or the skill to do something right, as in the case of an accomplished craftsman, but not care about doing a good job. Or alternatively one can care very much about doing a good job but not have the discipline or the skill, as in the case of an apprentice in a craft. There are skilled workers who don't care for the good, and there are workers who care about doing good work, producing a good cabinet, or writing a good poem but don't know how to do it.

5.2.1.2 The ideal craftsman or worker is the one who both cares about the good and knows how to achieve it. This is where the mutual inclusion, or the *circumincession, of knowing-truth* and *willing-good* into one another comes into play.

5.2.1.2.1 On the one hand, we have to say that willing the good presupposes knowing what the good is and knowing how to achieve it. In this sense willing comes after knowing. It is an appetite that follows upon something we come to know as good, either as desire if we do not possess it or as acquiescence if we do possess it. The willing is our response or the attitude we adopt responsibly with respect to something we have learned about as good.

Such a willing is distinct from the knowing it presupposes, which is concerned only with the truth of what is, and yet it cannot be separated from it. For if we do not know of something, we cannot desire it or acquiesce in it. At the same time, however, even though my response to or the attitude I adopt with respect to what I come to know as good is distinct from the knowing, I do inevitably respond in my own way or adopt an attitude with respect to what I come to know, whether it be a response of acceptance, indifference, or rejection. We can say, "I care a lot about this" or "I couldn't care less."

In this sense, willing comes under knowing, as the good comes under the truth, in that we have to know of something before we can properly will it. It is impossible to love something we know nothing about. Willing is a conscious and deliberate appetite, as we shall see more fully in the next section of this chapter on human knowing and human willing and also in our ethical consideration of selfhood in part two of this inquiry.

Insofar as the good comes under the truth, we also have to say that willing calls for some intellectual or rational discernment regarding the good. Not everything we will is ipso facto good. Willing of the good presupposes some knowing of what is truly good, as Socrates surmised in supposing that, if we know what the good truly is as rational animals, we do it.

5.2.1.2.2 On the other hand, or conversely, we also have to say that knowing the truth presupposes willingness or readiness to know and to think critically and reflectively, at least in any activity of scientific inquiry. In this sense knowing comes after willing, as in choosing a major for research in college. There may be some truth we know from the very beginning of our intellectual activity, but for the most part we have to learn most of what we come to know, whether in common sense or in scientific investigation. Truth is for us an object of inquiry and research and of critical reflection, which presupposes in us a desire for the truth we seek or else an acquiescence in the truth we find.

This presupposition of willingness for truth can be illustrated dramatically in the case of Helen Keller and how she came to know out of a desire for truth in the dimness of her self-consciousness, which no one in the family, not even Helen herself, suspected, but which Annie recognized in her as an intelligence still buried in darkness yet seeking to come out in the open, both for herself and for other selves.

Without that desire Helen would never have come to any intelligence of her own, much less acquiesce in the truth of any understanding of things and of selves, including herself, for what we are witness to in the "miracle" that transforms Helen's life and consciousness is Helen's own acquiescence in the truth of herself and of other selves as evidence of a prior desire that she herself or others did not know of and that only Annie tried to satisfy in spite of Helen's handicaps on the level of sense perception.

Here again knowing the truth remains distinct from the appetite we have for it. The mere desire to know does not guarantee the truth of our knowing. We may search without finding and we may acquiesce in falsehood as well as in truth. But knowing the truth has to be part of the good we seek as rational beings.

In this sense of the circumincession, knowing comes under willing, as the truth comes under the good, in that we have the desire to know before we actually come to know. This desire can become disciplined and deliberate and so presuppose some knowledge of its own, a knowledge of knowing, or an intelligence of intelligence, so to speak. Most fundamentally the desire is in the very nature of human intelligence, which has or rather is a natural desire to know in the self. As it becomes disciplined and deliberate in the exercise of one's own intelligence, it always presupposes some primordial conception of what it is to know and of what truth is.Insofar as the truth comes under the good, we have to say that truth remains part of the good for us. Knowing the truth is an essential part of our second perfection. Whether or not it is in some act of knowing that we achieve our ultimate perfection, knowing of some kind is surely part of that ultimate perfection we strive for in our activity as rational beings.

Thus, to the extent that *truth* and *goodness* represent two distinct objects or aims and to the extent that truth is the aim of knowing while goodness is the aim of willing, we have to say that knowing and willing are distinct activities. Truth can come under the good to the extent that it is something desirable for the self in its understanding, and the good can come under truth to the extent that it has to be known as good by the self to be sought. But the act that aims at the one as its object can never be the same as the act that aims at the other as its object.

This is why knowing and willing are irreducibly distinct acts even when they are most intimately intertwined with one another in one and the same self. I cannot separate what I want from what I know, nor knowing from wanting, but I can never do as if knowing were the same as willing or willing were the same as knowing, as distinct spiritual activities on the level of what we have called *spirit* or intellectual consciousness, as distinct also from sense consciousness, where distinct sense activities come into play in conjunction with the distinct spiritual activities.

5.2.2 We have already seen a certain distinction within the self between its activity and its substance in chapter 2. We arrived at such a distinction through a consideration of the diversity and multiplicity of acts in relation to the simple identity of the self in its substance. The distinction we are driving at here can be seen in a similar way, but now by reflecting more precisely on what the diversity of activities consists in, as we have just been doing in sections 5.2.1.1 and 5.2.1.2.

The diversity between knowing and willing is not the only one that can be brought out in the proper activities of the self, but it is certainly a crucial one pertaining to the rational aspect of human consciousness, and it is enough to bring out the outlook of two specifically distinct activities of the self as rational and as spiritual. Each one of these two activities, knowing truth and willing good, will entail any number of different acts depending on what particular truths or what particular goods one may be concerned with, but all will share in the specific outlook of the activity to which they belong. It is to account for such specific differences of activity that we are led to distinguish between powers in the self and powers that are distinct from one another in relation to one another and from the self in its substance as well.

The powers have to be distinct from one another because each one is the principle of an activity that is specifically different from the other. One has to do with *truth*, which is in the intellect as it relates to reality, including itself as well as other selves and other things. The other has to do with the *good*, which is in reality as desired by the rational appetite. I can exercise understanding only through my intelligence and not through my will, and I can exercise responsible decision-making only through my will, and not through my intelligence. When I am trying to understand something, I should not let my will interfere with the understanding, and when I am deciding something, it should be clear that this takes me beyond the limited understanding I may have of myself and of the world.

The intelligence and the will, as powers, also have to be distinct from the substance of the self because they are distinct from one another and cannot therefore be the substance itself since substance is one and they are two.

Taking either one of these two powers in abstraction from the other, it would be possible to suppose that only one of the two powers is an accident while the other is the substance, instead of both being distinct from the substance, or else one might take only one of the two, intelligence or will, as essential to the self and not the other.

On one side, the power of intelligence would be thought of as the substance or the essence, while the power of willing would be thought of as an accident or as inessential to selfhood. This could be viewed as a position that Socrates might want to adopt when he says that the problem of doing good or evil is ultimately reducible to a problem of knowing what to do and what not to do. If everyone knew the good, one might say according to this position everyone would do it. This would be like saying that every accomplished craftsman would always care about doing the best job possible. If people do not do the good, it is because they do not know it. Only learning, therefore, can solve the problem of good or evil; and learning alone is enough to solve it, as if to say that every craftsman as such always wants to do the good job that he knows how to do.

On the other side of the distinction, the will would be thought of as the substance or the essence, while the intelligence would be thought of as an accident or as inessential to selfhood. This might be viewed as a position that Nietzsche would adopt, since for him the problem of good or evil is basically a problem of the will to power and not a problem of learning having anything to do with truth. The so-called concern for truth, according to Nietzsche, is only a mask for a more fundamental will to power and self-determination that takes the self out of any communal existence based on mutual recognition, in a sheer transvaluation of values, supposedly beyond any distinction of good and evil.

But neither of these positions, that of Socrates or of Nietzsche, does justice to the identity of the self in the very diversity of its activity. Each is only one-sided, while the self has to be at least two-sided or a whole with two essential spiritual powers that are accidental to one and the same substance of the self, one of intelligence and one of will—two powers that weave into one another dialectically and complement one another in their historical circumincession among selves in communion with one another.

Each self comes to its proper second perfection, which is a sort of transvaluation of values in the self, in an exercise of both intelligence and will, with a reciprocal priority between consciousness of oneself and of the other as known values, on the one hand, and willful response to that value of oneself and of the other as good or evil.

The self is or makes itself what it is, neither on the basis what it knows alone nor on the basis of what it wills alone but on the basis of both at the same time and in their reciprocal relation to one another in the life of any self. I constitute myself in my identity through whom and through what I know and through the will I exercise with regard to whom and to what I know. The truth is important to me as intelligent. It is a value for me, but one that affects what I ultimately value as the good and how I value it.

The transvaluation of values is as much a problem of knowing as it is a problem of willing in the communicative interaction among selves. Socrates and Nietzsche should not be opposed to one another in a philosophy of human existence but, rather, confronted with one another in a discursive dialogue of mutual recognition.

Let us think back reflectively on how this reciprocity between intelligence and willing comes into play in mutual recognition as constitutive of self-consciousness in the presence of one another. In this discovery of oneself in the presence of another, there is a moment of separation of the one from the other self, on each side, where each one takes itself as the essential and denies the other as part of this essential good. Then there is the moment of denial of this denial, where each one realizes that to deny the other as essential to one's selfhood is at the same time to deny something essential to one's own self in attaining one's own second perfection. From this denial of a denial there comes the moment of recognition of the good that any other represents for the good of oneself and of the good that each one has to offer to the other in the desire for a communal good and in mutual acquiescence regarding such a communal good.

This can be illustrated in how both Helen and Annie come to a new level of self-consciousness in the presence of one another in *The Miracle Worker*. First, especially for Helen, there is a priority of coming to know Annie as another, on an intellectual level, objectively as it were, and to know herself, reflectively and no less objectively, as other than that other. This required a long discipline of Helen's intelligence where a premature intervention of appetites on the animal level can stand in the way of any discovery of another self as self as well as of one's own self as intelligent, free, and self-conscious.

The sort of immediate response to Helen's demands coming from a family unwilling to discipline itself as well as coming from Helen, stood in the way of Helen's coming to self-conscious intelligence of herself and of other selves. Their "love," as Annie puts it, stood in the way of not just discipline but also Helen's discovering the truth about herself and others as rational animals in the same way as particular self-interests can stand in the way of discovering the truth in scientific research.

Once the moment of truth has dawned for both Helen and Annie and for other members of the household, however, a priority of willing comes into play, letting the other go free as essentially good in itself as a self, and in willing the good of the other as well as the good of oneself, in a new kind of love—a love of friendship that is disinterested or selfless in the sense that it transcends the love of pleasure or the love of utility on the animal level. The miracle is not complete until Helen asks what or who Annie is as a self and until the teacher, for her part, says, *I love Helen*, which she was unable or unwilling to admit while she was only disciplining the child. In the same way, in recognizing that she had both gained and lost a daughter, the mother was letting her child go free and beginning to love her in a more disinterested way as a self in her own right.

All this was a significant culmination in the lives of Helen and Annie, who remained closely bound together for the rest of their lives. But it was also only a beginning, giving rise to further desires to know about or to wonder about other selves and about other things in the world, others outside the family, in the nation, and in the world at large, with whom more loving relations might develop: love of neighbors, love of science, love of all who labor in the search for the fullness of truth and for the betterment or the *transvaluation* of mankind in so many diverse ways and civilizations, where both intelligence and will come into play to complement one another in an expansive circumincession that adds rational cultures to nature in the constitution of selves around the world.

5.3 THE CONSTITUTION OF CULTURES IN THE HISTORICAL ORDER OF SPIRIT THROUGH THE EXERCISE OF INTELLIGENCE AND FREE WILL IN MUTUAL RECOGNITION

We have been reflecting on properly human activities as the primordial evidence for what we are as selves and what distinguishes us in our first- and second-person ontology from the beginning of our inquiry. Through the same reflection on properly human activities, such as intelligence and free will, we have also endeavored to show how the powers of rational knowing and willing must be taken as part of that first- and second-person ontology of selves no less than, and even more so than, the sense knowing and emotional willing, which we take to be characteristic of animals as such, both rational and nonrational, and that are directly related to the physical brain.

To show this relative transcendence of the intellectual over the sensual and of the willful over the emotional, we had to insist on what distinguishes the spiritual from the sensual in human activities with regard to both intelligence and will but without setting any of them apart from one another in the ontology and the existence of selfhood. It remains for us to reflect on how they do come together in the labor of going from a self's first perfection as a thing of nature to its second perfection in the communal good of one culture or another.

There are many ways of thinking about culture or cultures as historical phenomena. Some think of them as more developed or more advanced in certain families, clans, classes, or nations, usually their own, while they think of the less advanced or the less developed as not cultures at all, or at most as primitive or undeveloped cultures, if not underdeveloped and hardly surpassing the order of animal nature, if at all, with little or no capacity to exercise any functions of intelligence and will.

This represents only a particular conception of culture, belonging to a particular age or to a particular community, and not the universal conception we have been leading up to in speaking of intelligence and free will as proper activities of selfhood seeking its second perfection in more than just surviving as a thing or as a species of nature. The conception of culture we have been leading up to is one that includes a properly spiritual dimension that comes only with intelligence and free will as part of the communal first- and second-person ontology that distinguishes human beings from anything pertaining only to a third "person" ontology of any order, sentient or nonsentient, living or nonliving.

Wherever there is a living and mindful human being or a self, there is an other with whom there is communion in mutual recognition. And wherever there are selves in communion with one another with intelligence and free will, there is a culture, whether it is in the harshest conditions of nature or in the more temperate regions, even in the harshest struggle for survival. The struggle for survival by human beings is itself a culture that brings a spirit of comfort and communion to sustain the selves in their mutual recognition, as Helen and Annie did as selves in overcoming their handicaps with encouragement and love.

We will not try to describe here any of the remote cultures we are aware of, to show how those cultures yield evidence of intelligence and free will at their root and in their scope. We shall reflect only on how culture is constituted as part of our own historical existence as selves in one community or another, large or small, advanced or primitive, national or international, or in all of these. We shall do this with regard to the two powers we have distinguished as proper to the rational or spiritual soul: first, with regard to intelligence coming forth discursively from sense consciousness; and second with regard to the will taking over the emotions, each one of them, intelligence and will, both exhibiting one and the same structure of the soul rising above the material conditions from which it emerges in coming to its second perfection as spirit.

5.3.1 How the Reflective Self-consciousness in the Human Spirit Rises from Sense Perceptions to an Exercise of Critical Judgment regarding One Another's Understanding

We begin with what we have said before about human knowing or learning as beginning in the senses and rising to a twofold act of intelligence—that of understanding and that of critical reflection.

This is the essential structure that is found in all types of human knowing and learning, whether it be common sense or the particular sciences we alluded to at the beginning of this philosophy of human existence, or even the philosophy of human existence we are expounding here. Our aim is not to pass in review all that each one of us has learned through experience, understanding, and critical reflection, nor all the different kinds of knowing one could bring up such as can be represented by the different particular sciences, natural and social. It is rather to bring out the essential structure found in any complete exercise of intelligence as expressed in what we speak of as the *exercise of judgment*. What does such an exercise of judgment presuppose in the rational animal, and how do its different elements come together in a single act of knowing or learning?

5.3.1.1 How is all this to be conceived? We have already considered the structure of this act earlier in passing in order to arrive at the structure of the constitution of the self as a composite of form and matter and as a simple spiritual identity. But now we must look into this structure of knowing in greater detail than we did before, to bring out how human intelligence rises to the fullness of its critical ability toward truth. In doing so we shall not only be clarifying the structure of knowing in itself but we shall also be reinforcing our earlier understanding of the human soul as form of a composite, along with matter, and as spirit with a subsistence of its own.

We take human knowing, then, as the proper activity of a self having *truth* as its object, as we have distinguished it from the equally proper activity of willing having the *good* as its object. In this knowing there is an intentional grasp of reality in which knower and known become one in act. We say that this intellectual activity starts or emerges from sense perception or observation but is not completed in it. It is intelligent only as part of a reflective self-consciousness in which there is both understanding and critical reflection on experience as expressed in the terms of any direct exercise of judgment about something given in experience.

This implies a certain priority of the senses in relation to intelligence in human knowing, a priority that can be seen as either temporal (i.e., sensation comes before understanding) or one of dependence (i.e., understanding depends on sensation in some sense in the exercise of its own act). We assert a priority in both senses so that without sensation there would be no human understanding. But the discussion will have to determine more precisely in what this dependence consists. It should be clear, however, that sensation is only the beginning of human knowing and not the whole of it.

This is to say that while human knowing begins in the observation of facts through the senses, it does not end there, nor is the observation of facts, no matter how intricate or complex it may be or become, all there is to human understanding. There is also an intellectual accounting for the facts that comes into play in conjunction with sense observation. The relation between intelligence and the senses is like that between soul and body: one is the form of the other so that the act of intelligence is no less real in the observation of facts than sensation.

Conversely, this suggests that, to the extent that it is tied to human understanding, human sensation differs from the sensation of other animals even though in many respects it is bound to be the same in varying degrees of vividness. Even the sense consciousness of humans would seem to be specifically different from the consciousness of other animals in the same way the human body, in its neurological makeup, is specifically different from the body of other animals. Human sensation cannot be properly understood apart from its relation of openness to intelligence. Sense knowing is only a beginning of knowing for humans, a beginning that brings into play the added light of intelligence.

We speak of the sense powers of consciousness as tied to physical organs or to the material aspect of the self. These powers can also be distinguished as faculties to the extent that different acts of sensation can be distinguished from one another as seeing can be distinguished from hearing and touching from tasting, et cetera.

But it is important to keep in mind that a sense as such cannot be reduced to its physical organ; a sense perception entails an act or a form along with the organ that is its matter. There could even be a distinction between external senses, such as those we have just alluded to, and internal senses such as the common sense, which unifies what is grasped by the diversity of the external senses into a single perception, or the imagination, which can recombine perceptions, or the memory, which can retain sensations and perceptions. But we will not try to work out any such distinctions here. We are concerned only with the activity of sensation as a whole in its relation to the human intelligence that emerges from it.

Note that to the extent that sensation is already a level of consciousness and already includes some intentional activity, it cannot be purely material; it represents a certain degree of immateriality in the sense that the sensing being rises above its immersion in matter and is able to take in other beings intentionally. When I see something, I am not only myself but I become one with what I see, or it becomes one with me in the seeing.

When we say that human knowing in the rational animal rises or passes from one level of consciousness in the senses to a higher level of conception or understanding, we imply that the first or lower level is not closed in upon itself but is essentially open to the higher level in a way that the senses of nonrational animals are not open to any higher level such as that of intelligence. Fascinating as human sensation may be in itself and endless as it may be in its expansion, it cannot exhaust the human interest in knowing; mere information gathering never satisfies the self's concern for truth and meaning; information calls for and is always complemented by an intelligent interpretation that may be right or wrong, which then calls for critical reflection.

In other words, sense perception in human beings is open to questions for understanding and for critical reflection in a way that it is not for other nonrational animals so that we have to speak of a twofold act in the way humans come to know—not one of pure intuition, whether on the level of sense or of intelligence or of both one after the other, but one of discursive mediation in passing from one to the other, with intelligence probing into the senses and the senses lending themselves to the intelligence in the learning process. We do not discover the truth all at once but through a process of raising questions and seeking answers, as Helen did after coming to her own understanding of the predicate "water." Every answer or every conclusion comes as the completion of a rational act that began as a question in the rational sense consciousness.

By distinguishing two types of questions in this learning process for the rational animal, we shall be led to distinguish a twofold act to meet each type of question. However, to the extent that both types of question still aim at the truth—that is, at one and the same object—we shall not have to introduce a further distinction of powers in intelligence itself; the self exercises one and the same power of intelligence in pursuing the answer to both types of question.

When we speak of intelligence, we have in mind the power of knowing on the level of spirit, or the exercise of that power. As the first act of intelligence, understanding relates directly to what the senses present in answering the question *what*? or *how come*? regarding what presents itself in sense experience.

Questions for understanding can be very complex and can lead to prolonged investigations into what is given in experience, in view of explaining or accounting for what is presented through the senses. They give rise to scientific investigations of all sorts. Basically, however, the act of understanding consists in an apprehension of what is given in experience and in an endeavor to formulate what or to form the quiddity of what is so apprehended in a language that makes it intelligible to us. This first act of intelligence is relatively simple only in comparison to the second act of intelligence, which presupposes this first act and is mediated by it.

Critical reflection, as the second act of intelligence, arises from the first act and answers the question *whether* what has been formulated is true or not, verified or not, regarding being, or what is the case in point. This more critical aspect of intelligence consists in a more complex act of composing and/or saying yes, or of dividing and/or saying no, to the idea expressed in the relatively simple apprehension of the first act of intelligence, as to whether this idea supposedly corresponds to reality or composes with it, or whether it does not compose with it, in which case it is "divided" from reality by saying no to it. It is the act of either affirming or denying the truth of an idea we have already articulated in some language, or of agreeing or disagreeing with the formulation of some opinion in the understanding as to whether it is true or not.

This act of critical reflection seldom takes the form of a simple *yes* or *no* with reference to what has been properly conceived. More often than not it issues in a partial *yes* and a partial *no*, calling for a reformulation in the first act of intelligence and thus giving rise to a dialectical interplay between the two acts, the first and the second, in a learning process and in the progression of science as critical knowing.

Questions for understanding lead to questions for reflection where answers are partially in agreement and partially in disagreement with the opinion as expressed, which in turn leads to further questions for understanding, questions for reformulation, or for finding new terms to express what precisely we are trying to talk about or conceive. The process is not limited to a mere accumulation and retention of information but includes an interpretation and a critical understanding of interpretations. Yet the act of critical reflection, as distinct from the act of understanding, hinges on a simple *yes* or *no* with reference to what has been conceived or expressed in the terms of a proposition, as in S is P, or "this is a cat."

This relation between the two acts of intelligence can be illustrated in the development of any science that proceeds by formulating hypotheses and then seeing whether they can be verified experimentally or not. It can also be illustrated in the way we have proceeded in each one of our topics here in this elaboration of a theory of selfhood where we have been careful to define our terms precisely in formulating what is to be understood before going on to a discussion or a critical reflection as to the truth of those terms with regard to human existence.

Having clarified how we are to conceive the twofold act of intelligence rising from the sense experience in the rational animal, let us now turn to the more critical aspect of the judgment we are to make concerning the truth of this concept of a twofold act of intelligence in relation to our sense experience or our existence.

5.3.1.2 To focus our own critical reflection on the understanding of a twofold act of intelligence more easily, let us borrow a scheme of three levels of knowing that is modeled on physical science but that can be applied to any kind of scientific knowing. In this scheme all three levels are determined in function of one another as part of one and the same exercise of knowing or critical thinking.

The defining characteristic of the first level, which is the level of the senses and will be called the level of presentations, "is that it is presupposed and complemented by the level of intelligence, that it supplies, as it were, the raw materials on which intelligence operates, that, in a word, it is empirical, given indeed but merely given, open to understanding and formulation but by itself not understood and in itself ineffable."[1] This can viewed as the first moment of learning, having to do with matters of fact or of what is given in experience. Coming to know oneself for the first time in a confrontation with another self, as mentioned at the beginning of this investigation, can be viewed as such a first moment of learning.

The second level, "besides presupposing and complementing an initial level, is itself presupposed and complemented by a further level of reflection,"[2] so that the following scheme results:

TABLE 5.1. INTELLIGENCE

I.	Data. Perceptual Images	Free Images	Utterances
II.	Questions for Understanding	Insights	Formulations
III.	Questions for Reflection	Reflection	Judgment

The second level presupposes and complements the first. The third level presupposes and complements the second.[3] The second level can be viewed as a second moment of learning, having to do with the intelligent interpretation of what is given in fact, yielding concepts and ideas, including concepts or ideas of our own selves and of other selves, or even of simpler composites like "water" as in the case

1 Bernard Lonergan, *Insight*, Collected Works of Bernard Lonergan 3 (Toronto: University of Toronto Press, 1992), 273.

2 Ibid.

3 Lonergan, *Insight*, 274.

of Helen, all to be reflected on critically. The third level can be viewed as a third moment of learning, having to do with a critical reflection on the ideas we have worked out as they relate to the reality we are trying to understand, including the reality of selves in confrontation with one another.

To see the mutual implication of these three levels, one has only to reflect on the twofold order of questioning as it arises from experience. Presentations give rise to questions for understanding. Formulations for understanding in turn give rise to questions for critical reflection. Let us reflect on each one of these levels of learning one at a time.

5.3.1.2.1 On the level of the senses or of presentations, I know things in their singularity as *this, that*, or the *other* thing. I even know myself and you as singular things among other things, starting from ourselves as the first singular things I come to distinguish from one another, you and me here and now.

I perceive these things in relation to one another in space and time, as next to one another (or far from one another) and as coming one after the other (or at the same time). In fact, as Kant has shown, *space* and *time* are not just given or data but also forms of our sensibility. I not only find things as given in my world, but I situate them in a space and time relative to myself. Only thus can I come to perceive them clearly or objectively.

Even in the perception of a singular thing such as the table I am sitting at, I draw a space for it, which takes time, and at the end of the process pull it together or perceive it as a thing I can feel and lean on as we sit across from one another in confrontation.

For the things we are familiar with, we do this so quickly that we hardly ever notice the process. But when something strange comes into our experience the process can become quite deliberate and conscious, as for someone who might walk into the room without ever having seen a table such as the one I am leaning on. We look at it from different angles. We feel it from different sides. And in the end we put all the images together as the images of one thing, the thing I examined in such and such a place at such and such a time.

It is important to note that in this process there is a composition of both activity and passivity. Any knowledge of a thing we perceive involves a passivity on our part; the thing makes an impression on me, so to speak, through my senses. But the knowing or the perception is not a pure passivity, as an image is imprinted on a negative in a camera; it also entails an act on my part by which I situate the thing in space and time in relation to other things and to myself and by which I unify the manifold of impressions and images into the singleness of the thing I perceive. It is similar to reconstructing the time and space for a photograph I am looking at for the first time.

The senses are also the source of data and the means of information gathering, which is also by no means a simple process. In fact, it seems that computers or so-called artificial intelligence do little more than imitate the complex process of sense knowing. They gather information, store it in memory locations piece by piece, and then rearrange the data according to the instructions of the programmer.

Computers are "intelligent" in the same way as the senses are intelligent, except that they can be much more powerful in capacity and in speed than our senses. But they still require the direction of an intelligence in the same way that the senses open the way for intelligence and require the intervention of intelligence for their completion as human knowing. They do not measure up to a complete form of human knowing in themselves in that they cannot exercise any kind of critical reflection on an intelligent content, which they can only repeat or combine with other contents in accordance with input from a programmer.

The fact that human knowing begins in the senses hardly needs to be proven to anyone who has eyes to see, ears to hear, or a memory to remember. But if a critical reflection were to be sought to verify this assertion of sense experience as opening the way for human intelligence, it could be found in the reflection that intelligence for us always presupposes at least some sense activity. Questions for understanding always presuppose some data of experience, images, or utterances that give rise to such questions in the understanding of the learner, as the predicate "water" did for Helen. We become interested in understanding only after we have gone a certain way with the senses, even if it be only hearing utterances or perceiving them through signs with one's hands, as Helen did before she understood her first word so that she could then ask whether water was a proper identification for the thing she was experiencing through her sense of touch. The signing was a crucial occasion for questioning on her part, which had failed to materialize for her until then because of her sense handicaps.

Another way of seeing the *necessity* to begin in the senses would be to reflect on how we come to know the act of reflection itself. As we saw earlier in reflecting on how matter is a constitutive principle of the self in its substance, our reflection is never an immediate return into self or a pure intuition of one's own essence. It requires a certain activity on which to reflect. This activity for us is something that begins in the senses, which are irreducibly exterior to intelligence as such or to self-consciousness. It is our reflection on sense activity as such that makes us conscious of ourselves as bodies, as having and as being a body.

5.3.1.2.2 The level of understanding starts from sense experience but rises above it through an activity that begins with questioning in the understanding. There can already be a certain kind of questioning on the level of the senses to the extent that the quest for information or data, or curiosity like that of a dog sniffing around, can be called questioning. But such sense questioning or curiosity is not properly ordered to the understanding yet. It aims only at accumulating data, seeing more things, broadening one's experience. One can do all that for a long time without ever coming to much questioning on the level understanding or intelligence or without learning much from experience. Mere experience is not a guarantee of properly intelligent and critical learning, not even if one has the best vision and the best memory in the world.

One begins to learn from experience when one begins to try to understand by raising questions for understanding. One may not immediately understand to what length such questions may lead. The child, for example, who is forever asking, "*Why* this?" and "*Why* that?", may not yet know all it is letting itself in for, but it is starting a very different process than the one of just poking around aimlessly, as we see Helen doing before she comes to questions of her own even about things she can touch immediately, such as water or the ground. The truly inquisitive mind is interested in much more than just accumulating data; it wants to understand *what* things are and find an explanation or give an account for what things are. Besides knowing that something is, it wants to know *why* or *how come* it is *what* it is.

Understanding includes a wide range of activities from ordinary common sense to the most refined scientific theorizing. It can be purely theoretical or practical or both at the same time. We all have at least some understanding of at least some things, and those are the things that we think we know best. It would be impossible to give an adequate description of all that understanding can include, but it is important to appreciate the diversity of forms it can take and the essential role it has to play in our coming to know the truth in its fullness. Without ideas, concepts, or words as formulated in the understanding, we might remain in the dark about most of reality, as Helen did until she learned what a *word* is. Without formulating hypotheses of his own, the scientist could not advance in his search for causes, and without some concept of "the market," the economist could not discover how it works.

It is on the level of understanding that we see the essential role of language in the exercise of knowing. Without language our capacity of knowing is severely impaired and our range is limited to what our senses can reach. With language, however, not only is our capacity vastly expanded, but it becomes possible to overcome the limits of our senses, as we see in the case of Helen Keller. Because of her sense impairments she was not able to learn language in the way most people learn it. She was delayed, but when she did finally learn language, she was able to overcome even her sense impairments and range very widely as a world historical figure through her exceptional understanding.

Two things should be carefully attended to in this experience of language.

5.3.1.2.2.1 When we come to an understanding of something, we do not just take it in passively, as the senses might record and retain data. We come to understand by formulating for ourselves *what* is to be understood. We produce our own word, and until we have produced such a word we have not properly understood. And once we have understood something, we can always reproduce the word or some other word, even if we can't remember what had previously remained exterior to our understanding. We can explain what we have understood in new ways (i.e., different words that we produce) because the understanding is always active in creating its own word.

This is the reason why Annie Sullivan in *The Miracle Worker* was unable at first to simply transfer words into the understanding of Helen Keller, no matter how many times she signed them in her hands. Helen was able to begin understanding language and what it is only when her own understanding came into play—when she began to form words for herself self-consciously. Clearly Annie had a lot to do for this breakthrough to take place in Helen. Without Annie, the breakthrough might never have happened. But when it did happen, it could only happen with

Helen's own internal act of understanding seizing on a word and making it her own: *water!*

Once we reach this level of understanding and language, we discover not only our own act of understanding but also a whole new realm and capacity to explore and to grasp through new words, as we see Helen doing immediately once she has reached the level of understanding. Her mind begins to work much faster than her senses will ever be able to do.

5.3.1.2.2.2 The other thing to be attended to regarding language is that the presence of another self remains crucial as well in this experience. Without coming to her own understanding, Helen could not have been fully herself. But without Annie or someone else to enter into dialogue with her, Helen might never have come to that understanding. The word that one formulates for oneself is never a word purely for oneself; it is always a word one is sharing with an other self. The first word that Helen uttered—water—is a word she shared with Annie, and she was enabled to do so because Annie had found a way of sharing her own signed word—water—with Helen in the first place. Of course, the word *water* is not just their word. It is the word of anyone who speaks English. But that is not the point about words as coming from the understanding. One can hear words and one can retain them in memory, just as Helen could by repeating signs with her hands even before understanding what language is. *Water* became Helen's word when she first began to use it meaningfully with her *teacher* or sharing it with her and with her family. Moreover, the teacher herself was instrumental in her coming to do so by communicating or sharing that word, sedimented with intelligence, with which Helen could then enter into *conversation* with the teacher from her side. In fact, Helen's teacher was instrumental not only in that first act of understanding in Helen, the first of many that were to follow endlessly, but remained instrumental in many subsequent acts by feeding her new words in sign language for Helen to work with and by helping her put words together in new combinations, sentences, in conversation. These subsequent conversations were not just with the teacher but with many others in the world and about many things in the world she would never visualize for herself but would discover through words, not spoken to her but signed in the language she learned from Annie and to which she would add signs of her own to share with others.

None of us comes to our own understanding in a vacuum. We live and breathe spiritually in an atmosphere of words. Words and language are the element in which we live as intelligent beings. Our world is sedimented with language that already expresses an understanding and invites us to our own understanding in the way that Annie was inviting Helen through her repeated signing of words. We find ourselves coming to an understanding in the words that others have produced and communicated, with teachers of all kinds, in traditions and in cultures. We do not start from scratch, or *ab ovo*, literally from the egg, although we do have to start for ourselves at some point in our own understanding, which cannot be just remembering by rote. Without understanding, memory does not go very far and does not last very long, as science does in the understanding. We start with faith and beliefs in words, which we then formulate into more or less firm opinions, prior to any critical reflection on any of them.

Moreover, once we have started, we can also be helped along the way or speeded up by other understandings that we can plug into, artists and scientists we encounter in our reading or our schooling. This is why we go to school, for example, and learn the sciences others have developed before us. We learn with the help of teachers of all sorts who help us formulate words for our own understanding and combine them in different ways to better grasp *what* things are, *how* they function, *why* they are as they are, and so on.

While all the senses serve in this elaboration of experience for understanding in some way, it seems clear that hearing and memory have an especially important role to play. It is through hearing that we normally begin to clue into language and through memory that we retain what we hear at first. It is this association between words and hearing that led the ancients to attach a certain importance to that sense, even though it does not afford us the range that seeing does or the precision that touching does. They saw it as the sense associated with "discipline," that is, as the one leading best to understanding. Without hearing, one misses out on a lot of discipline that a child gets in the early stages of learning, a lack that can only be made up by another kind of sign language that does not need to be heard.

Deafness causes dumbness, and dumbness, which is only an inability to talk, is usually associated with a lack of understanding. Normal intellectual "discipline," therefore, begins through the ears and is extended through reading, where the eyes come into play normally, though not necessarily, since one can also read through one's fingers or sense of touch. Deafness can be overcome through other than audible signs. Words can be visible or touchable, as described by Dr. Oliver Sacks in *Seeing Voices: A Journey into the World of the Deaf.* There are ways of getting around deafness and dumbness, different disciplines, such as the one Annie devised for Helen, but they are different from the ones we are more accustomed to, and they require special care and attention. If they are not available, a deaf individual, often thought of as "dumb," has less of a chance of reaching a high level of understanding or may be perceived as slow even when she has achieved a high degree of intelligence, as Dr. Sacks discovered with many of his deaf patients.

5.3.1.2.3 Nevertheless, with all the refinement the act of understanding can attain, it remains only the first act of intelligence. It is complemented by a second act that begins as a critical reflection on the understanding and terminates not just in a word or a formulation but in a *judgment*, in an affirmation or a negation of what has been conceived as pertaining to reality. Knowing does not end in just having lavish and interesting ideas, even if they are one's own. The fact that one's ideas are one's own does not satisfy our quest for knowledge. One can be just as wrong with one's own ideas as with those of another. What we want is *true* ideas, ideas that correspond to reality, for truth is the object of knowing. Ideas and opinions about what is real may be true or false, and what we want to learn most are those ideas and opinions that are true as opposed to those that are false. That is why intelligence calls for an act of critical reflection on the act of understanding itself or on the word that is its outcome so that we may discern the true from the false in the understanding.

This is where the distinction between the two acts of intelligence comes into play. No matter how hard we may work at forming the *quiddity* of physical things, say, at understanding theory in nuclear physics as in Albert Einstein's theory of relativity or the general theory of employment, interest, and money, as in John Maynard Keynes's theory of political economy, we are always left with the further question of whether such a theory, or quiddity as formulated, is true or not. This further question can only be answered by a more complicated act than the simple apprehension or insight that has yielded such a quiddity to begin with.

The answer to this further question has to be one either of composition—saying *yes*—or of division—saying *no*—or a combination of the two in distinguishing some parts of the theory as verified and some parts as not verified, as we indicated earlier in speaking of critical reflection as the second act of intelligence relative to the first. The scheme from Lonergan we referred to at the beginning of this discussion helps us see this dynamic and dialectical relation between the two acts of intelligence.

The second act of intelligence we are now reflecting on is no less one's own than the first. Indeed, it should be even more so. It presupposes an understanding of one's own, but it goes one step further by asking whether the understanding is true to reality. In one way this second act is simpler than the simple apprehension of understanding since it hinges only on a *yes* or a *no* to be spoken with reference to a particular understanding or hypothesis, which may be more or less complicated. But to the extent that the *yes* or the *no* can only be said with reference to a particular understanding or hypothesis, which can be quite complex, it rarely issues into a simple *yes* or *no*. One may end up saying *yes* to one part of the understanding or hypothesis, *no* to another part, and remain in suspense for the most part, in wonder, ready to pursue the truth further through reformulation and reexamination of what is given in sense experience. Hence the idea of a constant revolutionizing in scientific theories in search of better or more true explanations of phenomena.

In modern philosophy, truth is frequently defined in terms of a correspondence between the mind and reality. But such a formula hardly does justice to what we mean by truth in the actual exercise of critical knowing. We seek the truth through questioning, and we think of it as an adequation of our thinking to reality, an attempt to grasp reality in all its fullness as well as we can critically and intelligently.

Hence the scientist is not satisfied with just formulating hypotheses, no matter how brilliant; he has to verify them or see if they are adequate to the reality into which he is inquiring. Empirical verification is the scientist's own form of critical reflection. So, too, in our own philosophy of human existence we have not been satisfied with just formulating propositions; we have tried to see if they were verified in our own experience of our self. And in this process of critical reflection, we have discovered that our ideas were not as clear as we would have liked them to be and still are not entirely adequate to the reality of self-consciousness in act, thereby requiring further probing into what human existence *really* is in act.

All this does not mean that there is no such thing as absolute truth or that all truth is relative. On the contrary, it implies an absolute truth, or perhaps what Lonergan calls "virtually unconditioned," even though our grasp of it may be relative or limited and we have enough of a grasp of this truth as absolute or virtually unconditioned to want to be critically reflective of our formulations, not to be satisfied with any answer to our questions, and to know that some answers are more true than others in many scientific realms. The fact that we do not have an absolute grasp of the absolute truth does not mean that we do not have any grasp at all and that we cannot tell the difference between true and false in critical reflection. Learning through critical reflection of our understanding of what things are thought to be implies that we know the difference between what we have learned already about the truth or the virtually unconditioned and what we have yet to learn.

It is easier to see how the presence of others can be instrumental in the act of understanding than it is in the act of one's critical reflection. It seems as though one can only be critical for oneself alone. And yet the presence and the help of a good teacher can be instrumental, not just in the act of understanding and formulation but also in the act of critical reflection itself through the recognition that is given to this act and through the effort to foster it in others as well as in oneself by demonstration so that the student, as well as the teacher, develops his or her own judgment and so becomes the equal of the teacher, and a teacher in his own right, a Ph D.

5.3.1.3 The position we have developed concerning the twofold act of intelligence is quite complex and could have any number of alternative views, but two are especially worth noting here by reason of their notoriety:

5.3.1.3.1 Descartes maintained that knowing depended on clear and distinct ideas that are innate in the soul and have nothing to do with the senses, such as the idea of the soul, the idea of God, and even the idea of body as *res extensa*.

5.3.1.3.2 Hume, on the contrary, insisted that knowing is a matter of vivid impressions and that ideas are nothing more than weak and confused impressions. For him, the act of understanding consists in nothing more than pulling together impressions into a bundle and giving the bundle a name. For example, the idea of the self is only the name for a bundle of impressions that I associate with "I" or "you" as found in the vivid impressions that affect the I.

It is from these opposed conceptions of knowing that both Descartes and Hume arrived at their opposed ideas of the selfhood in its substance. We took exception to both of these opposed ideas of the self earlier, partially on the basis of the conception of human knowing that we have just formulated, and partially on the basis of the conception of human willing, the concept of which it remains for us to formulate here as we have just done for the concept of human knowing. How is this second proper activity of the self as distinct from the proper activity of knowing in the self as rational soul to be conceived as distinct from knowing and as also rising from an activity of the composite by surpassing it, as human knowing does?

5.3.2 How the Reflective Self-consciousness in the Human Spirit Rises from Predetermined Emotions to Its Own Self-determination

There is no way of conceiving human willing except as a counterpart to human knowing—that is, as a twofold act of the power of willing emanating from human emotions, that is, as an act of *deliberate choice* and an act of *self-determination*.

5.3.2.1 To make this assertion clear, let us pause to reflect on how human willing relates to human knowing in the rational animal. Human knowing, as expansive as it may be in its enterprise of inquiry, does not exhaust by itself the activity of the self as a whole. In fact, it presupposes a certain activity of willing insofar as the pursuit of knowledge requires a certain determination to inquire on the part of the self, and it gives rise to an elicit form of willing that, as we saw in discussing intelligence and will as two complimentary powers of the human soul as rational, inevitably follows upon knowing. To the extent that our knowing is not immediately given to us, one has to be determined to seek it, and once something has been learned, one inevitably adopts an attitude of attraction or repulsion, one way or another, with regard to what we have come to know; one values it or rejects it or chooses to ignore it—that is, not to take it into consideration as either value or disvalue. One cannot learn anything new about what there is in the world without somehow becoming responsible in a new way with regard to the goodness or the badness of what follows from what one has learned.

Human willing thus is intimately intertwined with human knowing. But as a specifically distinct form of activity, human willing requires a reflection of its own to bring out its own peculiar structure and its proper function for the self as a whole.

Every being, in a sense, can be said to have its own "will", or a certain capacity or inclination to pursue a proper activity of its own in relation to other beings. Even things without consciousness have such a drive that derives simply from their natural forms. According to an old Scholastic adage, every form, natural or intentional, gives rise to some inclination.

Moreover, conscious beings, or beings with some power to know, also have, in addition to their natural form, intentional forms that also give rise to further inclinations. The sight of grain at the end of a barn gives rise to an inclination in the horse and sets him walking in that direction, and the sight of a bright new object in the world of a child sends it reaching for it. Not surprisingly, therefore, the self's higher ability to know will give rise to a higher ability to will and to determine itself. As it develops in self-consciousness it becomes more and more deliberate in its actions. To what extent will such willful self-determination be free? In what sense can it be free if it depends on something external to it such as the passions or the emotions in any animal, rational or not?

We have already had occasion to reflect twice on the kind of structure we shall find in the will, once in reflecting on the constitution of the self and more recently in reflecting on the structure of human knowing. Let us now examine how such a structure comes into play in the exercise of the will.

We take human willing to be the activity of the self that is distinguished from human knowing, though intertwined with it, and that aims at the *good* in things over and above the *truth*, as human knowing does. Though this activity of human willing stems essentially and necessarily from the power of willing in the soul as rational and as spiritual, we say that it starts from the emotions but is not completed as *willing* there. It starts where emotions let go, to make room, so to speak, for willing to come into play as a *rational appetite* amid a plurality of sense appetites or emotions.

Here, too, for the will as for human intelligence, this beginning implies a certain priority of the emotions with regard to the will in both a chronological sense and in the sense of a dependence. Here we also assert a priority in both senses that we shall have to determine more precisely in our discussion of the appearance and intervention of the will in determining human action. Without emotion there would be no human willing, but human willing is not merely emotional; emotions are only a beginning of willing, so to speak, and in many directions at once, depending on the diversity of emotions that present themselves.

The human will may communicate its own form to the emotions from which it begins, but it does not do so without assuming the foregoing movement of the emotions.

Nothing affects me, nothing interests me, unless it passes through my emotions. I have to have a "feeling" for something before I can relate to it explicitly or willfully. And yet just the feeling will not move me as a willful self. The feeling has to be projected intentionally in consciousness as a motive for taking action, as an objective I may want to fulfill. I have to see it as at least one among many objectives I may be interested in pursuing.

Human emotions are specifically different from those of other animals. That is why they can take on such immense proportions as are usually not found in other animals; they are plugged into the infinite range of human knowing and so can become quite disproportionate, even to the material form from which they spring. And yet as human, they cannot be properly understood apart from their relation to intelligence and will, which takes them beyond the range of mere emotions in a living composite of matter and form. The emotions are part of an infinite dynamic that requires careful sorting out and deliberation about how they are to be fulfilled in their diversity as parts of a whole. We call them emotions because we think of them as motions on the level of appetites tied to the material or the animal aspects of the self.

As for the senses, different theories of the emotions have distinguished between them in different ways. Aristotle, for example, distinguished between the *concupiscible appetites*, which had to do with things that are desirable, and the *irascible appetites*, which had to do with things to be feared. It is with reference to these two sets of sense appetites that he came to focus on temperance and courage as two cardinal virtues in his scheme of the cardinal virtues. Here we are concerned only with the realm of emotions as a whole in the etymological sense of *emotion*, or of "movement from," in the sense that the will takes its movement from them.

A similar distinction can be made along lines defined by Sigmund Freud as the *pleasure principle* and the *principle of aggressivity*. Freud, however, made a further distinction between conscious emotions or drives, those that are subconscious (those we are not presently conscious of but can readily be made conscious of) and those that are the unconscious (those buried so deep in our animal soul that they cannot be made conscious except through behavioral quirks, dreams, or psychotherapy). While this can be of some concern for the self and its proper sense of selfhood, especially in cases of mental illness or distress, we are not concerned with digging into this Freudian unconscious here. We can only reflect directly on emotions as they appear on the level of consciousness. It is only from this reference to this level of consciousness that the Freudian theory of the unconscious itself can be properly assessed anyway. The archaeology of the emotions would lead us back not only into the hidden recesses of the individual psyche, a fascinating study in itself, but also into the biological secrets of race and phylogenesis and the social influences of gender and economics. For us here, whatever that archaeology may reveal, it is enough that self-conscious or deliberate willing has emerged as the ground of our reflection and that emotions are a part of that consciousness in some kind of ferment.

Let us note, however, in connection with Maurice Blondel's *Action*, his 1893 study of human action, that it is through the emotions that all the forces of the universe impress themselves on the self and pull it in different directions. It is through the emotions that we are tied to the world and that the world and other selves tie into us. It is from such ties that emotions develop in our animal nature as a plurality of inclinations and aversions that we must contend with in our self-consciousness as we rise to a higher kind of motion of our own as selves from the side of our power of willing.

This implies that the level of emotions in the self is not closed in upon itself and does not account for the identity of the self by itself, as Freudians would have it; the level of emotions in the self is essentially open to the level of willing as deliberate and free; that is, as not determined by any one single emotion. Fascinating as the study of human emotions may be in itself, it cannot exhaust the power of the self to act and to constitute itself in its identity. No matter how strongly one might feel about anything, that alone is never enough to determine the self in its identity and its activity. When we say "rise," we are already implying a certain freedom in human willing from the determinism of emotions.

Here again, as in the exercise of human knowing, human willing is neither instantaneous nor a pure act of self-will; it takes place in a process of sorting out motives and choosing among them; it both relates back to emotions and looks forward to a determination of its own as voluntary. It presupposes a *power* of reflection—to hold the various competing motives at bay, so to speak, or in suspense momentarily—and a *power* of decision—to give itself to one of them and make it its own, the one in which it determines itself.

This twofold act of willing does not imply two distinct powers in the self since both acts aim at the same object, the *good*, at finding it in the first place and embracing it in the second. But it does entail a complexity of acts to complete the exercise of the one power. We call that power the power of willing in the soul on a par with reason and spirit, also spoken of as the rational appetite in contradistinction from the sense appetites.

The first act of willing is that of *choosing*, which relates immediately to the plurality of emotions as it holds them in check in view of *deliberating* rationally before choosing. The motions from the sense level flow from the light of sensation, but the power of reflective understanding is capable of holding this spontaneity in check so that each of the emotions, deprived of its immediate force, is given the form of an ideal or an intention to be examined as a candidate, among others, for realization at a given moment in a self's life. The light of understanding further clarifies each of these motives and their respective goods, comparing and contrasting them with one another, thus opening the way for deliberation, where intelligence comes into play as projecting into the future in terms of objectives to be aimed at.

Deliberation presupposes a plurality of motions and motives that appear in consciousness; the plurality of motions becomes, as it were, a plurality of possibilities or options for the self. If there were no such plurality in the emotions, there would be no place for deliberation and, inasmuch as the will can only determine itself by embracing one of the emotions and making it its own, there would be no room for freedom since the will would have to go with the one motion or motive that presented itself and that would absorb all possibilities for the self, as in the case of a fixed idea or an addiction, leaving the self without any originality of its own in self-determination.

With a plurality of motions and motives, however, the will is in a position not only to choose among them, thus conferring its power upon one of them so that it emerges triumphant from the pause of deliberation in consciousness, but also to create an order of its own in the tumult of the emotions, for in choosing one the will chooses not just one particular object but a whole order of priorities among the emotions. Any real choice of one motion among the plurality of emotions in one's consciousness requires a new discipline to be introduced into the system of emotions as a whole present in the self. A lack of discipline, on the other hand, can be the sign of an absence or a weakness in choosing.

The consciousness of free choice thus includes both the consciousness of other possibilities for taking action besides the one chosen and the consciousness that the one chosen will have to be inserted into a whole order of emotions and into the world as a whole through subjective effort and objective labor.

The second act of willing we shall call *self-determination*, the act of willing in which the self asserts itself in the identity it has chosen for itself. Mere deliberation and choice are not yet the complete act of the self's determination. After all, the choices or the options are still presented to it exteriorly and so determine it from the outside. Even if I can choose between A or B, I do not have a choice about having to choose between them, nor do I have a choice that it is either this A or this B that I have to choose. Even when I choose in such circumstances, my emotions are still determined by something outside of myself, and I am not yet fully self-determining.

To be fully self-determined, I must pass through this choice in a process of going out of myself, as it were—going into one option or another before me—in order to actualize myself. The reason for the choice I make as a self ultimately has to be my own self-determination. The more I approach true or complete self-determination, the more I determine even the options from which I have to choose, the more I find myself undivided within myself or in my character, habituated to go one way as a self and no longer tormented by emotions that constantly pull me in ways I have not chosen to actualize for myself.

5.3.2.2 To focus our reflection on human will further, let us use a three-level scheme similar to the one we borrowed in connection with the activity of knowing (cf. 5.3.2.1). In this scheme, as in the one used earlier, all three levels will be seen in relation to one another as part of one and the same exercise of human willing.

We say that willing begins in emotions *given* in one's consciousness at any given time in our experience, whether by nature, by the presence of others through nurturing or conversation, or even by our own past choices. This is the level of the human emotions or of the sense appetites. Each emotion, as a particular motive for action, has its own orientation toward a determinate future. As given, it is determined toward that one thing. But each one is also only one of many such determinations within one and the same consciousness, giving rise to the necessity of a higher motion in the self, that of the will itself or of the rational appetite with its twofold act and twofold level of motion, that of deliberation, and that of self-determination, as in choosing to marry and when to marry.

The plurality of emotions on the first level gives rise to the necessity of deliberation in the rational consciousness as a presupposition for free choice and self-determination of a self that finds itself in the presence of other selves as having to choose. Deliberation and choice, which presupposes a plurality of emotions given in consciousness, are thus a second level of motion coming from the will as rational appetite in a social self-consciousness. But the exercise of this first motion of the will proper, on the second level, as distinct from the level of the emotions, gives rise to a further necessity of actual self-determination, which is a third level of motion that presupposes the second level and complements it.

Thus, the second level, which is that of deliberation and choice of emotion, besides presupposing and complementing the initial level of the emotions, is itself presupposed and complemented by the further level of self-determination and decision. Hence we have the following scheme:

TABLE 5.2: INTELLIGENCE

I.	Feelings / Emotions	Motives	Objectives
II.	Motion of Deliberation	Means	Choices
III.	Motion of Self-Determination	Decision	Commitment

All three levels together constitute the exercise of willing as a whole. The twofold motion of the will rises from a plurality of emotions in one's consciousness. The plurality of emotions in one and the same consciousness gives rise to the necessity of deliberation and choice, which is the first level of motion for the will, though it is still directly related to particular emotions. The second level of motion for the will comes out of this first level of motion for the will, or this level mediating between the emotions and the proper motion of the will, on a level of self-determination, by deciding which of the emotions will be honored by the self and which will be cut off from the self in the formation of its character.

Let now analyze more distinctly how we experience each one of these three levels of motion in willing in relation to one another in one's own self-consciousness.

5.3.2.2.1 Like the senses, emotions such as love and hate, concupiscible and irascible, or pleasure principles and principles of aggressivity have to do with particulars—this particular good to be sought or acquiesced in, or that particular evil to be avoided or loathed. Each emotion, no matter how many there are, is determined in relation to its own particular good (or its own particular evil, since evil is the privation of some good). Thus, a plurality of emotions will always give rise to a plurality of motives or representations of corresponding goods to be aimed at in the consciousness of the self, each of which will stand for a particular emotion, or motive for a particular action, in the moment of deliberation. The intensity of the motive will depend on the intensity of the emotion to which it corresponds in the psyche.

Depth psychology has to do with the causes of such various emotions in an individual's psyche. It can show the origins of the different kinds of determinisms and fixation that have been set in motion in all of us who are disturbed in our consciousness by this variety of more or less intense emotions or motivations. It is not easy to trace the causes of the various emotions in a given psyche or to measure precisely their intensity in comparison to one another. Where they come from in the depths or in the past of the self, or how they acquired their relative intensity, may never be completely understood even in clinical analysis, but such a complete understanding is not necessary for a sufficiently rational deliberation in choosing an orientation for our lives. It is enough that a plurality of emotions have emerged in our consciousness and have given rise to a plurality of motives for action for us to ponder.

It is important, however, that there be not just one motive alone or that one not be so overpowering that the force of the others is simply lost or obliterated because one motive alone in one's consciousness does not lend itself to deliberation. It can only give rise to a fixation, a compulsion, or an addiction, which reduces the more universal motion of the will to a particular determination or determinism, that of the overpowering motive, since, as we shall see more clearly, the will cannot or is not free to determine itself otherwise than in that particular motion.

This is why we tend to think of someone with a fixed idea as somewhat less than sane and free and as probably requiring therapy while that same individual may think of himself as quite sane, rational, and free. The illusion of sanity and freedom, if that is what it is, is due to an absence or a suppression of any alternative motion or motive within the psyche. This is why also, when we have been carried away by some overpowering emotion, we feel we have not been ourselves. It is the part of the healthy psyche to give rise to a plurality of emotions to be held in check when the power or the act of deliberation comes into play.

It should be noted, however, that while this plurality of emotions is a necessary condition for the proper exercise of deliberation and choice, it is not sufficient by itself. In themselves, each one of those motions is determined and the whole set of them is also determined according to the relative weight or intensity of each one within the one psyche as a whole. Without the proper act of deliberation and free choice, the outcome or the future for the self would be strictly predetermined according to the relative force of the emotions, as behaviorism rightly claims, without seeing how deliberation breaks out of this predetermination. Deliberation brings an end to this predetermination on the level of emotions, while free choice opens the way to a new kind of determination that is from the self as a whole and not merely from the emotions.

Before we turn to reflect on that higher motion of deliberation and choice, let us note finally that our emotions are somehow the repercussion of the whole world within our consciousness. They are the way in which the world affects us or in which we are affected interiorly by different things and by other selves. In many ways we have no choice about how we are affected, just as we have no choice about our feelings as they are given to us immediately. We can only intervene and transform our affections and the world that affects us through deliberation and free choice and in that way become responsible, not for what is given to us in our rational appetite, but for what we make of it. The more we learn about ourselves and about the world, the more we may realize how we are determined by what is given to us, but the more also we can appreciate in what precisely our freedom consists.

5.3.2.2.2 The moment of deliberation appears as a break or an interruption in the predetermined flow of the emotions. It presupposes a certain amount of understanding and reflection on what is happening in that flow and a certain power to hold it in check, at least for a time, until the flow is given the direction of one's choice. Intelligence, therefore, provides a new level of force, so to speak, which enables us to hold the forces of emotion in check for a time and make way for what we are calling the *motion of deliberation*, a new and higher motion with respect to the emotions that will issue in a new and higher result for which the self will then be responsible even though it will express itself in some emotion or other, or in a particular set of emotions.

As an interruption in the flow of emotions, deliberation entails a certain kind of hesitation that could lead to a complete paralysis of motion. But that would be a perversion of the power of deliberation, which is by its very nature oriented to action of one kind or another. Paralysis of the will in the moment of deliberation, like fixation of the will, could be understood as a way of reducing the will to one particular emotion, such as anxiety or stress.

The true power of deliberation is a kind of universal force that can relate to any particular force and relate all particular forces to one another. This is why it cannot be reduced to anyone of them and why it can hold them all in check, at least for a moment.

This is why we also speak of this motion as *deliberation*. The hesitation it provokes in the flow of emotions serves not to stop it outright but, rather, to shift it to the higher level of motion, that of one's will itself, and it does this by first stopping the automatic flow and then giving it a new impulse of its own, which will have to overcome the momentum and resistance of what would otherwise be an automatic flow.

But in what does this new motion of deliberation consist? What does it mean to deliberate? And what do we deliberate about? In relation to our emotions, as we have just seen, it consists in a kind of sorting and ordering of what is given. We *clarify* our motives by comparing them with one another, by contrasting them. We project possibilities, which each one of them represents, for our future identity or our future options.

In consideration of this future identity of oneself, we also begin to *evaluate* them as means for our own self-determination. This evaluation is carried on not just through a comparing of motives among themselves but also in the light of an ideal or an idea of the good one wants for oneself; that is, in the light of what we value for self-determination. What I have to figure out, so to speak, is which of the tendencies that incline me one way or another here and now will better relate to the good that I want for myself and other selves in mutual recognition and how all the other tendencies will relate to that one, if it is actualized.

It is thus that options begin to define themselves for the self. Good deliberation does not just sum up possibilities from a given situation. It can also be quite resourceful and creative in coming up with new possibilities through recombinations, for example, of what is given through new insights into historical reality and through its own power of overcoming. Every choice always entails taking up a possibility that is given to the self, whether from the outside or from the inside, but it can also be a possibility that has been reshaped by a creative and inventive intelligence. Creating alternative options for oneself instead of just accepting them passively from the outside is a function of deliberation and represents a high degree of freedom. Ready-made choices may be better than no choice at all, but they may represent only poor expressions of one's original selfhood.

Besides being creative, deliberation can also bring with it a realization that choice is bound to be difficult and stressful. There are usually any number of tendencies in contention for being actualized in any moment of deliberation, many good alternatives to choose from, not all of which are compatible with one another. Choosing one means giving up the others. Hence the need to struggle against emotions that would move us in directions other than the ones we are choosing and the fear of giving up a good we might already have. On the other hand, there may be many ominous alternatives looming before us, not all of which can be avoided. Choosing which one to avoid means accepting the others for the moment.

Hence the need to struggle against the emotions of avoidance and the fear of giving up too much of what one has. Any choice I make inevitably has to favor one inclination or one set of inclinations over others and will inevitably encounter resistance from the inclinations that have not been favored and from the world outside that gives rise to these inclinations in me because of the plurality of motions that was the very condition for the possibility of deliberation and of choice to begin with. Every choice requires labor to be implemented in order to transform both the flow of emotions within the self and the world without, where the activity takes place.

But it is this labor or struggle, which go with choice, that may afford us our clearest consciousness of the act of choosing, which in turn brings deliberation to a close. This act consists in the election of what had been only a possibility before and what now requires a whole new order, a subordination of all other possibilities that had also been present with the one chosen. The choice defines a value for me and for a community, and it reorders all other values in relation to the one chosen in a sort of transvaluation. Nothing in the antecedent conditions or motions was sufficient to determine this choice of value for me or for my community precisely because choice is a new initiative inasmuch as all the previous determinisms were brought to a halt through deliberation so that the motion that emerges from choice is now a new motion charged with the power of the will as well as with its own predetermined energy. It is true that this new motion of the will inserts itself into a motion that preceded it, but the motion that results from this insertion of the will is of a different kind than the one that came before; it is a transformation of what was merely given; it is an expression of the self's own determination.

The precise act of choice is not a particular action as such but the interior core of any action where I am conscious of being the origin of my own action. This consciousness also includes a consciousness that I am free, that I could be doing otherwise, that this action is not all that I could do, not the only thing I was potentially able to do.

I have an immediate experience only of what I actually do, of what I actually choose, and not of possible "choices" I might have made but that I do not make. When I begin to think of those other possibilities, I may get lost in abstractions or be deluded about them, but I do have an immediate experience of my action as rising above the emotions as merely given to me. It is the consciousness of this transcendence, which is positive, that brings with it the consciousness of other possibilities, or of what has been called the negative aspect of our freedom as not determined to anything in particular, even the particular thing we are actually doing, the consciousness that we could be doing *not* what we are actually doing. The consciousness of our freedom does not begin in abstract possibilities but in the concrete possibility that we actualize by our choice, a possibility that can still be hemmed in by all sorts of determinisms.

Our reflection on the motion of deliberation and choice as first act of the will may leave us with the impression that it necessarily requires a long drawn-out and perhaps stifling process, as it can sometimes be, but that does not have to be the case. Though it can seem to run counter to nature at times, it can also be quite spontaneous and instantaneous. Prolonged deliberation is not essential to freedom in the sense that we must stop before each action. Such deliberation can in fact impede and diminish freedom of action by blocking all the spontaneity of the will itself, as well as of the motions on which the will must exercise itself.

For this reason, in discussing the freedom of choice, it is better not to insist on any particular action as such but, rather, on the experience of activity as a whole, which includes a multiplicity of actions, and on the consciousness that emerges more and more clearly that the self is indeed the cause of what it does and must accept responsibility for it. This consciousness grows from one time to the next, as we become more and more aware of the constraints on our freedom as well as of the freedom itself. What I know now about my freedom I did not know ten years ago, and what I knew then I did not know ten years earlier. This experience also leads me to think that I may not know as much about my freedom now as I will know in the future, nor yet be as free now as I may someday be, especially if I am still relatively young.

5.3.2.2.3 The act of deliberation and of choice of one among several possibilities is only the first act of the will carried on in the light of a second act that complements it, the act or the motion of self-determination. To focus properly on this second act, we have only to reflect on how none of the particular motions or motives that have appeared in consciousness properly determines the self's future orientation, even though one of them will be the way in which the self will determine itself. The only thing that can ultimately determine the self's orientation is the self's own *decision*.

Such an act of *decision* consists not only in cutting off, so to speak, the spontaneous or automatic flow of the emotions within the self but also in cutting off the energy that might have gone to some of the possibilities represented in deliberation and to redirecting that energy to those that have been chosen. Every self-determination is a negation or a self-abnegation, an asceticism, in view of something positively willed by and for the self and its community. That is what self-determination through decision means. This is also how one's character is shaped, for better or for worse.

As the self emerges from the conditions of its own freedom to arrive at its own self-determination, however, it does not enter into a realm of pure arbitrariness where anything goes, as Sartre seems to suggest in his existentialism. The self enters into the realm of its own spiritual identity where it also recognizes the presence of other selves similar to itself. The presence of these other selves has already made itself known on the level of understanding and deliberation where they had something to do with the formulation of possibilities for the self, but it is on this level of self-determination that this presence is seen most crucially in terms of mutual recognition. It is in my own self-determination that I encounter the other most profoundly on the level of selfhood, as the other likewise exercises his or her own self-determination. The dialectic of mutual recognition, which is constitutive of human selfhood, implies that self-determination inevitably entails mutual determination among selves.

This is why every self-determination is not only a *decision* but also a *commitment*, a going along with another, a recognition of a higher order of selves and an insertion of oneself into that communal order. True self-determination is not just a passing whim; it is an affirmation of oneself in the presence of others and a promise to others and oneself to abide by that affirmation. When one *commits* oneself to a course of action, one sets oneself going in the company of others—that is, in a communion with other selves.

This higher order of self-determination is not one that is ready-made or given by nature. It is one that is constituted by selves as such and can properly be called a human or *historical order* insofar as this can be distinguished from any purely natural order. As an order of mutual recognition, it presupposes a certain minimal equality of selves, though it does not guarantee it. Domination and enslavement are a possibility in this order, as actual history can well attest, but they are not according to the proper order of mutual recognition, nor are they part of what any human being is called to; they are possible but not justifiable, whether they seem benevolent or not. Neither is seduction, which is only an enticement of one unsuspecting self by another. Mutual recognition means letting the other be self-determining in the very act of determining oneself.

This equality in self-determination, however, is not something that can be immediately given. Like freedom itself, it has to be achieved in a dialectical struggle of confrontation for recognition, as exemplified in the struggle between Helen Keller and Annie Sullivan, a struggle that did not end with Helen's breakthrough but only began on that day, a struggle that became part of the historical struggle in which all selves must labor and struggle for self-determination and mutual recognition.

The motion of self-determination is, thus, at once an individual act in which I choose one of many possibilities for myself and make it a value for me and a social act in which I learn to value others as well as myself. Whatever I choose as value for me I always choose in the light of what I want myself to be ultimately as my own final end, but in doing so I am also choosing in the light of a transcendent historical order of spiritual selves, which raises the community of selves beyond the order of mere nature and determinism and beyond the order of mere emotions into an order of respect and love and forgiveness, where freedom and necessity are no longer opposites of one another but actually coincide.

If this motion of self-determination and commitment is difficult for us to grasp and can easily be overlooked in an examination of human action, it is because it is only a moment in the whole, albeit the essentially human moment, which no sooner than it has emerged from the play of forces or of emotions to assert itself in its originality must immediately plunge back into this interplay of forces to actualize itself by transforming what has been given to it and forgiving all seeming deviations from the communal order. There is no other freedom for the human self than this fragile and fleeting moment, but we must not think of it as anything less than the supreme triumph of human existence. The same moment of freedom is also the moment of a community, which must also express itself in a social structure, as we shall see more clearly when we come to speak of culture and of ethical life.

5.3.2.3 Different kinds of theoretical determinism in communal interaction can be seen as denying the position we have taken concerning human freedom. Let us briefly mention three kinds.

5.3.2.3.1 *Physical determinism* affirms an absolute determinism of human action according the laws of nature. This can take the form of pure physicalism, behaviorism, or Freudianism, and it flatly contradicts our assertion about freedom in human willing. It simply ignores the kind of experience and reflection we have relied on, as it naively affirms an absolute determinism of nature, allowing no room for any exercise of deliberation or free choice in self-determination.

We do not deny the reality of physical determinism. Human action is determined in many ways by nature and by other factors in human experience. We saw this in speaking of the flow of emotions. But that is not the only determination in human action. There is also self-determination through choice from among a plurality of determinisms, so to speak. In fact, the very consciousness of determinism itself presupposes a consciousness of freedom. If we were not free, there would be no experience of determinism as such, as we see in animals that are nonrational or even in individual selves who are fixated on one motivation without any other to contrast with it.

5.3.2.3.2 *Psychological determinism* sees the power of the will as rising above the determinism of nature but as itself determined by what is perceived as the greater good. This resembles physical determinism in that the good is reduced to something quantifiable, and deliberation is reduced to weighing possibilities or comparing them only among themselves without reference to the ulterior dimension of choice or self-determination, which can make of any possibility the supreme value for me simply by willing it to be so.

We do not deny that the will is an appetite and that deliberation entails an element of calculation. But we see the rational appetite as going much farther than a mere calculus of possibilities. Psychological determinism does not pay sufficient attention to the fact that free choice is ultimately a commitment of self in an order of self-determination as well as the choice of one particular good over another.

If I appear to choose the greater good necessarily, it is because I have chosen this particular good, rightly or wrongly, as more closely related to the final end that I am also choosing for myself. The so-called greater good for any particular act is greater only because of its relation to the final end that I am choosing in the same act. Thus, it is the "greater good" for me, the supreme value for me, as we have said, only because I make it greater by choosing it.

Psychological determinism mistakenly reverses the order of the motion of deliberation and choice. It is not any particular good that determines me but I who determine that this particular good that I choose will be the good for me. The determinism that psychological determinism affirms does not precede free choice but only follows it.

5.3.2.3.3 *Economic or social determinism* may be reducible to physical determinism but differs from it in that the action of human beings is presupposed. This is determinism in the historical order as such, which we distinguished from the merely natural order in speaking of the phenomenon of human life at the beginning of our reflection, and it can take the form of either capitalism or communism. It asserts that human action is determined by economic interests and that it is ruled strictly by economic factors. It reduces the internal aspect of self-determination and communion to its external aspect of choices and social structure, and it denies the power of commitment with respect and love or forgiveness among selves either out of cynicism (capitalism?) or out of desperation (communism?) in a master/slave dialectic bereft of respect and love or forgiveness.

While the influence of others on the self can be overpowering at times, it does not always have to be so, nor is it always so. The experience of self-determination we have referred to is an experience that overcomes such overpowering in actual respect and love or forgiveness among selves, which is a will for the good of the other as well as one's own in what we call communities or cultures.

Though social structures are a necessary condition for any communion among selves in history, they do not determine the life of a community unless the community chooses them to do so by legislation of some sort or by submission to some tyrannical force. When social structures become oppressive, it is usually because someone or some group is oppressing the community, but this is no longer just a theoretical denial of human freedom; it is a practical one as well. When a theory is devised to justify such practical oppression, it is called *ideology*, not a *culture*, which flows from a communal exercise of intelligence and free will in our historical consciousness.

It remains for us in this theory of selfhood to examine how all human learning and human desires, how human intelligence and how mutual regard for one another in free will pertaining to the second perfection in human existence, take shape in our historical self-consciousnesses as cultures for the betterment of our human spirit as soul of our body.

5.3.3 Culture as a Kind of Spiritual Framework in a Synthetic View of Human Existence in This World in Keeping with a Diversity of Second Perfections for Historical Self-consciousnesses

What results from all the activity of human intelligence and free will in the universe is *culture*, or more precisely a *diversity of cultures*, in what we have been referring to as the order of *history*, distinct from the order of *nature* in human existence. Culture is an essential component of human existence, along with nature, in the first- and second-person ontology of the human race we have been examining in this, the theoretical part of our study of selfhood. Before we move on to the practical part of our study, it is important for us to examine how the concept of culture comes to the fore as a principle for the study of selfhood put into practice, along with nature as first perfection for human beings in history.

We began our study by characterizing the human being as a self communing with other selves in the world. After trying to determine more precisely *what* the human self is and how it is constituted, we turned to its activity to see how the self actualizes and perfects itself through intelligence and willing and in what precisely these activities of intelligence and willing consist. In the process of reflecting on both of these spiritual activities, we were brought once again to the intersubjectivity of human action that we had seen in reflecting on mutual recognition as constitutive of self-consciousness. We encounter others in the very use of language to formulate our understanding of things and one another as well as our own selves and in the determination that makes us selves in the presence of other selves. Finally, we have seen how, through this encounter of selves, we constitute history as a properly human realm distinct from the realm of mere nature.

5.3.3.1 The question now before us is how best to characterize this realm of human activity as a whole and how to understand it in its various dimensions and polarities. Is there a term to sum it up as a whole? If so, what essential characteristics will it have to include in order to express the various dimensions of human activity in their dialectical relationships? Will it do justice to the fullness of the "communion of selves in the world", which we have been using as our basic frame of reference from the beginning?

To get to the full complexity of the dialectic leading up to historical cultures, we must begin from our experience of human activity as a whole, including not just that of intelligence and willing but also that of other powers or faculties with the effort and the labor that goes with all of them. It is from this complex fact that our theoretical reflection began; it is with it that it must end.

This is not an attempt to go back to some original primitive fact when rational self-consciousness first emerged from nature, however that may be imagined or represented in some evolutionary theory. It is rather a return to the abiding primordial fact of a reflective self-consciousness that emerges from its preexisting conditions in nature as a whole and as individualized and specified for this self-consciousness, yours and mine as well as for that of any rational animal we know. Even if we have risen above the mere fact of nature, with all its ramifications in our life and in our consciousness, thanks to the culture or cultures into which we have been initiated, we are still and always dependent and conditioned in this life on the natural ground from which we emerge, as any medical doctor, psychologist, neurologist, or epistemologist will tell us.

This is the fact for any reflective self-consciousness taken, not only as an individual in isolation from any other but as communal, in communion with other selves specifically as rational, through activities of intelligence and free will. This aspect of the primordial fact of human existence is significant for bringing out the cultural aspect of human existence as we come to know it. Just as it is through culture or cultures that we come to know and will human existence in its second perfection, so also communion among selves takes place in what we think of as *culture* or *cultures*, as the actual bond or bonds among selves within a horizon or horizons we refer to as the world or the worlds of different cultures. As such a bond, human activity is not abstract or external to selves. It is not superimposed on the self from a purely external activity. It is their concrete action as an intelligent and intelligible interaction among and within them, expressed through determinations of the selves themselves. The world here is taken concretely as the place in which selves meet, interact, and transform what is given to them.

5.3.3.2 The development of culture or cultures is found only where there are human beings already in communion with one another. Selves go from a state of being merely given by nature to a new state we think of as specifically *historical* through transformation initiated by the selves. This transformation is at once a self-transformation and a transformation of the world through the initiative of the selves. As human, this development can be called *humanization*, the humanization of nature or of the world as well as of human beings themselves by human beings themselves in communion with one another.

This transformation is sometimes characterized as a "second nature" for newcomers into a culture, as if humanization were a second form of naturalization. We even speak of the initiation or the induction of new citizens in a nation as "naturalization." My parents were naturalized as Americans in a ceremony at city hall when I was growing up, whereas I was presumably naturalized by my birth having taken place in the United States.

This idea of naturalization makes some sense in that our belonging to a nation is given as a matter of fact as part of one's communion with other selves in a nation. But it does not make sense in the proper sense of enculturation that we grow into, in communion with other selves, as we mature in our intelligence and free will as human beings. *Enculturation* is a spiritual phenomenon due to an exercise of intelligence and free will, that of my parents, my siblings, my neighbors, as well as my own. I am an American not merely by birth but by a communal exercise of intelligence and free choice with other Americans.Culture comes as a result of the self's own initiative and intervention in the processes of nature. To think of it only as a second nature is to reduce it from a first- and second-person ontology to a third-person ontology. It is to think of the world only as given by nature, not as transformed historically by the original and communal exercise of intelligence and free will in communities.

To speak of culture as a second nature for human beings allows us to speak of humanization as a naturalization as well. But this naturalization should not be understood as a return to what we now have to call our *first nature*, or nature as originally given, before the beginning of history as it were. There is no longer any such original nature to return to, as Marx pointed out against Ludwig Feuerbach; there is only a *second nature*, a cultivated nature at the stage of history in which we find ourselves, in the communities we have taken to as rational agents.

To speak of culture, however, is not to restrict ourselves to any particular culture or to what is often referred to as culture in an exclusive or alienated fashion, as if there was only one kind of culture that counted in history, such as modern European or postmodern. We speak of culture here in its broadest sense, primitive as well as sophisticated, coarse as well as refined: whatever has come as a result of human initiative at different times in history and in different parts of the world. Nor are we concerned with comparing or evaluating cultural differences here; in using a term that is often used in an exclusive and prejudicial fashion, we are trying to restore it only to its original universal and true meaning and not to only one particular form or another of human culture, abusive of all others. This is not a putdown of any culture, however advanced or regressed.

5.3.3.3 Culture is thus a pivotal notion that takes us from one order of the world to another, from the natural order to a more historical and spiritual order, but without detaching us from the natural order out of which we still have to make our way. As a pivotal order it entails two poles in dialectical tension with one another, one on the subjective side of consciousness and the other on the objective side of the world. What follows here in this exposition of the concept of consciousness for a historical consciousness of any kind is an articulation of what consciousness means as a whole, with two distinct poles, one subjective and the other objective. The transformation we have spoken of can be viewed from these two poles interwoven with one another.

On the side of the *subjective pole* is the self, any self, in its ontological constitution so to speak—that is, insofar as a self is a subject or the initiator in the cultural activity proper to a culture. From this side of the polarity, the transformation takes place according to the ontological structure of the self and includes three moments in the consciousness of those sharing in the culture: a moment of intelligence, a moment of internal disposition, and a moment of tastes or of preferences in the orientation of each one's desires for the good.

The moment of *intelligence* comes as a result of learning what is good for oneself as the member of a community and how to go about attaining that good in one's self and in other members of the community. This includes not just an ever-growing accumulation of information but also language itself and the exercise of understanding that goes with it, along with a habit of good and critical judgment in the exercise of intelligence. Every culture includes a fund of information and intelligent ways of dealing with it that come as a result of the culture's development.

The moment of *internal disposition* comes as a result of the exercise of willing and free choice in regulating our emotions and sense appetites for the natural goods of life in a community of rational beings. This includes habits of all kinds resulting from choices repeated often enough to give a certain stable determination to the emotions and the natural inclinations that come with a vigorous lifestyle. Such cultural dispositions, or virtues, do not take shape or are not fixed externally or by nature alone. They come by free choice in the rational appetite aiming at something perceived as a good for the community as a whole as well as for each member. From this we can assume a variance of virtuous dispositions going from one culture to another in keeping with a variance of intelligence and free choice of communities that vary in all sorts of ways.

The moment of *tastes and of preferences* in sense appetites for the good comes as a result of both knowing and willing in their repercussions on the corporeal aspect of the self. *De gustibus non est disputandum* (there is no point in arguing about tastes), but there is a point to saying that tastes are not just given by nature; they are formed and therefore subject to judgment and choice in different cultures. Education can be as much a formation of tastes regulated by reason as it is a formation of intelligence and character in the exercise of proper activities in communities.

On the side of the *objective pole* in the communal activity or of interaction among selves in a communal life, there are also three moments to be distinguished, each corresponding to the three moments on the subjective side. This objective pole is not related to the subjective as one self might be related to another self in the interaction between them; it is related as an external dimension is related to its internal dimension as we saw in considering the phenomenon of life in the Introduction to this inquiry into the primordial fact of human existence. This internal dimension is social as well as individual, as we also saw earlier, just as the external dimension is individual as well as social. Selves are related to one another in both dimensions, internal and external, subjective and objective.

This objective pole in any culture may take on a momentum or a determinism of its own, which becomes the object of many particular social sciences. Its pertinence to selfhood, nevertheless, has to be judged in the light of the subjective or the spiritual pole of culture since, as an exteriorization of the spirit of a community, it is relative to that internal and spiritual pole.

In this objective pole of culture there are also three moments to be distinguished, as implied in the three moments in the subjective pole. We specify these three moments of the objective pole in human existence as they correspond with the three moments we distinguished in the subjective pole.

Corresponding to the moment of intelligence on the subjective side of consciousness, we distinguish a moment of *works* conceived and produced by rational intelligence and ingenuity, beginning with language as a means of communicating among selves and representing a wide range of things for humans to produce for the satisfaction of their needs and desires and for expressing their originality as rational animals, including works of art of every kind, whether industrial, agricultural, literary, fine, or other, all of which are cultural artifacts of some kind.

Second, corresponding to the moment of internal dispositions on the subjective side of consciousness are *social structures* created by humans as they labor and interact at various levels of need and desire. This includes many levels of association as well as the political, which is usually understood as the overarching social structure that has taken various forms historically.

Note that structures are not the only thing that is social in a culture; they are only the objective pole of sociality, which also has a subjective pole—what we refer to as the communion of selves—and which take the form of all sorts of dispositions in the individual members of a community. A social structure properly understood is the externalization of a communion and is always relative to such a communion.

Third, corresponding to the moment of tastes and preferences on the subjective side of historical consciousness, there is a moment of *skills and expediency* acquired in the repeated production of works and social structures. The development of a culture entails not just an accumulation of knowledge but also an accumulation of skills in the application of knowledge to the satisfaction of needs and desires; these are embodied both in individual selves and in instruments that are an extension of the selves. A technology is a totality of such skills that can have a momentum of its own and may even overpower the community of selves that created it. Every culture has such a technology and runs the risk of losing itself as a community of self-conscious selves in it.

All of these moments on both the subjective side and the objective or worldly side of consciousness in a community have to be understood as weaving into one another in the historical consciousness of a community existing in the world among other communities. It is not our purpose in this philosophy of human existence as a whole to unravel any of these moments, as is done in particular sciences that seize upon one aspect or one factor in the human experience in abstraction from other aspects or other factors. Our purpose is more to understand the entire movement as a whole in its interweaving of moments on both sides of the historical consciousness that pulls them all together.

The movement or the development we refer to is not just a linear natural process; it presupposes the originality of human initiative as it intervenes in this natural process and communicates to it its own orientation; it is not merely evolutionary but revolutionary as well. We speak of it as historical insofar as it starts from within the self-determination of selves as we have spoken of it, originating from intelligence and free will. We speak of it as an interplay insofar as this self-determination is at the same time a mutual determination of many selves who are both free and interdependent.

The movement, as we understand it from reflection in our self-consciousness, originates interiorly in a moment of intelligence and free will that exteriorizes itself as a moment of intelligence at work in a suitable reality, shaped in accordance with tastes and preferences as shaped by our communion with other selves in a community. Reflection reveals to us the internal origin of the activity of selves, but we discover that origin only in its external expression; we discover ourselves and the nature of our activity and initiative only upon reflection or turning back from that external expression so that we always presuppose an exteriorization of ourselves or the community of selves in which we find ourselves.

This exteriorization, however, is never just a pure going out of oneself that ends there in the external side of our experience. There is always within it a movement of reintegration. Consciousness of exteriorization touches off and is itself part of a movement of return into self; reflection is not just a discovery but also a movement of recovering oneself in and through its exteriorization, a reintegration of the external into oneself. For the human self there is no pure integrity or integration; there is only constant process of reintegration to assure self-identity. Ultimate freedom, beyond mere freedom of choice, can only be an act of determining oneself in one's own identity, but such an act is possible for us only through choice and confrontation with other selves.

5.3.3.4 To focus our critical reflection on this interweaving of activity in historical consciousness, let us turn once again to a scheme that we have already used in connection with the activities of intelligence and free will and that will sum up now for us the various moments we have distinguished in both the internal and the external sides of historical and cultural consciousness, which we must now pull together in their relation to one another. Because we are only summing up a lot of what we have already seen in our reflection, however, we shall reverse the order of the levels that we saw in the earlier schemes. Earlier we were going from the bottom up into the internal aspect of intelligence and will, so to speak. Now we shall be going from the top down, putting the self as spirit at the top and at the center of the scheme:

TABLE 5.3: DYNAMISMS OF THE SELF

SUBJECTIVE POLE	POWER	SELF (as Spirit)	ACTIVITY	OBJECTIVE POLE
Information ←	Intellect ←	**SOUL**	→ Intelligence	→ Works
Dispositions ←	Will ←	**SOUL**	→ Decision	→ Institutions
Tastes ←	Senses and Emotions ←	**BODY**	→ Sensation and Motivation	→ Techniques

Imagine lines shooting out horizontally from the center column on both sides and curling back toward the center at each level, and then lines shooting down vertically from the top of each column and curling back toward the top, to represent the dynamic interweaving of diverse activities all at play in the shaping of diverse cultures.

Note, first of all, that this is a scheme for human culture as a whole. It includes both its subjective and its objective poles and centers them on the self. It also includes the intermediate factors of *activity*, on the one side, which not only gives rise to the objective pole but also ties it back to the self, and of *powers*, on the other side, which, as distinct from one another, tie the different moments of the subjective pole of culture into the identity of the self.

The curved arrows symbolize the movement of exteriorization and of reintegration. They go from the center out and curve back and move from the top down and curve back. They can be thought of as representing a kind of pulsating movement within the selves of a culture as a whole.

Perhaps the most serious deficiency of the scheme is that it is too static and too individualistic to represent the true historical movement of a community of selves of which a culture is only an expression. To correct for this deficiency, we must keep in mind the movement of mutual recognition that is constitutive of selfhood as such. The self at the center of the scheme is not just an individual but a community of selves sharing a spirit.

Moreover, it is clear that there are not just one but many and diverse cultures or communities of selves sharing in their different spirits in the world, and there has been a succession of such cultural communities in history. In thinking of such a diversity and succession, one tends to think of one's own culture and of the latest as paradigmatic and hence as privileged in any judgment about cultures, as if one's own or the latest were ipso facto the best or the highest. This should not, however, obscure the privilege or the dignity of other cultures in their own historical actualization.

History should not be understood as centering on only one line of succession among cultures or as culminating in only one culture, as it tends to be understood by Hegel and most Europeans, or so-called Westerners, where a spirit of domination over other cultures tends to color every judgment. Rather, history should be understood as a plurality of cultures, each struggling for recognition among the plurality of cultures and each with its place of privilege in world history. It is this that our proposition wishes to emphasize in speaking of any culture as a whole.

The truth of such a proposition is by no means self-evident. But to lay out the evidence for it hardly seems necessary for us at this point. And to do so would be simply to review the evidence for all the preceding propositions we have arrived at and to see this evidence as coalescing in one whole of human existence in which we find ourselves as agents of our own destiny. To understand this totality is to understand human existence as a whole. It is also to understand how human selves actualize themselves in the world in their second perfection as part of the highest perfection of the universe. A theory of selfhood would not be complete without an account of how cultures come to be as first- and second-person ontologies that take up third-person ontologies into the ambit of civilization in its communal spirit. We shall see more of how nature is assumed into spirit as we explore the practice of selfhood in its composing with nature.

PART II

Critical Reflection on the Practice of Selfhood

Introduction to Part II

The intersubjective philosophy of human existence does not end with the theory of selfhood as we have come to conceive it up to now; that is, in terms of cultures elaborated through human initiatives in historical self-consciousness. It requires a further reflection on the practice of selfhood as still ongoing in our *prospective* historical consciousness as future-oriented rational beings toward a second perfection that is at once communal and personal.

In the theoretical or speculative part of our reflection on selfhood, we started off by making a distinction between the self in its substance, or in its substantial identity as a self, and the self in its proper activities as a self of which we are more immediately conscious in our experience of selfhood. It is by reflection on what we took to be the proper activities of a self that we came to determine what the self is in its substance or in its essence as a union of body and soul understood as a composite of matter and form but where the soul was taken to have a subsistence of its own by reason of its proper activities of intelligence and will, whose essential dependence on the material conditions of the body is only extrinsic to its internal and spiritual initiatives as a self making its way in a worldly communion of selves. In other words, in this theoretical reflection on selfhood in the world, we were already presupposing an ongoing practice of selfhood in the world, the one that we took to be constitutive of ourselves as communing with one another in one of a diversity of cultures where we distinguish ourselves as partakers in one or several such cultures.

In this theoretical reflection on human activity, however, we were not considering practice the way we think of it in actual practice at any given moment of our existence; that is, in the way we exercise our own initiative as thoughtful or mindful human beings in history. We did see that the self in its substance at any given moment is constituted only in a first perfection as one who still has to work out its own second or final perfection as a self, even at an advanced age. This followed from the way we come to discover the self in its substance by reflection on its proper activities through which in fact it is moving toward an ulterior second perfection or its own final perfection as a self. But we did not see how that final self-determined perfection is conceived in practice nor whether the self-determination truly conforms to what we would call a perfection of selfhood or not. These are questions that arise for human consciousness in its practical orientation toward what it takes to achieve its second or final perfection by taking its own initiatives and in choosing what to do in the world and what not to do, or in choosing what to make of itself.

What we came to in the theoretical and speculative part of our reflection on selfhood is a better understanding of what it is to be a self in the world and of how we are ourselves a given in our own substance and how we exist in this world as given to us by nature and by our own past historical and social initiatives; that is, by taking action of our own as spiritual beings in communicative interaction with other selves, in mutual recognition, developing thereby in a historical interplay of exteriorization and communal reintegration into diverse cultures, each with its own particular spirit or spiritual identity. Everything we have found in this theoretical reflection tells us that we must look forward to the future in our historical consciousness as selves at whatever historical moment we find ourselves as selves, and ask ourselves what it is that we must do as selves in order to fulfill what we have spoken of as our second or our ultimate perfection as selves, whether as individuals or as communities of selves or, better still, as individuals participating in diverse spiritual communities. This means raising whole new kinds of questions about selfhood that will now have to be both practical—that is, having to do with the actual practice of human communities—and ethical—that is, having to do with the shared spirit of those communities.

THE PHENOMENON OF ETHICAL LIFE

THE PRACTICE OF SELFHOOD IS WHAT WE SHALL CALL ETHICAL LIFE. This is the same life we spoke of as human from the beginning with its intentional structures of polarization between something internal and something external, between a subjective pole and an objective pole, between an individual dimension and a communal dimension, and between a merely natural or animal existence and a more properly human or rational historical existence in its proper activities as a rational animal. When we speak of this life as *ethical*, we refer to what is specifically rational and self-conscious, something that is not found in other forms of animal or vegetative life. Ethical life as such includes a spiritual dimension of intelligence and will that transcends sense knowing and sense appetite, but not without taking in these lower forms of knowing and appetite, which is what makes it practical in the most concrete sense of the term as something to be actualized historically in this world.

In fact, the consciousness of *ethical life* we are referring to is very closely related to the idea of culture discussed at the end of our theoretical reflection on selfhood, which is actualized in diverse ways by diverse communities through diverse human activities. Consciousness of ethical life is a consciousness of one's culture as still oriented toward the achievement of some higher good in and for one's community and for humanity as a whole. There are many things, many different kinds of practice, that have gone into the development of the human culture one takes for granted in one's experience of selfhood, all of which have become part of the ethical whole in which one finds oneself, with its own objective pole as well as its subjective pole.

These are like sediments that affect one's historicocultural consciousness in the present as one deliberates and reflects on what should be done for the future good of oneself, of one's community, and of humanity as a whole. There are many things given to us in our culture and in nature as we try to figure out what will work in practice for our good and the good of other selves and what will not, always with the ethical idea and ideal of the higher good for human beings foremost in our mind. For it is from a conception of this higher good that ethical reasoning about what to do and what not to do in practice proceeds.

Included in the phenomenon of ethical life for our consciousness and for that of any communion of selves are customs and rules of behavior that have come down to us from the past experiences of rational communities intent on creating a better life for themselves as a second perfection. In civilizations deemed more advanced, such customs and rules are often elevated to a status of universal law or to a rule of law and of right in a form of justice.

Both the terms we use to speak of the higher good of selves, *ethics* and *morality*, are derived from the ancient idea of custom as formative of a community. So-called traditional societies are usually those that remain explicitly conscious of their origins in the customs arrived at by their elders or their predecessors in the ongoing life of the community. But even in communities where constitutions and bylaws have been enacted, there remains a lot of reliance on custom and common acceptance of practices for managing most human affairs, even in theoretical science and research. What we take to be the ethic of a community, or of a profession, for example, is often little more than a long-established custom for that community or that profession. Georg Wilhelm Friedrich Hegel speaks of custom as defining the spirit of a community or a people.[1] We could also speak of custom as defining the spirit of any profession as well or of any association of like-minded people together in some practice for a common purpose.

Custom, however, or even enacted law, is not enough by itself to determine the practice of a rational agent or a self in a community. As free and as deliberative, this agent has to exercise some critical evaluation, not just of the means at his disposal for taking some action in the present or of the action itself he or she is about to take, but also of the established customs or laws that might induce one to act one way rather than another in coming to one's own self-determination. This evaluation has to be done not in the light of a higher custom or law, such as Immanuel Kant's "moral law in the heart," for example, but in the light of the higher good of selves that we are seeking, their spiritual and communal good as well as their socioeconomic good in history. Custom and law, as rooted in the past, are not sufficient to define this higher good of selves as such. This higher good is a matter of a rational appetite seeking an infinite good for selves in a community, albeit through taking particular actions one at a time. It is the part of critical practical reasoning to find the means or action that will lead to that end and to refuse the means or action that will lead away from that end. What we have to do here, in this practical and ethical

1 See the long section on Custom in his chapter "On Spirit" in *The Phenomenology of Spirit* (1807), leading to the section on Morality, and then to the chapter on Religion.

part of our reflection on selfhood, is examine how we think of this higher, ethical good of selves in a community and how we go about determining our human initiatives practically as rational selves in the light of that good.

THE SCIENCE OF ETHICAL LIFE AS A WHOLE

What distinguishes the practical science of selfhood from the theoretical science of selfhood is that the practical science is oriented toward action, toward what the self does as a self, or has to do, rather than just toward the truth about the self, or about what the self is in its identity, or how it is constituted in its historical actuality, as we have seen in the theory of selfhood. The truth we saw about the self is that it has to be active, with a practice of its own, to achieve its second or final perfection as a self. This is true not only for our own selves but also for all selves of the diverse human communities we know of in history. Practice is an essential actualization of selfhood. What this means, however, for the science of selfhood as practical is that practical science must look toward what human action or practice aims at, what we have already spoken of as the *good*, in distinguishing the power of willing from the power of intelligence. Beyond the question of truth about selfhood, we must raise the question of what is the good for self-consciousness and the question of how a rational self-consciousness goes about realizing this good for itself, for other selves, and for the world in which all self-consciousnesses find themselves.

We should note that philosophy is not the only practical science of selfhood we have to mention here. There are many other practical sciences having to do with the good of selfhood in the world. Most of the sciences we speak of as social, as distinct from the natural sciences, are practical rather than just theoretical in that they have to do with some good of selves and how better to achieve it. Medicine, for example, is largely a biological science having to do with the good of health for human beings and how best to achieve it, to preserve it, or to restore if it is failing. Economics, on the other hand, is a science having to do with the good of commodious living in the world for human beings and how best to achieve that through labor, appropriation, and the production and distribution of commodities we have come to require for life in a highly developed modern world. These particular sciences are only two of many other social sciences, each having to do with a particular aspect of the human good to be achieved or maintained in history. There is something philosophical and ethical about all of them in that they are social and they have to do with some good for human beings in history, though none of them has to do with that good as a whole or as ethical for selfhood as such.

In our philosophy of human existence, we distinguish the practical science of the good to be achieved by and for selfhood as a whole from the other more particular sciences having to do with particular aspects of that good, not in order to separate philosophy or ethics from them, as if in total abstraction from them—or as Kant would say, as if it were purely a matter of intentions determined as categorical imperatives and nothing else in a domain that is purely ideal and remote from the real aspirations of selves in the world, such as the desire for health and for commodious living in the world—but in order to integrate these particular sciences into the higher perspective of selfhood as such, or of humanism, which we are trying to elaborate in a science of the ethical whole.

Here again, as in the theoretical science of selfhood, we do not think that the practical science of ethics as a whole can replace or ignore what is proposed by social sciences, such as those of economics, medicine, psychology, or sociology. The good that ethics has to consider is not some other good than that which is considered in these particular sciences, not some pie in the sky. It is the pie of all these goods taken together. Humanism, even as flowing from human existence or activity, the way Jean-Paul Sartre speaks of it, is not absurd or irrational. It is made up of the rationality and the sense that comes from all of these particular sciences taken together existentially; that is, in a properly human practice. And it is for ethical science to work out discursively the rationality and the sense we make of this whole in our self-consciousness.

What we start from, then, is not some disembodied spirit or some pure practical reason emitting categorical imperatives in the void. It is rather the consciousness we have of ourselves and of others as selves in the world. This consciousness includes not only an awareness of presence to one another in what we have called some first perfection but also an awareness that each self is at the same time striving to achieve a second perfection of its own. Each is a project unto itself, sometimes in competition with other selves, sometimes—and perhaps more fundamentally—in conjunction with other selves in that mutual recognition is constitutive of self-consciousness as such, as we have seen at every step of our reflection up to now.

This is what we have found in our reflection upon the most basic human experiences of intelligence and free will. It is all part of our clear consciousness about our selves. In the conjoining of our consciousness with the consciousness of others, all of us somehow striving to achieve some good of our own, there is a coming together of responsibility toward the good of these many selves striving toward a good that is common to all of them, the common good of a community in communicative interaction. From this sense of the human good as common to many comes what we call *con-science*, a co-consciousness of responsibility toward the good we share in mutual recognition of one another.

Consciousness and conscience are very closely related in our self-consciousness. That is why we often confuse the two words when we want to speak of ourselves in our self-consciousness. But we do not speak of "self-conscience" in the same way that we speak of our "self-consciousness." That is because the idea of conscience already contains the idea of individual self-consciousness, as does the idea of individual responsibility toward the good. The idea of *con-science* adds the social or the communal dimension to the idea of consciousness by adding a prefix meaning *with* to the word we use for intellectual knowing in our experience—that is, for science. We do not think of all this play on words in coming to our self-consciousness, but whoever speaks of *con-science* has to have in mind a plurality of selves in a community of selves.

Nor does the idea of consciousness as such imply the idea of conscience. There can be consciousness without conscience, not only in lower animals but even in individual human beings who show signs of being amoral in their consciousness—that is, of lacking any conscience or sense of responsibility toward the good for human beings as rational or as intelligent and free agents—just as they also show signs of being asocial. It is quite possible for a scientist to be amoral in his attitude toward the particular good he is working toward, even when he has a clear conscience and responsibility with regard to the good of the community of scientists he is working with and with regard to the broader community of which the community of scientists is a part. The more normal thing, however, or the ethical thing, is for conscience to dawn and to develop in conjunction with self-consciousness in the pursuit of any human activity, whether theoretical or practical, as a matter of responsibility toward the human good as such in a community.

This is what is commonly called coming to the age of reason in human consciousness, and it dawns in consciousness at the same time as self-consciousness itself, through the dialectic of mutual recognition and communicative interaction with others in diverse communities, as we have seen. It is possible, for example, for a scientist to be amoral in his attitude toward the particular good he is working toward when he ignores the clear conscience and responsibility he has or should have as a member of a community of scientists in the pursuit of some truth or means to better the human condition, not to mention the broader community of which the community of scientists is a part, or the problem of the crisis we are experiencing regarding climate as a whole. The scientist can also be immoral by violating the canons or the rules of procedure that have been set up by these communities in the pursuit of such particular goods as part of the human good as a whole.

The primordial fact we start from in our reflection on the *ethical* whole of human existence is no less complicated than the one we started from in our *theoretical* reflection. But it is a fact we take to be no less established than the fact of self-consciousness itself. We do not have to create it for ourselves at this point. We have only to focus our attention on it. It has been part of our experience of ourselves ever since we became conscious of our selves and of other selves as rational, and our consciousness of it has developed apace with the development of our self-consciousness in all of the properly human activities we have engaged. When we become self-conscious as human beings in communicative interaction with others, we become *conscientious* at the same time in the commitment we make to other selves on the level of self-determination, the second of the twofold act of willing mentioned earlier in our theoretical reflection regarding that twofold act of willing. This follows from the way in which we come to our self-consciousness; that is, through mutual recognition with other selves.

Becoming fully conscientious, with a full sense of responsibility to the community we live in, does not come all at once normally, not any more than becoming fully self-conscious. It usually comes in stages, gradually, in almost imperceptible breakthroughs with the dawning of new light in our consciousness as rational beings. It is like coming of age in our community by accepting new responsibilities and being recognized by others as having these new responsibilities. We do not choose this new sense of responsibility as we come to the age of reason, whether gradually or in sudden leaps and bounds, as happened in the experience of Helen Keller. We simply find it within ourselves, as we find our will, which follows our reason as our rational appetite, and as we find ourselves in the fullness of our self-consciousness.

Conscience can be very faint at first in human consciousness, but it should grow with age and experience and with reason, hopefully. It can also develop in many different ways in different people. But it is an essential aspect of the fact of human self-consciousness as a whole, which we have to take for granted here in our reflection on the practice of selfhood as ethical. If there were no properly ethical or intentional behavior in the communal life of selves, there would be nothing to reflect on in a science of ethical life as a whole.

In the introduction to his *Nicomachean Ethics*, Aristotle remarks that young people are not ready to engage in a scientific reflection on the subject matter of ethics. He thinks of young people as still too inexperienced in leading an ethical life in their behavior and as ruled too much by their passions rather than by their reason. Historians tell us that what he had in mind was almost everyone short of middle age or short of maturity in the ordered life of the community, such as juveniles and almost certainly college-age students. The reason for this exclusion of the young from the scientific reflection on the ethics of the community was that they lacked the rational experience of ethical behavior as such, or of a clear conscience of their own, which is a prerequisite for a practical science of self-consciousness on which to reflect.

This is perhaps too harsh or too critical an assessment of what young people are capable of in their behavior as human beings, not unlike the assessment Aristotle made of slaves in Greek society. We do not have to agree with this rather high rational threshold set for entering into ethical life, let alone for a systematic reflection on such a life. We have just seen that there are many thresholds to be passed between the ethic of a child in a family, say, and the ethic of a full-fledged or mature member of a political community with one's own sense of responsibility toward the communal good. Most people in our society, including college students and many high school students, find themselves at different degrees between these two extremes of self-consciousness and of conscientiousness with regard for one another.

But for our purposes here, as we begin this scientific reflection on properly ethical life, it is important to recognize that at all of these degrees, there is a real experience of ethical life in the communal living that begins for us in childhood. Children may not have enough of this ethical life as such in their conscious experience to begin to reflect on it systematically, as we are about to do, but they do have a beginning of it, and we have more of it, at whatever age we are, to share and to learn from one another. And that is what we have to start from in this inquiry into what makes for ethical life in reflective self-consciousness. In this practical part of our philosophy of human existence, as in the theoretical part, it is still our own experience of selfhood as ethical at this time that is the text to be examined.

In another remark at the beginning of the *Nicomachean Ethics*, Aristotle also points out that in this science of human practice or of communal behavior we should not expect to find the same kind of mathematical exactness as we look for in the more theoretical sciences of nature. Modern science makes the same kind of distinction among the sciences in terms of hardness and softness, where physics is taken as the model for hardness in science, and social sciences—as we have already seen—are for the most part practical sciences, generally taken to be soft in comparison to physics. Other theoretical sciences of nature, such as biology and psychology, generally try to approximate the hardness of physics in their method, frequently at the expense of freedom and spontaneity, not to mention originality, in their respective domains, while among the social and practical sciences, some, such as economics or sociobiology, will boast of being more hard-wired or more like physics than, say, sociology or political science, where statistics and decision-making are far more open than anything we find in physics or biology.

This does not mean, however, that we should set aside any ideal of exacting confidence we set for ourselves in the first part of this science of the human phenomenon in history for this second, more practical part of our inquiry. There is still a fundamental experience of ethical life—a primordial fact of human existence—for us to start from, and there is still a need to define as exactly as we can the parameters of this phenomenon and the principles that make its various parts work as they do and as they should. Predictability in this science may not be as stringent as it is expected to be in the natural sciences, given that the agents in this phenomenon are infinitely resourceful and free in making decisions of their own, but something like predictability will have a lot to do with figuring out, providentially or prudentially, what works for the good and what works for the not so good of human society. What we have to figure out in this science is everything that goes into the making of good practical judgments for the ever-present and future good of our humanity.

6

Conscience, Responsibility, and the Human Good as Second Perfection of Selfhood

Our first task in this science of ethical life is to establish the fundamental fact of this phenomenon as a whole or to specify the subject matter of our inquiry, which we will then proceed to unpack in our reflection on this practical experience of selfhood. We begin here in the same way as we began in the more theoretical part of our reflection on selfhood, but with a lot more to work with in our consciousness that has been elaborated about the self and its proper activity as self-conscious in our theory of selfhood.

What we start from in this practical part of our philosophy of human existence is no longer just the bare fact of self-consciousness communing with others in the world as given in our consciousness. Included in this fact of actual self-consciousness now is that the self as self in its self-consciousness is active in pursuit of its second perfection or its ultimate good as a rational being and that this pursuit is a matter of its own self-actualization for a consciousness or for selfhood. Also included in this fact is that this self-actualization is a matter of rational pursuit for the self out of its rational appetite, requiring deliberation and choice amid a plurality of ways that present themselves in the moment of freedom and deliberation, options that result from the many determinisms at work in the psyche of the human subject at any given time in its experience so that self-actualization for the self can only take place through deliberate choice and self-determination.

These are all elements or ingredients in the fundamental fact of ethical consciousness as such that we should elaborate on in our reflective analysis of this fact. But at the outset we must see how they all come together as simple aspects of one and the same ethical phenomenon in human existence. Three such aspects must be distinguished: *conscience, responsibility*, and the idea of a properly human or *rational good*, all of them relating to one another in the practice of selfhood. What we propose to show, therefore, is that as reflectively self-conscious, the human being acts out of a *conscience* in communion with others, with a sense of *responsibility* toward actualizing and maintaining a *good* that is spiritual as well as physical, biological, and economic.

6.1 CONSCIENCE

We begin with the aspect of conscience as something we come to have in our self-consciousness, something having to do with how we should act or should not act in pursuing our second perfection as selves in communion with other selves. It is sometimes confused with consciousness, but not all consciousness entails conscience. There is no conscience in nonrational consciousness, and even in rational human beings there can sometimes be consciousness without conscience. In the normal course of events, however, we usually find conscience in rationally self-conscious beings when there is a question of their taking some action of their own. When I am about to do something, I ask myself not only whether it will work for what I want but also whether what I want to do is truly conducive to the good I intend as a rational being, the good of myself and of other selves who come under the scope of my influence and my action in our communicative interaction. Different actions can work toward different kinds of second "perfection," but not all of these may be in keeping with the perfection that is appropriate for rational self-consciousnesses. In the deliberation of rational self-consciousness, there is always an ethical factor to be weighed along with the more narrowly conceived factor of utility or of pleasure in some particular physical, biological, or social undertaking.

We act out of conscience in the same sense and to the same degree that we act out of self-consciousness. Self-consciousness is the measure of spiritual maturity or humanity we have reached in the exercise of our intelligence and will. It allows for varying degrees of maturity or perfection in one's own development as a human being or in the development of diverse human communities. As merely reflective upon itself and its own activity, self-consciousness is speculative and theoretical. As it looks toward its future in practice or in the exercise of its proper activity, however, it becomes *prospective* with regard to its second perfection or to the good it chooses to aim at for itself and for other selves. For every degree of self-consciousness in properly human activity there is a corresponding degree of *conscience* that comes into play in the prospective outlook of consciousness, to assess rationally whether and how the actions we have taken or are about to take measure up to the good we hope to achieve as rational human beings in communion with one another. In this sense, conscience is an ongoing judgment we exercise on the ethical goodness or badness of our own actions and of the actions of others in our diverse communities or in the community of all people as a whole.

Though we distinguish conscience from merely speculative self-consciousness, we cannot separate one from the other. We cannot attain any degree of self-consciousness without at the same time attaining a corresponding degree of conscience. The development of conscientiousness as one progresses in a science or an endeavor in communion with other selves active in the same science or endeavor is not a matter of choice for us, as we shall see more clearly in developing the corresponding idea of *responsibility* in human action. It is a matter of *circumincession* alluded to in speaking of how knowing of truth and how willing of good feed into one another and enhance one another in human action and when intelligence and will—or truth as object of intelligence and good as object of the will—are mutually inclusive of one another. On the one hand, we can say that the reflective self-consciousness comes under the *prospective* self-consciousness of intelligence, just as the skill or the understanding of a craftsperson comes under his or her will to produce a good work for a community. But on the other hand, we have to say as well that the prospective self-consciousness comes under the reflective self-consciousness, just as the will to produce a good work comes under the craftsperson's skill or understanding in the execution of a good work. As the craftsperson improves his or her skill to produce good work, the willingness to do good work should grow proportionately as a matter of good conscience. It is a matter of bad conscience for a skilled craftsperson not to do as good work as one can. Similarly, as we grow in reflective self-consciousness, what we do as human beings ceases to be a matter of indifference with regard to the good we aspire to as selves. Everything we do as selves becomes a matter of *good or bad conscience* with regard to the good we will to achieve, or may fail to achieve, as human beings in communion.

We should note also that we come to good or bad conscience in the same way as we come to self-consciousness, through a *dialectic of mutual recognition* with other selves. Conscience, as the etymology of its name implies, is a knowledge we acquire *with* others, as we acquire self-consciousness itself in the presence of others. We made the case for this earlier with regard to reflective self-consciousness as such. The same case must now be made regarding conscience as well. Just as we come to consciousness of ourselves only in the presence of other selves, so also do we come to conscience about right and wrong, good and bad, in human action, only in the presence of other selves. The formation of conscience in a child starts from the first moment of recognition between infant and mother—with a smile of approval or a look of disapproval that is reciprocated on both sides. It continues in all sorts of subtle ways in early family life for a child, where different forms of approval and disapproval regarding different actions and attitudes are internalized by different members of the family, so that each comes to share in a common ethic about what is right and wrong for the good of the entire family.

An ethic, or a good conscience, is a shared way of thinking and doing things among members of a family or a broader community. Children show that they have internalized a family ethic consciously when they show approval or disapproval for actions they observe or hear about outside the family as well as actions within the family. When a child says, "We don't do that sort of thing" or "People don't do that sort of thing to one another," or "This is the sort of thing people must do for one another," she or he is usually expressing the ethic or the conscience that has developed in the course of a family life, which has brought her or him to her or his actual self-consciousness in that family. Parents can often be surprised by how much their children have learned from them in their practical attitudes and in their conscience.

Moreover, this formation of conscience in one's self-consciousness is not limited to the immediate circle of family life. The formation of conscience in self-consciousness takes place wherever there is any real recognition of other selves in a common endeavor in the broader society, in one's town, in one's nation, and even on the international level—wherever there is any real communicative interaction among selves.

Coming to one's self-consciousness in the presence of other selves does not take place only within the family. It takes place in many broader social contexts of school and work, of political organizations, and of foreign relations, where the other is at first a stranger but through human contact and recognition becomes someone more familiar, so to speak, another self like the selves one already knows, including one's self—others who may be a friend or an enemy but with whom one must deal as one would with any other self.

Conscience is not just something for the family. It is something that develops at every level of communicative interaction among selves, in the nation as well as in the family, and even in the international community, so that it comes into play in judging the good or bad of action even at its most universal level. Conscience comes into play in every realm of human activity, whether it be work or play, scientific research, or technical implementation, wherever there is collaboration or teamwork in human endeavors. Wherever there is organization of people for any practical purpose, there is an ethic that forms among and for the participants in pursuit of a common goal. There is nothing we undertake rationally in human society that does not become a matter of conscience for a self-consciousness. From this comes the idea of rendering humanitarian aid for the victims of disaster even in the remotest parts of the globe.

Even though the Greeks did not say much about conscience as such in their reflection on the life of the *polis*, political self-consciousness was very much a matter of conscience for them as we are shown by the way Socrates felt, or rather reasoned, about ending his life in Athens instead of running away to escape the sentence of death that had been imposed on him by Athens. We know that he was tried and found guilty of charges brought against him that he thought were contrary to what he had done for the good of Athens, his community. He had argued that, far from being punished after the condemnation had been handed down, he should rather be rewarded by the city for all the service, military and civil, he had performed. When his rich friend Crito came to rescue him from prison through bribes, as the day of his having to drink the hemlock approached, thereby giving him the chance to run away from Athens and continue to care for his children in a foreign land, another community to which he did not belong, he found no good reason for abandoning the community that had nurtured him as a human being, as an Athenian specifically, in the face of death, not even for the good of his children. The only reason, or *logos*, he found compelling for him—in conscience we might say, even in the uncertainty he found himself in concerning an afterlife—was to continue living as an Athenian under the laws of Athens that had condemned him, even though he had argued against the condemnation and the sentence of death.

Socrates stayed to drink the hemlock as a man of Athenian conscience, unlike Aristotle, who was not an Athenian by birth and who would later leave Athens when he found himself in danger of being condemned by the same city, giving as a reason that he did not want to be the occasion for Athens making the same mistake of condemning its critical philosophers to death a second time. Even in running away from Athens, Aristotle was following an Athenian conscience that would allow him to return to Athens in more favorable circumstances, for he too had been nurtured in his conscience by Athens. Conscience does not end at the doors of the family home or when one leaves the place of one's origin. It expands with the communion we experience with others in a homeland and in the world at large, where other communities and homelands are to be found and recognized for their selfhood. The science of ethical life as a whole must give due consideration to all of these dimensions of social existence as a matter of conscience, no less than as a matter of practical necessity or utility in a global framework.

6.2 RESPONSIBILITY

INCLUDED IN THIS IDEA OF *CONSCIENCE* in human self-consciousness is also a sense of *responsibility* that relates it to the good we are concerned with in taking action of our own as rational beings. This sense of responsibility too is something to be reflected on as part of the initial fact of our ethical life as such. With the development of conscience as it relates to the concerns of more universal communities, there comes a higher and more expanded sense of responsibility with regard to taking action in the world for our own good and for the good of others in what we have to think of as our broader, more universal historical consciousness.

Coming to one's own self-consciousness in an encounter with other selves always entails a call to action to which we respond in mutual recognition. The recognition that takes place is never purely passive or purely speculative. It always entails an action in response to the other, from both sides in the encounter, which commits both sides to achieving some good that can only be realized by both in communion with one another. The child who becomes conscious of itself and of its mother on the level of selfhood through the smile may not know it yet, but it is entering a whole new world of reason and communion, or of *spirit*, that it will discover for itself as it comes to its own reasonableness. As mentioned before, this will normally take place over time gradually, but it can also take place suddenly at different times, as a new spurt of reasonableness, when a higher, more universal sense of responsibility emerges regarding the good of other individuals as well as one's own. We can see this sort of thing happening in the story of Helen Keller, when at the end of the play *The Miracle Worker*, or at the initial confrontation with Annie Sullivan that brings both of them to a new level of self-consciousness or of what we also have to call a new level of reasonableness, both become reconciled to one another not only in love but also in mutual responsibility for one another for the future.

Without going into the question of love as essential for this moment of reconciliation for the time being, let us reflect on how this sense of mutual responsibility emerges in our historical consciousness in a new moment of reasonableness between selves. It does not come just as a matter of fact. It comes as a matter of necessity, following upon the new level of self-consciousness, which itself came as a matter of necessity from a dialectic of mutual recognition. We do not choose to become self-conscious spirits with intelligence and will and with a conscience. We accept it as coming with the new and higher state of reasonableness, or we recognize it as part of what we are in our rational nature. Nor do we choose to become responsible with other selves in our historical consciousness. We recognize our sense of responsibility as part of what comes naturally and necessarily from the way we come to our self-consciousness. We accept responsibility as part of what it means to be rational in our activity. The sense of mutual responsibility may have to be ingrained in us as part of our upbringing, but when we get it we do not get it as something imposed on us from outside; that is, apart from our own reasoning. We get it as part of our rational conscience in the process of being formed through a practice that is communal at the same time as personal.

Much has been made of responsibility as integral to our ethical self-consciousness in modern social science and philosophy. Max Weber advocated an ethic of responsibility, at least in politics, rather than an ethic of absolute ends of the sort that comes from Kant's idea of pure practical reason.[1] The latter tends to pass over the historical consequences of our actions and of policies set in motion by decision makers in human society by thinking only of some absolute ideal or some categorical imperative dictating some action or prohibition, as if it did not have to be actualized in real historical circumstances. A truly responsible ethic is one that looks to the future good of humankind and seeks means and measures in the present that will serve that good effectively. Hans Jonas has shown the importance of moving ethics in this direction of responsibility, away from a pure Kantian formalism, in the face of consequences from modern technology and scientific research that are destructive of the human good for many or for society as a whole, with the single-minded idea of the "absolute end" they have in mind in taking action or laying down the law.[2]

The ancients spoke as little of *responsibility* in the formulation of their political ethic as they did of *conscience*, but Aristotle expressed a similar idea at the beginning of his *Nicomachean Ethic* when he took exception to Plato's way of talking about the good as something absolute rather than as something we are hoping to achieve in our human activity. The good we have to speak about in ethical science is not some absolute Good beyond the reach of human beings but rather the good as operable by human beings in society or in community, a good that will always be something rather tentative in our present historical life. It will have to be a good that many can enjoy in this life, even if it is not perfect and assured for all and for all time. We shall have to give due consideration to this idea of the human or rational good we start from in our conscience later on, but let us keep in mind that the sense of responsibility we show in our practical attitude as human agents in the world relates directly or intentionally to that good as a good to be achieved in communion with others.

1 Max Weber, *Essays in Sociology* (London: Routledge & Kegan Paul, 1977).

2 Hans Jonas, "Technology and Responsibility: Reflections on the New Tasks of Ethics," in *Philosophical Essays: From Ancient Creed to Technological Man* (Englewood Cliffs, N.J.: Prentice Hall, 1974), 3–20.

Our insistence on *responsibility* as an integral part of our ethical consciousness stems from our relatively modern insistence on self-consciousness, where each self is understood to have its own sense of responsibility, not just in the family but in the broader civil society as well. This sense of responsibility is part of the democratic spirit we associate historically with the French and the American Revolutions and that we find spreading to other parts of the world as well through revolution. It was first highlighted in political discourse, for example, by Alexander Hamilton in the *Federalist Papers*. Responsibility has been called the ethical corollary of human beings as makers of history.

As such, however, this spirit or this sense of responsibility is anything but individualistic. Born of mutual recognition among selves, it is essentially a mutual responsibility corresponding to the greater social awareness of selves among themselves in diverse communities such as the family, the nation, or what we have begun to speak of as the international community, with the advent of global commerce and communication among peoples.

It is through our ethical sense of responsibility that we are open to the good of other selves as well as our own in working toward our ultimate second perfection. This expansion of our ethical consciousness comes to us through language, in the very words that we use to communicate ideas, and through dialogue, where we encounter the other as other and as possibly quite different from ourselves in our way of conceiving the good and how to achieve it, not just within one and the same culture or community but also among different cultures and communities. In theory, our sense of responsibility toward others and ourselves opens the way to a better understanding of other cultures and communities as well as a better appreciation for the more fundamental and more universal principles or goods that bind us together as human beings in a sort of universal communal practice. In practice, it gives a better historical sense of where we stand in relation to other cultures and communities that have gone before ours or that we still encounter in the world in the pursuit or in the promotion of a human good that is for all peoples.

Through the same ethical sense of responsibility, we also come to recognize the rights of other communities and of individual self-consciousnesses in these diverse communities, universal human rights that we are still in the process of defining and beginning to take into account in the interactive communication taking place among the diverse communities around the globe. Rights are not anything in the world except as *recognized* and proclaimed in relation to self-conscious individuals and communities. They may not be the entire good that diverse communities happen to be seeking in the world, but they represent the most basic goods without which a self cannot be a self and without which a human being cannot be at least minimally human, spiritually as well as physically.

We shall have more to say about human rights when we come to the subject of justice later. But before we can come to that, we must give more thought to the idea of the human good as it enters into the way we conceive our ethical task in the world. Human rights are only one aspect of that good. What more do we have in mind when we think of the good, both rational and animal, as the guiding principle for our ethical reasoning and our ethical behavior?

6.3 THE HUMAN GOOD AS PRINCIPLE OF REASONING CONSCIENTIOUSLY AND RESPONSIBLY IN TAKING ACTION AS RATIONAL HUMAN BEINGS

We first of all should think of the human good as something to be achieved through human endeavor. As we have seen from the start in our reflection on the self and its proper activities, such a good comes only as a second perfection for the self through the exercise of its proper activities. If we think of this second perfection as something we are seeking, we can say with Aristotle that it is happiness, fulfillment, or satisfaction for the rational appetite. But happiness or satisfaction for a self does not come any which way, as if by fortune or good luck. There are things that bring us happiness and satisfaction without our having done much about them, though these are more often than not the doings of other selves. A surprise gift that fulfills something we were looking for or a celebration of some accomplishment by oneself does bring much human happiness and satisfaction that we cannot get on our own. In this sense other selves, and even other things, can make us happy, such as a beautiful sunset or a friendly pet. But none of this happens without a person willing for the good that will bring happiness and enable one to find satisfaction through that person's own striving for perfection, so to speak.

Aristotle illustrates all this through the example of the flute player who is not satisfied with just making noises haphazardly with his flute.[3] What he strives for is playing it in a certain way that will express a composition to perfection. And it is in the performance of the piece that he finds happiness and satisfaction as a flute player, though an enthusiastic applause from an appreciative audience will also enhance that happiness and satisfaction. It is only in the actual performance itself, usually in front of an audience, that he experiences his deepest satisfaction as a flute player.

Such is also the case in the performance of ethical life in the existence or the practice of the human being as a self. We reach moments of happiness and satisfaction through doing things and doing them well. That is when we experience the good we are seeking in our striving as human beings. The experience may be fleeting most of the time, subject to many misfortunes that may befall us. But it is an important experience for a self to have, both to get some idea of the good we are seeking in human action and to sustain us in our striving, even if we think we can never attain perfect happiness and satisfaction in this life. For, as the Greek saying goes at the end of the story of Oedipus, who suffered the worst misfortunes imaginable for a family, count no man happy until he is dead.

To get a more typical idea of the good we are striving for as ethical human beings, we have to turn once again to the proper activities of selfhood and to the *appetites* of the self from which they flow, both rational and sensible. Appetites are understood as orientations in consciousness to a good. The good is understood as what we desire when we don't have it, and as what we acquiesce in when we do

3 Aristotle, *The Politics*, book 3, section 1282b.

have it. We distinguished between two kinds of appetite in the self: the will, or the rational appetite, and the emotions, or the sense appetites. We arrived at that distinction by distinguishing two kinds of proper activity of the self: one, the rational soul as spiritual, with a subsistence of its own in its operation, and the other, the composite, operating in composition with bodily organs. Both, however, were taken to be essential for the self according to its nature so that now we have to think of two kinds of good as essential for the fulfillment of the self, one that we shall have to take as rational and spiritual and one that we shall have to take as composite of soul and body, which will include such things as health, physical well-being, sensible or emotional satisfaction, and aesthetic enjoyment of any kind. These are all elements on the subjective side of any human culture or civilization that we must now consider as elements of the good we are striving to achieve through what we now refer to as our ethical activity.

In this initial reflection on the mere fact of our ethical consciousness, we cannot speak of these goods in any great detail as we must do in deliberation and in our actual practice. We can speak of them only generally or typically, as Aristotle says, as they relate to the appetites we start from in our activities as human beings. The task of the scientific exploration of this fact will be to show how we have to come to particular determinations of the ethical good for ourselves and for our communities. For the moment, we are only trying to show how the question of the good becomes a matter of practical concern for historical selves and how far afield that concern can range in the historical context of human activity as a whole. What we have to understand first about the ethical as such in human activity is that it has to do with a certain excellence in the performance of our typically human activity as it affects the various aspects of human life on Earth, both spiritual and physical, as with the performance of the flute player or of anyone else who has a role to play in a community; and that satisfaction or happiness for a self-consciousness will come only through the performance of the good we take to be ethical in a community where all are performers as well as audience for one another.

The other thing that should be said concerning the specification of the good that comes into view in ethical self-consciousness is that it has to be a social or a communal good in principle. This follows from the way we come to our self-consciousness and our conscience, through a dialectic of mutual confrontation and reconciliation. Conscience, as we experience it ethically, which is characteristic only of self-conscious human beings and not of other nonrational animals, is something that takes shape in a community among individual self-consciousnesses, and it relates all individuals to one another and to the community as a whole with its own universal precepts and principles for communicative interaction. When we exercise our conscience in judging our own actions and the actions of others, we do so always in the presence of other selves, explicitly or implicitly, in search of approval or disapproval from others as well as from ourselves. This is because the good we are seeking in our ethical self-consciousness is always the good of other selves as well as the good of our own selves. It also explains why the enjoyment and the satisfaction individuals take in the performance of their ethical tasks in communion with others is enhanced by the enjoyment and satisfaction other individuals take in that performance in response to one's own performance. The things we seem to enjoy doing most as human beings, such as good humor and love, are things we do with other human beings or want to do with other human beings even when we are alone.

There are two aspects to this ethical good as social and communal—one external and the other internal—according to a distinction we made from the beginning in the phenomenon of human life as a whole. The external aspect has to do with social structures in which we find ourselves in interdependence with other selves. The internal aspect has to do with the actual sharing of communion itself in mutual regard and respect for one another. Both are taken to be essentially social in their actuality and both are essentially related to one another in that social structures do not make human or ethical sense except in relation to the *internal spirit* of a community, and in that the internal spirit of a community cannot organize itself historically except in a social structure, however it may choose to do so. Our task here will be to examine how communities as ethical wholes organize themselves in coming to their own spiritual self-consciousnesses, with special attention given to the family as an ethical whole, the nation as another kind of ethical whole, and the possibility of an international society as yet another kind of ethical whole comprising humanity as a whole—present, past, and future

7

Freedom and the Necessity of Right Reasoning in Ethical Consciousness

Ethical consciousness is self-consciousness as oriented toward actualizing its second perfection or toward realizing a properly *human good* in the world. It is self-consciousness as practical in the most fundamental and the most humanistic sense of the term. It is self-consciousness as creating culture or cultures in the world that can satisfy human aspirations to what we have been relating to as the human good, spiritual as well as physical and emotional. Our first question in the critical examination of the ethical phenomenon we have begun elaborating as a whole is to ask where precisely this ethical fact takes hold in our experience of selfhood.

In the theory of self-consciousness we distinguished between two kinds of proper activity of the self: those that are proper to it as a composite of soul and body—sensation and sense appetites—and those that are proper to it as soul having a subsistence of its own—intelligence and will as rational appetite. We did not distinguish these as separate layers of actuality within the self, piled onto one another as it were, but rather as interweaving with one another in any human action as a whole that is at once spiritual and physical or emotional, as well as theoretical and practical. The place or the moment in self-consciousness in which we saw this interweaving most clearly is in the deliberation that precedes any free choice of a course of action and that comes with a plurality of motives for choosing one course or another, in scientific reasoning as well as in practical reasoning. This is the place or the moment of consciousness in which the phenomenon of ethical life would seem to present itself most emphatically in human existence. How can this be demonstrated in our ethical science, and what sort of necessity would follow from this demonstration?

There is reasoning that takes place in deliberation: theoretical as well as practical, reflective as well as prospective. We began with the theoretical and reflective aspect of this reasoning in the first part of this philosophy of human existence. But that is not how reasoning begins concretely in human experience. Reasoning begins as practical and prospective, as we face or deliberate over problems of everyday life, problems of survival or problems of human enlightenment. Even children face such problems to the extent that they have begun to exercise reason for themselves and to deliberate in their interaction with other selves, their parents, their teachers, and others they encounter in their human pursuits. It is through this prospective reasoning that ethical consciousness as such emerges, as the child develops an ever-broader sense of the good we are seeking as selves or as rational agents in communion with other rational agents, for we must not forget that we are all selves only in communion with other selves.

What sort of necessity, if any, governs the development of this higher rational or ethical sense, and how does it relate to the sense of freedom and autonomy we also develop as human beings? Is the ethical sense only an imposition from others or from the community as a whole, or is it something we come to in the freedom of our own reason? To answer these questions let us begin by reflecting once again on the existential situation of the self as deliberative and free in its historical consciousness.

7.1 HUMAN EXISTENCE AND HISTORICAL CONSCIOUSNESS

If we go back to the notion of human existence as we have articulated it from the beginning (cf. Part I, chapter 2.2 and 2.3), we are reminded that the self is not just a given in its existence. Even as a given in its essence, it is as one actualizing itself through an activity that is its very own. We do not discover what it is to be a self by some sort of direct intuition into the essence or the identity of our own self or that of another. We discover what it is to be a self only by reflecting on the activity of selves as *existing*; that is, as going or as having to go beyond what they are as given essences. This existing is something essential about selfhood that calls for a priority of existence over essence in the way we come to know the self, as existentialism has claimed. What we are as selves is what we make ourselves be in actualizing ourselves through our proper activities as human beings. There is no truly human essence closed upon itself. There is only one that is open to actualizing itself in the presence of other selves who are also actualizing themselves in communion with one another.

This is not to say that there is no human essence whatsoever. Nor is it to say that there is only a human essence constituted in itself in isolation or in opposition to every other human essence, as if it were also constituted in itself in isolation or in opposition to every other. It is to say that there is a human essence, or a humanism, constituted historically by the interaction of selves in different communities or cultures, all of them sharing in a common human essence or a common humanism constituted by a characteristically human action of intelligence and will. The consciousness that is shared in this characteristically human action is not just a natural consciousness, such as that which we share with other animals, though that is not excluded from what makes up human activity. It is more what we should call a *historical consciousness*, which we share with other selves as rational agents in the world; that is, as operating out of deliberation and free choice in shaping our lives as selves in a community.

Though we speak of human consciousness as natural as well as historical, we should not think of it as purely natural any more than we think of it as purely spiritual. *Historical consciousness* is a unique kind of consciousness that combines both the natural and the spiritual in one and the same self-consciousness. We have seen how human activity is spiritual as flowing from intelligence and will, but it is not purely spiritual in that it has to play itself out in some sort of physical or natural activity, even if it be one of sense perception or of intervention in a world that would otherwise follow its own natural course.

There is a tendency in modern philosophy to think of nature generally as that which is in conformity with reason, but this is to stretch the idea of nature beyond what it stands for in the world, or else it is to turn reasoning into nothing more than a natural process unable to distinguish itself from any particular process that may be at work or in motion within a particular self, as in a particular emotion or in a particular conception of evolution. Natural science or natural ethics in this kind of reasoning ends up as nothing more than a recitation of what is taken to be the way things are and the way they have to be, necessitated as it were either by some natural law or by some emerging probability in a universal struggle for survival. This is reasoning reduced to some form of essentialism, or an absence thereof, in a recourse to randomness as a substitute for what is otherwise taken as a matter of rational explanation.

In the historical consciousness of selves in communion with one another, which is the locus for properly ethical consciousness, there is so much more to reasoning than this attempt to stay as close to nature as we can in our research and in our ambition concerning the human good we are striving for. We have seen how reason relates to the plurality of determinisms that penetrate our consciousness from the world and from society in the form of particular mobiles and motives for action from the standpoint of a consciousness with a universal movement of its own as a whole. We have seen how reason relativizes each one of these particular determinisms as partial and holds it in suspense at least momentarily in order to deliberate and to choose which one, or which combination of them, it will give itself to or make its own in the pursuit of its own more universal good as a self. We see this kind of reasoning and discussion even in the elaboration of alternative forms of action to be taken in the practice of scientific research prior to taking one course or another, since scientific research is itself part of the ethical endeavor in pursuit of the human good by a community.

When we speak of historical consciousness as a whole, we mean the kind of rational consciousness that is found in diverse human communities, diverse cultures and humanisms, and contains much more than what is given by nature. It contains a lot that has come to be through the historical initiative of these communities and, on a more universal level of history as a whole, a lot that has come to be through human achievement across the ages that nature could not produce. Ethical consciousness has to do with all of this human achievement or failure, no less than with what is given to us by nature.

That is why we have to consider ethical consciousness as *historical* and not just as natural. Strictly speaking, there has never been a state of pure nature for human beings as such. The moment we step out of infancy into self-consciousness, we step into history. It takes each one of us a long time to realize this fully, just as it has taken many civilizations a long, long time to appreciate themselves as a historical whole in conjunction with other civilizations. We are only beginning to develop what we could call a worldwide self-consciousness, or the consciousness of a global village. We should understand, however, that at every level of communal self-consciousness, there are ethical exigencies that rise above merely natural exigencies, just as the exigencies of our second nature arrived at through communal habituation of one kind or another rise above the exigencies of what is first given to us by nature.

7.2 THE NECESSITY OF REASONING WITH OTHERS IN HISTORICAL CONSCIOUSNESS

How then does ethical consciousness come to be out of *historical consciousness*, where every human being takes its stand as a self-conscious and responsible maker of history? Reflection on how we come to act as human beings in the world brings out two aspects of deliberation—one that is personal or individual and one that is communal or social—where we discover our freedom to choose as we will. We have seen how this moment of deliberation gets articulated at the center of our self-consciousness through intelligence and will. Let us now examine how reasoning takes place in this centered moment of our practical self-consciousness.

As we come to self-consciousness we become more and more deliberate in our action. We take deliberateness to be a marker for being human and for being responsible agents in a history that is our own as well as that of others. As rational agents we understand that there are many avenues of development open before us and that we must choose the one that we will make our own. That is how we come to reasoning about ourselves, about the future, about the good we are aiming at as human beings, and about what means we must take to achieve that good as we conceive it. Practical reasoning of this sort is integral to self-consciousness in every kind of human endeavor where some good or some aspect of the human good is at stake, scientific or artistic, utilitarian or altruistic.

Reason functions in two ways in this process of deliberation. First, it is the power to entertain different courses of action that might satisfy the many desires that move us as human beings. Other nonrational animals do not have this power. They are driven by a single desire for a determinate good they seek more or less intermittently, such as a certain food, in their ecological habitat. They survive and prosper as animals to the extent that they succeed in obtaining that determinate good nature has set for them. They become endangered as species when they lose access to the one good, however complex, nature has determined for them. The rational animal is not so constricted in its desires and in the good it can envision for itself at any given moment of its existence. To be sure, there are many ways it is constricted, needy and endangered, even more than other animals, especially at birth and in infancy, but reason provides many more ways of overcoming these natural limitations, including aspirations to higher goods that nature alone could never satisfy. At the beginning of a human life there is little more than nature and instinct to get the not-yet-rational infant to do the right thing to survive and to prosper, but once reason begins to dawn through mutual recognition with other selves, many new desires, many new motives for action begin to emerge in the consciousness of the child that will free it from any single determination of nature and require choices to be made as one matures to adulthood in the way of self-consciousness.

Studies in human development and child psychology have done a lot to show how different forms of natural determinism come into play in this maturing of self-consciousness for individuals in our communities, but we should not overlook that all these determinations are gathered by reason within the consciousness of each individual self-consciousness as partial determinations for one and the same consciousness in which deliberation and choice have to take place. What is liberating in all this is not that we escape or deny the natural determinisms that move us in real life but that we come to see that we are not determined by any one of them, which is always only one among many, and that we come to envision not higher determinisms but higher possibilities for human fulfillment that nature alone could not begin to suggest, more humane possibilities as well as more technical proficiencies.

The second function of reason in the process of deliberation has to do with how deliberation itself takes place. Able to relativize the various impulses to act that present themselves in consciousness, reason also has to evaluate them, sort them out in relation to one another and in relation to the future good of the self as a whole. For each impulse it formulates an idea of some good to be strived for, a motive for action in one's consciousness. In doing this, it also begins to compare and to contrast the various impulses, now seen as motives in consciousness, not only in the light of the good that each one represents for the self but also, more importantly and more significantly for ethical consciousness as such, in the light of the good for the self as a whole in its self-consciousness. Each particular impulse is in fact an impulse of the self. But none of them is isolated from other particular impulses in one and the same consciousness, though some may be stronger than others. If one of them becomes totally dominant over all the others, reason loses its hold as a power of liberation from the determinism of impulses. Responsibility fades into fixation and obsession.

Reason maintains its hold in this process of deliberation only by representing for the self some idea of the good that will encompass that of the self as a whole, that of the rational appetite as well as that of the sense appetites. For, along with the impulses of the sense appetites in this process of liberation and deliberation, there also comes the movement of the will or of the rational appetite for which the good is that of the whole human being and not just that of one part or another at the expense of another.

This is where, in deliberation, the rational agent exercises its freedom, which is also called *liberum arbitrium* in Latin. Having stopped all natural impulses in their track, so to speak, reason is prepared to arbitrate among them and to impose itself or its choice on them through the will. Free from the determinism of any of its inclinations, it negotiates which one of them, or which coalition of them, it will choose to go with in its pursuit of the good for the self as a whole. Each one of the particular appetites represents a special interest in the parliament of rational self-consciousness and for the individual consciousness. As a universal faculty concerned with the good of the whole, reason brings these special interests into a debate, so to speak, in which some compromise will be found for the self to go forward, perhaps a new kind of interest that none of the special interests could have come up with in isolation from the other special interests.

Thus reason comes to dominate the particular or the partial inclinations of the self, but not absolutely or in abstraction from them. It comes to rule over them as a ruler rules over subjects who have a will of their own, in the manner of politics, as Aristotle says, and not of pure dictatorship. Reason does not try to simply suppress particular inclinations, especially not those that are deeply ingrained in the nature of the self. Rather, it tries to reorient them and to moderate them in relation to one another in a way that will be rational as it searches for the way to move forward in the present moment through a kind of consensus among all of them, or a kind of coordination that will give priority now to one, now to the other, in an effort to adjust them to one another, with the goal of integrating them, natural appetites as well as rational, into the single unity of an actualized self.

Ethical life for a self thus consists in a performance of reason in which all its appetites and emotions are brought into a sort of concert with one another we call character. It starts in a struggle with one's emotions, and it develops into a labor with these emotions, wherein reason comes to penetrate the very fibers of our sense appetites through the development of habits or dispositions that are conducive to the good or the happiness of the human being. If the human being finds his or her good or happiness in performing as a cultured human being, as the flautist finds satisfaction in performing as a good flautist, it is only by bringing the excellence of reason to bear in all of one's inclinations and finding satisfaction in such a living performance of whatever we do as human beings.

There is a strong element of self-satisfaction in the performance of ethical life, but it must be understood as pertaining to reason and not just to one or another particular interest of the self. Our rational self-interest cannot be identified with any one of the many particular interests that move us in our consciousness. It is not the self-interest of a selfish gene, as this has been represented in some evolutionary theories. Nor is it the self-interest of any particular emotion in the self, which is selfish by nature, and not universal, as reason should be in its concern for the human good of selves as a whole. Selfishness sets in for a human being when reason becomes identified with one or another particular emotion in oneself to the exclusion of other particular emotions or interests that reason has made possible in one's consciousness. This can happen by deliberate choice, as when one simply gives in to a particularly strong emotion or by a lack of clear assertion of reason and its responsibility in a process of decision-making, as happens when we are only coming to the age of reason in our human behavior. Insofar as reason distinguishes itself from all the particular interests it recognizes within the unity of a consciousness, it is not selfish as any one of them is by nature. It is universal and regulative for all of them in view of the total good of the self, which is comprehensive of many particular goods, all of which must be coordinated in the good of the whole.

We shall see how *virtue* develops in the various appetites through this regulative function of reason in the formation of character, but before we can do that we must take into consideration one more dimension of rational self-consciousness, its social or communal dimension, which is a condition for the emergence of reason itself in ethical consciousness and for the development of virtues in the appetites.

We have seen how the human self is constituted in its self-consciousness through a dialectic of mutual recognition among selves. We do not come to self-consciousness, as Georg Wilhelm Friedrich Hegel says, except in the presence of another self-consciousness. We saw this clearly illustrated in the dramatic case of Helen Keller and Annie Sullivan. What we must understand now is that this is the story of reason itself in self-consciousness and not just of reason isolated from other self-consciousnesses and absolutized in its self-centered isolation. What comes into being through mutual recognition is rational self-consciousness as such so that reason itself is social or communal from the start no less than self-consciousness. We discover our reason and that of others and we learn to reason in the same moment as we discover our own selfhood and that of others, so that the human good we seek rationally as selves will always be the good of other selves as well as our own, the good of a community as well as the good of the individual self-consciousnesses who recognize one another in that community.

We do not come to the age of reason in our self-consciousness out of a state of war of everyone for himself against everyone else, as Thomas Hobbes puts it, or in a spirit of competition with everyone else for what are taken to be scarce human goods, as John Rawls puts it in his *Theory of Justice*. We come to the age of reason as we enter into communion with others through *language*, as Helen Keller did in a sudden flash of enlightenment with Annie Sullivan, or as most children normally do in a gradual process of enlightenment through interactive communication with their elders in community. We learn to reason from the perception of a good that is communal, or common to many, and from that we grow in our self-consciousness through regard and respect for the other as well as for our own self, so that ultimately we find satisfaction and happiness as human beings only in communion with other human beings. This is what we strive for ethically, not just in our youth but in our adulthood, in the whole of our lives in our historical consciousness. Without this perception of a common good for humankind, there would be no rational self-consciousness, no ethical consciousness. How, then, is this communal good conceived in relation to practical reasoning in ethical consciousness?

7.3 THE IDEA OF THE COMMUNAL GOOD AS PRINCIPLE IN ETHICAL REASONING

THERE ARE MANY LEVELS OF COMMUNAL GOOD to be considered in the experience of our historical consciousness, depending on the different kinds of community we identify with as selves. Each one of these communities is an ethic unto itself in that it has a view of the communal good shared by all members in it and a way of working toward that good that is also shared by all in it. There are many such ethical communities in which we find ourselves as selves for coming to different kinds of human good, such as the enjoyment of sports activities or the development of science and the arts. Not all of these communities are of equal significance for the development of a universal ethical consciousness, but we would insist on three of them as especially significant for the development of such a universal ethic in historical consciousness: the *family*, the *nation*, and the *international community*. All communities can be said to be ethical, even a band of thieves or a for-profit corporation, in the sense that they share a common sense of a good to be achieved for people and a common way of working toward that goal, even where there is a division of labor. What makes some of them unethical is that their sense of the good and of working toward it is not in conformity with the sense of more basically rational communities such as the family, the nation, or the international community.

It should be understood, however, that the communal good we are talking about in an ethical consciousness is not one that is opposed to the good of individuals in the community. On the contrary, the communal good is inclusive of individual goods. It is nothing else than the good of individuals recognizing one another as selves and committed to promoting that for one another. Opposition in the good of a community is usually found between the good of one individual and the good of another individual, or of one particular group and another particular group. When there appears to be opposition between the communal good and the good of one particular individual or group in the community, it is usually because one particular individual or group has taken over the idea of the communal good and reduced it to its own particular good in totalitarian fashion. That is, it has replaced the inclusive communal whole with its own particular good and interest by representing that particular good and interest as the good of the whole and by excluding the particular good and interest of others from consideration and from due regard. This happens not just in societies where a tyrant or a dictator takes over but also where a majority rules without due consideration and regard for the good and the interests of minorities and of individuals who are part of the ethical community in their self-consciousness.

The idea, or the ideal, of the communal good that comes with mutual recognition among selves cannot be restricted to any established social structure of "law and order," which may be required for the communal good as we shall see later but which cannot adequately define that good independently of the *spirit* at work in the community moving it toward an ulterior good. Any system of law and order is bound to be particular, appropriate perhaps for a particular time and place. Whether it is good or not for an ethical community in the long run has to be judged in the light of the communal good that it is supposed to serve not dictate. It is not a community that has to serve its constitution but, rather, the constitution that has to serve its community or the spirit of a people.

The ideal of the communal good is thus the good of persons and selves as such joined together in mutual recognition. It is both personal and communal at the same time. Instead of thinking of the personal good as opposed to the communal good, we have to think of the personal good of diverse individuals and groups as a participation in the communal good. Though the personal good of various individuals taken discretely is not equal to the communal good, there is no personal good for selves in mutual recognition without the communal good. This is not just a matter of the whole being greater than the sum of its parts. It is also a matter of the discrete parts, persons, sharing in the communal good in diverse ways and in different proportions in keeping with the different initiatives taken by each in communicative interaction.

The Greeks spoke of the communal good as the good life for human beings in a community, not as individuals in isolation from one another, much less in hostility with one another. Luxury, which introduces an element of competition among the members of a community, was not included in that idea of the good life, though some aspects of physical and economic well-being were. The good life for them, as for us in any community, was something to be actualized by human endeavor and to be esteemed in the light of a good communally envisioned. To be sure, this included the struggle for survival in a harsh world and the satisfaction of individual needs. But it was not limited to that or to the realm of money-making. The good life for the human being is more one that is led according to *reason*, even in the struggle for survival and the satisfaction of one's needs and with mutual regard and respect for one another as selves, with justice for all, and ultimately with diverse friendships of all sorts. All this is included under the idea of communal good in ethical consciousness not just as an ideal any human community is striving for but also as something that is already living in any community where mutual recognition has begun to take hold, as it did in ancient Athens.

The question for us now is to reflect on how we reason in our historical consciousness from this communal good we aspire to as human beings.

7.4 ETHICAL REASONING FROM THE COMMUNAL GOOD

Practical reasoning in historical consciousnesses differs from theoretical reasoning in scientific consciousness. Theoretical reasoning is *reflective*. It proceeds from principles that are taken to be true and necessary to demonstrate conclusions as also true and necessary in consequence. Practical reasoning, on the other hand, is *prospective*. It starts from the conception of a good that is to be attained, an end that is intended and investigates what means may be chosen for the attainment of that end. When it yields a plurality of means that could be chosen for attaining an end, it not only frees the rational agent from the necessity of any particular means so that it can choose freely which means to take but also makes it necessary for the rational agent to choose since the agent cannot advance toward attaining its end without taking some means or some particular action in the historical moment of consciousness. If the rational inquiry into means toward an end, or toward a good we intend as human beings, yields only one means available for that end, then there is an ethical necessity to choose that means, even if one is free not to choose it or if one is not determined by nature to follow that course of action. The more means we can find or invent in the pursuit of our human good, the more free we are to choose and the more likely we are to succeed as rational agents in attaining some form of that good. But there always remains in historical consciousness an ethical necessity to choose and to choose means that are conducive to a desired human good, not just any good.

This way of exercising practical judgment, which is at the same time ethical for historical consciousness, can be illustrated in the way we practice health care as a community. Health is an integral part of the good we care about as human beings. Rational investigation into means that might be conducive to that good, or into those that might be nocent to that good, has gone on in every human community we know of in history and has yielded a great variety of results by way of medicines, from natural herbs to artificial drugs of all sorts, from acupuncture to radical surgeries, from the simple clinic to the large medical center. In modern society the search for means in health care has developed into a large scientific and technological industry. Even as it continues to advance in the search for ever more efficient means to do things in health care that have been impossible up to now, it already has a vast array of means in place for us to choose from in our caring for health as a human good.

All this is rational investigation on a universal scale of science and technology. It arises out of a practical concern about health for human beings in general, but it proceeds in the mode of scientific research, which is no longer immediately practical for a historical consciousness but, rather, theoretical and technical, applicable but not yet chosen as a means for anyone in particular. When one becomes ill, however, or concerned about one's own health or that of others in any way, one then has to do a rational investigation of another kind in the light of the good or the end one intends for oneself or for some other individuals. In this investigation we take the good as intended for a particular individual or for a community as a whole as the principle in our reasoning, and we search from the wide plethora of means made available by scientific experts in health care, doctors, pharmacists, nurses, and a host of other clinicians and therapists for means that are conducive to the health and good life of one individual or another in question or of the community as a whole. If we come up with a plurality of available means relevant to the health of an individual or of a community, we have the freedom to choose, but we also have the ethical necessity to choose. And if we come up with only one possible means conducive to the good of that individual or the community at a given moment in time, as in the case of an urgent need for surgery to save a patient's life, then we have the ethical necessity to choose that means, even though we are free not to choose. Even when there is no urgent need to choose a particular means, human beings go through this sort of practical reasoning on many levels of their existence, spiritual as well as physical. It is something we have to do as rational beings, and that characterizes us as human beings in more ways than one.

Our illustration speaks of reasoning mainly with regard to finding and choosing means relative to the particular good of individuals, but it is not restricted to envisioning the good of individuals in isolation from one another or from the community in which individuals are recognized as human beings. In fact, practical reasoning in the choice of means for an ethical consciousness has to start from an idea or an ideal of a communal good that has priority over any particular good of individuals, not in a despotic or totalitarian sense, but in a sense where the individual good is seen as a participation in the communal good.

This priority of the communal good as the principle to reason from in ethical consciousness follows from the way we come to our individual self-consciousness in communion with other selves through mutual recognition, where we get our first conception of the good we have to strive for as human beings. This is the good, not just of one individual self over against other individual selves but of the two or more individual selves coming together, or communing, in their self-consciousness, recognizing one another in their individual right. In this recognition, there is already the ideal of the human good as communal, to which even those who give absolute priority to the good or the right of individuals pay negative tribute when they say that the exercise of one's rights should not interfere with another self's exercise of its rights, as if that were possible in a state of war or of sheer opposition or hostility between selves. Selves in communion with one another pay a much more positive tribute to the communal good as the ideal or the principle from which to reason in ethical consciousness, and it is from this higher tribute that liberal individualists derive their lesser tribute as a limitation on the absolute right of the individual to which they give priority.

It is sometimes said that the first principle of moral reasoning is do good and avoid evil. This is similar to saying that being and nonbeing is the first principle of scientific reasoning in the sense that we have to come to *what* is the case and avoid saying anything that is not the case. The whole enterprise of Socratic cross-examination or critical reflection in science rests on this principle. Both of these principles, as stated abstractly, seem very remote from anything particular in practical decision-making or in theoretical inquiry, but in every process of reasoning, practical or theoretical, they are brought into play in distinguishing the good from the bad as well as the true from the false. Whatever a particular case may be, it cannot be both good and bad or both true and false at the same time in one and the same respect. To inquire into anything is to inquire where the good or the truth lies and to recognize the privation of good as well as the privation of truth in anything else that might be thought on that same subject matter.

It is important, however, to recognize a certain positive content in these first principles, especially in that of practical reasoning if not in that of theoretical reasoning as well, a content to which every particular case of reasoning, whether practical or theoretical, has to be related. In the case of practical reasoning, that positive content has to do with how we conceive the *good* as something we have to do. The Latin version of the first principle of practical reasoning, *bonum est faciendum*, is far more expressive in this regard than the English version we have cited. It does not say just do good formally, whatever that might be, but, rather, the good is what must be done.

This hearkens back to how we come to the idea of the good in the first place, as the object of an appetite that drives us forward as selves, as something we desire if we do not have it, and as something we acquiesce in if we do have it. The good is what we all have an appetite for, *id quod omnes appetunt*. We are conscious of appetite in ourselves both as rational, namely the will, and as sensible, namely the emotions. The good we have to think about in our ethical consciousness, however, is not just one that is given to us, as we might say our present good or goodness as essences is given to us. It is a good that has yet to be achieved by us through initiatives we have to take as self-conscious deliberative beings in any historical moment. Happiness for a human being is not something simply handed over on a platter, so to speak, by someone else or by an object of desire. It comes more as something deserved by our action, as a satisfaction we have to reach for even when it is attained only in communion with other selves. Others can make us happy, but only if we are striving to achieve the good we must as human beings, which is the good of others as well as our own.

This is how the sense of duty comes into ethical consciousness as the first principle in what we speak of as moral as well as practical reasoning. But the content of that first principle or of the good that must be done, or that must be accomplished ethically, is not as determinate or as a priori as we might wish it to be in our speculative or deductive consciousness, whether we think of it as the good for an individual or the good for a community. Even for an individual alone, the idea of the ethical good cannot be reduced to any particular good relative to any particular appetite or motive for action that may appear in one's consciousness at the moment of deliberation, along with many other particular appetites or motives for action. For the rational appetite that must decide freely among all these particular appetites and goods, which ones to cut short, which ones to go with, the good is something indeterminate relative to those particular appetites, something infinite relative to the plurality of finite motives.

Free will is not attached a priori to any particular good, but as free it is still oriented to a good that has something of the infinite dimension of its power to deliberate and to act on its own. In this infinite dimension of the good for itself, an individual free will can and does include the good of other free wills as well in its self-determinations and in its commitment within some particular community or other, or even within the community of human beings as a whole, even though that does not necessarily exhaust the infinite dimension of the good for its rational appetite.

That infinite good for the rational appetite as such may include something that surpasses or transcends even the universal good of history. But even if we stay within our conception of the immanent good of history, we find ourselves at a loss for rationally determining the good of free wills, or of our own free will in isolation from other free wills already communing with us in our deliberative consciousness. The good each one is seeking to determine in a community of free wills is always at the same time the good others are also seeking to determine. This inevitably brings a dialogical dimension into the free act of deliberation that must not be overlooked in any attempt to arrive at what is the good for us as rational beings and at how we are to act in taking means to achieve this good. It is to this dialogical dimension of deliberation that we must now turn, to show the necessity of some communal prudence as the first virtue required for a community of rational beings seeking to achieve the good or the excellence proper to them as rational beings.

7.5 THE NECESSITY OF TAKING COUNSEL IN ETHICAL REASONING

To understand this dialogical dimension of deliberation in ethical consciousness better, we would do well to consider deliberation as an exercise in taking counsel, *consilium*, as Thomas Aquinas calls it in the *Summa of Theology*, I–II, q.14, a taking counsel that takes place before coming to choice, *quod electionem praecedit*. At this point in our reflection on human freedom and deliberation, then, the question arises: taking counsel with whom?

We have tried to open up the question of deliberation and freedom in human practice as widely as we can, to whatever might seem possible or appealing in any moment of true deliberation in the life of a self-conscious subject intent on actualizing itself and having to decide what will be its final perfection as a human being. This is a moment when all sorts of particular determinations come rushing into the consciousness of the ethical subject, with none of them equaling the infinite power of the willing subject who remains indeterminate in this power but who must come to some determination in its free self-determination. This is a serious situation for any reflective self, and if the gravity of it is fully appreciated, it is not surprising that a need to take counsel should occur to the reflective self-consciousness. But with whom to take counsel, and about what?

7.5.1 In answer to the first question, about whom to take counsel with, we have to say certainly with oneself and with one's own emotions. This is where the need for taking counsel begins, within the self, before seeking counsel from others. The self, however, is not a pure form or a pure self-determination, not a pure identity, so to speak. It is an identity with many emotions and many determinations churning within, seeking to become the determinations that become real for the self. In the moment of critical deliberation for the self, the self must take counsel with these emotions and these particular determinations, take them into account in the decision it is about to make, just as a political ruler has to take into account his or her subjects in determining what will be for the political good of the community. The human subject cannot advance toward its ethical good as a whole without enlisting its emotions into the project and bringing them into its own rational order.

Even before going out of oneself as a subject, taking counsel with one's own self is not as simple as one might think at first. Nor is it as purely formal as Immanuel Kant would have it in his *Groundwork for a Metaphysics of Morals*, when he sets reason off in opposition to inclinations in establishing what is for him the first principle of all moral reasoning, the purely rational sense of duty, or the categorical imperative, as he calls it, bereft of any content having to do with action in the concrete of historical consciousness. Inclinations or emotions are what gives rise to diverse motives for action in human consciousness over which we deliberate in decision-making. The sense of duty or moral obligation we experience in practical reasoning has to do not so much with pure reason, where the absence of self-contradiction is the only criterion for discernment, but with reason trying to assess particular courses of action in relation to the good it intends as rational.

Obligations and prohibitions in ethical consciousness are not purely formal, as Kant seems to suggest in *Groundwork*. They are always relative to some course of action that comes up for consideration in ethical deliberation, which can be viewed as either conducive or necessary for the good we intend and therefore as *obligatory* or as deleterious to that end as our communal good, and therefore as *prohibited*, according to the first principle of ethical reasoning in actual practice, which says that good is to be done and evil is to be avoided.

The fact that a plurality of courses of action comes up for consideration in any historical moment of deliberation in human consciousness is due to the plurality of inclinations and emotions that move us psychologically in one direction or another. Each one of these motives for action represents a good for us, but not all are ordered rationally to the human good as a whole as they occur spontaneously in our experience. It is reason's task in deliberation to find the way in which they can be so ordered by choosing some and repressing others according to the different historical circumstances in which we find ourselves and thereby working toward our final self-determination as selves. In this process reason does not function in abstraction from emotions but, rather, takes counsel with them in deciding what to do and what not to do and shapes them into an ever more rational whole under what we call the *virtue of prudence*.

7.5.2 Subjective emotions, however, are not all we must take counsel with. We must also take counsel with other selves in our ethical consciousness. This follows from the way we come to self-consciousness in the first place, through communion or through mutual recognition with other selves. Prior to going into the question of which other selves one might take counsel with at any moment of one's life, we should understand why we must take counsel in our ethical consciousness with any other self or with some other, whoever that self may be at the moment of taking counsel. One does not take counsel in one's ethical consciousness in isolation or apart from any other consciousness, not any more than one comes to one's self-consciousness in isolation or apart from any other self-consciousness.

As we illustrated earlier, in the fifth chapter of our reflection on the theory of selfhood, one does not come to one's self-consciousness except in the presence of another self-consciousness who is also coming to its own self-consciousness, if not absolutely from an absence of self-consciousness, at least in a new way, in the presence of this other self-consciousness referred to in the first place. Taking counsel with oneself for either of two self-consciousnesses will necessarily involve taking counsel with the other, as we see illustrated at the end of the play *The Miracle Worker* in the case of Helen Keller's coming to self-consciousness in the presence of Annie Sullivan as the other self-consciousness. Far from each one going off to take counsel by herself in that first or new moment of self-consciousness for both of them, they find themselves taking counsel with one another for the first time after a long struggle in which there was anything but taking counsel with one another.

Helen is taking counsel with Annie in the expansion of her budding self-consciousness, not only for naming things in the world but even for discovering and recognizing her parents as other selves for the first time in her self-consciousness, as she had begun doing as an infant before going blind and deaf. Annie is taking counsel with Helen in what she has to do next as a teacher with this student who is finally breaking out in her own self-consciousness. What is happening is the beginning not just of a friendship that has been long in coming and that will go on for a long time in an extraordinary life of communing between the two of them but also of the two taking counsel with one another on what they will do together for the rest of their lives. Not all selves who enter into some communion with other selves will become as closely interlocked with the other as these two did, but all who enter into such communion find themselves taking counsel with and from one another in their practice as human beings, especially when the communing turns into friendship. Friends are always those we want to take counsel with most, either explicitly when we call on them or implicitly when we ask ourselves what they would think if we did one thing or another.

There is another way of seeing the necessity of taking counsel with other selves in ethical consciousness—through the idea of the discrete communal good that selves are in fact seeking as selves—but before we come to that, there is one more point to be made about the necessity of taking counsel with other selves in one's ethical consciousness.

Taking counsel with another self does not necessarily result in both selves making the same decision or taking the same course in life. Taking counsel with another self, especially when it rises to the point of mutual recognition, enables each self to be free in its choice. It may result in both selves joining together in some practice of life, or it may result in each self going its own way, each one following its own inclination or choice as the other follows another, without losing the benefit of taking mutual counsel with one another and without leaving behind the friendship that may have begun in that mutual taking of counsel, as we see happens a lot among old school friends who have their separate lives but are always ready for a reunion with these friends from earlier days. What the mutual taking of counsel does is raise each self to the platform of its own freedom, so to speak, so that each can make its own decision—whether to stay joined with the other or to go its own way in search of other counsel with whom to join. For in every move of an ethical consciousness there is always a search for counsel with another of one kind or other.

7.5.3 If we ask now who are the other selves with whom one must take counsel in ethical consciousness, we cannot say that it is only with friends, though there is more necessity to take counsel with friends than with anyone else, as we shall see when we come to discuss friendship as it relates to the necessity of justice in ethical consciousness. Friends have a much higher idea of justice with friends than with anyone else. That is why it is always worse to steal from friends and clients than from strangers or competitors.

For the question of who is the other with whom I must take counsel, which is similar to the question of who is my neighbor, we must answer that it is with anyone we enter into communion in mutual recognition. Teachers must take counsel with their students as Annie did with Helen and as Socrates did with those who followed him around, taking counsel with him reciprocally. Parents must take counsel with their children, political rulers with their subjects, first-world people with third-world people in the so-called global village, and always reciprocally in all cases.

There is no preset limit to the number or to the kinds of other people one has to take counsel with as a rational being in a lifetime of historical practice. To be sure, one has to begin somewhere, and that will always be with those one enters into communion with more immediately, as the infant with its mother.

The circle of communion and of reciprocally taking counsel begins in one's family, but it does not end there. It opens up into one's neighborhood and into one's school, with other students as well as with teachers, into one's workplace, and beyond all these, into one's nation, where one comes to take counsel with many more different selves who are fellow citizens. The reason why we pay special attention to the circle of the family and the circle of the nation in this constantly expanding ethical consciousness is that each one of them affords an essential sphere of consolidation at different stages of the expanding ethical consciousness, the one familial and the other political, at least as ethical consciousness has been understood in Western civilization.

Even these essential spheres of the family and the nation, however, each with its own ethical exigencies and its own rights, so to speak, in the universal order of historical humanity, are not closed in on themselves absolutely, independently of one another and of a yet broader sphere that would embrace the whole of humanity in which there also has to be some communing and taking counsel among selves in an ever-increasing global practice. Such a universal sphere should not be excluded from ethical consciousness as such, as it was by Hegel and other Euro-centered thinkers in modern history, to the detriment of those we now call the third world as a result of the two-pronged modern imperialism that is capitalism and socialism. If there is any recognition of people as selves in the third world, as there must be when we enter into real communion with them, then there must be a readiness to take counsel with them in our ethical consciousness as well as with anyone else in the first or the second world. Just as the familial sphere of ethical consciousness mediates the political sphere, so also the political sphere of ethical consciousness has to mediate an international or a universal sphere of properly ethical consciousness in which community with other selves has to take place, along with some reciprocal taking counsel that has to be institutionalized. If there is a world spirit in history, it cannot be particularized in any one nation or group of nations at any stage of its incarnation.

7.6 THE GOOD AS OBJECT IN THE TAKING OF COUNSEL

With whom to take counsel, however, is only the first question that arises in ethical consciousness. A second question arises at the same time as this first one: taking counsel about what? This is the question that brings us back to the idea of the good as what we are deliberately striving for in human practice. What is the good we are striving for as human beings, and how do we go about deliberating about steps or means to be taken toward that good? These are the fundamental questions we must raise in right reasoning about what to do and what not to do in our lives—*recta ratio agibilium*—or in what we all call *prudence* as a fundamental disposition in the way we experience self-determination.

7.6.1 There are many goods to be considered in deliberation prior to taking human action, the good of one's own self, the good of other selves, and the good of one's community as a whole. Even when we begin our consideration with the good of our own self, there are many different goods to be considered, corresponding to our different needs and our different appetites. Different goods for us correspond to different needs and different appetites in our lives, as we saw in our first approach to the idea of appetites and of the good. In taking counsel before taking action, therefore, we must take these many goods into consideration, goods of the senses as well as goods of the spirit, the good of health as well as the good of freedom, the long-term goods we are made aware of by science and philosophy, not to mention religion, as well as the goods we are more immediately aware of in our reflective self-consciousness.

Ethical practical reasoning starts from the goods we have conceived in our lives as human beings, goods of the soul as well as goods of the body. We take action in the world, not just to make history for the sake of making history, but as part of a plan we have for our lives. As we mature, the plan becomes more and more explicit in our consciousness, with different stages of the good to be achieved along the way becoming more and more articulated. Even when we are younger, nevertheless, when plans are still implicit or in the process of taking shape, we are thinking in terms of goods we want to achieve, of ways we want to perfect ourselves.

At the core of all this planning in practical reasoning, in our ethical consciousness, there is concern for the good of our selves as a whole, as a human being in some ultimate second perfection that would sum up all other second perfections realized in our selves along the way. Just what that ultimate good will consists in may not always be entirely clear, but some conception of it governs our thinking in prudent practical reasoning along the way, as the first principle from which our reasoning proceeds in making decisions and choosing courses of action in the different activities we engage in as human beings. This is especially so if we think of that ultimate good as the communal good for human beings in communion with one another, but it is already so, even when we think of it as the good of any single human being as a whole. At the root of all our practical reasoning, and encompassing all the different kinds of practical reasoning we engage in, there is this first principle that we must do the good for the human being as a whole—*bonum est faciendum*.

What we reason about before making decisions and choosing courses of action in ethical consciousness is not whether there is such a first principle for practical reasoning. In our ethical consciousness, we begin from such a principle. That is where the sense of obligation starts from in our conscience, before it is brought to bear on particular courses of action that must be taken or that must be avoided. The first principle of ethical/practical reasoning has a negative side—*malum est vitandum*, evil is to be avoided—as well as a positive side—*bonum est faciendum*, good is to be done. With our first principle in mind, with our sense of obligation concerning good and evil, we take counsel concerning options that present themselves, not just about how or whether they will work pragmatically for some particular goal we may have in mind but, more importantly, ethically speaking, whether they will serve the human good as a whole or take away from it, which is to be avoided if we can and as much as we can.

This is reasoning not about the good we are seeking as human beings as a whole but about options that present themselves historically as means toward that good we are envisioning for ourselves. In any rational plan of life there are many goods we envision as intermediate between the final good we envision for ourselves as a whole and any more immediate good we may have in mind in a particular situation, such as something to study here and now in a research project or something to go for that is immediately at hand, such as a pile of cash.

Our conception of intermediate goods, such as succeeding in a career or increasing profitability for a corporation, can be used as principles for practical reasoning in particular spheres of life but not for reasoning about human life as a whole. As conceptions of some good, they can be principles for reasoning taught or learned in a particular sphere of good or another. However, as intermediate such conceptions have to be understood, not as the ultimate good of the whole but only as a means to that good, subject to taking counsel as to whether or how they serve that ultimate good. Success in a particular enterprise, as good as it may seem in itself, is not necessarily in keeping with the principle of the human good as a whole. It is only a part that may vitiate the whole instead of enriching it as such. It has to come under prudent counsel in an exercise of ethical reasoning, as any historical exercise of one's options must.

When we speak of intermediate goods, therefore, we do not mean that they cannot be conceived as principles of practical reasoning in any particular sphere of human life and enterprise. They are so used, and rightly so, for that particular sphere of the good. However, taking counsel in ethical consciousness does not end or begin with reasoning from such intermediate principles or conceptions of the good. It starts in the first or the ultimate universal principle, or the conception of the human good as a whole, even as it descends into particular spheres of human initiative where decisions have to be made. At the same time it leads back to that first principle, as the good we intend ultimately in assessing the relative goodness or insufficiency of any particular sphere of good under consideration. It does not become subordinate or intermediate to these particular considerations of what is good or bad but, rather, assumes them into to its own universal sphere of human life as a whole, which is the first and last good for ethical consciousness as such.

It is not enough to be good businesspeople. We must also become *ethically* good human beings, with prudence and justice in our reasoning.

Intermediate goods, such as the good of a career or the good of an enterprise, even though they may be more universal and more rationally compelling than the more immediate goods that may entice individual selves, are still only partial goods in need of some higher discretion on the part of ethical consciousness as such. No matter how many such intermediate goods or principles one may conceive in one's life plan, each one more universal than the previous one, they are all still in a relation of means to our first and last *good* as ethical human beings. They do not escape the need to be taken into counsel as we ponder what will serve that ultimate good and what will not.

Such intermediate goods cannot be taken as absolutely good for any human life as a whole. As partial, they are relative to other partial goods that have to be taken under consideration in taking prudent counsel about the life of any human being on the whole. If there is any absolute good to be taken into consideration in taking rational counsel, it is this universal good of a self, and nothing less, difficult as it may be to conceive, though it is often spoken of in terms of inalienable human rights, the right to freedom, the right to a life of one's own, the right to commune with others, and so on. Our conception of this universal good for a human being is the light in which we much judge the relative merits of any particular course of action.

Every particular course of action to be taken by a human being, in any particular sphere of goodness and enterprise, is always like a means to an end or to the ultimate good of the human being as such, as conceived in ethical consciousness. Stated this way, the idea of means to a universal end in human action seems very abstract, but the idea becomes very concrete for an ethical consciousness when we come to deliberate and to take counsel about any action we contemplate taking as rational beings. In every decision that we consider as human beings, there is always at stake not just some particular good we are concerned about but also the universal good of our lives as a whole. We do not always invest the whole of ourselves in all of our actions, but when we do, deliberately and conscientiously, we bring into question the good of ourselves as a whole, as we would like to see ourselves in the end, and we commit ourselves to a course of action with the whole of our being in mind.

We should note here in passing what it means to relativize a particular good to a good conceived as the end one intends in an act of practical reasoning. The overarching idea of the good one intends is the one associated with the end, not with the means one has to decide about. This is evident in practical reasoning even in a particular sphere of the good or of human activity, such as doing research or taking care of patients. The good one intends ultimately in such activities is the good of patients, not the good of researchers or the good of caregivers, which is usually associated with the means researchers and caregivers have at their disposal for providing health care. It is not that researchers and caregivers should not have ends of their own, such as finding new means or gaining a reputation for successful interventions in the lives of patients or even just making a good living for themselves with their work. These too are good ends in themselves, along with having the good of patients as their first and last end in health care. But such particular ends or means should not trump the end of health care as such, which is the good of patients, not the means as such one has to decide about in providing health care.

The means themselves may have a certain goodness about them, especially in a highly developed health care delivery system, but that goodness is not the absolute goodness, so to speak, in the light of which health care providers have to reason in caring for patients in the present or future. The absolute goodness in the sphere of health care is the good of patients, and it is only in the light of that good, regardless of how we conceive it, that any particular means can be deemed good, no matter how technically perfected it may be. If a means does not work for the good of a patient nor of patients on the whole, it is not good in the sphere of caring for patients. In reasoning about what to do or what not to do with patients, we cannot proceed rationally without asking whether or how the means we may be contemplating will work for the good of the patient. The practical goodness of means in health care does not consist in how impressive or how powerful they are in themselves but in how or whether they work for the good of the patient, which is the object or the good of health care as a whole, the absolute good to which all means in health care are totally relative.

The good of health care, however, is only a partial good, relative to the universal good of a human being as a whole, about which we have been speaking. If we think of that universal good as the absolute good of ethical life, the first good to be intended and the last to be achieved, we then have to think of all partial spheres of goodness and enterprise as somehow means or as mediating for that absolute, which always remains difficult for us to conceive concretely in our historical circumstances. There are many partial goods we could think of as mediating the universal good of human being as a whole beside the good of health, such as the good of education, the good of labor and production, the good of commerce, the good of justice, and even the good of friendship. We do not have to go into all of them now to see how they, as partial, are in a relation of means to the end we conceive as the good of the human being as a whole, as its happiness, or as its ultimate second perfection.

Every act, every activity we engage in as deliberate human beings, not only goes out to others in the world but also remains in us to shape our ethical identity. The way we act now, ethically, determines the way we will be in our final perfection as human beings. If we act peacefully now, we will be at peace in the end. If we act virtuously now, we will be virtuous in the end. If we act violently or viciously now, we will be violent and vicious in the end. In whatever we do, we are making ourselves the kind of person we will be in the end—good or bad but not indifferent.

For an ethical consciousness, there is no act that is ethically indifferent; that is, that would be neither ethical nor unethical. Taken abstractly, some acts or some activities might be thought of as ethically neutral or indifferent, just as certain procedures in health care might be taken as medically neutral or indifferent from the standpoint of the good of a patient. But when it comes to concrete engagements of ourselves and of other selves in the real world, there can be no ethical neutrality or indifference. When we use a medication on a patient, we are affecting that patient for better or worse. That is why medication should not be prescribed lightly or for no good reason. The same is true for anything else we undertake as human beings. Even the most trivial act we perform can have a profound effect on our character, not to mention the character of other selves around us.

Concretely and practically speaking, in the life of a rational or ethical being such as a self, there is no act that is irrelevant to the total good of that human being, no act with exigencies of its own in a particular sphere of activity that is also not without some ethical merit or demerit. Scientists and experts often think as if their particular spheres of activity were exempt from their ethical consciousness. But in their ethical consciousness as human beings, they cannot remain in that abstraction. When they take action as human beings, even in their particular sphere of expertise, they engage themselves ethically in their action as it relates to their conception of an ultimate good for their lives. Not all activities they engage in may raise ethical questions for them. But some do, at least for some scientists or experts. And when they do, we see evidence not only of an ethical consciousness in them but also of how it is impossible to keep one's scientific or expert consciousness separate from one's ethical consciousness, even in activities that do not seem to raise ethical questions on the face of them. The ethical dimension of our consciousness as it relates to the final good of our being as a whole is at work, at least implicitly if not always explicitly, in all activities that are part of our plan as rational beings for our life as a whole. We shape ourselves ethically in all that we do in the pursuit of a career or our hobbies, in our relations with others, in our family, in our nation, in humanity as a whole. If we are not doing it now in all that we do, we will never have another chance to do it. In fact, if we are not shaping ourselves ethically, chances are we are shaping ourselves unethically, which should be troubling for any ethical consciousness. There is no way of remaining neutral or ethically indifferent in one's action, which would mean being neither ethical nor unethical, in taking counsel about one's life as a whole.

7.6.2 The universal or communal good we have been speaking of thus far as the object in taking counsel or as the first principle in our practical reasoning as ethical consciousnesses has been the good of a self as a whole with a life plan for achieving its second perfection. This is a good that is already difficult to conceive in all of its details and in all the aspects that it must include as the good for a human being in history. One comes to a proper conception of such a good as object only after a long experience in taking counsel. But there is a further dimension of that good as object in ethical reasoning that must not be overlooked and that makes it even more difficult to conceive in all its details and all its aspects, the *communal* good as a whole for selves in *mutual recognition* of one another. The good we seek in our ethical consciousness is never just the good we seek in isolation from others or in competition with other selves. It is a good we seek in communion with others, which as we have already suggested makes it even more difficult to conceive and requires a broader experience still in taking counsel or in prudence.

We have already spoken of this communal good as an idea we start from in our practical reasoning as ethical beings. Taken as an idea or as the first principle in our practical reasoning as ethical beings, it appears distant and remote from where we are in taking counsel about actions or about means to be taken in particular. It is even more universal as an object for us to aim at than the universal good or final end for a single human being as a whole. Yet it is the universal good we must reason from in deliberating about the subordinate goals and the particular aspects of the good we envision for ourselves as we elaborate plans and decisions to be taken in our lives, just as the universal good for a self as a whole has to be the principle of reasoning for assessing any particular means or option that presents itself in the course of a lifetime.

The communal good we have in mind as the principle of our practical reasoning in ethical consciousness is not another one than the final good we are already thinking of as the universal for any self as a whole. These are not two separate goods in contention with one another in our ethical consciousness. They are one and the same final universal good that is at once personal and communal for selves in mutual recognition with one another. As such, they are a single universal good to be aimed at by all human selves in any sort of communion with one another and by each self in particular in its advancement toward its own personal good, which is at once a communal good. Hence the necessity of taking counsel with others in fashioning the conception of the good we are aiming at in the way we conduct ourselves concretely in life.

The universal good we conceive as personal and communal cannot remain abstract and remote in practical reasoning when we come to deliberate over what to do and what not to do in particular. The universal and the particular in practical reasoning cannot be taken as opposite goods, so to speak. If there are particular goods in the life of an ethical self, it is only as they relate to what we speak of as the universal or communal good of the self as both personal and communal. In this relationship, the final universal good is the absolute, and all other goods have to be understood as relative to it. When we deliberate as rational beings, we do not deliberate about the universal good of a human being as such, not any more than a health care provider deliberates about health as such. The health care provider deliberates about what means to take in caring for health, and in doing so looks for a course of action that will lead to the good of health or serve in the achievement of that goal for a patient. That is the way we proceed in every sphere of human activity as rational and ethical agents. We take counsel with the idea we have of our ultimate good as human beings in mind, and we look for courses of action that will lead to that good or serve in the achievement of that goal for ourselves as well as for others.

The universal good of selfhood is the first in what we intend, *primum in intentione*, even though it may be last in execution, *ultimum in executione*. In the interim between intention and execution, there is a mediation that takes place, a dialectic of practical reasoning in which we bring our idea of the intended good to bear on courses of action that are open before us at different junctures of our lives and in which our understanding of what is possible with the means we have at our disposal to work with within ourselves as well as without gives us a more concrete, realistic sense of the ideal of the good we intend for ourselves and for others. We do not fully understand the first principle we start from in practical reasoning, especially as it applies in concrete historical circumstances. In trying to apply it in concrete circumstances, however, we grow in prudence and come to a better appreciation of its importance in keeping our lives on course toward the good of our selves as a whole.

The mediation we are speaking of takes place at many intermediate levels of practical goodness between that of the universal or absolute goodness of the self as a whole and that of particular goods for a self in concrete historical circumstances. Practical reasoning does not always start explicitly from a universal conception of the good of selfhood as a whole. It usually starts from intermediate goods, such as the good of a family, the good of an enterprise, the good of a profession, or the good of a nation, which are conceived as essential aspects of the universal human good or as means to that ultimate goal. We reason more from what we think would be good for our family, for our undertakings in communion with others, or for our country than what we think would be for the good of humanity as whole. This is in keeping with the diverse cultures in which we find ourselves. It is legitimate ethical reasoning inasmuch as these intermediate goods are conceived as essential or necessary aspects of what we take to be the universal good of selfhood as a whole. It is a way of bringing the exigencies of the universal communal good down to the level of particulars in decision-making, as it raises every decision taken in any self-consciousness to a level of ethical responsibility for better or worse.

The conscientious self thus reasons from several culturally diverse conceptions of the ethical good within the overall universal conception of the ethical good as such. There are times in a self's life when some of these conceptions may seem to come into conflict with other conceptions of the ethical good or with the universal conception of that good as a whole, thereby provoking a crisis of conscience for the self. If two goods deemed to be ethical are thought to be in conflict with one another, how can the rational being choose either one without violating the other? Or, to state the crisis even more acutely, if the pursuit of an intermediate good appears to be in conflict with the pursuit of the ethical good of selfhood as a whole, how can one justify continuing to pursue a specific intermediate good if it is in violation of the ethical good as a whole and no longer a means to that end? There are ways of mediating such cases of conscience in practical reasoning, but for an ethical consciousness it is important to keep in mind that some means may be justified ethically or rationally, and some may be simply unjustifiable in the light of the ethical good as a whole. Unless one is willing to accept this possibility that some courses of action may be simply unjustifiable or evil, one cannot honestly raise the ethical question about any action without obfuscating the ethical issue of right or wrong altogether.

7.7 THE NECESSITY OF CHOOSING PRUDENTLY IN ETHICAL CONSCIOUSNESS

In reflection on the dynamic of our rational consciousness, we find our selves driven by many appetites or inclinations toward many different goods rising from our nature and from the historical circumstances in which we find ourselves, in communion with other selves. Our freedom comes out of this plurality of inclinations or motions as they are projected in our consciousness as motives for future action. It is a freedom to choose which one or which set of these motives we will follow in the pursuit of our good as selves and which one or which set we will decide against in choosing our course of action in life. Each one of these inclinations and motives represents a certain determinism toward some good in our consciousness. They emerge in our consciousness unsolicited, and each one, if left to itself, unrelated to other inclinations and motives in one and the same consciousness, could and would determine as the sole motive the future action of the self. We see this happen with people who are driven or fixated by a single idea, unable to pause and reflect on what drives them because they have no alternative motivation to deliberate about. They do not experience themselves as determined. They see themselves as free, but this is the freedom of nonrational animals who are in fact determined to one thing, to one course of action that will favor their survival in the struggle with other animals or different kinds of animals, each with its own instinctive way of action.

When we say that the rational animal or the rational self is free or not determined to one thing or to one course of action, we presuppose that there is in its consciousness a plurality and a diversity of motives for action for it to choose from in its self-determination after due deliberation on the diverse courses of action opened before it. This plurality and this diversity of options is not limited to those that rise from nature or from our past. It also includes ideas as motives for action that come from the creative imagination of the rational animal and from reason itself as prospective of greater and higher goods to be achieved in civilizing the world. This is all the more reason for saying that the rational animal or the self is not determined to one thing when we think of the rich diversity of civilizations that have been brought forth in human history.

We must recognize, however, that the rational self-consciousness does not remain entirely undetermined in the course of a lifetime, as it may find itself in its initial sense of freedom. It comes to deliberation in its consciousness as one that must choose to act one way or another. It takes counsel with itself and with other selves recognized as selves about the good at stake in different moments of choice that present themselves existentially as well as historically. In such moments, however, it cannot remain indeterminate. It must choose and come to its own self-determination, and therein lies the question of *prudence* or of what that determination should be in relation to the total good of selfhood as a whole or to the communal good we have spoken of as the first principle in practical reasoning.

As given initially, or as it first appears in the moment of deliberation for a self-consciousness, this total good of the self is an empty form, a mere formality that must exercise itself and give itself body in one or another of the motions that are agitating for actualization in the self's consciousness. In other words, freedom is realized in the self only by going out of itself into some determination that it must adopt as its own. Each one of the determinate motions in its consciousness represents some good for the self, but not all of them can be adopted at one and the same time, and there may be some that should not be adopted at all, as unjustifiable in the light of the good we are pursuing as rational selves. Proper self-determination for a self in communion with other selves thus comes about, not in just a single act that takes place once and for all, but in a series of acts that become habitual for a self in the way it comes to its own self-determination through particular choices of one determination or another or in the way it shapes its character as an ethical consciousness. Reasoning and taking counsel have everything to do with this process of self-determination and shaping of one's character. They come forth in every moment of deliberation and they develop as an excellence in what we take to be proper activities of the ethical self as such or as the virtue of right reasoning in taking human action—*recta ratio agibilium*—which is called *prudence.*

The process of practical reasoning in a deliberative ethical consciousness we have been reflecting on is one that finds its perfection through prudence, which from this point of view could be termed the proper second perfection of the self as self or as rational agent. The self who has attained prudence in every respect of human endeavor could be called one who performs most perfectly as a human being and who finds most satisfaction in that performance, especially when he or she is acknowledged as such by other selves, much as the perfect flute player finds satisfaction in his or her performance and in the applause received from the audience.

However, who can we say is perfectly prudent in this life or in the communities we find ourselves? This is a much more difficult question to answer than one about who is the perfect flute player. There are varying degrees of prudence, just as there are varying degrees of excellence in flute playing and those who have not attained a relatively high degree of prudence are not in any position to judge who is more prudent than others. Prudence or right reasoning about what is to be done in human initiative is not given by human nature or even by the capacity to reason and to deliberate that discloses itself in our self-consciousness. As a *virtue in our reason*, it has to be learned or acquired through repeated acts and through a long experience of hit or miss in attaining our ends as human beings. We have to put it into practice in order to learn it and have it as something we can count on in our deliberations.

As selves, we start off with a plurality and a diversity of impulses and inclinations that occupy our consciousness, so to speak, and leave us torn asunder by many attractions pulling in different directions. With reason and the capacity to deliberate, we are able to bring this stirring of appetites to pause for a moment or to free ourselves momentarily from the particular determinisms that they represent so that we may be able to choose which ones to actualize or which ones to cut off or decide against rationally; that is, in the light of the universal good we will for the self as a whole. As the rational appetite intervenes in the play of the sense appetites through deliberate choice, the will is not without some representation of the good for selves in communion with one another, but the representation at first is only "typical," as Aristotle puts it, without the vividness of details that particular sense appetites bring to the forum of consciousness. Even as it neutralizes all or most of the appetites in the moment of deliberation, the will remains undetermined in its universal scope and looks for ways of determining itself among determinisms given at different particular moments. In doing so, it tries to relate the various courses of action that open up before it in consciousness to the good it envisions for the self as a whole so that it can choose the one that will be conducive to that good as one seeking to provide for that good. At first it does this tentatively in various realms of human activity, but over time and with experience in this kind of decision-making, it acquires or grows in the *virtue of prudence*. It comes to a better understanding of what the good is that we seek as rational beings in communion with others and a better appreciation of the ways that lead to that good or of ways that may turn us away from that good.

We do not learn prudence in an instant by reflecting on some abstract sense of duty or on what Kant calls *categorical imperatives* in which no formal contradiction is to be found. We learn about obligations in ethical consciousness as we learn what actions are deemed necessary for the communal good of selves, as we see in the obligation to speak the truth for the good of a community, to use one of Kant's own examples of a categorical imperative. If we take prudence as the first moral virtue in practical reasoning, we see that all obligations and all so-called moral imperatives are hypothetical in the sense that they presuppose that we will the good for which the obligatory actions, such as truth telling, are deemed necessary according to prudence as relating means to ends. Prudence as the *habit of right reasoning* concerning what is to be done or not done is not only at the head of all the moral virtues, it is also at the heart of all the other virtues, for there is no way of being truly just, truly courageous, or truly temperate without being prudent in all these regards. We shall see how this comes about when we reflect on those virtues as well, but for the moment it is important to understand what precisely prudence brings to human action as ethical.

Prudence brings measure to what we do as it relates to our final good as selves so that we do not exceed the mean by doing either too little or too much. It brings balance and poise to the self so that it is ready to take action whenever and wherever it is called for. It sets the mean not just for the other virtues but also for practical reasoning itself, so that it does not fall short as merely cautious or rush too quickly ahead as overly daring. It functions on two levels: first, on the *pragmatic level* of consequences that will follow from one choice or another, and second, on the *ethical level* of how different choices and their consequences will affect the good of self-actualization for selves, both for oneself and for other selves. In other words, it is concerned with what works and what does not work for whatever particular end we have in mind in any moment of deliberation, and at the same time it is concerned with how that particular end or consequence of action will affect the self-actualization of the self as such, whether in itself or in its relation to other selves.

As a *disposition of practical reason* it functions, consistently, constantly, and often creatively in every moment of true deliberation on these two levels of consideration, the *pragmatic* and the *ethical*, keeping both levels always in suspense and in balance with one another. Such a disposition is not given by nature, as the power itself of reasoning and of deliberating is given to the self. Nor is it a disposition that comes in an instant as one begins to act more or less rationally. It comes only gradually through repeated acts in which the self pauses to deliberate and then to take action in view of its final end as well as in view of particular ends that enter into its plan of life. It is learned, or it becomes a *habit* of the mind, on both levels of practice, the pragmatic and the ethical, not so much by indoctrination, though some of that goes on for every self in its communion with other selves, as by one's own exercise of practical reasoning as an ethical self. In this regard, it should be seen as a call to self-actualization in the fullest sense.

Prudence cannot be taught directly to anyone who does not have it already, as Socrates said of any virtue. Nor can it be imposed exteriorly as if by law or an imperative from on high or outside of self-consciousness. Prudence has to be learned interiorly through different stages of deliberation where one elaborates one's conception of the good for one's self as such and for other selves as well in mutual recognition, at the same time as one elaborates and as other selves also elaborate, different particular conceptions of the good—such as the good of health, the good of learning, the good of character, the good of culture—that selves want to include as parts of the good of selfhood or as intermediate ends to the final end of total self-actualization in a community of selves.

Prudence takes many different shapes, especially at the pragmatic level, where it has a lot to learn about how things work in the world of nature and of mutual interaction among selves in society. At this level there is a lot that can be taught in science and in politics or in a culture as a whole. But this is in keeping with the rational process as *taking counsel* with oneself and with one's own nature as well as with other selves in mutual recognition. There is a lot to be learned from others as the habit of prudence develops in oneself within a culture of like-minded selves. But all this learning takes place for a reason that is fundamentally oriented to a good that is proper to oneself as a self-consciousness communing with other selves as to its proper end as a self from which it begins to reason as from its principle.

The actualization of prudence as a disposition in one's exercise of true deliberation concerning both ends and means in one's life plan is one whereby the self begins or continues to determine itself freely and willfully as a self. It is also an excellence of the rational animal as such, a *virtue of reason*, wherein the self already finds some satisfaction and some happiness in its own self-determination. We see this among the elders of different communities who are viewed as prudent to the highest degree of integration and to be emulated in striving for a prudence that is at once principle and end for an ethical consciousness.

We could ask whether such exemplary prudent selves in a community have actually attained their final satisfaction or happiness as selves or whether there is not some higher end for perfect happiness to be attained by selves, one that cannot be properly conceived by reason as such but that would take us beyond the level of ethical discourse that takes the communal good of history as its principle or, as Aristotle says, in opposition to Plato's idea of the separate Good, the good that is achievable by man. We do not deny or even question that there may be some higher good for a self, or for the entire community of selves in history, to be seeking.

But before raising such a question for ethical consciousness, there is a lot more to be reflected on in ethical consciousness as historical and as still caught up in the struggle—not just for survival and some commodious form of living but also for recognition as selves in diverse forms of communion or culture.

8

The Necessity of Justice and Friendship in the Will as Rational Appetite for a Communal Good

As the virtue of *right reasoning*, prudence is the first of the virtues required in ethical consciousness as setting parameters for human action in pursuit of the good, but it is only the first of several virtues required for the formation of a truly ethical character. As the virtue in reason itself, or as right reasoning concerning what is to be done in human action, prudence is a general virtue that has to inform all the appetites that drive human action, both rational and sensual. The complexion of these appetites as given by nature in the human subject is not determined to one thing as it is for nonrational animals in their struggle for survival. With reason, in the moment of deliberation, that complexion gives rise to the conception of a plurality and diversity of goods for the human subject to strive for and of ideas for action as the means for achieving those goods in the presence of which the rational animal is free to choose which course to follow or which line of the good to pursue at any moment of its existence.

Right reasoning in the light of the communal good of the self as a whole is not a matter of instinct given by nature. It has to be learned and become habitual as a way of determining ourselves in our pursuit of that good. Prudence as such is a form of enterprise in the pursuit of the human good as it relates to our appetites, whether rational or sensual, any one of which is a call to action in pursuit of some particular good at the same time as to the universal good of the self as a whole in communion with other selves.

In deliberation, the free rational agent is called in *conscience* to choose from several or more particular courses of action in the light of a more universal good for oneself as a whole and for other selves as well. It is possible to choose one course of action or to follow one particular appetite, as if it were the be-all and end-all of one's life, but that is not in accordance with right reasoning. Right reasoning starts rather from a universal perspective on the good for selves, which includes many particular goods, not all of which are compatible with one another or with the universal perspective on the good. In right reasoning, the deliberate conscientious agent seeks out the particular goods or the ways and means that will be conducive to the universal and communal good of selves and chooses those he is prepared to undertake, sometimes out of a sense of duty because they are perceived as necessary to maintain or to enhance the good life of one's community.

Always in our ethical consciousness we are choosing not just one particular good or another but also how that particular good is to be part of the communal good we are committed to in our rational self-consciousness. In prudence, there is not only comparative reasoning among particular goods relative to one another but also reasoning concerning particular goods with reference to the communal good that takes priority in ethical reasoning as such. It is by reason of this necessary reference to the communal good as principle that prudence is found as a general virtue in reason itself shaping all choices of particular goods, making them right for that communal good as well as for the particular good of individuals. To be sure, there is also a particular side of prudence, when it is in the service of determining ways and means for achieving the particular good of some undertaking, such as profit in a business enterprise or results in a scientific experiment, but even as particular or as more utilitarian, this particular prudence comes under the rule of prudence as a general virtue by reason of its relation to the communal good and its priority with regard to any particular goods, especially those pertaining to the sense appetites. In right reasoning, particular goods are viewed as part of or as ordered to the overarching communal good of selves.

What we find in human consciousness, therefore, is not just a reason in need of rectification for it to become consistent in the pursuit of the communal good of selves as a whole but also appetites that also need rectification, in line with the universal good of selves, appetites with some virtue of their own to make them consistent with one another in the pursuit of the universal good as a whole for a self-consciousness in communion with other selves. This need for rectification or for virtue is especially true of the sense appetites, which seem to pull the self in such divergent directions from one another, but it is also true of the rational appetite or the will, which as free is supposed to be in control of the sense appetites and not be controlled by them, as unfree or as determined by them.

In fact, it should be said at this point in our reflection that prudence itself does not develop as a habit of reason in self-consciousness without some simultaneous development of conscience and other habits in the appetites themselves to orient them toward the better rather than toward the worse. We saw earlier how reason has to take counsel with the appetites found in our self-consciousness, with our emotions and our will, in prudent deliberation leading up to an exercise of free choice. What we take counsel about is the good as it relates to the appetites as given in our consciousness at one moment of our existence or another and about ways and means for actualizing some higher good for ourselves. We conceive of different goods or different kinds of good in accordance with the different appetites stirring within us. That goes for goods of the body as well as goods of the spirit. In taking counsel, rational ethical consciousness is looking for a mean, or means, among the various appetites that will keep them in balance within themselves and with one another with regard to the universal good of the self as a whole. Such a balance is not given by nature. It must come from reason taking hold amid the natural turmoil of the appetites in a rational self-consciousness.

If, however, reason finds only turmoil among the appetites or exaggerations of one kind or another, either by way of excess or by way of deficiency, it will have no way of determining the good relative to the different appetites or of establishing a mean for achieving that good for the self or for a community of selves. Human nature does give some indications for determining the physical good for a human being such as health, for example, and for establishing means to maintain that good but not for determining the human good as a whole on the cultural or the historical level as a whole or for establishing a mean, or proper means, in our action for the spiritual good of selfhood. One's natural temperament and nurturing may also bring certain predispositions toward some aspects of the good or of virtue within oneself, but it is for reason to recognize these as such. It is also for reason to develop further dispositions in one's character to keep one on a course of fulfillment for the good of the self as such, if not a satisfaction of all its human appetites, rational as well as sensitive.

Perfect happiness or the lasting satisfaction of our human desires, which cannot be indiscriminate, is not to be expected for the self in its historical existence, but it is an ideal we strive for as selves by fine tuning our emotions in keeping with an order consistent with the universal good of selves in communion with one another, whether in a family, a nation, or humanity as a whole. The development of moral virtues in our appetites comes as a result of this fine tuning that takes place historically in different communities and in different cultures as well as in different individual selves. When it takes place successfully, it makes for peace and satisfaction in a community of selves, but it does not take place without a struggle with competing appetites that must be brought into line with the universal good of selves in communion with one another. Virtue, or some refinement, is a necessity for the appetites as well as for reason in ethical consciousness. And it is to this necessity of virtue for the appetites that we must now turn in our reflection on the practice of ethical selfhood.

We have distinguished between two levels of appetite in the historical self: that of the sense appetites and that of the rational appetite, or the will. Each level follows from a distinct level of consciousness, that of sense consciousness in which there is only partial self-reflection, and that of intellectual consciousness in which there is what we have called total reflection in actual reasoning, whether in theory or in practice or in the exercise of one's intelligence and of one's self-determination in willing. The question of virtue for the appetites, therefore, breaks down into two parts: that which pertains to virtue in the sense appetites and that which pertains to virtue in the rational appetite, or for the will. In our reflection here we shall go first to the latter part of the question, having to do with the virtues that pertain to the rational appetite, before going to the first part of this question, having to do with the sense appetites, in keeping with the total reflection we can exercise in our act of willing and in the act of shaping our will into certain dispositions deemed necessary for discerning the communal good of the self as a whole and for finding the mean in our action, external as well as internal, that will serve that good.

8.1 JUSTICE AND FRIENDSHIP AS GENERAL DISPOSITIONS OF WILLING IN A COMMUNITY

How, then, are we to conceive of the communal good as it relates to the rational appetite in self-consciousness, and what dispositions does attainment of that good require in that appetite? The question arises for us in our ethical consciousness from the way we conceive ourselves, not abstractly as if in absolute isolation from one another with only our individual self-interest at heart but concretely as selves already in communion with one another through *mutual* and reciprocal *recognition* of each one having personal as well as communal interests.

If we think only of our sense appetites in this relationship with other selves, we are drawn back into subjective dispositions that are different for each individual as emotions in search of their own peculiar fulfillment in accordance with their own particular determinism. These subjective appetites or emotions, as we shall see, have to be brought under the sway of reason through the moral virtues of courage and temperance. But if we understand the will as rational appetite, we are drawn forward into a more universal conception of the good, capable not only of relating the good of particular emotions to the more universal good of the self as a whole but also of joining the personal good of different individuals to the more universal aspect of these personal goods as they relate to one another and to the communal good itself as a whole.

Reflection on this level of subjectivity in the rational appetite of the self in communion with other selves brings us to a level of objectivity with regard to the good that we cannot imagine on the level of the sense consciousness or of the sense appetites. It brings us to a level that takes priority in ethical reasoning as more necessary and more universal than all other considerations having to do with particular subjective dispositions for individual selves. To speak of *necessary* dispositions in the rational appetite of selves in communion with one another is to speak of general dispositions required even for determining the proper dispositions of the sense appetites such as courage and temperance, just as prudence is a general disposition in practical reason itself required for determining the proper dispositions of all human appetites, natural or sensible as well as rational.

We distinguish two such general dispositions of the will or of the rational appetite to go to in any existing community we take to be ethical. One we name *justice*, and the other we name *friendship*. Both we take to be general virtues in that both relate the rational appetite directly to the communal good, the conception of which is the principle for all practical reasoning in ethical consciousness, as shown above. What distinguishes them from one another is the different aspects of that communal good to which they relate, one external and one internal.

Justice has to do with excellence or rectitude in external action and interaction among selves and in the way things are disposed for the personal good of selves in a community. It implies an idea of rights recognized for each individual in a social structure or in a right ordering of things and of interaction among selves toward the communal good.

Friendship has to do with the free exercise of communion in self-determination among selves that begins once a modicum of justice has been established in a community and some human rights of other selves have been recognized. It comes into play internally among selves only once some equality of human right has been recognized. Friendship can also promote greater justice in human relations, as we shall see, as well as make injustice in external relations appear even worse than where there is hostility or competition for more than what is right for oneself and no friendship.

We shall examine each one of these general dispositions as required for the communal good of selves in typical historical societies one after the other before showing how they are in dialectical relation with one another in constituting the historical communal good of selves in different kinds of human community. We shall show also how in each one there is a dialectic at work analogous to the dialectic of mutual recognition that gives rise to the need for these general dispositions in any sort of communal life.

8.2 GENERAL JUSTICE AND INJUSTICE

Consciousness of the need for justice in human relations begins in the moment or moments of mutual recognition, when we first come to consciousness of ourselves and other selves at one and the same time, moments of an emerging sense of responsibility as well as self-consciousness. These are moments in the struggle for mutual recognition among rational animals, and they are moments in which our rational appetite opens up to the good of another as well as to one's own and moments in which we begin to communicate with one another in our striving for the good life as human beings. In one sense they are already the beginning of that good life in communion with others, but they are only first steps taken in that life of a *spirit* that still has to struggle and labor in the world to actualize itself more fully. Only a rational appetite, or the will, can open up to the good as it relates to another and not just to oneself to a universal or communal good, as we have been saying, but it does so without losing sight of its own good. In *mutual recognition*, the good of each self comes into view as communal.

It comes into view not only as something given for our self-consciousness but also as an ideal to be realized in history through human action and labor to create the social conditions for such an ideal to flourish. In the initial moments of mutual recognition we see ourselves not only as relating to one another in our struggle and our efforts but also as independent individuals taking initiatives to better ourselves and our conditions of life. At the same time, we recognize one another as having rights and creating rights in relation to one another in working toward a higher communal good: the right to respect as self-conscious rational beings, the right to ownership of things, the right to take action for oneself as well as for others, the right to education, the right to health care, and all sorts of other human rights that can emerge in the historical progression of a communal consciousness. It is the idea of such human rights that brings us to the idea of a need for justice as a general disposition in the rational appetite or in the will of selves struggling in the world in communion with one another. Without such a disposition or without a will for justice in the world, there can be no realization of any communal good for selves in history or in any community.

We should note, however, that this will to do justice does not arise out of individual selves taken in isolation from one another, each acting with only its self-interest at heart, in competition with other individuals also acting only with their own self-interest at heart, as this has been represented in modern social contract theory or in John Rawls's more contemporary theory of justice.[1] The general disposition of the will as rational appetite comes to the fore, not in the context of hostility or of sheer competition in taking advantage of one another. Rather, it comes in a context of mutual recognition of each other in a family or an association. It has more to do with cooperation with one another in the management of things and of what is given in our experience for the advantage of the communities as a whole, even when that advantage of the communal whole allows for relative advantages and disadvantages among the members of a community as long as the disparity does not become so great as to marginalize the disadvantaged from the community to which they should belong by right. *General justice* as a disposition of the rational appetites in communities has more to do with creating social structures for the benefit of all individuals recognized as selves than just resolving conflicts of interest when they arise in communities. Conflicts do arise in communities where there are always individuals prone to claim more than what is their due or their right, and justice has to step in to adjudicate where the proper order or the proper mean lies in the use of things for the communal good rather than just for the good of one individual at the expense of and to the exclusion or marginalization of others. But in doing so it is only going by the general conception of the social order that is thought of as prevailing and beneficial for all in a community.

Aristotle spoke of universal or general justice as *legal justice*. But that was with the understanding of law as a rational enactment in society, an external social structure supposedly in view of the communal good. We shall see more on that when we come to speak of the necessity for law in moderating the interactions among the members of a community. Here, however, we should note that in the correlation between justice and law, it is not law that dictates justice but, rather, justice as a general disposition or as a virtue in the rational appetites of selves recognizing one another's rights that dictates the law. If there were no general disposition of justice in a society toward all its members there would be no law in the proper sense of the term because the rule of law itself is a social structure instituted to serve the good of communion among selves, a rule that should not be preempted for the excessive benefit of any individual or of any class of individuals at the expense of others in the community.

Here we should speak of *general justice* as social rather than just as legal in the sense that justice requires a social order and social institutions in the rational and cooperative endeavors of the members of a community. It is the rational ordering

1 John Rawls, *A Theory of Justice* (Cambridge, Mass.: The Belknap Press of Harvard University Press, 1971).

that follows from right reasoning in a historically enterprising community aiming at higher communal goods or benefits. As such it can take many different cultural forms, depending on the different conceptions of the external cooperative good that bring individuals together, employees and employers, in their endeavors for a good that is both communal and personal. We do not have to elaborate on the many forms that social cooperation has taken in the past or that it could take in the future through reasoning from particular goods we envision as well as right reasoning from the communal good. We should note, however, that our own conception of the external social good and of the ways we see open before us to achieve such a good has been formed within a particular culture that does not exhaust all rational possibilities for conceiving such a good. History and our day-to-day experience in the global village, so to speak, put us in contact with diverse cultures and diverse ways of conceiving the communal good and ways to cooperate in realizing it, all of them more or less rational, like our own, all of them with some general disposition of justice that binds them together in their cooperation for their social and communal good.

If we think of cultures as different kinds of community taking initiative in history in view of some communal good, we have to think of them as having their own form of right reasoning in practice and their own form of social justice regarding selves in their community. General conceptions of justice can vary from community to community, but insofar as they stem from mutual recognition and mutual regard among selves, they must extend to all selves equally in the communal good of the whole. This would be true of any private group or club organized for the pursuit of a particular good, such as a business enterprise or an association for the pursuit of some leisurely activity like a chess club or a golf club. There has to be some social justice for all such cooperative endeavors. But this is especially true for the kinds of social endeavors we take to be fundamental or essential for the pursuit of happiness or of the communal good in the human community as a whole, the endeavor of the family, the endeavor of the nation, and the endeavor of a global economy, which is little more than the result of competition among multinational corporations still far removed from anything like a community with a sense of justice and friendship for all, including employees as well as employers.[2]

Each one of these essential endeavors has a culture of its own, even though they might be subordinate to one another, and right reasoning for each one requires an order of justice that regards every self or that gives every self its due from the least to the highest. In the family, it means giving due regard to children as well as to the spouses on a basis of some rational equality and autonomy, where dialogue—taking counsel with one another—is the rule and not abuse of one kind or another. If too much inequality or domination on one side or the other is allowed, there is injustice and deviation from the communal good. The same would be true of a clan or a tribal society. The communal good of a familial society is never the exclusive

2 For a brief and authoritative account of how the current consolidation of large multinational corporations has taken place and continues to dominate global economics at the expense of workers and society at large, see sociologist Robert Reich, *The Common Good* (New York: Alfred A. Knopf, 2018).

good of its head or of any one of its parts. It consists in a rational organization that is conducive to communion among all the members.

Similarly, in the nation there has to be a rational organization of historical practices that shuns excessive inequality or injustice in what is supposed to be a community. There are many sorts of coordinated endeavors that go to make up the communal good of the national whole. These endeavors interlock with one another, each having a particular good of its own in view, often in competition with other particular endeavors seeking a greater share of the common good or of the wealth of a nation. Right reasoning and the general disposition of justice in a national community may allow for certain inequalities in the allotment of functions and of wealth that comes from different individuals, different families or tribes, different kinds of workers in the national endeavor to improve the national good, as long as this allows for everyone in the national community to gain a decent or a proportionate minimum share of respect and benefit for that community. When, however, the inequalities in the attainment of these external goods, whether of respect or of wealth, become so great and excessive as they have become in many modern nations, especially in the third world, we fall into systemic marginalization and injustice.

This is evident, upon reflection, even when we think of the excessive inequality between the rich and the poor in what we think of as the more advanced nations in creating wealth and power. In this struggle for recognition and well-being, inequality between the rich and the poor, to put it in its simplest terms, has grown with every step along the way. This inequality continues to grow in what has been recognized as a downward spiral into poverty for the many, even as the few who have gotten the upper hand get richer and richer, while the rest are left to struggle more and more not to fall back into poverty and not to become increasingly marginalized, left without any regard as citizens and selves and without the necessities required for surviving alongside an economic structure of excessive wealth and power. For right reasoning in terms of working for the communal good of a nation, this can only be viewed as injustice, structural and social injustice, in need of rectification; that is, in need of bringing the extremes closer together in what we think of as a community and as what the Greeks thought of as a *politeia*, under the leadership of those who exercise a political function in the nation in or out of the government.

Our aim here is not to explore how such rectification is to take place in our modern nation. That should normally be the burden of political debates in times of elections, which Aristotle spoke of as times of revolution in a political community. Our aim, rather, is simply to point out the situation of systemic or general injustice in which advanced nations find themselves when they allow such excessive inequalities, not just with regard to impoverishment of the many but also with regard to opportunities for self-betterment through the exercise of one's own initiative or proper activity. This is the injustice that undermined the ancient Roman Empire, and it is undermining the postmodern multinational monolithic empires built to subvert local communities and economies around the globe in developed as well as underdeveloped countries. True progress in human history can only take place through the improvement of justice in economies where many different individuals and groups come together in mutual recognition, to work toward a communal good defined by the communities and not just by those who only benefit from the communal good and offer nothing back in justice to the employees as well as to the community that makes their profit possible.

The modern general injustice we speak of is found not only within different advanced nations but also among the nations themselves, which also fall into two extreme groupings: those that are extremely rich and those that are not only extremely poor but also extremely indebted to the rich nations or to the multinational financial institutions that operate out of those supposedly rich nations. The situation of inequality and injustice is even more flagrant among the nations than it is within particular nations, rich and poor, where we find a widening gap of inequality between the few nations that are enriching themselves and the many who are falling deeper into poverty, in a race of economic takeovers that is sweeping across all national boundaries, in a neo-colonial global economy in the hands of multinational corporations competing with one another, not only for market share but also for the least expensive raw materials and the lowest wages possible in dehumanizing sweatshops.

In this existing global economy there is a lot of practical reasoning going on for profit taking on an ever-wider scale but with little or no concern for the communal good of the nations being exploited, which includes the good of people as well as the good of natural resources being drained. In other words, there is little or no right reasoning in view of the communal good of anyone, whether it be of families, workers, local communities, or nations. Even governments, for the most part, that should have the communal good of their people upper most in mind end up playing this game of economic domination to get ahead with these multinational corporations or just to stay in power, at their service, with no concern for demanding the just wages, the just remunerations, the just working conditions that their people have a right to as participants in what should be a communal good for selves rather than just a slave-holding in favelas. Instead of the justice, or at least the semblance of some equality and mutual regard among persons or among parties in the struggle for recognition, one finds only injustice, a lack of respect for the other as a self, a contempt for the communal spirit that animates any community, and a willingness to run roughshod over economic initiatives taken by local communities.

There is talk of an "international community" coming into being as a result of globalization in a market system coordinated by large multinational corporations, but we have to wonder whether what has come about as a result of this globalization so far is anything like a community. To be sure, people and peoples from all around the globe have been drawn into the net of the economic system created by the multinational corporations, aided and abetted by the World Trade Association and the International Monetary Fund, created by these same corporations to solidify their hold on nations in all parts of the globe. People associated with these large corporations in the centers of power often assume that the society in which they find themselves is one that is basically just, but that is a justice only for the rich and for those who stand to benefit directly by their association with the centers of power and wealth in the world. It is not justice for the whole world or for the vast majority of those who are marginalized around the world. In fact, for the vast majority and for a growing number of people around the world there is more injustice rather than justice and, consequently, a lack of community that trickles down and undermines local communities and local systems of justice as well as their local economies for the greater profitability of the multinational corporations.

What does exist on an international level at the present time, if we prescind from institutions such as the United Nations and the International Court at The Hague or from the organizations of humanitarian aid for victims of natural disasters, is a system of economic competition among powerful corporate agents reaching out across borders in pursuit of ever greater profitability for the corporations, with little or no concern for the communal good of the people or the peoples they are roping into their system. What we are left with as a result of this aggressive global reaching out so far has been a massive dislocation of human communities across the world that are left in a state of injustice without the means to advance in any sort of good life for themselves, marginalized and dehumanized by the very system that has overtaken them and their means of livelihood.

Economic analysis can explain how this has happened rationally, but it can do so only for the benefit of those who are in control of the system. It cannot do so for the benefit of those who are marginalized by the system. It can only explain that they are marginalized and why they have been marginalized as they are by the system. It cannot conceive, let alone explain, the gross injustice of the current global economy as it affects people in their selfhood. Only right reasoning in the light of a communal good yet to be achieved can do that. There is a lot of such reasoning that takes place in international aid organizations as well as in institutions such as the United Nations and the International Court, even among economists and some corporate executives who show some humanitarian concerns. But the reasoning is not always seen as rigorous enough to take precedence over the prevailing practical economic reasoning in view of ever greater profitability for corporations, as the sense of general justice for an international community would require.

What right reasoning in view of a communal good means is setting standards in a framework of active cooperation that will allow and require a greater equality, a greater recognition of those who remain marginalized, and a greater opportunity to reap the benefits of their participation in the communal endeavor. As we saw earlier, right reasoning in view of realizing a communal good means achieving a balance among goods that is neither too much nor too little, finding a mean between the two extremes of either excess or deficiency. For individuals in a community, this means striking a proper balance in the exercise of one's emotions, finding the mean between excess and deficiency for the different emotions that move an individual to action. For a community as a whole this means striking a proper balance in the way different individuals contribute to the communal good and finding a mean between excess and deficiency in the way that the external social good is allocated among selves, including the good or the right of recognition as well as the good or the right of ownership for all participants in the community.

On the part of individuals coping with their emotions, the means has to be a subjective one, depending on the state of one's emotions, as we shall see when discussing the moral virtues of courage and temperance. In thinking of *justice*, however, whether as general or as particular, we have to say that the mean has to be more objective, more on the side of things and on the side of profit for the other as other, rather than just on the side of what moves each individual subject in himself or herself. In fact, right reasoning cannot arrive at the right subjective mean for different individuals in a community without due consideration for the *objective mean* of *general justice* for the community as a whole, as we shall see when we discuss the other moral virtues. But before we come to that, we must understand how the objective mean of justice is something in things and in how they are related or due to selves as other than one another in a community.

In the case of some particular justice in a community, the objectivity of the mean is easy to recognize. When someone borrows or purchases something from someone else, a certain imbalance or inequality results in the way things relate to the borrower or the buyer on one side and to the lender and the seller on the other. Justice is done or balance and equality are restored, however, when the borrower returns the object in good condition to the lender or when the buyer pays the just price for the object purchased. Justice is restored no matter what the subjective dispositions are of the borrower or of the buyer toward the other to whom something is owed.

In the case of general justice, however, the objectivity of the rational mean is not as easy to determine or to restore if it is missing. It depends on how social relations are conceived among individuals and on the social structure that has taken hold in a community or how the means of production are organized for the good of the community. The rational mean of justice, or the way of organizing exchange relations among selves in a community, can vary greatly according to different cultures or different ways of conceiving the communal good. What general or social justice requires in all of them is a certain respect and regard for the other on the part of all and for the right of everyone to a fair share of the communal good, which implies a certain basic equality of standing for all in the community. When there is excessive inequality between the rich and poor or between the different factions or classes in a society or a corporation, we have to say there is no justice worthy of a community.

That is why we have to say there is no international community as such because of the excessive inequality wrought by multinational corporations in the global economy among rich and poor nations and among the rich and the poor within the diverse nations. If there is a system of justice in the corporate global economy, it is a system for the rich only and not for the many who don't just happen to be poor anymore but who are being kept poor, at a distance from the counsels of power, deprived of any due regard as selves and without a chance of making their voice heard or of benefiting adequately from their labor. It is a system of reasoning that takes counsel only with itself and not with the other who may have another system of reasoning and a more communal sense of justice. The suggestion that the poor, or the least advantaged, may be better off as a result of the spread of this corporate economy into the remote parts of the world changes nothing with regard to the questions of justice or injustice on the communal level. What counts most in that question is whether there is excessive inequality, which makes any sort of fundamental social justice and community impossible. The poor and the oppressed have every right to think of the global economic system as unjust. Right reasoning is on their side in the struggle for recognition and for a communal good, international as well as national and familial. They have been caught up in a system that exploits them at the same time as it denies them recognition, a system totally lacking in basic social justice.

8.3 THE TWOFOLD RENDERING OF JUSTICE IN A COMMUNITY

THERE ARE TWO GENERAL VIRTUES AT THE CORE of ethical consciousness in a community. One is *prudence*, or right reasoning, in practical reason itself as it relates to the communal good as a whole. The other is *justice* in the rational appetite as it also relates to the communal good as a whole. Right reasoning in the light of the communal good is required for ethical consciousness in all human action and enterprise. If the reasoning isn't right in the light of the communal good, the action, in whatever realm, will not be ethically good or justifiable. Similarly, if there is no social justice, there will be no concern for a right social order among selves in the rational appetite that moves people to act; there is no communal good that can come of the action. Human action in history is always about particulars, but as ethical or communitarian it has to be ruled by the general concerns of right reasoning and a rational appetite that is right or rectified. For human action to be ethically right it has to come from a will disposed toward just social structures.

Precisely what the just social structures are or should be concerning the just price, the just wage, or just taxes, for example, remains a question for us as for any community engaging in any action and deliberating or taking counsel about what to do or not to do in its economic initiatives. Insofar as human action is always about particulars, however, and about the good of individual selves, the general virtues of prudence and social justice have to come down to particulars in practices that affect individual selves as well as the community as a whole. Consequently, along with the general virtue of right reasoning in view of the communal good, there has to be a particular prudence for particular realms of human action and interaction. And along with the general virtue of justice relating to social structures in human interactions, there has to be a particular justice in rendering each individual self in a community his or her due. In other words, in a rightly ordered society, justice must be rendered to individuals recognized as participants in the communal goal, whether on the level of the family, the nation, or the international community, wherever there is community.

If we start from the general or the social conception of justice, we can see that this rendering of justice has to take two forms: one that has been called *distributive* and the other, *commutative* or retributive. One has to do with what is owed to individuals from the community as a whole. The other has to do with what is owed to individuals from other individuals in the community, always under the overarching norm of general justice and what is for the communal good as a whole. The reason for this twofold rendering of justice in a community lies in the way a community of selves is constituted historically through mutual recognition among the selves as selves, each with its own rights and responsibilities, in the advancement of the communal good, again whether on the level of families, other local communities, or modern states, where we find a subordination not only of individual citizens to a more universal community but also of local communities, families, and particular organizations, all of which are ordered to the communal good of the whole of humanity as well as to their own particular communal good.

It is easy to see how *commutative justice* is supposed to work among individuals or particular associations or corporations. The mean or the measure there is a matter of strict equality in recognizing the rights of one another as selves or as groups with a self-interest in the disposition of external goods. In buying and selling goods, for example, justice in the transaction requires retribution on both sides so that each one gets as much as he or she gives. If I take something worth one hundred dollars out of a store, I must pay one hundred dollars, assuming that this is a just price for the item taken. The same must be said with regard to respect for one another, which is also an external good in a community. In commutative justice, we must also show respect for one another and one another's rights, no less than for ourselves and for our own rights inasmuch as the good of each one is a participation in one and the same communal good.

The question that remains always for *commutative justice* is how do we arrive at determining what is the necessary level of equality in the disposition of external goods, such as ownership and respect, in the various commutations that the members of a community engage in? Is that something totally negotiable among the parties to a transaction no matter what inequalities or disadvantages may exist in the negotiation for one side or the other, in a supposedly free exchange of goods, labor, or respect for one another? Or is there a minimum level of equality in a standard of living and mutual recognition without which or below which there can be no genuinely human communal life?

The problem of setting a minimum level of equality in all social transactions is one that arises in any theory of justice, especially in those that make justice a matter of negotiation among supposedly free and equal rational agents in a supposedly fair system of exchange. It arises because there is never a simple equality among all the members of a community interacting with one another through negotiation. There are always those who have some advantage over others, whether of wealth or of power, who can force an agreement that would seem just in their view but that could be unjust for the community as a whole and would in effect marginalize those who are disadvantaged in an exchange or a deal that they have to accept for the sake of survival, even if it be in a standard of living and respect that is well below that of the community, in what Thomas Hobbes has called a state of nature that is "brutish, nasty, and brief." What is unjust about a state of such disadvantage is not that it is brutish, nasty, and brief but, rather, that it marginalizes the disadvantaged or excludes them from a communal good of life and respect to which they are forced to contribute without just remuneration and restitution. When only the advantaged dictate the terms of the agreement, without due regard for the disadvantaged and their rights in a community, it is not just the disadvantaged who suffer. It is the whole community that suffers and that should stand up for the rights and welfare of the disadvantaged and restore a minimal standard of life and respect for all in a community, a standard that is decent according to the level of communal life that has been attained historically in the given community.

From *commutative justice* we thus pass over dialectically to *distributive justice* for individuals in a community. Unlike commutative justice, distributive justice is not a matter of restoring or maintaining some kind of equality in transactions among individuals in a society, much less between individuals and the society as a whole, such as a corporation or a state, taken as another individual. Far from being purely egalitarian, distributive justice recognizes the differences in the standing individuals or particular groups with special interests can have within a community. It takes those differences into account in reckoning not only what is owed to those individuals and particular groups in the community, including honor and recognition as well as remuneration for their contribution to the communal good, but also what service and support, such as taxes, they owe to the community by reason of what they get from the community. The equality that distributive justice seeks to restore or maintain is one that is proportionate in each individual or in each particular group to its relative standing in the community with regard to both rights and duties without transgressing on the rights and duties of other individuals or their particular goods, which can be unequal for different individuals and groups in the community as long as they are not so unequal that the disadvantaged are marginalized or cease being part of one and the same community of selves and become hostile to one another in a struggle to dominate and enslave the other, where the winner gets more than his or her fair share and the loser gets barely enough to survive as a beast of burden, without recognition as a self and as a rational contributor to the communal good as was thought to be the case even for slaves in ancient societies.

We have already seen how such a state of affairs in a society is in violation of general justice as it refers directly to the communal good, no less than it is in violation of distributive justice as it refers to what is owed to individuals, families, and particular groups in what we assume to be a national community. To think of a modern nation or a modern sovereign state as a community requires a certain stretch of the imagination and of right reasoning in the light of a communal good to be achieved by a nation or a state. But it is precisely in such a stretch of the imagination and of right reasoning that our conception of justice, both general and particular, in the form of both distributive and commutative justice is seen as essential and necessary for the social structure of action and interaction among the members of a community. Without some sense of justice and recognition of others each in their own identity as rational selves, as a general disposition in a population, there can be no community of the sort we have been presupposing in this reflection, as the Greeks did in developing their own sense of justice for the *polis* viewed as a *koinonia* or a community, and as we still have to do for the modern nation as a community. It is only in the context of a real historical community that a proper sense of justice can be developed as necessary and binding on all its members, advantaged as well as disadvantaged, just as there cannot be any real community in historical actuality unless it is grounded in justice as a general disposition in the will of its members and a readiness to render each his or her due according to both commutative and distributive justice.

8.4 FRIENDSHIP AS NECESSARY GENERAL DISPOSITION IN THE ACTUALIZATION OF A COMMUNAL GOOD

JUSTICE IS ONLY THE FIRST OF THE GENERAL DISPOSITIONS REQUIRED for maintaining and promoting a communal or ethical life in the self-consciousness of human beings. *Friendship* is another general disposition that may be even more crucial and more necessary in the actualization of a communal life that is free and committed in its self-determination. It is usually not numbered among the four cardinal virtues of prudence, justice, courage and temperance, which make up the social backbone of a truly ethical consciousness, but it has to be considered as essential for all of them and for the communal life that they determine in its historical consciousness, whether as familial, national, or international. Friendship is an integral part of the goal or the good all virtues aim at in a human community, which not only comes at the end of the historical struggle for mutual recognition but also enters into the struggle itself as an anticipation or as a partial actualization of that goal, inclining every communal self-consciousness to a fuller actualization of the goal. As justice looks to the *external structures* in the struggle for recognition of the communal good in self-consciousnesses, friendship looks more to the *internal spirit* that motivates the struggle, the desire for communion among selves rather than just its institutionalization in social structures.

Aristotle introduces his discussion of friendship toward the end of his *Nicomachean Ethics*, in Books VIII and IX, before going on to consider contemplation as the ultimate end of human purposive action in Book X as a sort of transition from the discussion of those things that are unto the end, such as virtues in the communal self-consciousness, to a discussion of the end itself, which he conceives as an exercise of the self's highest faculty or function in his view, namely the speculative intellect. He speaks of friendship as greatly enhancing the enjoyment of that end, speculative though it may be, just as we enjoy any good that satisfies desire all the more in the company of friends, including the enjoyment of a good joke, a good meal, or a good victory all in one. Even if he does not consider friendship strictly as a habit in a self's character, as he does all the virtues, Aristotle does speak of it as a quasi habit, or as a part of a disposition one finds in the mind or the will of members of a community as a bond among them.

If we are to think of friendship as a general disposition in the life of any community or as a quasi habit that adds quality to that life, we must still think of it as distinct from general justice, which has more to do with the ways members of a community relate to one another in their external relations with one another.

Friendship has more to do with the spirit in a community than with the social structures of its historical operations. Indeed it is an essential ingredient in the communal good we are aiming at as the second perfection in our self-consciousness. Friendship among selves will enhance our enjoyment of that end or the happiness we strive for in our human activity. But we do not have to wait until the end for that enjoyment. Friendship can begin in the struggle for that happy end and, as a general disposition of the will in a community, can make that struggle, even for justice, more enjoyable along the way as members all work together to better their lives. We enjoy friendship together as we labor for some communal good because friendship is an anticipation in the present of the happiness we hope for in the end.

Friendship enhances the practice of justice in historical communities, smooths the way for it, and makes it more likely to succeed in the end. As actualized in a community, friendship is an anticipation of the communal good as our end, and it brings better insight into the good we have to reason from in right reasoning about what to do and what not to do in our historical initiatives, in matters of commutative and distributive justice. That is why we have to think of it as a necessary general disposition in our ethical consciousness, along with prudence as right reasoning in matters of human action and with justice as readiness to render to others what is their right and their due in our cooperative endeavors with them.

8.4.1 Friendship as Reciprocated Love

How then are we to understand friendship as such a general disposition in the life of a community? We have to think of friendship as a kind of love for others in the members of a community. Love in this sense implies a certain desire for the other as good for oneself and some acquiescence in that good or some enjoyment of it when that good is somehow possessed. If there were no love among the members of a group interacting with one another, if there were only aversion regarding one another, or only competition in each one asserting only one's own self, there would be no community, no communion among them. Friendship exists in a community only if there is love in it among selves.

Friendship, therefore, always entails love. However, love does not always entail friendship. Love can be one-way, going from one to another, but finding no love in return, no reciprocity of love from the other. Such love may be very noble and very generous in generating community, but it does not have the fullness or the richness of love that is the basis of a community, the love of friendship in which mutual recognition is transformed into a communion among selves. A love that is unreciprocated by another falls short of true communion with another. It can turn back on itself and even lose sight of the other as good and therefore as the object of love. The love we speak of as a general disposition in the spirit of a community is one that is requited reciprocally among its members and that keeps each one open to the other as well as to oneself. The experience of friendship is so much a part of the spirit of community among selves that those who are lacking in it, those who never make friends with anyone—not even their closest relatives—seem to be lacking in any sense of justice, in any respect for the other as other, and in any moral or ethical sense whatsoever. Even if they do nothing immoral or contrary to the spirit of a community, they seem to be amoral without any love or interest in the other as a good for them.

This reflection on amorality on the part of one without any experience of friendship leads us to another essential trait of friendship as a general disposition of the will. If the amoral individual is a loner, someone who does not communicate with others, the moral person or the one conscious of living in a community of selves as a self is one in constant communication with other selves. Real friendships develop through actual communication among selves. The reciprocity of love we are speaking of in friendship is one that is quite conscious and communicated in all sorts of ways in the interaction among selves through words and through actions. It shows itself even in the need for taking counsel with one another in deliberations and right reasoning about what to do and what not to do in view of a communal good that encompasses the good of each one of the friends. It is in friendship that we best appreciate the commonality of the good for each one of us and the necessity of taking counsel from one another even as a matter of right and justice.

One other trait required in the experience of friendship we are speaking of is that of a real presence to one another in *mutual recognition*. This real presence may begin through immediate contacts, and it has to go much deeper than just a glancing, external contact, where the other is seen as no more than an object or a means to some particular end we have in mind, such as closing a deal or making a profit. Actual friendship is a presence on the level of consciousness, person to person, recognizing one another and joining together in a common endeavor. Such presence cannot be taken for granted. It has to be actualized through effective communication between people in a certain acquiescence in one another through dialogue and mutual love in the common pursuit of happiness.

Such presence to one another also has to be nurtured and maintained, to become habitual as a disposition in the self-consciousness of each individual so that it does not disappear in times of absence or separation from one another. Friendship can have varying degrees of intensity with different people in different circumstances of closeness and distance, but it always entails a certain circularity in mutual self-consciousness with others far and wide as well as up close and intimate. This will become more evident as we consider the different kinds of friendship we can discern spiritually in our social existence as selves.

One final trait we should note about the love of friendship is that it is something properly *spiritual*, on the level of self-consciousness, and not something merely physical or sensual as it may be for nonrational animals, if indeed there is friendship properly speaking at that lower level of consciousness or at the level of those who have not yet come to a full recognition of the other as another self, in mutual recognition. We sometimes see this when we relate to others only sexually or in some other possessive way of dependence on the other, when one cannot let go of the other, whether as a parent with a child, a child with a parent, or in the case of Helen Keller and her family before the final breakthrough, when true reciprocity finally became possible in their love as a family. True friendship begins within the family as well as outside the family, only when the love is reciprocated among selves who have reached a certain level of self-consciousness and independence from one another so that each can respond to the other freely and responsibly as to another self.

Short of that, human beings in association with one another tend to become manipulative, competing with one another for dominance through seduction, force, violence, even rape of one another in some form, hardly what we have come to think of as a community among selves, which requires a general disposition of friendship as a corrective against these abuses of goodwill toward others, the willingness to enter into loving human relations with others.

8.4.2 The Three Kinds of Friendship as Reciprocal Love

Three kinds of friendship have been distinguished, going all the way back to Aristotle, on the basis of three kinds of love and three kinds of corresponding goods or objects of love that have been observed among selves in communion with one another: the love associated with pleasure, the *bonum delectabile*; the love associated with utility, the *bonum utile*; and the love associated with the good of the other precisely as good in himself or herself, *ipsum habens bonitatem*, the *bonum honestum*. Another division has it so that the first two are understood together as the *love of concupiscence*, whether for pleasure or for utility, in contrast to the third as the *love of benevolence*, where the will is for the good of the other as other than oneself in the reciprocal love of each one for the other.

The third kind of love is usually thought of as the disposition of friendship in the fullest sense among members of a community. That does not mean that the first two are not dispositions of friendship as well among individuals who find themselves in need of one another in different ways of associating with one another, whether in the family, the workplace, or political life. The notion of "love" running through these distinctions into two or three kinds is not a univocal term. It is analogous in the sense that each kind is understood as it relates and compares with the other, with the highest kind being taken as love in the fullest sense so that the notion as a whole can be understood only through the dynamic relation that ties the three together in the historical consciousness of a community.

For human beings in communion with one another, friendship does not blossom forth in its fullest, most authentic sense instantaneously. It comes forth only through a process of generation that starts in a friendship of both pleasure and utility, presupposing a *just* form of mutual recognition between one self and another. If we think of the relation between an infant and its mother prior to the smile of recognition, we may not find a reciprocal love of friendship yet, but we will find a love of pleasure, or at least of satisfaction, at work in the relationship. At first the relation is mainly or generally physical or biological. The infant has biological needs, loving or seeking whatever satisfies those needs—the breast of the mother or some substitute form of nourishment provided through a nipple. The mother, whatever else may be going on in her consciousness, brings satisfaction to the infant's needs by supplying her breast or some substitute, which the infant latches onto as a means for satisfying his or her need. Whether there is pleasure or not for the infant, there is absorption in and of whatever gives satisfaction, a simple consumption of that good, which disappears and ceases to be as an object of desire. When the desire or the appetite for more nourishment returns, attraction to the breast and to the good that it provides will return time and time again, because satisfying one's physical hunger can never be done once and for all, whether it be hunger for food or for any other commodity of life.

Once the smile of recognition between the infant and the mother or other caregiver comes, however, a new kind of desire springs forth for the infant, a new need that seeks satisfaction, done only by some recognition of the new self that is emerging, coming from the mother or another caregiver who must now attend to this new need even more than to the need for physical and biological care. This is to provide care to the child that cannot be consumed and that remains as the child grows in his or her self-consciousness, not only finding satisfaction of a need in the caring proffered but also taking ever more pleasure in it and giving back pleasure to the other through a smile and an eagerness to learn all the other things required for participation in a communal good of selves, of which the child is only beginning to become conscious. As close as this satisfaction of a higher need of recognition of the child as a self may be to the satisfaction of its physical and biological needs, it rises to a higher kind of pleasure that can already be characterized as one of friendship among selves even though it still depends on pleasures that come and go and that may not be lasting for a lifetime.

Besides the natural desire for the good of nourishment in human beings, there is also the natural desire for the good of sex, which comes up later in life but seeks its own satisfaction no less than the desire for nourishment. This instinct, too, can be satisfied in a way that is purely physical and biological, with or without a sexual partner, but with little of what Sigmund Freud calls "libido" or the "pleasure principle" in human beings. Nonrational animals seem to get all the sexual satisfaction they need that way but with little of the pleasure human beings look for in sexual intercourse with another human being, presupposing some conscious recognition of the other as other in communion with oneself. In sexual intercourse, rational animals look for something more than just carnal satisfaction. They also look for recognition from their sexual partner, which brings its own spiritual pleasure or satisfaction to the rational animal along with that of carnal satisfaction. But this pleasure, too, may not be lasting for a lifetime because it is immediately associated with an instinct that waxes and wanes even among sexual partners who remain faithful to one another. A friendship based only on such a love of pleasure would not be as lasting as one based on love of the other as good in himself or herself as a self, as we shall see presently.

The pleasure that we experience with the satisfaction of such basic needs or desires as hunger and sex is bound to be momentary. It comes with the satisfaction and it goes once the satisfaction has taken place. The immediate object of desire has been consumed or possessed, and instead of acquiescence in a good that is no longer, we have satiety until the desire or the urge returns. Upon reflection, we come to understand that such acquiescence cannot be complete or continuous as one might wish in the human quest for happiness. It has highs and lows and times when it has to be put off, times when the "pleasure principle" gives way to what Freud calls a "reality principle." In a Freudian outlook, this appears as putting the immediacy of love aside or off to a future time, as reason and civilization take hold, setting up distances between things and people beyond the immediacy of the pleasure principle and opening up another way of ordering the objectivity in some utilitarian or technological fashion. Different historical cultures thus appear as a consequence of different forms of reason and science breaking out of the immediate circle of physical, biological, or psychological needs and satisfaction, supposedly toward higher, more civilized circles of pleasurable life, though civilization itself can also bring its discontents, as instant gratification has to give way to the more utilitarian reality principles of instrumental reason.

This turn to a reality check, however, is not a turn away from the love of pleasure or the so-called pleasure principle. It is a postponement of instant gratification in order to work for perhaps higher and more complete gratification, more commodious living, and a fuller kind of communion among selves. It is still a kind of love but of things and of others as useful for attaining some future good. As opposed to the love of immediate satisfaction, it is a love that takes pleasure in reasoning itself, in knowing how things and people work and in making them work for some good or other we are aiming at, in calculating and manipulating reality toward ever more complex achievements. This love on the level of instrumental reason also has pleasure of its own, which is not essentially different from that on the first level of sense gratification. It falls within the love of concupiscence, as the ancients saw clearly in a less technologically complicated world, because it does not turn away from pleasure in turning to utility. Behind the reality principle as Freud saw it, there remains the fundamental pleasure principle we have seen operating on the immediate level of concupiscence. The love of utility in the other is simply a love of concupiscence on a broader scale than the more immediate love of pleasure.

Part of the pleasure we take in pursuit of the *bonum utile* comes from the fact that we are working toward that good in communion with coworkers who can also become friends. As coworkers in an endeavor, of whatever kind it may be—educational, sporting, professional, commercial, or political—individuals take rational pleasure and pride in doing their job well and in being recognized for doing so. Individuals also take pleasure in recognizing others as also doing their job well. What comes from this recognition is a certain esprit de corps that pervades the utilitarian cooperation in the production of all sorts of social goods in the economy of family, nation, or international society as a general disposition requiring not only justice in the way these social goods are distributed to the different individuals cooperating in the utilitarian enterprise but also respect for the other and his or her rights as a self contributing to that social good. Satisfaction of these spiritual or ethical needs and requirements in any form of utilitarian cooperation where individuals serve as means to the good for one another gives pleasure to the selves involved in it, from which a certain love for the other, who is coworker in the enterprise, can arise. Wherever such love is reciprocated among two or three or more coworkers, as frequently happens in different workplaces, there is friendship that expresses itself in camaraderie and facilitates the pursuit not just of social goods but also of social justice for all in the distribution of those goods once they are realized.

Friendship on the basis of the *bonum utile* thus can extend to a much broader circle than the one based on the *bonum delectabile*, which satisfies such immediate desires as those for nourishment and sex. Even as it does so, however, this friendship of utility remains within the circle of the *bonum concupiscibile*, still only satisfying need, albeit on a broader economic scale in association with more and more coworkers, in the task of meeting broader social and economic needs. Friendships that result from association in such utilitarian cooperation wax and wane also as the need for such cooperation waxes and wanes or as the opportunity for changing jobs presents itself. They last as long as the need for cooperation in one endeavor or another lasts, and they tend to disappear when the necessity of working together disappears, as when people change jobs and go to work in another cooperative enterprise. New coworkers come on the scene and may become new comrades or new friends at the same time as old friends associated with former jobs are lost sight of unless a higher, more lasting form of friendship has emerged, based on love for the good of the other as good in himself or herself, the *bonum honestum*, which does not wax and wane as the satisfaction of needs does but remains constant, as does the good of the other who remains constant in reciprocating a love of benevolence grounded in an excellence that has become habitual on both sides.

Similar to everything else that is of truly spiritual or ethical value, one does not—or, rather, friends do not—come to such enduring friendship without some struggle with their immediate natural desires and impulses and their need to participate in the utilitarian struggle for survival or for the more commodious living humans can create for themselves. Friends do not simply fall in love, though something similar to that seems to happen at the first level of friendship based on the love of pleasure, as mother and child do in the bonding that takes place at feeding time or as lovers do when they first begin to feel some sexual or affective attraction for one another as selves.

Friendship may begin in such first moments of falling in love, but it does not reach its perfection there. It goes through a second moment of utilitarian cooperation concerning goals to be realized in a common effort, even if it be simply that of creating a life for themselves together, whether in a family, in an enterprise, in a nation, or in an international community as a whole. In creating such a communal life for themselves, friends at the same time develop virtue within themselves, especially the virtue of justice, which makes them good in themselves at the same time as it facilitates their doing good for others as well as for themselves. And it is this good of virtue in the other as well as in oneself that becomes the object of love in the highest kind of friendship we find at the heart of a communal life that is constant and lasting, the closest thing to perfect happiness we can think of as human beings in our historical actuality.

Aristotle observes that base men, lacking in any appreciation of the *bonum honestum* or of the good of virtue in others or in themselves, cannot truly be friends. What they see in others is just a good to be exploited for one selfish advantage or another, not for the good of an other or of a community as a whole. On the other hand, Aristotle also remarks that if true friendship with other selves is not alone what final happiness in one's second perfection will consist in, it will nonetheless be associated with whatever joy or satisfaction that happiness will consist in, even if it is one of pure contemplation. Friendship will be a complement to that joy. It will enhance it as a joy in a way we cannot find when we are alone to enjoy any good that comes our way in life, whether it be a good joke, a good meal, good sex, good health, learning, a job well done, or any other good that we experience as selves in a communal life, including the good of virtue and excellence, which we recognize in other selves and gives added joy in our relations with them as others recognize in us the same virtue and excellence, which in circular fashion gives all added joy in the friendship or the reciprocal love that binds all together in a communal happiness.

We see why base men cannot be friends, at least not in the highest sense of the term, which presupposes and embraces the real goodness of virtue and excellence on the part of the friends. We see also why this sort of friendship is not given by nature as the satisfaction of desires for pleasure or for utility from others in a love of concupiscence that shapes so much of the interdependence in our social life. Friendship on the level of the love of pleasure we desire from others, or on the level of utility that others add to our productivity of social goods, does not rise to the level of friendship on the basis of the *love of benevolence* for the dignity and the virtue we encounter in one another as selves perfected in a communal way life.

Infants start off not only as speechless but also as incapable of experiencing human love and friendship as long as they have not reached a stage of mutual recognition with their caregivers and of self-consciousness able to respond in a human way to the human care and affection they are being given. This kind of regard for the other as self, and for itself as self no less, comes only with the first smile and the first use of language for a child, which releases the infant, so to speak, from its absorption with satisfying its immediate animal needs and frees it for the satisfaction of its desire for recognition by other selves and for the possibilities later on of friendship. If infants experience pleasure in the satisfaction of their immediate natural needs, it is not yet the pleasure of friendship on a level of rational self-consciousness.

Children, on the other hand, who are coming to some rational self-consciousness through language and a progressive mutual recognition with other selves, can attain some level of friendship in conjunction with the love of the pleasure they are experiencing with their caregivers, their siblings, their friends at play group or at school, at the same time as others take pleasure in showing them such human care. This can be seen as true friendship when the love and the interest is reciprocated. But it is only a beginning based on some passing attraction and not on the enduring goodness of virtue or excellence in a self. Young people who have not yet entered into any responsibility for social tasks to be performed for promoting some social good, also tend to find themselves at this first level of friendship, moved this way and that way, wherever the changing allure of pleasures takes them. What makes theirs true friendship is that it is already a reciprocated love in some mutual recognition between oneself and another, which distinguishes the satisfaction or the happiness these young friends feel when they are with one another from anything nonrational animals may feel in following their own instincts or in the satisfaction of their natural desires. We do not find among the young of lower, nonrational species the same kind of exuberance and enjoyment young friends can generate for one another in friendships that may come and go but that affect their spirits profoundly, as witnessed by the way such moments of joy are remembered later in life when the young have become elders in their communities.

When individuals enter into more utilitarian relations with other selves having to do with providing some good necessary for the betterment of a community, whether on the level of the family or of civil society, a more mature kind of friendship may develop among coworkers but one still tied to a satisfaction of needs in a broader social context. Here again, as we saw earlier, some personal attraction may develop among workers who are thrown together for utilitarian purposes to serve some other social good but who also begin to show some interest in one another, some reciprocal love in mutual recognition at least for as long as they are associated together in performing their utilitarian tasks. This is a higher form of friendship than the one based mainly on the reciprocal love of pleasure, but it is still one based on pleasures workers take in working with one another. It could also be based on the beginnings of habits of virtue, especially of justice, that workers find in one another as friends and comrades.

Though these lower forms of friendship do not measure up to highest form based on a reciprocal love of benevolence for the good actualized as virtue in those who are friends in the truest and most lasting sense of friendship, with internal dispositions or traits of character that are not easily removed, they are still genuine moments of friendship that can be identified as such in a dialectic that begins with recognition of the other as satisfying basic needs, from which pleasure is taken as well as advantage for the survival of the self as living and for effectiveness in producing social goods. The final moment of friendship, which crowns the final achievement of communal happiness, so to speak, rises only from these earlier moments, as is evident from the way we have come to the state of communal happiness in which we find ourselves as selves. It is not perfect happiness, but it is real happiness enhanced by the degree of friendship we have attained in our respective communities.

With this dialectic of friendship there is also the dialectic outlined previously between general justice and the two particular forms of justice, distributive and commutative, to be taken into account in our historical consciousness. It takes time and experience for both justice and friendship to establish themselves firmly as general dispositions in the will or in the historical consciousness of the members of a community, each with its respective dialectical moments. The question then arises as to whether there is not a dialectical relation between the two of them as they come together in the formation of a single spirit to animate the existence of a community.

8.5 THE HISTORICAL DIALECTIC OF JUSTICE AND FRIENDSHIP IN COMMUNITIES

WE HAVE BEEN SPEAKING OF JUSTICE AND FRIENDSHIP as actual dispositions of the will that constitute communities in their historical actuality. There are no properly human communities in the world unless they are spirited by dispositions of justice and friendship in those who make up the community. As spiritual or as voluntary, such dispositions do not simply evolve from a natural process. They are not given by nature but, rather, come from rational initiatives taken by selves in mutual recognition of one another, where communal life as such begins, not as a new stage in a natural evolution from potency to act but, rather, as something revolutionary in the world, a passage to a historical actuality of selves communing in the world at a level inaccessible to nonrational animals. When we speak of justice and friendship as general dispositions of the will in communal life, we do not think of them as given by nature but as acquired through a practice or through repeated acts that build community from the inside out. What we have been reflecting on is how such dispositions are actualized in the consciousness of individuals who are members of one community or another. To speak of a dialectic between justice and friendship, therefore, will be to explore how the two of them relate to one another in the process of a community becoming intermittently more just and more friendly rather than simply competitive or hostile toward other societies

It is possible to do this because of the open nature of justice and friendship as general dispositions of the will in a community. Neither justice nor friendship are fully established in any community we know of in practice. There is always more of the general spirit to be acquired by different members of the community, and there are always more individuals to whom justice must be rendered and friendship proffered. At any given moment in the history of a community, justice may be more advanced than friendship, or friendship more than justice. Whatever may be given of one at any moment may also serve to promote the development of the other where existing friendships may reinforce the move toward greater social justice or existing justice may occasion the possibility of new friendships among people, both enhancing essential aspects of the communal good, internal as well as external. Justice and friendship, as we know them in communities, can thus condition one another and serve to reinforce one another in the historical tension that makes a community move in the direction of a greater communal good on both scores, internal as friendship and external as justice.

The key idea that serves as the pivot for this dialectic is that of *equality*, which, as Thomas Aquinas notes in his commentary on the treatise on friendship in the *Nicomachean Ethics*, is last in justice but first in friendship—*ultimum in iustitia, sed primum in amicitia*, as Aquinas puts in his commentary.[3] Friendship begins from a perceived equality among individuals, whereas justice aims at realizing such equality on a level of selfhood. Friendship, which is at the core of any communal

3 Thomas Aquinas, *Sententia libri Ethicorum*, Book 8, Lectio 7.

life, therefore flourishes only where some condition of equality between selves has been reached, and it takes justice to create that condition where it does not exist.

We do not have to presuppose, as modern social contract theorists do, that there is only inequality and injustice, not to say open hostility, at the start of any social life for human beings to arrive at their principles of justice or of commonwealth, or as Hegel also does, even after describing the dialectical conditions for coming to self-consciousness in the presence of another self-consciousness through mutual recognition. If, rather, we reflect on the experience of mutual recognition as a loving confrontation between selves and as constitutive of their self-consciousness, we come not just to a new kind of differentiation between one self and another but also to a kind of equality between them as selves from which a new kind of reciprocal love or friendship can spring, as we see occurring between Helen and Annie at the end of the play *The Miracle Worker*, whatever other inequalities may still remain between the two selves. This shows that the self is not a social animal like any other but that he or she is capable of friendship, of a reciprocal love among selves, from the very beginning of its self-consciousness, a love that becomes an added motive for righting the inequalities or the injustices that remain in society, in line with a communal good that respects differences as well as equality.

What this means is not that friendship takes priority over justice on any level of communal life but, rather, that even on the first level of communal life in mutual recognition, there is already enough equality for friendship to begin, enough also to see that there is a lot more inequality to be dealt with through humanitarian aid, through education, through financial aid, through social enterprises of all sorts—all matters that come under the aim of justice as presupposed in friendship. What principles of justice aim at is a decent minimum level of goodness and equality for all members of a community, which all have a right to in a community and from which they can proceed to develop friendships as they enjoy the happiness of a real communal life.

It is important to keep this lexical order in mind as we think of promoting the communal life in a society that has not yet attained the minimum of a decent social justice or equality on a broad scale, such as on the national or the international scale, where the differences between the haves and have-nots have become so enormous that the very idea of a communal life has become unthinkable, not to say undesirable, as the global economy has been conceived thus far. When differences between the haves and the have-nots, between those at the center of social developments and those left on the margin, between the developed and the underdeveloped are as great as they have become in modern society, on the scale of both national economies and the global economy that supersedes them all, there is such a fundamental lack or loss of social justice or equality in what some may still wish to call a community that there is little or no community worthy of the name at any level of an economy that results in such disparities and inequalities among subjects and agents. A niggardly improvement in the living and working conditions of the poor cannot make up for what is lacking in equality, especially in a society that has acquired so much wealth at the expense of both nature and the poor marginalized by the economy.

A decent minimum of social justice for a community is one in which all the members of a productive society can have some equal opportunity to enjoy benefits accrued by their labor and their contribution to the communal good, benefits they have a right to, at whatever level of development a society may have reached rather than just at some bare minimum from which humans are usually supposed to have started in coming together, as if from some state of pure nature where life was "brutish, nasty and short" or as if from behind some "veil of ignorance" where nothing is known about belonging to a community. Where there is economic progress and development, there has to be a proportionate progress and development in social justice and equality, sufficient for mutual recognition to take place effectively among selves as a condition for the development of true friendship among the members of a community.

Concern for the poor, the marginalized, or the victims of natural or economic disasters is not entirely lacking from the centers of wealth and power that rule over the global economy. It is a part of the ethical consciousness of those who still find themselves in solidarity with a suffering humanity that expresses itself in philanthropy and charitable giving to the needy and the helpless. But there are those who think they can pass to this mode of giving to other selves, for which friendship would be the only motive, without first going through the exigencies of justice and mutual recognition for beneficiaries who are in fact victims of predatory practices in the financial and labor markets of the world. If equality is what justice aims at, and if friendships begin only from a basis of equality among selves, charitable gift giving as an expression of solidarity and friendship cannot begin without having met requirements of justice in social and economic relations. In the dialectic of justice and friendship, the obligation to render justice to the other comes before the obligation to render charity to one's friends or to strangers. Charity without justice is false charity, when justice and causes for disaster in social relations are ignored. It is more a salve for one's bad conscience with regard to justice as a disposition to render to the other his or her due, especially when the gift is only a fraction of what is actually owed in justice. Charity and gift giving in community is always good as a sign of friendship. But it is not a substitute for social justice for all its members who are owed the conditions that will make a decent, respectable standard of living possible for them.

There is, nevertheless, in the communal life we experience at various levels of communion with other selves, enough of the general spirit of justice and friendship to show how the development toward greater justice and toward higher friendship can mutually reinforce one another in a historical promotion of the communal good for all. The friendship we experience at one level of communal life, such as the family or a local political community, and the genuinely human happiness that goes with it motivates us to raise the level of equality and justice that the friendship presupposes in the community itself and to work toward greater equality and justice, a higher decent minimum level of enjoyment of the good produced through cooperation, for those outside the community, on the periphery so to speak, but who are recognized as other selves with basic human rights of their own that fall under justice. Through friendship we also become all the more sensitive to the injustice done to our friends and to others who might also become friends.

Community, the justice, and the equal respect for our human rights we experience at one level of community life frees us to enter friendships with others that are more satisfying to us as rational selves. At the same time it also intensifies the feeling of alienation, if not of guilt, toward others recognized as selves but excluded unjustly from participation in the goods necessary for a decent minimum level of communal life in a society otherwise flooded with a wealth of goods. From this feeling of alienation and guilt, based on a perception of social injustice not just for one's closer community but also for the broader community of the nations and of humanity as a whole, we find ourselves now in the thralls of struggling with a global economy thrust upon it by multinational corporations in competition with one another for control over world markets. In this world-historical struggle for justice, the general disposition of friendship we find already actualized in our local communities adds a dimension of hope that justice can be done in the more universal community of the nations and of humanity as a whole.

Thus, given the various dispositions of justice and friendship we experience in our conscience at various levels of communal life in the world, familial, local, or national, we find ourselves at various stages of a historical dialectic in the promotion of a universal communal life for humanity as a whole. We think globally but we have to act locally where we find dispositions of justice and friendship already reinforcing one another in their respective spheres of higher achievement and spurring us on to a more universal form of social justice as well as a greater intensification of the friendship that ties a people and peoples together into a shared communal life.

Both justice and friendship revolve around a sense of some basic equality due to all selves, a will for justice leading up to ever higher levels of equality in the good life, and friendship adding depth to this human equality in its internal dimension of love and happiness here and now. There remains a historical tension between the two, but not one that leads to war or to animosity between classes, races, genders, or nations. Wars and animosity do not result in any enhancement of communal life, whether within the warring factions themselves or on the larger scale that brings confrontations between them. They stem from a harsh, self-enclosed disposition of justice bereft of friendship that sees only an opponent in the other or from a base sort of friendship that is suspicious, not just of its enemies but also of its allies in a struggle for survival. In the more rational struggle for a communal good of nations, families, and other intermediate organizations of one kind or another, the open dialectic of friendship toward a reciprocal love of benevolence based on the goodness or the virtue of selves keeps the sense of justice and equality from being too closely identified with only one group, one class, or one nation, in opposition to others, too exclusive of the other as other, while on the other side the dialectic of justice to be rendered to all individuals to be recognized as selves, regardless of their difference from ourselves or from our particular faction, keeps friendships from becoming too particular or from foreclosing on the possibility of other friendships with other selves in a wider circle of communion. What we have, then, in our historical consciousness, as we seek to advance to a higher second perfection in our communal life as human beings, are two general dispositions of the rational appetite: one toward the *good life of justice*, or a decent minimum level of equality among selves in a communal life, and one toward the *good of friendship*, a higher level of communication in reciprocated love. Between these two general dispositions there is a tension in which each one supersedes the other in a dialectical progression toward greater justice and higher friendship.

Justice supersedes friendship in the sense that friendship is a kind of justice inasmuch as friendship entails a certain proportionality or equality among friends. Friendship is an exchange of love in which there is a form of commutative justice between one individual and another. As an act of communication between two individuals, it is a form of commutation or of mutual exchange that has to be expressed in some external social structure and that therefore comes under the mediation of justice. On the other hand, however, friendship takes us into a higher form of communication among selves than that which is satisfied with some minimal level of equality in an external social structure. Presupposing a minimal level of equality among selves, it raises that equality to a higher level—a level of love. It consists in an equality of love, especially in the love of benevolence rather than just an equality of rights, which it only presupposes. Thus in a community where there are both justice and friendship, actual communication, or communicative interaction, brings justice and friendship together in a historical dialectic spiraling upward toward a more perfect communal life.

This dialectic stands as a caution against those who would speak too easily of the love of benevolence as taking place directly from person to person on the basis of an internal good found or recognized in the other. Such communication between persons in the love of benevolence does not take place historically without some external expression in language and in some structure of social defense. This ties the love of benevolence not only to the love of concupiscence but also to justice itself, whose function it is (not love's) to rectify the order of extreme social dislocations and institutions. Even in its highest and most intimate forms, friendship still has to be mediated by justice. There are rights as well as rites to be observed, as required by love itself, at any level of communication. These rights and rites are not only necessary for the practice of true friendship; they could even be said to be constitutive of friendship itself. They are in a real sense the minimal content of reciprocated love—*minimum caritatis*, as some ethicists would say. Without them at any level of friendship, there is no real human love of benevolence for the other as other.

The same dialectic also stands as a caution against those who would struggle for justice or against injustice without any thought of love or friendship in relation to the other. If the other is seen only as one to be feared, against whom one must protect oneself and assert one's rights while conceding as little to the other as possible, there can be little or no mutual recognition, no genuine communion among selves on a basis of equality from which friendships can develop in a community or a commonwealth. There can only be a truce that is enforced by the winner or the master in the struggle for survival or for some advantage over the other or by a higher force that holds both winner and loser in awe, as Hobbes put it, in a continuing ambiance of fear and hostility that is ever ready to break out in the open.

If a community or a commonwealth were constituted in the stark terms of a social contract as described by Hobbes or Rawls without some mediation of friendship among individuals entering into what is better called a covenant, there would be no communal life in it. It would be only a mechanism for controlling violence by institutionalizing violence as a social force without taking real communion and friendship among historical selves into consideration as the primary social bond. In fact, it would be rendering any such communion and friendship suspect from the standpoint of whoever is seeking only to control violence, whether as master in a hierarchical household of slaves or as sovereign in a commonwealth where subjects live in constant fear if imminent death or ruination. Such is not the ideal of the communal good we have to reason from in our ethical consciousness, nor is it the communal life we start from in our experience as rational selves in communion with other rational selves. Even as we strive for some minimal equality of justice in mutual recognition, there is already at work in the members of a community a disposition of friendship that takes us beyond justice.

Moreover, this disposition of friendship, when actualized among selves who recognize one another as equal, magnifies the justice or the injustice from which it takes off. It is a motive stronger than justice itself, for seeking justice, and it makes injustice among friends a worse evil than injustice among strangers. Injustice between two friends, such as stealing or lying, is worse than injustice between strangers even though from the standpoint of justice there is the same objective measure of rightness and wrongness and the same obligation to make things right where there is injustice. Treason or betrayal of a friend is worse than betrayal of a stranger or an alien, though it may have the same general consequences for the betrayed. Conversely, one feels more bound to do justice to one's friends than to strangers, though it may cost neither more nor less in either case. Indeed, one is usually pressed to do justice for one's friends in a community before doing it for others even though there may be a more pressing need for justice on the part of others who are not yet friends.

This dialectical interweaving of friendship with justice can be seen as having far-reaching consequences for the advancement of social justice in and among communities operating in their own self-interest in ways that overlap with one another. It takes a keen sense of justice, as well as a precise understanding of how particular social and economic systems work, to perceive a given social order as unjust and exploitative. The poor and the marginalized frequently have this sense of justice much more acutely than those who only think of manipulating the system in their own self-interest without thinking of what would be fair or just for the disadvantaged in the system.

The sense of injustice coming from the system will be greatly heightened when there is also an experience of friendship in a community among the disenfranchised with an added urgency to find justice for one's friends as well as oneself. In a global economy such as we have now, where the many have become conscious of being marginalized and disenfranchised not just as individuals but also as communities, but where there is also a growing possibility of a global communicative interaction among the poor and those who are deprived of their livelihood, a new sense of global community can arise to join all these individuals and communities scattered about the globe, victims not just of natural disasters but also of the globalized economy together in one spirit of cooperation and friendship to restore some balance and equality in the distribution of the accrued economic and social goods and to promote a better communal life for all who belong to the human race. Such a new spirit in the human community as a whole will inevitably enhance the demand for a universal social justice, as it has led to greater indignation at the injustices of the present socioeconomic system, even if such injustice is not imputable to anyone in particular. From the universal sense of friendship comes a whole new dimension of responsibility in seeking social justice of the strictest kind.

8.6 THE HISTORICAL NECESSITY OF DIALOGUE AND LABOR IN COMMUNION WITH OTHER SELVES

There are, of course, immense problems to be resolved in the passage to a more just social order, problems magnified by the inextricable complexity of a global socioeconomic system organized to maximize profitability for large corporations that stand to benefit from that system. Many see this system as a coalescence and cohesion of natural forces, much as Hobbes conceived the natural state as a state of war and competition, impenetrable to reason and love. Some think of love and friendship in this so-called natural state as an "impossible possibility" (Reinhold Niebuhr), especially for large groups on a global scale, as if there were not already some love and friendship to fall back on in smaller communities from which a disposition toward greater social justice on a national and an international scale can also arise dialectically even among the most disadvantaged by the current system. The rationality that has been built into the so-called natural social forces of an economy that rages on without due consideration for the human good of people engaged in the system, whether from the center or from the margin, is not the only rationality there can be. The reason of mutual recognition and friendship, as found in smaller but real communities inspired by leaders such as Mahatma Gandhi and Martin Luther King Jr., can find ways of circumventing the limitations imposed by an oppressive economic system.

The historical social reality in which we find ourselves is not an impenetrable natural whole. It has come to be only on the basis of intentions transcending nature from the beginning, including that of creating a more commodious form of communal life for ourselves. The historical reality in which we find ourselves and one another is a moving reality, and an important part of that movement has come from an actual sense of justice and friendship, general dispositions of the will that have long shaped selves into communities of mutual recognition and communicative interaction. The current global socioeconomic system tends to ignore or to override these real dispositions in diverse local communities in order to amalgamate them into a standardized system of mass production and mass marketing, thus marginalizing what justice and friendship has already been built up in local economies, if not simply destroying it to make room only for itself among the survivors. To be sure, there is always much more to be done in existing communities, large and small, in terms of justice and friendship as well as economic progress. The social structure of justice may be falling far behind the new exigencies of technological and economic progress in many communities, but the solution to this problem will not come from abandoning the sense of justice and friendship that brings communities together. That would leave us only in a worse state of injustice and isolation from one another. A truly ethical solution will come only by raising the standards of justice and friendship to a higher and more universal level using the new means of communication and cooperation that technological progress has provided in a fair trading system, where the right of everyone to a decent minimal standard of living and working is recognized with a possibility of creating friendships and peace for all peoples. Technological progress has given us the means for a truly universal communicative interaction. The spirit of justice and friendship in our ethical consciousness now requires that we work at making these benefits available for all people to enjoy.

This is not to say that there are an infinite number of possibilities open to us at any given moment or that the future will take care of itself. There are constraints on what we can and cannot do. But there are also initiatives to be taken in the promotion of justice and friendships among people and peoples. There is a logic in the dialectic of these two virtues that should affect the course of history for diverse communities and for the global community that is now only beginning to take shape. This logic cannot be limited to the present system as it stands, only to perpetuate it in its current state of injustice and competitive hostility. The dialectic of justice and friendship is a logic that requires us to begin envisioning new possibilities for an ongoing communal life and new means for making these possibilities real for all people. The experience we already have of justice and friendship is open to a future we have yet to see. The limitations we find in our present historical state are due to the social structures given in the present. Such structures are necessary by reason of the material and external conditions in which we find ourselves. But such conditions are not fixed in some absolute state by nature as those who wish to maintain control over social structures they have put in place for their own benefit would have us believe. Our experience of justice and friendship under the constraints of these socioeconomic structures is limited, but it remains open to a better future as part of our historical consciousness. It always remains for us to transform them in our ethical consciousness into something more conducive to a communicative interaction that is more just and to a communion that is more friendly, peaceful, and enjoyable for *all* selves concerned.

The good we aspire to historically as human beings and that we must reason from in our ethical consciousness is not one that can be given by nature or by a sheer interplay of forces in a social power structure. It is a communal good that can only come about by human beings reasoning together and laboring together or taking initiatives to better the human condition in the world, both internally and externally. As communal this good can only happen socially through the inventiveness and the efforts of many coming together as a community. From the exercise of such social inventiveness and effort in diverse communities come not just results we call civilizations and cultures in the world but also the general dispositions of justice and friendship we have been speaking of in a community as habits of mind and of spirit for the members of this community.

It follows from all this that practical reasoning from the communal good can never be purely individual, focused only on one's own self-interest. It has to be social, or better still *dialogical*, where each one takes counsel with the other in justice and friendship as well as with oneself in conceiving the good to be realized for the other as well as for oneself and in determining the mean of justice that is called for in relations of production and exchange regarding external goods. No one can conceive of a communal good alone in isolation from any other. Nor can anyone dictate or determine the mean of justice for another without the other standing up for himself or herself in a dialogical confrontation and being taken seriously as a rational self, no matter how poor or economically marginalized he or she may otherwise be.

There is such a rich diversity of ideas, talents, gifts, and visions within particular cultures as well as in the diversity of cultures that no adequate view of the good we are seeking concretely and historically can be achieved by anyone in isolation from others, no matter how firmly and well grounded one's principles of practical reasoning may be in an abstract idea of the communal good. The real, practical value of the principles themselves or of the general dispositions of justice and friendship has to be illuminated anew, in taking counsel, and can come only from an other in history, whether that other be one of the same culture as oneself or of an unfamiliar culture in the confrontation of cultures. Our knowledge of the end in the idea of the communal good is undeniable, but that knowledge remains open in each self for enrichment from other selves, which happens only from dialogue, where the word of each one is taken seriously in equality and friendship in coming to any sort of communal self-determination. The word of the other, even of one who has been marginalized, is as crucial as one's own in determining the mean of social justice in a community. It must be heard if there is going to be justice and a decent communal life for all. Hence the importance and the necessity of truly open dialogue among the members of a community, which is already an actualization of friendship, for the sake of justice and the communal good.

Now, it is possible for us to see the historical necessity of this dialogical openness in responsibility to the other grounded in both justice and friendship. For if the other is truly a norm, as he or she must be in justice and friendship, the other must then enter into the counsel-taking that must precede any exercise of free choice and self-determination. Taking counsel with the other who is encountered and recognized as a self is more than an abstract consideration of one's moral principles. It is taking in the other in the formation of one's own conscience, which is a conscience shared with the other in one's community, whether local and cultural or universal and global. The other, in a true community, has a conscience as well, also in need of being formed and informed by an other through dialogue, cultural and intercultural.

Right reasoning in view of the communal good takes shape in a community through such mutual formation and information of consciousness on a level of rational dialogue among selves. This is not to say that there has to be complete agreement among selves at every historical moment of practical reasoning in a community. There can be real, even irreconcilable, differences in confrontations among selves, especially over matters of justice, at any moment in the historical consciousness of a community. But justice and friendship, as general dispositions in the will of a community, require that some reconciliation be worked out through negotiations and judgments by courts of law in a manner that is dialogical, where the rightful claims of everyone are heard and listened to equally as well as responded to. Every community has its own way of reconciling differences that set one member or one group at odds with another. But in all of these ways there has to be a readiness, an openness to dialogue with the other as a self equal to oneself no matter what the difference may be between the two.

Gandhi tells the story of an episode late in his life when he was asked to intervene in the settlement of a strike against a manufacturing firm by the workers actually striking against the firm. He was by then a powerful ally to have on one's side in such matters in India. He accepted to join in the confrontation but not without first working out a discipline with the striking workers on how they were to act in a nonviolent way and on what they were to claim as their right. This took some time in the lives of these workers, but it prepared them for entering into dialogue with the managers of the firm. When he finally brought the claim of the workers before the managers, however, they did not take the time to listen or to consider the rightfulness of the claims. They immediately gave in to the demands, thinking that they could not win against Gandhi. The workers were pleased at this outcome. They had won, thanks to Gandhi. But Gandhi himself was not as pleased because of the way he had won. He was disappointed that they had given in so fast. Management had entered the negotiations without any willingness to hear or to listen to claims of the others in some sort of communicative interaction with the others, who remained purely marginalized in their minds, objects of contempt rather than selves in a community, which should include workers as well as management. Gandhi was not interested in just winning the way he did. He knew that it would only be a matter of time before another struggle unto death broke out between labor and management in the part of India where this one had. He was more interested in forming a community where management, a leftover from the British colonial occupation, and workers could cooperate for the communal good of all Indians of whatever class, color, or religion, including the untouchables, the most marginalized of the marginalized.

But making history and creating civilization is more than just talk. It is also *labor* and making plans about what to do with what a community has from nature and from those who have labored in the past to form a civilization. Human culture transcends the forces of nature, no matter how dialogically, only by reshaping nature or humanizing it, according to its spirit, and to serve its purposes. When that spirit is one of contention and competition for the upper hand in appropriating the forces of the resources of nature, it tends to be destructive of nature as given and indifferent toward the good of its survival, thus giving rise to ecological crises of every sort. When the spirit is more one of communion with nature as well as with others, scientifically as well as aesthetically, it becomes more constructive of nature even as it uses it for its own amelioration in the world.

Using nature with due regard and respect means laboring with it and developing it in ways that it could not take with the intervention of human labor, which is practical reasoning applied to nature, even as manual labor. The hand is the perfectly adapted instrument of nature for the animal that is rational in its historical essence. That is why the manual laborer is not without his own dignity as a rational self. He or she is an essential contributor to the communal good, not just of the family but of the nation and of the international community as well. As such manual laborers are deserving of much greater recognition and remuneration than they have ever received, whether in ancient society as slaves or as craftsmen or in modern society as farmers or as wage laborers.

A society where the division of labor is such that all manual labor is left to one class and none would be required of any other class would hardly be a community any more than one in which extreme poverty is the lot of most and wealth, especially extreme wealth, is the lot of fewer and fewer people. In modern society, matters of justice and injustice are closely related to the way labor remains divided between the intellectual and the manual and to the excessive advantage the intellectual has taken over the manual. If there is any social justice to be restored, it will have to come from the side of manual labor claiming its rights with or without the agreement of the other side that has set itself apart from manual labor and the poverty associated with it.

We should keep in mind that even manual labor, as human and rational, has an intellectual component when it is performed as part of the communal good in a community where dialogue prevails over sheer brutality associated with only slave labor. In a community where dispositions of justice and friendship prevail over the struggle for survival and domination or for just gaining the upper hand and taking advantage of the other, language takes precedence over labor in dialogue. This is to say that truly human labor, under conditions of justice and friendship, is not just a matter of sweatshops organized to get things done under dehumanizing conditions for the laborers, allowing for little more than survival in a life that is short, brutish, and nasty. It is more a cooperative endeavor of the many in a struggle for recognition and human rights for the betterment of all. There is no just society without labor relations of some kind, and there are no human labor relations in right reasoning without language, which in the process of labor negotiations should take the form of a dialogue in the light of our conception of a communal good.

When we speak of labor as something more than just talk in making history and creating civilization, our historical good, we should not think of it as taking shape brutally, as it does for brute animals caught up in a sheer struggle for survival that does not transcend the ecological conditions for survival, much less result in a higher communal good or a civilization, for self-conscious, rational animals. In a dialogue, we become conscious of the other and of the need to collaborate with the other in the bettering of the human condition in the world for all. We recognize the need for a general disposition of justice for the other and for oneself as well as a general disposition of friendship in collaborating for the communal good of all.

In actually collaborating historically, we cultivate not just the land or the material conditions of our human existence but also the internal dispositions of justice and friendship, which take the shape of a culture or an ethic in our self-consciousness or our conscience, a way of conceiving the communal good for a community and of working or collaborating toward that communal good. This is how particular communities and cultures come into being in history. And this is the way a global human community will have to take shape around the world, with dignity and mutual recognition and a decent minimal equality of benefit for all.

With dialogical planning and labor and the discipline they presuppose, we complete the circle of the historical effort required for the communal good. With dialogue as their context and as their center, they constitute a structure for the process by which human beings strive for the good both effectively and fittingly, according to right reason. While dialogue assures a certain quality in the struggle for mutual recognition, one that does not exclude reconciliation, planning and labor assure that the dialogue has real history as its subject and not just some utopic vision. In this way the real exigencies of the communal good can emerge in the light of justice and friendship, to be met through the common dialogical initiative of rational self-consciousness in history.

9

The Necessity of Authority and Law in the Free and Communal Exercise of Self-determination

We began our reflection on the phenomenon, or the fact, of ethical consciousness by focusing on *conscience* and *responsibility* regarding the human good in the actual practice of selfhood as makers of our own history. This led us to consider virtues as necessary or essential constituents of our ethical consciousness in a communion of selves beginning with the virtue of prudence, or right reasoning from the communal good, then proceeding with the virtues of justice and friendship as necessary dispositions in the rational appetite of selves for finding the means to work toward any sort of communal good or human happiness in a community.

The virtues we have articulated, however, are only internal dispositions of subjects or of selves in a community and say nothing of the external social structures that assure permanence and continuity in the identity or the external culture of a community, especially if we consider only the general disposition of friendship and not the general disposition of justice, which starts from a recognition of the other as another self and therefore as an equal to oneself in some basic sense of having human rights in the historical community or communities of humankind, as much as I do. Even as an internal general disposition of the rational appetite or the will, justice requires respect and regard not just for the other as other but also for what we call *law*, or the laws, which govern social relations as they affect our use and our appropriation of external things, including mutual regard in the pursuit of a good or a happiness that is communal as well as personal.

Modern considerations of ethical consciousness, such as those of Thomas Hobbes or Immanuel Kant, as well as those of Jürgen Habermas and John Rawls, usually start more from the side of law and legitimation or of moral law and obligation rather than from the side of internal dispositions or virtues that make for a good communal life in history. Kant, for example, speaks of the heavens above me and the moral law within me, not virtue. Hobbes speaks of the necessity of a power to hold everyone in awe through law, to come to a state of peace and avoid reverting back to the natural state of war. Rawls speaks of justice as a matter of legal procedure or procedural justice that will allow for everyone to get their fair share of external goods, regardless of inequality in social advantages and disadvantages.

The connection between virtue and law lies in the historical consciousness of communities, especially in the general disposition of justice, to work with and to reflect on ethical discourse. The consideration of justice does lead to a consideration of law, just as the consideration of law can lead to a consideration of justice as a general disposition of the rational appetite in a community of selves. Both are essential ingredients of what we have called the phenomenon or the fact of ethical consciousness. But the question arises as to which one of the two should have priority in determining that phenomenon for a community—virtue or law?

Here we have proceeded from the side of virtues as necessary dispositions within selves communing with one another in the pursuit of some communal good as their second perfection. We have established the necessity of such dispositions for actualizing a good that is at once personal and communal. The actualizing of such dispositions in a self, however, does not come instantaneously, nor is it given by nature. It has to be communicated from generation to generation in diverse communities, and it has to be acquired by individuals through repeated acts of self-determination in keeping with right reasoning from the communal good and with dispositions of justice and friendship in relation to others in a community. Such reasoning and such dispositions are not given by nature. They are acquired by practice in the exercise of deliberation that precedes free choice and of self-determination that follows free choice in the formation of one's character and one's dispositions in communicative interaction with others. They become part of a second nature, so to speak, in the historical consciousness of selves who shape themselves into cultures as they pursue their own communal good.

The virtue ethic we are reflecting on is not one that flows simply or deductively from what is spoken of as "natural law" in the modern, more legalistic approach to ethics or morality. Ours is a virtue ethic that develops historically in self-consciousness thanks to right reasoning from the communal good of selves in the practice of a community and thanks to dispositions of justice and friendship that follow from such reasoning in the rational appetite of selves disposing themselves to seek an ultimate good that is communal as well as personal.

There is a sense, however, in which such an ethic can be said to flow from nature or to be grounded in nature so that the ethic of a community is not something totally arbitrary or something purely conventional, as the Stoics or Kant might put it. In deliberate practical reasoning, no matter how creative or conventional it may be, reference always has to be made to nature and to our natural appetites to see what possibilities they allow for in the pursuit of the good and our second perfection, whether communal or individual. Deliberation always starts from some understanding of what is given to us by nature and by our natural appetites for us to organize and to decide about. Thinking about the communal good in practical reasoning is not just a matter of dreaming. It has to be realistic, with reference to nature and therefore to natural law as it affects human behavior, in thinking about possibilities for the future and the need for caring for our own health and wealth, such as they may be.

Moreover, we could say that it is natural for reason to do so, even in its own terms, as a given in human and ethical consciousness. Even if we don't have prudence or right reasoning by nature, it is in the nature of human reason to move in the direction of right reasoning from the communal good, as we tried to show earlier in our reflection on the nature of right reasoning from the communal good. Kant did not speak of categorical imperatives as matters of natural law, but in speaking of them as matters of moral law and obligation, in pure practical reasoning as such, in conscience or in the sense of duty as such, he was referring to pure reason as a nature unto itself, distinct from nature outside of human consciousness whose determinism is the object of speculative reason, not of practical reason. In that sense, he could have spoken of the moral law within him as also a natural law of practical reason, as distinct from pragmatic or utilitarian reason that gives rise only to hypothetical imperatives: if you wish to accomplish this or that good, such as health, you must choose this or that means.

Here we shall speak of law as flowing from reason but not in abstraction from nature. It is a matter of nature for reason to command human action, and it is a matter of right reasoning to do so in ways that are conducive to the communal good and not in ways that are obstructive to the communal good. Even if right reasoning is not given by nature but rather acquired by repeated acts in taking counsel with ourselves and with other selves before taking action of one kind or another, it still has to contend with nature as a matter of expediency for the rational animal in this world.

Moreover, it also has to contend with our natural inclinations, also known as passions and emotions, in determining what is for our human good, both personal and communal. Not all of the inclinations and appetites that arise in us naturally or according to the determinism of our nature are compatible with one another or with what we take to be a personal and communal good. We do not choose these inclinations and appetites that arise in us spontaneously, such as candidates for the election of reason at any given moment, calling for attention as we deliberate over what to do and what not to do. The diversity of these emotions and inclinations in the human soul is what gives rise to the need for deliberation and choice in the rational animal, as we saw in our discussion earlier of the first act of willing. Rational self-determination does not take place in human action except by choosing what candidates will be admitted and in what order. For, as Aristotle says, reason rules over the passions and emotions like a political ruler over free subjects by favoring some and by placating others not favored but ultimately by bringing them into the line of reason itself or of the communal good.

We shall see how this sort of negotiation with our emotions in right reasoning takes place when we come to speak of the virtues that pertain to the emotions—courage and temperance—in addition to those that pertain to reason itself and to the will—prudence and justice. For the moment we must reflect further on how *law* issues from right reasoning as an institutionalized external social structure to be heeded in conscience and deliberation or in deliberative self-consciousness. As such, law is to be understood as a dictate of reason, and as a dictate of right reasoning it has to be ordered to the communal good, the principle of right reasoning. The question thus arises as to how law is constituted in our historical consciousness as an external institution to complement the internal general disposition of justice that binds individuals in a community in mutual recognition of one another.

A first answer to that question can be found in the idea of *customs* or *mores* that take shape in any living community. As right reasoning develops in the historical experience of a community, it not only discovers new ways of realizing what it conceives as its communal good, it also develops customary ways of its own as a community of mutual recognition conducive to promoting that communal good internally as well as externally. Institutional structures thus come into being that are taken for granted, or presupposed, as necessary or binding for the continued good life of the community. Figures of authority emerge whose reasoning is recognized as more apt for the communal good. And from these authorities come more formal statements, or laws, than can be found in mere custom to guide and enhance the way to the communal good encompassed by customary mutual recognition.

These laws issue from human reason in the historical order. As such, they are contingent on the historical circumstances of the community and on the relative prudence and justice of those who issue the laws. To say that these laws are rational implies that, while these laws relate to nature as a whole, they do so only as understood by the lawmaker. They also relate to the natural emotions of individuals in the community, including those of the lawmaker as well as of others. In this sense they can be thought of as "natural laws" but only in the sense that they are binding in *conscience* or on reason itself as embodied in a particular constitution that is political rather than just natural.

With this insistence on the historical constitution of laws in human reasoning, we shall begin by reflecting on the historical constitution of authority in a community from which the constitution of human law follows. Then we shall turn to the two ways in which law flows from authority: first by way of conclusion from natural circumstances in which we find ourselves, and second by way of creation of new forms for the development of communities.

9.1 AUTHORITY AND THE COMMON GOOD

Everyone in human society is called to exercise right reasoning from the communal good and to promote justice for others as well as for oneself in one's action. That is how we come to be free and rational in our self-consciousness in communion with other selves at the same time as we constitute ourselves in such diverse communities. This communal exercise of these general dispositions of prudence and justice in our reason and our will is the very foundation of the communal existence from which we begin our reflection on selfhood in one community or another. It is the essential ingredient of our decision-making that gives rise to our sense of responsibility as well as our conscience in the way we relate to other selves in the world.

In a way, this call to right reasoning and to doing justice in our action is found in all members of a community to the extent that they come together for a common purpose. It is addressed to all equally, and all are equal in it in that they are called to right reasoning and to doing justice like every other being communing in right reasoning. The call, however, is not shared in equally by all. It is not given by nature or by the powers of reasoning and willing as such in any individual self taken as supreme in its isolation. It comes only with the acquisition of dispositions or habits of right reasoning and doing justice in one's historical consciousness. And that can be quite uneven or unequal, including among the individuals of one and the same community, such as a family or a clan, as well as among different communities within the human community as a whole. This is where the question of some authority external to oneself in the exercise of one's reasoning and one's own decision-making regarding rightness and justice arises; for *authority* in a community always entails the power of influencing the reasoning and the decision-making of one or of many by another who has this special power.

Now, being influenced by another self in one's reasoning and free decision-making is not contrary to either reason or free will in a community of selves. It is part and parcel of taking counsel with others in the process of deliberation prior to taking any action on one's own. What is special about authority is that the influence has to be taken in or accepted by the one being influenced, which appears contrary or heteronomous to the spontaneity or to the freedom of one's own reason and will. Whence is this *necessity of authority* for human subjects in a community, and how can it be justified?

Hobbes, who does not recognize the idea of the communal good as the principle from which right reasoning proceeds, argues for the necessity of authority as a power or a force that can hold in awe all those willing to enter into some social contract or agreement, lest they fall back into their natural state, which he conceived as a state of war of everyone against everyone else or as a state of composition of everyone against everyone to get and to hold onto as many resources necessary for survival in this world as possible. As a substitute for the idea of a common good around which a community can coalesce, Hobbes falls back on a "desire for peace" amid the constant state of war of everyone against everyone, where each one is looking out for oneself alone and is always under the threat of being killed by another or by a horde of others no matter how strong or powerful he or she may be in oneself. From this abstract desire for peace comes a truce or a willingness on the part of many not to exercise their right to whatever they want to the same extent that others are willing not to exercise their right to whatever they want, neither more nor less. This social contract does not end the "natural state of war" and/or competition but limits it to those things not included in the contract, where "force and fraud" continue to be the rule as in any state of war.

From his conception of the state of nature as a state of war of everyone against everyone, Hobbes argues for the necessity of an absolute sovereign or of an authority as a force to hold those entering into the social contract at bay from one another, in awe or in fear, not of one another since that remains under the rule of "force and fraud" in their persisting state of war and competition but of the *authority* as such conceived as a higher force or power that can hold those who have entered the contract to abide by what they have agreed to. Without that superior force in place, there can be no social contract, no security in agreements, no mine nor thine. There can only be what each one can hold onto by force or fraud against all others. And if, once the authority is in place, a decree should come down that is unacceptable to an individual contractant, least of all a decree of death, then the individual has only to revert to the state of nature from which he or she came, with force and fraud, toward the authority as well as toward all others, including those still under the contract.

This is hardly a picture of authority befitting a community of selves in communion and in cooperation with one another aiming at a communal good or some second perfection for itself and all its members. It ignores the dispositions of right reasoning and of justice and friendship we have indicated as constitutive of a communal life in both subjects and rulers and proposes instead a pure force, abstracted from community and in opposition to all its members, where might alone makes right, leaving all members no alternative but to knuckle under as slaves or else reverting back to a state of war of everyone against everyone without any possibility of communion in either case.

Who would exercise this sort of power in a society is a problem for any community, large or small, for it could be anyone who rises to a position of power and domination over all others by whatever means and for whatever reasons of personal advantage, either as a conqueror in war or as the winner in a competition for market shares, who can then dictate what is right and just, what should be done and what shouldn't be done, in one's own terms and for one's own advantage, openly as a tyrant or as one operating secretly behind the scene of public opinion through manipulation of market forces without regard for any communal good. This is what comes from considering the just society as only a solution to the problem of war or of unequal competition in the distribution of scarce resources. It is justice for the conquerors and the winners and not for the rest who are defeated, losers and marginalized by those who have taken control.

The problem lies not just in who defines justice and right but also much more fundamentally in how justice and right are defined. Might alone does not make right. Justice does not follow only from those who have the upper hand in society. It follows more from right reasoning in view of a communal good by whomever holds the reins of power in a community, not in secrecy behind closed doors or in councils of war and competition plotting against an enemy or a competitor but openly and in transparency before the community so that it can be recognized as for the communal good and therefore as binding for whole communities, on those in authority as well as on those who have only to obey as well as they can. Sheer might without this sort of recognition does not make right in a community. It only distorts whatever dispositions of right reasoning and doing justice might already exist in a community into something irrational and unjust or warlike, not communal peace of any sort.

There is, of course, always an element of force and coercion in the exercise of authority in a community, legitimate as well as illegitimate, just as well as unjust. We refer to law as something to be enforced. But this is felt mainly by those who have not yet entered into the dispositions of right reasoning and doing justice proper to the ethic of a community, such as children or immature persons who have not yet learned to act responsibly in their community or criminals who have decided to go against the ethic of the community in what they do and think.

The purpose of coercion in the exercise of external authority, however, is not just to protect the good of the community or to rectify injustices that have been done but also to get individuals in need of coercion into habits of right reasoning for the communal good with due considerations for the good of others as well as their own, either for the first time for those still growing into such dispositions or as rehabilitation for those who have fallen into vice due to a corruption of such dispositions. Sheer force and coercion as described by Hobbes or as exercised brutally against human beings do not and cannot foster what is called for in view of a communal good. It cannot do this since what is in question is the development of internal dispositions of reason and will in the self-consciousness of individuals. It can only drive people deeper into a state of war against the people of a community. But when administered rationally and fairly toward the one being coerced, it may help him or her to enter into the internal dispositions of right reasoning and doing justice that characterize the more mature and responsible members of a community. It may also help convince the criminal that he or she deserves to be punished in keeping with the right reasoning and the justice against which that person has offended and to which he or she must convert if that person is to be rehabilitated as a member of the community.

The use of force and coercion by authorities against others in an ethical community founded on internal dispositions of right reasoning and doing justice should never come as a brute reaction to an offending subject. It should only be part of a strategy, devised by one disposed to right reasoning and doing justice to all, to induce and persuade individual selves to enter deeply into the spirit of the community as selves who will do so only if they do so rationally and freely, not as slaves or prisoners of war in the proverbial war of everyone against everyone.

The exercise of authority in an ethical community requires highly developed dispositions of right reasoning and doing justice to others in the leaders who assume the responsibility of authority in a community. The use of coercion should be an integral part of that exercise, not just with regard to the young or the beginners in the exercise of a communal life of virtue or to criminals who have offended against that life but also with regard to all others who may be tempted to depart from that life and strike out on their own at the expense of others and of communal life as a whole, as in the case of those who seek only to profit from the lawful order or from those in authority who make the laws, as large corporations do in lobbying for laws favorable to them and in funding elections of candidates that will be favorable to them.

There are many kinds of human associations. Some call themselves communities but are not communities in the true sense of the term. They are little more than truces for survival in a state of war or mergers to assure domination or growth in a competition for scarce resources or for market share, as described by Hobbes and other social contractarians. Those that are communities in the sense that we have been presupposing here are the ones that have developed or are developing a shared form of right reasoning and a shared form of doing justice to one another as selves, what the Greeks called a shared *ethic*. Communities do not exist as communities without such shared dispositions among their members.

When one joins a community as a self communing with other selves, one agrees to enter into the form of right reasoning and of doing justice that characterizes that community or that gives it its ethical character shared by all in this community of rational selves. When one finds oneself as a self in a community, as children in a family, in a clan, or in a neighborhood; as young people in a nation; or as immigrants and newcomers in a country or a culture, one finds oneself developing new habits of reasoning and doing justice such as those that build up and maintain a community in its historical consciousness. That is how the development of selves ordinarily takes place in communion with other selves.

There are many kinds of community that a self can belong to, usually interweaving and interlocking in the historical consciousness of selves and in their conscience. We have singled out some as more essential to intersubjective human existence in the world, such as the family, the nation, and now perhaps a global community to go with the global economy, where war and competition still seem to be the prevalent dispositions. Individual selves may also single out other particular communities as essential for themselves as selves on the basis of shared particular interests with others, such as sports, education, music, work, or just simple friendship for getting together on a regular basis. But for all of these different kinds of community there is also a characteristic form of right reasoning and doing justice proper to each one, as well as a characteristic form of exercising authority in view of the communal good.

Everyone in a community of fully constituted selves is called to right reasoning in view of the communal good and to doing justice socially as well as individually in keeping with one's responsibility as a participant. Concern for the communal good in its most fundamental sense thus belongs to the community as a whole and to each member as disposed to right reasoning and doing justice. Without such concern, there is no way of sustaining community without falling back into a state of nature, war, or sheer competition masked as a truce for coexistence. But the concern or the dispositions of right reasoning and doing justice for all are not found equally in all members of the community so that some may be more apt for exercising that concern for the community as a whole than others are. From that inequality comes a need for authority vested in one individual or in a group within the community, or possibly still in the community as a whole—a need for some kind of governance to keep the community on track with regard to some communal good.

The idea of *authority* or of governance here is not entirely different from the idea of *responsibility* toward the communal good to be found and fostered in every member of the community. The person or persons in authority should have more, not less, concern for the communal good and ideally should have more highly developed dispositions of right reasoning and doing justice to all others, contrary to what the tyrant would think or do, who would only keep people in awe or in fear by his actions with concern not for the communal good as such but, rather, for the tyrant's own individual good. The idea of authority does entail a capacity for influencing the will and the reasoning of others, as we have seen, a certain might over others from which comes the twofold question of how such might is acquired and whether such might is enough to make right whatever an authority may declare. These are questions that arise even in the most genuine of democracies, where it is always a party or a faction that rules over a community, whether as a majority or a minority, whether openly before the members of the community or secretly behind closed doors.

There are many ways of gaining power over a community: by conquest, by coup, by takeover, by merger, by winning an election in a democratically constituted society. Having the power alone, however, does not make the authority right in whatever it thinks or decrees. However necessary the power of coercion may be to maintain peace and cooperation in a community, as we have seen, in the face of those who have not yet entered into the spirit or the ethic of the community or in the face of outright criminals who are in defiance of that spirit of cooperation, that does not justify whatever may come to mind in the exercise of some authority. Might alone cannot make right. Authority in a community of selves must be recognized as serving the communal good first and foremost and as serving the individual goods of its constituents through administration of distributive and commutative justice as part of communal justice. We have seen that right reasoning from the communal good and doing justice to others are fundamental dispositions necessary for all who would make up a community in history. Those in authority in a community are not exempted from this necessity. If anything, they should be held to a higher standard and responsibility in regard to both reasoning from the communal good and doing justice for all. One hates to think of what happens in a community when those in authority cannot reason rightly about their constituents in any kind of transparency or dialogue, in the exercise of their function, and show no interest in promoting social justice of any kind. But we are not without much of such abuse of and by authority in our day.

No matter how they may have attained their position of power, as long as authorities exercise their function in a spirit of right reasoning with the community in view of the communal good and a spirit of doing justice to all first and foremost, not in Machiavellian fashion but seeking to promote such a spirit in the conscience of all, they can and should be recognized and followed as true leaders in a community. Conversely, whenever authorities fail to exercise their function in a spirit of right reasoning with the community and of doing justice to all in the community, again no matter how they have come by their position of power, whether by succession or election, they forfeit their power to influence the reasoning and the will of others as authorities in a community and open the way to revolution on the part of constituents who are themselves exercising right reasoning in view of the communal good and seeking justice for all in the community. This is not a revolution against the community but a revolution within a community against people in power who are no longer reasoning as true members of the community and no longer seeking justice for all or who have not even begun to do so from their position of power. Revolution is often a power struggle within a community that must take a violent turn of power against power, given the abuse of power over subjects it starts from, often resulting in the uprising of an other would-be authority that is often also abusive, not just of the entrenched authorities but also of others in the community in whose name it claims to be acting.

But revolution in a community does not have to take such a violent turn, even when it is deemed necessary and therefore justified for the sake of all in the communal good. It can take a more peaceful turn through elections, for example, where people can come together to choose a new authority through a process of right reasoning and doing justice that is itself communal and dialogical in formulating the kind of change they deem necessary. This, of course, presupposes that the people in a community have attained a certain maturity and character of their own in right reasoning and doing justice and that would-be leaders or authorities seeking election appeal to such traits and dispositions in the voters interested in a regime change.

To the extent that voters have not reached a sufficient level of maturity in this regard, however, or fail to enter into the requisite dialogue for learning what the issues are in an election and what changes are likely to ensue, if any, by the election of one candidate rather than the other, they leave themselves open to manipulation by the powers that come to be through appeals to their emotions, their uninformed self-interest, and their selfishness, so that no revolutionary change can take place in the interest of the communal good. Campaign reform becomes a problem along with governmental reform—and a necessity for any true revolution to take place. Without a true and open dialogue between leaders and their people in a community, not just before an election but also after the winner has gained control in which both the leaders and their followers learn from each other what is to be done, there cannot be any authentic revolution or step forward toward a higher communal good. There is only playing politics among power brokers trying to gain, to maintain, or to regain a power that, far from seeking recognition from a community disposed to right reasoning and justice in an open dialogue, remains in control hidden behind the scenes, unseen and unrecognized. Even when it appears to go from one hand to another or from one party to another, it remains a form of tyranny over people, unchanged and promoting only its own particular interests rather than those of the communal good.

It is important to keep in mind that for authority to function properly in a community, it must take counsel not just with itself or with the secretive or unseen power brokers but with the community as a whole, which can happen in a monarchy or an aristocracy as well as in a democracy. No human authority in history is so superior that it can do without the right reasoning of its subjects in the just pursuit of a communal good. It cannot work in isolation from its people, nor without the people's own disposition toward some social justice. In a human community authority has to be exercised in conjunction with the people who are already disposed to right reasoning from the communal good and to doing justice for all; in other words, a people ready and willing to exercise their own responsibility in the promotion of a personal life that is communal. Justice attained without the active participation of members of a community is not truly communal justice. It only gives the appearance of justice and equality as injustice and inequality become more deep-seated.

The exercise of this kind of communal authority can take different forms in different kinds of communities such as families, clans, neighborhoods, cities, nations, and even what we have begun to recognize as the international community in defense of basic human rights for all human beings. Parental authority differs from the authority of the chief in a clan or of the government in a nation. Civic authority can also be institutionalized to serve different functions in a balance of powers such as the executive, the legislative, and the judicial. It is not for us to elaborate on the exercise of any of these different forms and functions of authority in world historical communities. That is the task of more particular disciplines having to do with history, political science, or jurisprudence. Our task is more to reflect on the fundamental aspects of communal and ethical life as found in any community properly so called and, here more specifically, on how authority plays an essential role in the shaping of a community. Every community, every nation has a story about the way it came to be with the kind of authority or authorities it requires to fulfill its historical task. But in all of them there had to be some kind of authority to take hold in the right reasoning of a community and to lead down some path of social justice for all. This is the conclusion we must come to in this reflection.

Another conclusion is that the members of a community should expect a higher degree of right reasoning and of working for social justice from authorities, and when they have a chance to say who will be in authority—at election time, for example, and at other times as well—they should look to see who would have the higher degree of prudence and concern for all and not just to those who would serve their own particular interests, regardless of consequences for the communal good or the good of others. It is important for an electorate not to let itself be duped by name calling, distortions of fact and of character, and appeals to their lower instincts rather than to their own dispositions of right reasoning and concerns for a more just society. In a community all are called to exercise right reasoning and caring about justice for all, both in choosing or recognizing true leaders for the community and in responding conscientiously and responsibly in the exercise of their own freedom as members of the community in accord with the dispositions of right reasoning and doing justice, which they have acquired as members of the community, even if it means protesting and rebelling against certain dictates of authority or against the given authority itself as not reasoning and acting in the interest of the communal good. The life of a citizen in a modern democratic community can no longer be one of simplistic complacency before whatever powers there may be in authorities or behind authorities, bending them to their special interests. As citizens of a community, we must all be active in the rational pursuit of a just communal good and in seeking or supporting leaders for whom that good is the guiding principle of their policies and their action.

9.2 HUMAN LAW AS RATIONAL ARTICULATION OF FUNDAMENTAL SOCIAL PRINCIPLES

Law and authority are very closely implicated with one another in the ethical consciousness of a family, a clan, a nation, or any community. On the one hand, law is understood as issuing from a duly constituted and recognized authority. On the other hand, every particular authority in a rational community, including the highest, is understood as coming under the rule of law, no less than everyone else in the community. Authorities may change the law at times, but when they do, they change it for themselves as well as for everyone else. This is due to the nature of law as part of the external social structure of a community along with authority, both of which are seen as necessary in the dialectic of justice and friendship building up to a rational communal good.

We have seen how the exercise of authority in some form of social structure is necessary and good for a community. In principle at least, authority is supposed to keep members of a community focused on the communal good in their reasoning and collaborative planning for future action and labor. But authorities come and go in the life of a community, and there is no assurance that they will always be true to their purpose of finding the proper or just mean for actions to be taken in the community. They can be sidetracked by their own inordinate affections and particular interests or by the special interests of others who have an undue influence on them in the social arena and divert the concern of authorities from the communal to the particular good of some regimen of society, usually the most affluent, at the expense of the more disadvantaged in the community.

Right reasoning from the communal good is first and foremost a community affair. As such, it dictates not just particular commands to do or not to do at a given time for individuals in a community relative to the communal good but also certain general principles or laws requiring or prohibiting certain behaviors in community relations over time. It is right reasoning from the communal good that is the true origin of law for a community and not just some particular authority at any given time in the history of a community. What makes law universal for all in a community is that it is conceived as useful or necessary for the communal good. This holds true for any sort of community, large or small, including the universal community of mankind.

There is need of a more steadying influence in a community than just some particular form of authority, whether it be parental, monarchical, aristocratic, or majority rule. It is an influence that will attend to the good of all members of a community, minorities as well as majorities, the disadvantaged as well as the more advantaged, those less able to exercise their own human rights as well as those who think only of exercising their own individual rights from a position of power. Such a steadying universal influence can only come from *reason* itself expressing itself as *law*, to moderate the activity of a community as a whole, including the way it comes to choose or recognize its authorities in accordance with a distinctive ethic for a people calling for an institutional or constitutional form of leadership or authority to keep what we have been calling right reasoning on an even and universal keel, a condition for keeping self-interested national members loyal to a community.

Right reasoning from the communal good in deliberation has to do not just with deciding and choosing particular actions to be taken at a particular time but also with developing ways of acting that will consistently yield the good we are seeking. Over time such customary ways of thinking take the form of dispositions in our consciousness or of what Kant calls maxims for what to do when certain options present themselves. Though such dispositions and maxims may remain open for revision upon further experience, they also have the form of universal principles for guiding action as circumstances vary for individuals. Kant says that law is a maxim that a rational being would want to be the maxim for everyone, as if the consciousness of law arose first only from an individual in isolation from other selves in a community. In contrast to this, the consciousness of law we wish to speak of is the one that arises only in a community where mutual recognition of one another is the foundation of both individual rights and law to protect those rights and to promote them for everyone—that is, universally.

That is what we have simplified in the very idea of right reasoning from the communal good. We could call this the first principle of practical reason in ethical consciousness. From this principle we derived the necessity of a disposition for right reasoning and taking counsel or of prudence in all members of a community and of a disposition of true regard or of justice for all others selves. From this principle we have also derived a necessity for authority in the external social structure of a community to promote right reasoning and taking counsel in the community and to give it direction, as well as a necessity to heed such authority as part of the right reasoning of everyone in the pursuit of a good that is at once personal and communal. And now we are deriving a necessity of institutional law as part of the same external social structure, to promote a disposition of justice in everyone toward everyone as an essential part of the communal good and to effectively moderate the interactive relations among members of a community according to a mean that is objective and real in keeping with the rational exigencies of the communal good and not just to a mean that is subjective and shifting in the right ordering of one's passions and emotions, as we shall see in reflecting on the cardinal virtues or courage and temperance in ethical consciousness.

The law we are reflecting on is not a law of nature as such, in the way natural scientists speak of laws. Nor is it properly a natural law, as modern philosophy and theology have spoken of ethics or moral laws, as if they were absolute and given in human nature as something to start from in moral reasoning, coming from a supreme lawgiver for all that exists. We take reason as rising above nature in the historical and ethical consciousness of a community that may be particular as well as universal to include all human beings, and we take law as stemming from reason as it transcends nature in right reasoning from the communal good. That is why we speak of *human law* rather than any supposedly given natural law social scientists may come up with in their reflection on social structures in human behavior. And that is why also we speak of only human law and not any divine law that may also be at play in the historical consciousness of diverse communities in the world.

We do not exclude any references to nature in our reflection on human law in the spirit of a community, as Kant did in his reflections in *Critique of Practical Reason* or *The Metaphysics of Morals*. Human reasoning, even if it is of the highest or "purest" practical form, does not take place apart from nature or external social structures. Those are the grist for reasoning in any historical consciousness. Right reasoning has to be utilitarian as well as true to the communal good. It has to seek an objective mean in the distribution of real external goods in keeping with a good that is communal as well as personal. We could say that this pertains to the nature of right reasoning but that it would not make reasoning a thing of nature. Practical reason is about ordering nature for the good of communities in history. As such, it is not arbitrary or contingent on what happens in nature or in external social structures engineered by human initiative. It has its own exigencies, which are those of a community, that of the whole human race, or one that only participates in that whole, not of nature or of any existing social structure.

Nor do we exclude the possibility of some divine law at work or at play in the historical consciousness. Right reasoning is the exercise of a certain *prudence* or providence in view of a good conceived communally by a community. Different members of a community may have different takes on what that good should be, some perhaps higher or more altruistic than those others. In highly integrated communities, one would hope that those in authority would have the best, most comprehensive view for the highest attainable communal good for a given community.

One could also conceive of a higher authority still, one that has created the universe and the whole of mankind, that still could have a higher communal good than anything human reason can conceive of for a chosen people or for humankind as a whole and that would also enable human beings to strive for that higher good through higher-than-rational means. This would be a higher kind of providence working through human providence for a communal good, but it would not be a providence we can reflect on directly as we are doing here in the historical consciousness of ourselves and others in communion with one another. All that we have to reflect on directly is the right reasoning that binds us together as selves in communion with one another.

Taking that as the first principle of our practical reasoning in ethical consciousness, or as the most universal law of right reasoning in relation to a communal good, we have to see not only how we derive commands for execution through human action but also how we derive certain intermediate principles or laws, precepts for taking or avoiding certain actions, to bring the universality of the first principle of ethical behavior to bear on the particularity of choices we have to make as the conclusions of our deliberations. Actions are always particular and cannot be governed ethically by a principle or a law that says no more than "do good and avoid evil," the "categorical imperative" par excellence. Practical reasoning has to figure out where the good lies and where evil lies in ever-changing particular circumstances, and to do this it needs more and more particular principles and laws to adapt the universal law to more and more particular circumstances of action and decision-making.

Thomas Aquinas compares the process of rational decision making in human action to the process of coming to conclusions in speculative scientific discourse. In the latter, we start from known principles to investigate whether propositions about different subject matters are true or false. If we demonstrate that a certain predicate is proper to a particular subject, we come to a conclusion about the truth of reality. In practical reasoning, we proceed similarly. We start from known precepts about what is good or evil to inquire about different courses of action to see which ones would be conducive to the good we want and which ones would be contrary to that good. What concludes the deliberations is a decision to act in a way that is supposed to be conducive to the good of a community as a whole

For the most part, in our day-to-day life we do this starting from intermediary principles or precepts, either in particular sciences on the side of speculation or in particular spheres of action on the side of practice, principles, and precepts that eventually connect to the first and highest or most common principles and precepts on either side of reasoning, speculative or practical. On the speculative side of reasoning, reflection will lead back to a first principle connected with the understanding of being and nonbeing. Here, on the practical side, it has led us to a first precept about doing good and avoiding evil. When we speak of human law as a whole, we refer to an entire corpus of precepts and principles that have been articulated through right reasoning for human communities in their wide cultural diversities and for the human community as a whole in its intersubjective existence. In reflecting on the ethical consciousness of these communities, we have been elaborating on the first principle or precept as we come to know it through mutual recognition of one another as human beings.

There are many degrees of complexity and subordination in the law of any community going from its first principle to its application in particular cases of rational decision making in the wide realm of human endeavors. But we must always keep in mind that it is not the law that makes community. It is community that makes law, to serve its own purposes—namely, to promote the communal good—which is a spiritual good of dignity as well as a material good of well-being. In his philosophy of history, Georg Wilhelm Friedrich Hegel claims that a people is not a people or a community of historical significance unless it has a written constitution of its own. That is to emphasize not only the centrality of reasoning in the formation of a people but also the historical necessity of formulating laws for what we have been calling the external social structures of a community as distinct from its internal *spirit as rational and free* at the same time as communal. What we have been arguing for is a first principle that states the necessity of formulating laws or precepts to guide and to judge particular actions in various spheres of human endeavor in accordance with whether and how they serve the communal good or not, as simplified in a dialectic of justice and friendship.

The role of law in a community is closely allied with its sense of justice. It sets limits in the ways members interact with one another to keep them from injuring one another, and it determines retribution and penalties for those who transgress the justly defined limits. More importantly, it assures, by force if necessary, that people will live up to their commitment in agreeing to live and work as members of a community, always ready to give their due, at least in justice if not in friendship as well. In a sense, law is akin to the virtue of justice to the extent that it is internalized by the members of the community and becomes part of their habitual thinking, but it is not strictly a virtue or an internal disposition of reason or of will in the sense that prudence and justice are as the basis of existing communities. Law remains only a dictate of reason to bring external social structures into conformity with the spirit of a people or of a community, which is at the discretion of the community as a whole and not just that of particular lawmakers. This implies a very definite limitation of how we come to conceive a plethora of laws and on what they can be expected to do for the good of a community.

If we first ask who are the lawmakers, we should say the community as a whole, the multitude of those whose communal good is at stake, or all those capable of right reasoning in conceiving a communal good for all and in conceiving just measures conducive to that good. That would be similar to holding the entire community in permanent constitutional convention to formulate laws and judicial procedures for all that is done in the community, outside the courts as well as inside. If a community did that formally on a permanent basis, there would be very little time or opportunity for anyone in the community to do anything for one's own good as well as the good of the community. It would also have to presume that all are equally disposed to right reasoning and to respecting the good of others as well as their own in their transactions, which is not likely to happen spontaneously in a large convention of any kind. It may happen in smaller conventions, such as a New England town meeting or the launching of a club or a social movement, but town meetings meet only once or twice a year for a short time, as members take up different tasks in pursuit of their goals. Not all members of a community can be concerned with lawmaking all the time, least of all those who have not yet attained a degree of right reasoning or of caring for the good of others.

This does not necessarily mean that the community as a whole is totally deprived of a voice in lawmaking for itself. It finds its voice in leaders and authorities who come to stand out from the multitude but who come to be recognized as expressing what is conceived as the communal good and what has to be done or avoided to achieve or maintain that good in the community. How leaders or authorities come to stand out, whether by heredity, by proven excellence, or by election, is not the most important thing about the role they have to play in lawmaking for a community. The more essential factor is that they are *recognized* as expressing the thinking of the community and its aspiration to a communal good, as we have already seen in speaking of the necessity for authority as part of the external social structure of a community.

Lawmaking flows from some kind of authority in a community, even when that authority is established by an election or a choice of the people and not by the sheer force of circumstances. However we may think authority is established in a community, it has to be recognized as legitimate only insofar as it serves and promotes what a community conceives as its communal good. Similarly, however, as human law is enacted in a community, it is recognized as binding in conscience of all members of the community only insofar as it is seen as necessary for the communal good. If a law does not serve or promote that good, as Aquinas remarks in defining human law, it is not a law. That is why lawmakers always have to invoke the communal good to justify the measures they impose on people.

Thus, human law has to be seen as a dictate or a directive always ordered to the communal good as to its end, emanating from the reasoning of a community, either as a whole or as speaking through some authority but with the further proviso that it be promulgated for all in the community to know. This proviso introduces a further aspect of lawmaking that has an additional advantage for a community as well as certain limitations. The articulation of principles and laws to govern behavior in interpersonal relations can be viewed as a kind of teaching for the members of the community as well as a kind of coercion to bring newcomers and outlaws into the fold or keep them from harming the community.

Everyone knows the first principle from which we all start in moral or practical reasoning: do good and avoid evil. But not everyone knows the principles that follow from that for the various spheres of social life and economic activity as parts of communal life as a whole. We all know that it is necessary to do good and to avoid evil the moment we come to self-consciousness in mutual recognition of one another, but then we have to learn what doing good and avoiding evil entails in the many things we do as human beings. Communities have to learn this through intelligence reflecting on their experience and through reason deriving more specific principles for judging what is good or evil in the diverse spheres of human activity, both natural or economic and historical or political, as well as communal.

In this reflection on experience, practical intelligence comes to see certain spheres of activity as essential or necessary in the communal good and therefore as requiring the articulation of principles of their own for discerning between good and evil, right and wrong, just and unjust in each particular sphere, laws to promote or require certain activities in a certain way and to prohibit other activities. Thus, we reason to the necessity of certain practical principles to guide our action in different particular spheres, much as the scientist reasons to the necessity of certain particular conclusions in the diverse spheres of being, whether natural or social. Authorities as lawmakers, therefore, should be seen as teachers and leaders in this process of deriving more and more necessary particular principles for guiding the actions of members toward the communal good—necessary not only in the sense that they are required for promoting the communal good but also in the sense that they follow from the first principle understood as the foundation of a community. As leaders in this respect of deriving particular principles from the first universal one, they should also be seen as teachers for the community at large in matters that all should come to understand for themselves, at least with regard to principles that are presented as following necessarily from the first principle or what are also called natural law principles as derived by practical reasoning from its first principle as the foundation for human community.

Here, however, a caveat should be expressed regarding principles as enunciated in particular laws. They do not all follow from the first principle with the same necessity, just as conclusions in diverse sciences do not always follow from the first principle of speculative science, which is that we cannot say that something is and is not at one and the same time and in one and the same regard. It is a long way from the certainty and necessity of this first principle for anyone who has the use of intelligence to the certainty and necessity of conclusions arrived at rationally, say in cutting-edge physics or economic theory. And there are many intermediate laws and principles that have been discovered along the way that have led to the enunciation of these most advanced principles. The principles that follow more immediately from the first principles as found in particular sciences such as physics and economics, to name one natural science and one social science, have more of the certainty and the necessity about them of the first principle of reasoning than those that are later brought forth, usually after much debate, when more and particular factors have been brought forth so that reason finds it more and more difficult to keep track of all of them and to synthesize them into conclusions about individual events with total certainty and necessity. At the cutting edge of inquiry in such sciences, even the most exact, we find conclusions that are uncertain and tentative, asserting statistical probabilities as the closest thing they can come to by way of principle or law.

In the process of right reasoning for human action, we find a similar gradation of certainty and necessity, going from the universal certainty and necessity of its first principle, which says to do good and avoid evil, through intermediate principles, usually taken for granted in a community as constitutional to a final conclusion, which in the final analysis is to take a decision to take some concrete action. The first principle is most certain and necessary. It is what gives rise to right reasoning as such in relation to particular spheres of human activity, such as family life in which procreation and education of future generations takes place and economic life in which the management of external affairs and material goods take place for the well-being of the community as a whole and of individuals and families through the coordination of labor and commerce. For each of such activities recognized as essential and necessary in the pursuit of the good for human beings, rational societies discover or derive regulative principles to make them work for the good or at least to prevent individuals from injuring one another and the community as a whole, laws deemed necessary for maintaining order and rightness in the pursuit of the good.

In other animal species, which are also in pursuit of their own good, such regulative principles may develop naturally, so to speak—that is, uncritically and without self-consciousness—only as conditions for survival. Species without the "right" kind of regulation in their behavior do not survive. But for the human species there is more at stake than just survival of the species. There is the higher good of communal and personal life for which we have reason to set us on our way, over and above the nature we share with other animals. Reason is for us the "natural law" we derive from our first ethical principle as it relates to the communal good. Among the principles we derive in the sphere of family life, there are some that follow immediately, such as those that govern the institution of marriage with regard to sexual relations, the procreation of children, and their education, which enable us to discern right from wrong, good from evil, in what we do pertaining to this sphere. These are seen as certain and necessary almost as much as the first principle, but only for this sphere of activity and not for other spheres. They are the first principles for the discernment of good from evil in the sphere of family life, hopefully recognized by both the family and the broader society. From these particular first principles other principles will also emerge through reason to address more particular questions yet of good and bad in different aspects of what is to be done in this sphere of activity, questions of policy regarding one thing or another amid the plethora of things to be done, which can go on indefinitely in the concrete practice of a family or a small community.

As we move further and further away from first principles and closer to the complex requirements for particular actions, however, we also move farther and farther away from certainty and necessity of the first principles in our reasoning, into matters that are difficult for reason to encompass clearly and that therefore are open for discussion. Principles and policies formulated at this level of practical reasoning are similar to conclusions at the cutting edge of the more advanced speculative sciences: they cannot be seen as certain and necessary in the same way as first principles are or as those that follow immediately from these first principles for the different spheres of human activity, as we find them enshrined in written constitutions, for example. At the cutting edge of human enterprise in social activity, rational lawmakers cannot know or anticipate all the conditions and circumstances that will affect the good of all members of society any more than most members do. Even if laws or policies still have to be enacted at that level of uncertainty in practical reasoning, the law has to remain flexible and open to revision, and it has to allow for exceptions that do not come under the law when they come from a higher wisdom and prudence in relation to the communal good.

Thus, even when it is seen as following necessarily from ethical and natural first principles, so to speak, in the prudent exercise of practical reasoning, human law is bound to be changeable and open to adjustments in many respects. With regard to the first principles from which it operates, human law does not change. It cannot abandon any of these basic principles in which it is grounded as right reasoning. They are the foundation of what we call the *rule of law* in society. But as the laws, or lawmakers, draw closer to particular cases and to particular spheres of human activity, they have to formulate additional principles and guidelines to fit the more particular historical circumstances of social interaction, realizing that these are not the only way that a rational society could go in its pursuit of a human good and that members of the society still have their own reasoning to go by, which is not reducible to the reasoning of the lawmaker, even as it relates to the communal good.

The prudent lawmaker does not enact law without taking counsel with those who come under the law, not just to secure allegiance to the law in society at large but also to produce a better, more rational law that will better serve the communal good. Even then, however, the law that is produced, necessary as it may be for the moment, can never be the final word in an evolving historical community. There is always a need to review the law in any community and to add or to subtract from it, to amend it in keeping with the changing requirements of the communal good and with the changing degrees of internal virtue in the members of a community. At the limit, the more dispositions of prudence and justice are found in the members of a community, the less law it requires in its external social structure. This is the obverse of saying that authority and law are necessary to coerce outlaws or others still not integrated into a community into acting like members of the community, even if they do not have the internal dispositions of right reasoning in dialogue with others and of justice toward all others.

Virtue is the bond of community, not law. What brings members together and keeps them in unison with one another are internal dispositions of right reasoning and of regard for the good of one another. Law is necessary as a guide mainly for those who do not have those dispositions to the extent that such dispositions are not fully developed or remain unsteady as a community develops its way of living and of making a living in the world. We have seen that law is an external regulation for what has to happen in a community for virtue and the communal good to take hold. As such, law is not an internal disposition of character or virtue, though there can be a habit of judging according to the law that is laudable among the members of a community and necessary for the communal good, which makes law a matter of internal conscience for the members of a community.

The question arises, then, as to whether law, an external social constraint, can cause virtue, an internal disposition acquired not by nature or by any external constraint but only by repeated acts of right reasoning in relation to the communal good and of willing the good of others as well as oneself in any and all social interactions. In other words, the virtues of prudence and justice we have referred to, not to mention friendship, develop from within the members who form a community in communication with one another, not by any external constraint as such. Strictly speaking, then, as only an external constraint, law cannot cause virtue in any self-operating out of a rational free will. It can only create social conditions in which rational free agents may or could act in a manner that is reasoned rightly and justly on a consistent and regular basis.

This is not to say that law has nothing to do with conscience or responsibility or, more precisely, that conscience and responsibility have nothing to do with law. On the contrary, lawmaking has to do with forming conscience and responsibility in a community, and members have an obligation to take the law into consideration as they come to their own judgments about good and evil social interaction since, as we have seen, lawmaking is a necessity for right reasoning in pursuit of a communal good. The question as to how much law can do to foster, or perhaps to prevent, the development of a genuinely communal spirit remains. It can help, by coercion, those who remain outside that spirit to enter into it, but it can also hinder, also by coercion, those who are well advanced in that spirit by preventing them from entering more deeply into it. We can legislate matters of justice required for friendship, as we have also seen, but we cannot legislate friendship, an essential ingredient of the communal good. Attempts to do so usually degenerate into unjust favoritism and a consequent deterioration of the communal good.

In the other sphere of human activity we have alluded to—the economic over and above the natural or the familial—there is also a necessity to articulate laws to maintain a just equilibrium in human communities, but such laws or principles will not be derived directly from nature as given to us in family or tribal life or as natural law in the sense that we have been speaking about it. In economic activity, the rational animal rises above nature as given or as a result only of evolution or survival. Through labor, human beings transform the things of nature and use them to create a better world, a better life for themselves than they would have if they remained mere animals only adapting to a given ecostructure. In doing so they appropriate things and exchange them within the framework of a communal life, each one for oneself at the same time as in communion with others. They make history for themselves and their community.

In this sphere of activity there is room for a lot more freedom and enterprise than we find among other animal species just barely making a living or surviving in a world of give and take. In the sphere of the rational and enterprising animal there is room for revolutions of every sort—agricultural, industrial, and technological—all of which add new levels of development and communication within and among communities. But it is important to note that all their activity does not take place without a great deal of invention, cultivation, buying, or selling—not just of goods but also of labor and services. Economic activity is an eminently social activity, and justice requires that everyone in the community gets his due from it in goods, in wages, or in compensation of any kind. And it is for every community to determine the principles on which this due is to be calculated for each one in the community as producer and as consumer.

To do this, a community must start from the same first principles we have been advocating from the beginning of our reflection on the practice of selfhood: *right reasoning* from the communal good. From its conception of that good, however abstruse it may seem at first and as first, it must proceed to formulate more specific principles of justice for the various phases of negotiation and exchange in economic activity—not natural laws as such, since we are now reasoning not about nature or from nature but about history and from history, nor the so-called laws of the market in a modern economy that hardly rises above a jungle warfare among competitors—but rational laws seen as necessary to preserve and to promote the communal good of all for everyone in the community.

These would be laws that specify basic human rights under justice for all members in order to protect those rights by enforcement, in addition to laws that promote the exercise of those rights by all, the least advantaged as well as the most. They would be laws that a community arrives at by reasoning on its historical experience and that of other communities in different stages of economic development. Those that follow more immediately from the first principle would be seen as more certain and more necessary and therefore as unchangeable insofar as they are constitutional. Those that come after, as economies become more and more complex and liable to fall into the hands of more and more powerful operators such as large corporations, will be seen as less certain and necessary but will still have to rise to the need of assuring justice for all in negotiations and commerce of every kind: just prices, just wages, just benefits, just representations of goods and services on offer, and so on to protect consumers as well as providers and buyers as well as sellers and to keep the economy from falling apart from the excesses of its most powerful agents, the managers of excessively large corporations whose concern for social justice in any community has all but disappeared.

It would seem that the only community capable of dealing with large modern corporations or conglomerates of corporations is the nation, not the family and not the tribe. Smaller, more local communities need the nation to keep these large economic operators within the constraints of social justice as well as of individual case justice that has to be brought before courts. Only a nation can write law or establish objective norms for just pricing, just wages, just benefits, just representation of goods and services, and just profits in view of the communal good in an economy for players who might otherwise run wild and self-destruct as well as do injury to others and to social justice. Modern economies have shown many examples of this kind of self- and social destruction. Whatever reasons may be given for such recurrent injustice—whether greed, arrogance, or stupidity on the part of agents in the economic systems—it is part of right reasoning in nations to articulate laws and formulate principles for judging what will be allowed and what will be forbidden in the entire gamut of economic transactions on the basis of what has been found to work and not work for the communal good. Such laws are deemed to be necessary for advancing and maintaining the communal good, though they may not be as certain as the principles and laws from which they are derived as adapted to the changing circumstances in which the communal good is to be sought. The problem here is not one of choosing what sort of economic system we are going to have, capitalist or socialist. All economic activity is socially interactive and works only with accumulated capital. The problem is finding and making laws and regulations that will make it work or keep it working for the good of all and not just for the few who use it only for profit for their own personal aggrandizement. That is what the disposition toward social justice means and requires in a national economy.

The emergence of large multinational corporations as controlling agents in an economy that they have created and that cuts across national borders presents many problems from the standpoint of just lawmaking in any nation, large or small. How can any nation legislate in the face of a power that overwhelms it and that shows no regard for the communal good of any nation, least of all for the local economy that is sustenance for any local community? This is a problem not only for small nations, which are usually the poorest and least developed, an easy prey for large corporations to take over and draw into their own corporate economy, leaving every semblance of a just national economy in shambles for it to better serve the economy of the megacorporation, ignoring all the economic regulations that have made other nations not just more rich but also more just. It is also a problem for the larger nations and the more socially as well as economically developed who constantly have to fight off efforts of takeover by the rich and powerful corporations who are constantly jockeying for positions through elections and through lobbying in national assemblies so that they can write their own laws for the nation, without regard for social justice and the communal good, as if their own corporate good were the only good that counted in society.

This is not the place to elaborate on how this totalitarian takeover by relatively few people takes place in rich as well as in poor nations. But it is the place to remind authorities and lawmakers in any nation, large or small, rich or poor, that they have as their responsibility to provide for the communal good of their people, or at least a decent minimum level of social justice for all. That is what defines them as authorities and lawmakers in a community that is rational and just. If they do not stand up for their people—all of them, no matter how poor and destitute—they are not reasoning rightly, and they are not just in whatever lawmaking they indulge in, especially when they legislate in favor of the rich and the mighty at the expense of the poor and the powerless, the marginalized by a totalitarian economic system kept in place by multinational corporations. This is something leaders must be concerned with in any community, above all on the national level, against the incursions of large corporations, since there is no higher authority or constitutional law to grapple with the machinations of these multinational corporations in a global economy they have created for themselves.

9.3 HUMAN LAW AS DETERMINATION OF HISTORICAL SOCIAL STRUCTURES

THE LAW WE HAVE BEEN REFLECTING ON SO FAR is the law rational communities derive from necessary first principles by way of conclusion from historical experience in the way they labor over nature and develop economies of exchange among themselves and with other communities. In its most basic forms, this experience begins with the cultivation of fields and bringing produce to market for exchange so that all in the community may have the opportunity through buying and selling to satisfy their diverse needs through a diversity of goods produced by human ingenuity. From this experience, communities learn that personal ownership of fields, more than just possession without recognition of that right, is necessary for the communal as well as the personal good. For, as Aristotle argues against Plato, fields commonly held are commonly neglected and consequently never get to serve the higher human good of community.

Similarly, from this experience, communities also learn the necessity of buying and selling for sharing privately held goods with others in the community or with other communities and the necessity of establishing common objective norms, or what Aristotle calls a *real mean* or measure for comparing objects or services that are not of the same kind, so that equality will be maintained in exchanges no matter what the subjective intentions are of those entering into the bargain. These are fundamental principles of justice that then have to be refined as the economic experience of a community develops and as systems of exchange become more complex, internationally as well as nationally, but that nevertheless come as consequences or conclusions derived from those first principles, giving rise to private ownership of means of production and to fair pricing in all exchanges of labor and services as well as goods. These are frequently referred to as natural law principles in discussion of human law, but we have described and prescribed them as principles of justice derived from historical experience through right reasoning from the communal good.

There is, however, another kind of human law in human communities that is not derived as a matter of consequence or conclusion from first principles taken as either natural law or the law of justice in economic exchanges of external goods but that is also deemed necessary for the communal good. This is commonly referred to as *positive law*, in contradistinction from so-called natural law or the law of nations that govern basic social relations in accordance with equity and decency or fairness to all. It is deemed positive in the sense that it adds determination in realms of social structure where the fundamental laws of social justice remain indeterminate. This is said in contrast to what more specific laws add to the first principles in right reasoning, in keeping with more developed economic and social circumstances of the means of production and the exchange of external goods.

The specification of human law we have been talking about up to now is arrived at as a matter of consequence or conclusion from the first principles constitutive of a community through right reasoning, in accordance with the historical experience of economic development. Tentative as this reasoning may become as it addresses more and more complex relations of production and exchange, it still has something of the necessity that attends the principles of right reasoning in a community. It is deductive, so to speak, in the way that conclusions are arrived at in speculative reasoning. Not so, however, with the second kind of law we are trying to get at now. It does not merely follow from historical experience as we know it. It is more constructive of new experience, adding determinations that foster new forms of freedom and self-determination in communities and that maintain a higher spirit of unison and friendship among the participants.

Concerning this second kind of human law in communities or in nations, two things should be noted. First, although they denote a higher degree of freedom and originality in the way they come to be formulated, they are still derivative from the first principles of right reasoning that make lawmaking a necessity for the good of a community and a nation. This presupposes that some positive lawmaking is deemed necessary for the communal good and it implies that when such *positive laws* are duly enacted in view of the communal good, they too become obligatory in conscience for the members of the community. They become part of what individuals have to respond to in their own deliberation about what to do and what not to do in social transactions.

Enactment makes laws part of what members have to take into consideration in their own practical reasoning from the communal good. They are not merely external impositions that can be ignored in the internal realm as long as one is not caught violating them, as is often thought in the case of traffic laws, for example, or tax laws or laws defining punishments for particular crimes. Conscientious observance of such laws is part of what is necessary for the communal good, but so too is conscientious objection to such laws when they are judged not to be conducive to the communal good or to social justice for all. Serious conscientious objectors in a community, such as Mahatma Gandhi and Nelson Mandela, who show concern for the communal good are never just revolutionary or troublemakers. They are lawmakers in their own way, setting communities on new courses of action.

The second thing to be noted about this second kind of human law for communities or for nations is that they are bound to be proper to the community in which they are duly enacted by a process of self-determination. This means that, to the extent that different communities and nations take an original and distinctive shape of their own through self-determination in history and in different geographical locations, they cannot and will not have the same form of legislation to govern their social affairs. Each is bound to have a form of legislation or a way of legislating, different from others—customs that may evolve with the experience of development in the community but always in keeping with what is original and determinate for this or that community in its place of origin.

We see here how lawmakers can and should have a creative role to play in a community or a nation, such as founding fathers and mothers or reformers setting new courses of action for their community or new ways of acting in consort with one another, as in the case of the Greek *polis*, the modern state, or the emerging nations of the Third World. True lawmakers foster a new spirit of cooperation and communion among people otherwise dispersed or at odds with one another. And in doing so they are bound to particularize human law in more and more diverse ways so that we should not expect humans to be the same in all nations and in all communities. Right reasoning in the construction of law for a community has many directions to choose from, some of which it may find already given and some of which it may have to invent in the light of the communal good it is pursuing. What results from this is a rich, historical diversity of ways in pursuing the human good that are irreducible to one another but that should complement one another rather than be in contention with one another, as in the case of multinational corporations in competition with one another.

There is a sense in which human law should be the same for everyone in that it is necessary as a social means for pursuing the communal good and in that it entails recognizing basic human rights for everyone without which there can be no community of selves. This would be true of human law in both the senses we have distinguished—the one that concludes to more particular principles from first principles in practical reasoning and the one that invents or determines new principles to keep new forms of interaction on track toward a communal good. But to the extent that human action itself is innovative and even revolutionary in human history, human law has to change in keeping with different cultures that emerge without losing its capacity to shape the external social structures in a way that is conducive to the communal as well as to the personal good of communities. This is especially true of a human law that determines new principles for social behavior as communities come to an understanding of their own in history distinct from what they are by nature and from what other communities have made themselves. There is a need for continuous and creative lawmaking and for judging according to law in making history for any community or nation.

This kind of lawmaking is in the class of genuine artistic creation where selves are called to express themselves in external social forms that will better represent their universal aspiration to the communal good. It is an integral part of historical initiative in what we have come to call the art of politics, where lawmakers and judges show true leadership in response to the aspirations of their time.

We could ask where nature or where the law of nations leaves off and where the creative art of politics begins in historical lawmaking. What in human law is arrived at strictly by way of conclusion from experience and first principles of practical reasoning, and what is arrived at by way of free determination in human initiative? Posed in this way, the question seems to presuppose that we can abstractly separate the historical from the natural in our experience, when in experience and in practice they are caught up together in a dialectical process of conceiving a good we aspire to and choosing the means required for achieving that good. The decisions we make affect our experience, which in turn affects the knowledge we derive from experience by way of conclusion. Our decisions can and do in fact lead us to new conclusions that were not clear in our first awareness of first principles in practical reasoning but not directly as decisions, for that would make the conclusions arbitrary and not rational or necessary in guiding human action toward the good. They do so only indirectly by giving way to new experiences as calls for a new interpretation of what is necessary for the communal good in light of the results and the consequences of our prior decisions.

This is how rational selves learn what it takes to be ethical as they take new initiatives in pursuit of their good. They start off with only a vague notion of the good they want as human beings, which they cannot conceive more clearly apart from the means they have to choose from in pursuit of that good. Choosing means is a sort of experimentation for the rational self to see which one works better for the good intended and which one does not in a process of clarification for articulating what Kant calls maxims in different spheres of action that then come to be seen as laws for each particular sphere—for oneself and for others in the community. In this ethical experimentation, historical consciousness cannot do as if it stood at the end of history, with a complete and final knowledge of the good we are aiming at and of the only means that can lead to that good. It has to learn by trial and error what principles to stay with as good and what principles to discard as bad, as historical right reasoning from the communal good requires.

This is already true in the first form of human law derived from first principles as necessary conclusions, but it is even more true of human law derived from those first principles as determinations in the more creative spheres of human activity, where the means themselves are devised by human initiative in history rather than by just nature alone. History is a mixture of human initiative and nature. There is simply no state of pure nature to start from in historical consciousness. Everything we find in reason to deliberate over is always a product of nature and human labor. Attempts to keep the two separate lead to skepticism and cultural relativism. Because we cannot find nature or reason in isolation from everything, we say that whatever comes to be is arbitrary or indifferent, neither good nor bad. We do not see that there is nature and reason in human initiative itself, as we have been seeing throughout this reflection. The social reality or the culture we start from is indeed open to the free initiative of selves with its positive orientation toward a communal good in the making. As we look forward to envision what that good will be, we also reflect back on what shape our initiative is to take so that we are enabled to judge between good and evil even in the realm of the most creative initiatives where selves transcend nature.

As human beings invent new ways of coming together as communities, they must also invent new laws of extreme social cohesiveness such as we find in cultures of all sorts. Instead of thinking of the two kinds of human law we have distinguished—those that are derived by way of conclusion in practical reasoning and those that are derived by way of determination in taking new initiatives in history—perhaps it would be better to think of them as coming together on a continuum of law with two extremes, one where the law is clearly a matter of conclusion from natural and rational first principles concerning human rights in a community and the other where the law is clearly a matter of free determination in an original way of coming together for selves laboring in common to create a new life, with a middle where one extreme passes gradually over into the other in a historical dialectic. This would explain why there is one basic human law for all human societies, a law of nations so to speak, or a *jus gentium*, and also why there have to be different human laws for different human societies depending on the different ways they have cultivated their own affairs, external as well as internal.

In any given culture, let alone the multiplicity of cultures, it is impossible to draw a sharp line between what is from nature and what is from human creativity or from perversity and destructiveness. For the historical being that we are, there is simply no state of pure nature from which to start. Everything we find in any society is a product of both nature and reasoning. Attempts to keep the two separate in reflections lead to either absolute tyranny, as according to Hobbes, or absolute cynicism, as according to libertarians, concerning any human law. Right reasoning from the communal good requires lawmaking on both levels of human activity, the natural and the historical or cultural. Human nature is not closed in upon itself as in a narrow circle of survival, the way it is for nonrational animals. It is open to new initiatives, freely conceived for the betterment of selves. On the other hand, human freedom is not independent of nature or of the mutual recognition that is constitutive of ethical consciousness. Both come under right reasoning and lawmaking for the communal good.

It is reasoning that makes the distinction between the two extremes on the continuum of law in its twofold relation to nature, that of concluding and that of determining or deciding. But it is also reason that holds them together in their distinction as it passes from one extreme to the other, back and forth, in its historical task of learning and inventing what is necessary for the greater communal good at one and the same time or in alternating phases. The distinction is important because it clarifies the various aspects of reason's lawmaking task in history, while the continuum from one extreme to the other represents the horizontal dimension of law as it affects external social structures into which a vertical dimension is introduced for the sake of a spiritual communal good. It is for each society to work out its own law, both rationally and freely, starting from nature as given and going toward an end it shares with all other societies, the spiritual good of history. It would be insufficient to rely on nature alone to give a society its human law, but it would also be imprudent or irresponsible on the part of reason to fly in the face of nature or of the necessity for law even in its boldest initiatives.

The question of human law as free determination in external social structure recognized as necessary for the communal good brings us back to the question of *authority*, for law does not take shape in a community except through the mediation of selves who care about the communal good in their historical consciousness. That is why *responsibility* for the communal good is of the essence in any definition of authority or of law in any community. Such responsibility pertains to everyone in a community as a whole, as it would ideally in a perfect democracy of virtuous citizens perfectly disposed to right reasoning and to justice in their dealings with one another. But in less-than-perfect societies with less-than-perfect right reasoning and justice for all, this responsibility is delegated or devolves to leaders in a community who, supposedly, can better express the aspirations of the community and the historical means necessary for reaching that happy or happier state.

Just as there are two ways of proceeding from first principles in practical reasoning, so there can also be two ways of exercising authority—one that consists in authentic interpretation of what can be concluded as certain and necessary from those principles, which gives rise to a *jus gentium* or a law of nations common to all in the exercise of their human rights, and one that consists in a simple declaration or determination of what will be right or wrong for a particular society in its historical and cultural circumstances.

It is important to keep these two ways of lawmaking clearly in mind, especially in comparative law studies, so that we will not confuse the law of a particular society with the law as it pertains to all societies and, even more importantly, so that we will not lose sight of the law common to all societies in intercultural and international relations. For the latter there is no universally recognized authority for propounding the law and providing rightly owed humanitarian aid, not to mention mere protection of human rights, such as we find within the boundaries of particular nations. But with the increasing globalization, not just of the economy but also of culture and religion, the need for such a global law of nations and of an authority to propound and enforce it, is coming to be recognized more and more, to regulate what multinational corporations have wrought and make it serve better the communal good of all human beings around the globe, with justice and friendship for all rather than just the private good of those who profit from so-called private corporate activities thanks to scores of workers who are not even counted in the calculations.

Chief executive officers of multinational corporations and their cohorts are not in the business of caring for the communal good. That is the business of political leaders and authorities within the diverse nations in control of their own diverse economies. Nor can we say that international associations of these multinational corporations, such as the World Trade Organization, the International Monetary Fund, or the World Bank, are any more in the business of caring for any communal good of selves around the globe. They are in the business only of facilitating the operations of multinational corporations across national borders, usually at the expense of all the nations in which they operate, rich and poor. The only agencies in the business of caring for the communal good on an international level seem to be those of the United Nations, such as the World Health Organization or UNESCO, and the so-called nongovernmental organizations (NGOs) dedicated to providing humanitarian and developmental aid wherever it is needed, seconded by the United Nations (UN) in doing so. These agencies in and out of the UN have no officially recognized lawmaking authority of their own except such as is granted by treaties or by international agreements, but they can be seen as leaders in making new laws in effect to bring humanitarian aid to people and to protect them against the abuse and the despoliation wrought upon them and their natural resources by reckless foreign exploitation. They are shapers of a more just international social structure rallying people from all walks of life and all parts of the world in opposition to the rampaging of multinational corporations and redistributing wealth in a fairer fashion.

We can speak of these NGOs as lawmakers insofar as we recognize them as caring for the communal good on an international level where there is no government supposedly caring for any communal good but where there is much need for law and order in a jungle of corporate warfare. Recognition of this need is the first social bond that draws peoples around the globe together, the bond of justice that leads to peace and friendship. Law is an organization of external social structures seen as necessary for the communal good of selves. It flows through prudence or right reasoning from the communal good in leaders or authorities recognized as such by selves in a community. Recognition confers upon law a certain universality and objectivity that transcends the idiosyncrasy of those who make it, for once a law has been recognized as such, it becomes binding on its authors as well as the other members of the community. It becomes an objective social bond that ties members together and binds them in a conscience shared by all equally.

As recognized in conscience, law brings some assurance of stability amid the fluctuations of subjective dispositions that can pull individuals apart from one another as they compete for survival and thus are set at odds with one another. It serves the communal good by helping persons transcend their subjective partialities. It is universal, not as something generic and common to everyone in the human species but as coming under the communal good, as a means to that end. In this sense law is a good for society, not just a necessary evil we have to obey extrinsically when we are caught up in it, as in a purely penal conception of law. When human law is recognized as determining what is for the good of a community, it plays a mediating role for reconciling individuals with one another in the conscience they share as a community without, however, collapsing external positive law into internal conscience or internal conscience into external positive law.

There are two ways in which this kind of collapsing can take place: by accepting some external positive law as the sole norm for conscience or by making one's subjective conscience the only law there is to obey. These two attitudes, the first found in Hobbes and the second found in Kant, are the direct opposites of one another in the modern liberal conception of law, and they feed on one another in their opposition. Both flow from a common confusion about how law and conscience relate to one another. One recognizes only external law dictated by an absolute tyrant deemed necessary for the survival of subjects, otherwise caught in a war of everyone against everyone without adverting in the least to anything like conscience in anyone's historical consciousness where reasoning is grounded in some concern for the communal good. The other ignores the reality and goodness of external positive law deemed necessary for the communal good and falls back on a purely internal conscience as the only law of moral consciousness without adverting to any necessity of taking external action in following one's conscience. But neither takes into account the crucial role *virtue* has to play in this mediation between internal conscience and external positive law.

No community of any historical significance exists in a state of pure nature without virtue of any kind in those who make it up. Neither does virtue exist by nature in the rational animals that make up a society. Virtue comes into being in free, rational agents only through repeated acts of right reasoning and of willing justice for the other as well as for oneself in the perspective of a communal good, as we have seen repeatedly in our analysis of ethical consciousness. What constitute human communities more than anything are *acquired virtues* of prudence and justice in mutual recognition of a reciprocal good among subjects in community with one another. It is these fundamental virtues that more than anything else beget human communities, which then in turn reinforce these virtues and bring them to new heights of perfection in the way selves come together as selves in peace and friendship as makers of their own history. Historically speaking, the two—virtue and community—have to be seen as developing apace with one another in a properly conceived whole.

The virtues we have been talking about, however, are internal dispositions of reason and of will or of the rational appetite in self-consciousness as these relate to other self-consciousnesses in community. There are other virtues as well that have to be acquired and developed under the guidance of reason in the management of sense appetites for selves living in community. We will address these later under the heading of courage and temperance as cardinal virtues that go with prudence and justice. For the moment, we should note that it is the internal dispositions of right reasoning and justice that require some form of authority and law in the external social structure of a community to assure a higher fulfillment of the communal good. Without some external control, some heteronomy, the pure autonomy of rational self-consciousnesses will result in chaos or anything but ordered peace and prosperity. This does not mean the kind of absolute authority and law Hobbes reasons to in his social contract theory. But it does mean a necessity of recognizing some external authority and law in the conscience of a community, especially under the requirements of social justice, in the management of external affairs and of transactions among the members of a community, not to mention transactions with other elements of the broader community. Hence the need for a special prudence for lawmakers in a community and a special commitment to justice for all, which has to be reckoned with in any conscience but that does not become internal to any purely individual conscience as such.

The positive determinate law emanating from any authority in a community must remain external and objective relative to any subjective conscience, even one disposed to right reasoning and social justice. Even if it has to be reckoned with in taking counsel for prudent and just action of one's own, it is not reducible to conscience as such in what it requires and in its sanctions, as Kant would have it. Mutual recognition of one another as selves in our transactions is what mediates between the external and the internal, between the objective and the subjective in a shared concern for a communal good.

Keeping this distinction clearly in mind between the external and the internal, between the objective and the subjective, is important for understanding how human law, objectively promulgated, relates to virtue or a formed conscience and to the communal good it is supposed to serve. We have seen that authority and law alone, as externally imposed, cannot cause virtue in subjects. At best, they can only create social conditions in which virtue may develop through repeated free acts as commitment to pursuing a good that is communal as well as personal. Much less can they create that communal and personal good itself. Pushed to their extremes, as in Hobbes or in Kant, external laws and individual experience can only make that good impossible to attain.

The good we are speaking of for a human community is a spiritual good, one that includes the good of friendship as well as the good of justice. External authority and law, prudently articulated and justly administered, can go a long way in creating conditions for such a historical good to take shape in the consciousness of selves, but they cannot legislate that good itself any more than they can legislate virtue itself. Even if they can legislate some aspects of justice, they cannot legislate friendship, peace, or happiness. That comes only through an internal, spiritual initiative of selves that takes hold when certain minimal but decent external and material conditions are actualized in a social structure that is just and externally assured by some authority and law.

All of this implies that authority and law are bound to be different in different communities, in subordination to the different spirits that move them. There is no one fixed concept of external law that fits all nations, let alone all communities. Neither is there any fixed concept of authority for all time. Not even God is such an authority. The spirit moves much more freely in a community than the law can so that the law has to be constantly adjusted and revised to keep up with the needs of the spirit for two rather obvious reasons: one on the part of reason itself, which makes the law, and one on the part of selves, for whom the law is made.

To begin with, then, as a product of human reason at a given moment of history, law shares not only in the human spirit's creativity but also in its limitations. In practice, reasoning proceeds from principles to conclusions only gradually, one step at a time, finding its way to more particular principles only tentatively, as one reflects on the historical experience of a community. On the side of establishing more positive determinations of law, the prudent lawmaker has to proceed even more tentatively, not knowing exactly how subjects will implement the law or what will be the outcome of their implementation. As brilliant and as genial as lawmakers may be in the positive determinations they bring to the law, they cannot know ahead of time all the ways the law will come to fruition or fail to meet the changing needs of a community. The laws they put in place have to be firm if they are to provide stability for the community. They should not be easily changeable, especially if they are fundamental and constitutional, but they should also be flexible and adaptable to new situations as the social structures evolve in unpredictable ways. New laws have to be instituted to meet the requirements of the communal good and to protect human rights of selves in the new circumstances. Old laws need to be let go or reinterpreted when they no longer serve the basic human rights of large segments of the society.

This takes away nothing of the genius of original lawmakers. If it is done rationally and honestly or transparently, it should improve on the law instituted by the founders of a community on the basis of its growing experience, letting go of principles and determinations that have proven to be wrong or ill conceived and adding new principles and determinations more in keeping with the requirements of a changing communal good so that law remains a necessary component of the social structure in a community working toward its historical good in conjunction with other communities also working toward their own historical good.

The second reason for flexibility and openness to positive change in the law of a community comes from the side of the selves at whom the law is aimed or for whom it is intended. If law is meant as a discipline for selves who may be at odds with the rational and just spirit of a community, it must adapt to the changing dispositions of those selves as they relate to the communal good. Strict laws and strict law enforcement are necessary for those lacking in right reasoning and in the sense of justice for others, but as selves develop dispositions of right reasoning and of justice of their own in a community there is less need for law to be overbearing. Brutal law enforcement can offend against the communal good building up in the community and can become irrational and unjust, the opposite of what law is for.

Law is supposed to provide a certain stability in social relations, but it can do so only if it takes into consideration the different dispositions that different selves exhibit in their behavior, good and bad. Mature people who are reasonable and just in their dealings with others do not need to be treated as children or as criminals. Nor can children or criminals of any kind be forced to become virtuous in their reasoning or in their dispositions toward others. Virtue comes to selves in a community only through a free exercise of repeated acts that is beyond the control of external authority and law. Learning and teaching virtue, which is bound to be different not just for individual selves in a community but also for different communities at different stages of their development, follows a pace of its own to which authority and law must adapt. It is not selves who are at the service of law and authority but authority and law that are at the service of selves in community with one another.

This is not an argument against law and law enforcement in any community of selves as such. We have seen how human law and law enforcement are necessary and good as part of the external social structure of a community. We even have argued that, as relations of production and exchange become more and more complex in a society or in history as a whole, there is more and more need for laws to regulate and to define what is just and unjust in these relations and for real enforcement of those laws. This is an argument for recognizing the limits of what external law and authority can and cannot do for the spiritual good of a community.

Law and order as such are not the communal good we are seeking in community life. They are only means to that good, and they are conceived as good only as necessary means to that good and only insofar as they are conducive to that good, which transcends the scope of law and order. As such they cannot be absolute or fixed in any totalitarian fashion for any segment of society, even if it is a majority. Even if law and order are just at any given moment, they are not the internal dispositions that make for justice in a community. Much less are they the makers of such dispositions. They can only open the way for such internal and subjective dispositions in selves that make up a community, who in turn have to conceive the communal good for themselves and the way they will actualize it in peace and friendship.

To this extent we have to say that external authority and law enforcement must will their own end when they are no longer necessary or when they can no longer lead the way. There is much more to leadership in a community than what authority and law can provide, coming from the selves who have acquired the social virtues of prudence and justice and who are still working toward their second perfection as a community. Authority and law must not only maintain social conditions for such spontaneity to occur. They must also make way for it by stepping aside and by willing their own end as an imposition on a community that no longer needs them. One may wonder whether such a happy state can ever be reached by any community in history, but the fact that some communities have attained relative states of happiness and peace for a time at least, over and above what authority and law can dictate, suggests that there is more to the idea of the communal good than anything authority and human law can provide, let alone dictate, and that the validity of human law ends where that more begins.

9.4 CONSCIENCE, LAW, AND REVOLUTION

Having seen this limitation of what determinate human law and authority can do in the pursuit of our communal good, it remains for us to consider how we still have to recognize it as a historical means to be consulted in taking counsel prior to taking action for our future good. We spoke about taking counsel earlier as part of right reasoning in mutual recognition among selves engaged in the task of making their own history, personally and communally. We included in this necessity to take counsel selves from every walk of life in a community or a nation, subjects as well as rulers, juniors as well as elders, laborers as well as entrepreneurs, and whoever else is involved in the initiative of the community in a truly democratic spirit, presuming that all have a rational interest in pursuing their communal good. Everyone's word should be heard in the dialogue that moves the cultural action of a community forward.

We did not, however, include the enormous baggage of principles and determinations that accumulate in the external structures of communities and that they must carry with them in taking counsel. These many particular principles and determinations, as we have seen, are derived from principles on which cooperation and interaction are grounded in a community, the first of which is to aim at the communal good, as resulting in conclusions from experience and in decisions taken freely in the course of a community's history. They are established residues, so to speak, from past experience, but residues arrived at rationally that can shed some light on future experiences for those who are still only beginning their journey. They are the leaders from the past who have become authorities in lawful social structures or principles pointing the way to a better future. In other words, by reason of the rationality expressed in them, as they stand and give stability to the community, they remain always as part of what those in a historical community must take counsel with.

This is a long way of saying that, in deliberation at any given moment, selves in a community must take counsel not only with other selves but also with conclusions, principles, and determinations arrived at by their historical forbears and predecessors. This is not to be done as a matter of strict adherence to the conclusions and determinations of the past in the way conservatives often think about legacies from the past. We are referring to principles and determinations that have to be flexible and open to new ways of doing things, as we have seen, and as those in deliberation always have to see when they come to new initiatives of their own in a communion with other selves. Neither is deliberation over what is to be done to be conducted without any due consideration of what has been done and learned in the past, as libertarians would have it frequently, as if they were not selves with a past in communion with others selves. Without mutual recognition with others in the past, they would not be the selves they have become, able to deliberate about their future. In the moment of deliberation and practical reasoning for future action, all of our presuppositions—those from the past as well as those of the moment—have to be brought into question in the light of a community's good as such, always the first principle of conscientious practical reasoning.

As the members of a community take counsel with the law in deliberative decision making, they must not think only of abiding by the law and the authorities who have promulgated it as something given and fixed once and for all. Many laws are written for particular situations in the history of a community, often to serve the particular interests of one class or another, not that of the community as a whole. It is the responsibility of rational decision-makers to ask not only what should be done in ever-changing new social circumstances but also whether the standing authority and law is still relevant to the historical situation of the community and whether it is really serving the communal good rather than that of a ruling class or a tyrant. In other words, decisions have to be made about authority and law itself as well as about actions necessary for the good of human beings.

This implies that laws themselves, and the authorities that promulgate them, have to be tested to see if they still apply in the cases to be decided, as in courts that have to decide about punishments that may or may not fit the crime or in cases of action that were not envisioned clearly by the original lawmakers, or to see if they are truly conducive to the communal good and not just to the particular good of some individual or class. Human action is always about particulars, and human laws always have to come down to particulars in their articulations and determinations. As law goes from its more universal and necessary principles to more particular spheres of human activity, it becomes less certain as law and less clearly applicable to different kinds of action being contemplated, which means that particular laws become matter for deliberation themselves along with the action under deliberation. Changes in the directions of one's action might require changes in the law for future action, which no responsible rational agent should take lightly as long as law remains a necessary means to promote the communal good even in a progressive society.

The necessity to decide about law itself as well as the action it is supposed to guide also implies that the lawmakers themselves test themselves as lawmakers, whether in the community as a whole or as individuals playing lawful leadership roles, to see if they are truly fulfilling the purpose of law, which is always and everywhere to promote the communal good. This is a problem arising from the very first principle of ethical reasoning, which can never be completely resolved at any historical moment for a community. Lawmakers, even when they are recognized as having the communal good at heart, never have just that interest at heart. They also have other particular interests for themselves as individuals or for particular classes of society or even for particular political parties. And the question always has to arise for rational decision-makers as to which one of those interests actually prevailed in the enactment by an individual, a class, or even the majority in a democratic society that need not be in keeping with the universal interest of the community as a whole.

Hegel speaks of the acting consciousness or conscience (*Gewissen*) as secretly working for its own good and not that of the community, but also as confessing its sin before the community in the expectation that the judging consciousness or conscience will also recognize its own particularity and confess its own sin, as lawmaker, also acting only for itself and not for the good of the community.[1] This confrontation of the acting and the judging consciousness in a communal conscience for Hegel yields a dialectic of sin and forgiveness in mutual recognition that results in what he calls religion or religious self-consciousness. For our discussion, it brings us back to the necessity of always examining our particular conscience and what it recognizes as laws, to see whether these are in fact focused on the communal good and social justice and whether there might not be other laws in conscience and other authorities that might better serve our future communal good in human interaction.

We have seen that there is an obligation in conscience to take existing laws into consideration in deliberating over what action to take as members of a community inasmuch as law is conceived as a necessary means for keeping the community

1 Confer the last part of the section on morality in the long chapter on spirit in Hegel's *The Phenomenology of Spirit*, which concludes with the dialectic of two consciences, one that confesses its sin and the other that does not, as it condemns the other for its sin, the confessing consciousness and the judging consciousness, leading thereby to the human spirit as religious.

constant in its orientation to the communal good and social justice. This does not mean, however, that we have to accept them at their face value regardless of whether or not they are in fact conducive to the communal good and social justice. We have to examine not just what they say but also whether they do in fact serve the communal good and social justice and how they do so, if they do. This comes from being rationally responsible subjects in communion with others. Not all enactments of lawmakers in a society meet the stipulation about serving the communal good in the definition of law. Some, if not many, may be so ill conceived that they go against the communal good at the expense of large segments of society who are unjustly excluded, disadvantaged, or marginalized because of the special interests the enactments actually serve, often because of lobbyists twisting the language of a statute so that it serves only a particular good and not the communal good.

We do not have to go into all the ways that the corruption of true law can take place or has taken place in modern society, national and international, in this reflection on how law is supposed to function ethically or in conscience. We have only to see how in conscientious deliberation as rationally social agents individual selves cannot simply set the question of law aside, as if they had nothing to do with it or it had nothing to do with their good or that of others. The question of law is intricately woven into the conscience of every rational member of a community and must be dealt with along with every other issue in decision making. Society cannot be changed for the better without changing its laws for the better. Such changes in the law may begin simply as *conscientious objection* to existing laws for reasons recognized as good by the community, but they inevitably take the form of *revolution* against some given laws and the authorities that enforce them, by war, coup d'état, or some electoral process whereby new authorities are chosen with a different set of laws and policies in mind. In any case, an old regime of laws is set aside and a new one is put in place that hopefully will better serve the communal good and social justice, all because authority and law are important factors in the communal good of communities. This is why war and politics are never just games we play or contests to see who will come out on top, as they are often reported in the news media. They are also matters of conscience in which the good of communities is at stake, as they seek better ways of promoting a communal good and social justice for themselves and for all communities of selves in world history.

The conscience that binds members of a community together as one spirit in mutual recognition does not require only that they are in conformity with the law, no matter what it says or what purpose it serves, which may be enslaving rather than liberating. To be sure, there has to be a presumption in favor of the law in rational deliberation, but that can go only so far. Law and order as determined in the past are not the final good of any community. Nor can that good be defined purely in terms of law and order since law and order are only means to that good, not the good itself. When a particular form of law and order is found to be wanting in this regard or to be exclusive of too many selves with regard to the communal good or social justice, conscience requires some kind of revolution to bring them into line with the purpose they are supposed to serve. This may be recognized by those in authority, but it is more often recognized by those who have been excluded or marginalized by the powers that be, as in colonialism, segregation, or apartheid.

Conscientious revolution in a community usually begins from the side of those who have been left out of the planning, neglected, or excluded unjustly from the benefits of communal life—the oppressed as they are often spoken of in the third world. In particularly harsh circumstances of violence, as in colonialism, it often begins as sheer violence directed at the violence of the oppressor, as Frantz Fanon brings out at the beginning of his account of how revolution takes place in *The Wretched of the Earth*. But it does not end there, even for conscientious advocates of violent revolution like Fanon, Mandela, or Malcolm X. What they see happening in the initial act of violence is the revival of a communal spirit that had been lost or destroyed under colonial oppression. The action, deliberately taken, becomes the occasion for recognizing others taking the same kind of action, against an oppressive system of law and order, and for entering into communication with one another in an effort to restore a community life of their own through dialogue and mutual recognition.

This second side or second phase of a violent revolution that is conscientious is not always seen for what it is—the beginning of a new communal spirit that has to restore or develop for the first time its social structure of authority and law independently of the old oppressive colonial structures; a new nation, for example, in control of its own resources and of how it will use them for the benefit of its citizens. There are many different ways in which this can be done, but it will serve the good of the entire community only if all members of the community are brought into the dialogue and all are willing to exercise their human rights at the same time as they recognize the rights of others in some kind of dialogue.

That is what revolutionary leaders like Gandhi and Mandela advocated as uppermost in their revolutionary movements. They were struggling for a higher communal spirit even among their own adherents, let alone those they were opposed to. Before any action was taken, they were intent on forming the conscience of their own followers or on raising their consciousness to a higher communal level inclusive of all, including the oppressors as well as those who were most oppressed, like the untouchables or the totally marginalized. They did not start with violence of any kind, but they did resist in the name of the communal good against laws and authorities that were not serving that good or preventing it altogether from taking shape in any social structure. And even when they did resort to some violent or military means, as in the case of Mandela, it was only to bring the standing authorities to their senses about the gravity of the situation and the necessity to renegotiate older agreements. There was always the hope for them that the standing authorities would give up their opposition to new proposals and laws to guide action and interaction in the newly emerging community, something legitimate authorities should always be willing to entertain in a community.

Revolution should never be undertaken lightly in any community, given the importance of law for maintaining equilibrium for that community. Nevertheless, it should come as no surprise in a society teeming with actions and interaction of every kind in all sorts of conglomerations. That is why in modern democratic nations we schedule elections to take place on a regular basis, to allow for revolutions when they are needed or when too many things have gone wrong with the law and the policy of standing administrations and lawmakers. Whether something or anything better always comes from elections is, of course, very dubious. Not all the voters take the time or make the effort to get a well-informed view of the issues or assess them conscientiously, much less have a dialogue about them as members of a community, which itself hardly ever results in much unanimity. But it is a matter of conscience for all responsible agents or activists in a community to join the dialogue that ultimately leads to setting policies and laws of one community or communities, familial, national, and international. That entails much more than a simple obligation to vote mutely in the secrecy of a booth, especially if we are simply giving in to emotions unregulated by reason in the light of the communal good.

10

The Necessity of Courage and Temperance as Dispositions in the Sense Appetites of Ethical Consciousness for a Rational Participation in the Communal Good

Virtues are an integral part of ethical consciousness as oriented toward a communal good for rational selves in search of their own second perfection in communion with other selves. They are not given by nature as are the powers that give rise to such endeavors in fully constituted human beings. They are acquired by repeated actions motivated by these powers, such as intelligence and will, and regulated by reason in view of some good that is at once communal and personal. That is how selves rise to their own second perfection and come to their own ultimate good as dictated by reason and by nature.

We have seen how two cardinal virtues come into play in the pursuit of this ulterior perfection by rational selves, each one perfecting a distinct power of the spiritual soul, namely prudence (perfecting practical intelligence for what is required for the communal good) and friendship with justice (perfecting the will in its communicative interaction with other selves). But as essential and crucial as these two may be for ethical consciousness, there is more to the powers of the soul. Those powers, which we refer to as passions or emotions, must be taken into consideration by a science that purports to be about the whole of ethical consciousness of the rational animal.

Unlike what the Stoics or Immanuel Kant thought, these lower powers of the human soul are not opposed to the rational powers of intelligence and will in the human being, nor are they extrinsic to the moral intention of ethical conscience as such. As integral to how the human being is constituted in its ethical consciousness as both body and soul, they must be regulated by reason in view of the total good of ethical consciousness, and they add a dimension of their own to the quality of the second perfection or the communal good for the rational animal. They are part of what counts for human happiness when regulated by right reasoning. Human intelligence and will cannot add to their own second perfection in ethical consciousness without somehow elevating passions and emotions to something rational in ethical self-consciousness itself. And this is where two more cardinal virtues come into the scope of ethical consciousness in ethical self-consciousness, that of *courage* or fortitude and that of *temperance*, to bring the complex of passions and emotions churning in reflective self-consciousness into line with the personal as well as the communal good of selves.

There are many and diverse passions and emotions at work in the development of human beings as rational animals. These passions and emotions, or however else one might wish to characterize them, are principles of action and reaction to other selves and to the external world of objects in human experience. We shall speak of them as *emotions* generally that are stirred up in our consciousness by what we experience of the world and other selves. They are sense appetites in response to sense perceptions of one kind or another as well as feelings of attraction or repulsion with regard to a wide range of objects that present themselves for our consideration and that give rise to reasons for taking action to perfect ourselves further or to find satisfaction for our appetites.

Much indeed has been written of these sense emotions and appetites over the ages, and still more in our own times, in the particular sciences of psychology and phenomenology, including how they are associated with and influenced by neurological conditions in our body, but we shall not go into much of that here. We shall take it all as a matter of fact in our nature, not as pure spirits by any means, but as self-conscious rational animals who have to work their way through this huge baggage of emotions and appetites to find the good that will satisfy their rational appetite reasonably and responsibly in communion with other rational selves. The question will be to examine not only how reason and free will, as rational appetite, emerge from this contentious and interlocking plurality of emotions and appetites, each with its own absolute object, so to speak, but also how much intelligence and free will contend with all of them in the search for a cosmic cultural good.

It is interesting to note in passing that just as our theoretical science of selfhood presupposed a certain plurality of particular sciences, opening the way to our intersubjective science of selfhood as a whole, so also our practical science of selfhood leaves us with a certain necessity as rational animals to go into particular virtues of all sorts pertaining to two kinds of sense appetites and emotions:. one having to do with goods we simply desire as good for our selves, animal as well as rational or spiritual, and the other having to do with goods difficult to maintain or even to attain as good in our historical circumstances, whence the necessity for two more capital virtues pertaining to the sense appetites and the emotions to complement the capital virtues of prudence and justice: those of *temperance* with regard to good we simply desire and those of *courage* with regard to the goods difficult to maintain or to attain in keeping with Aristotle's distinction between the two kinds of sense appetite and the two corresponding capital virtues of temperance and courage.

We shall not elaborate on any of the particular virtues that come under the capital virtues of temperance and courage, which require particular knowledge of particular conditions of selves in right reasoning in view of the communal good as well as of the personal good of the particular selves, as Thomas Aquinas does in the two volumes of Part II of *Summa Theologiae*. We shall refer to these particular virtues generally as they enter into the realm of conscientious behavior. But we shall show the necessity of such virtues in the sense appetites and in the emotions for a soul or a spirit that is still animal in the process of right reasoning and of deliberation prior to taking action as a self in the world.

10.1 THE PLURALITY OF PARTICULAR SENSE APPETITES IN TENSION WITH REASON AND THE WILL IN THE RATIONAL SOUL

There are many sense appetites that come into our consciousness and our conscience in the course of our decision making as rational animals, some directly from the nature given to us as individuals and some mediated by various aspects of culture in our communion with other selves. They are a necessary part of our lives, for it is from them that incentives to take action for our own good come to the fore in our consciousness.

There is no need to sort them all out here or to figure out where they come from in the archaeology of the subject as it relates to the world. Wherever they come from or however they find their way into our consciousness as desires and sense appetites, we have to recognize their presence there, in our consciousness, along with the object of their desires, for as impulses in a consciousness they are merely blind drives and impulses without any projection of some object that would satisfy them. It is only in a rational consciousness that they take the shape of objective goods to be striven for or as motives for taking action of one kind or another.

We must not only recognize that there are normally many such emotions and appetites in each rational consciousness, each with its own object as a motive for taking some particular action. We must also understand that they are in contention with one another to be actuated at any moment of the living consciousness, ready to go forward in its life toward its second perfection. Not all are equally relevant to that ultimate good, but they are all brought to a halt, at least momentarily, in the moment of deliberation by consciousness by the universal or comprehensive power of reason, which contains them all, as a responsible self-consciousness intent on a good that is both communal and personal.

Not all of these emotions or passions can be activated equally at once, nor should they be at any given moment of responsible self-consciousness. This is where the power of free choice in the rational appetite comes into play and has to intervene to determine which of the many contentious sense appetites will be activated and which will be set aside according to right reasoning concerning the sense appetites as well as the rational appetite in its orientation toward the communal and personal good. The sense appetites are not in contention with the rational appetite, nor are they left extrinsic to the moral good of the rational appetite, nor to the goodness of justice and friendship as willed by free choice. They become moral by reason of the choices we make in keeping with justice and friendship or immoral by reason of bad choices we make, not just with regard to other selves but with regard to ourselves. They are part and parcel of one and the same ethical consciousness we all share as rational animals, which is why there has to be right reasoning concerning our emotions as well as our social or communal relations, for the rational soul is the principle not just of reasoning regarding the communal good but also regarding our sense appetites as animals seeking ethically to become ever more good rationally.

Hence the necessity of inquiring further into the necessity of virtue as a properly ethical perfection in the sense appetites of the human soul or of making our sense appetites rational analogously in their own domain as sense appetites.

10.2 THE REGULATION OF SENSE APPETITES IN THE RATIONAL ANIMAL THROUGH REASON AND FREE WILL

We should note first that most of what we have said about virtue in ethical self-consciousness so far has had to do with the *spiritual* powers of the soul, reason and will. Sense perception and sense appetites are not spiritual powers as such; they are powers of the composite soul and body, or more precisely powers of the soul as form of its body. That is why moralists such as Kant and other idealist philosophers tend to leave them out of consideration in talking about pure practical reason, relating only to some absolute good in the abstract and not to the particular goods that may present themselves for particular emotions to seek. Such emotions are plentiful not only in any human consciousness, each one seeking its own objective fulfilment and each one in contention with the other emotions in one and the same consciousness, as we have already observed in describing this complexity of sense appetites in the rational consciousness.

Such complexity and such contentiousness are not found in the same degree in other lower animals, who are also moved by sense appetites. For the rational animal it comes from the power of reason, which besides its power to bring any sense appetite to a halt also has the power to conceive higher objects to satisfy appetites, such as the appetite for warmth in a cold climate or the appetite for beauty in a dull setting, and the power to conceive higher or better ways to satisfy tastes in these appetites. All this adds to the complexity and to the contentiousness of sense appetites that we do not find in lower animals. And it brings us to the problem of free choice in satisfying our human sense appetites, for no single free choice of one appetite over all the others can satisfy the complexity of the emotions or sense appetites of a fully vested rational animal.

With the problem of free choice regarding our emotions there also comes the problem of regulation of these appetites: which one or ones to go with and which to push back; which ones to go with first, here and now, and which to put off until later; and so on in setting a plan of life for ourselves, not absolutely at any given moment but rationally open to the richness of life itself or the life of the spirit. The key thing is not so much to suppress emotions, though that may be necessary for some in certain circumstances, but, rather, to regulate them according to an order set for them by reason.

Regulation of emotions according to reason is a key factor in any exercise of free choice. In fact, that is where the regulation of the emotions begins for the rational animal. We do not exercise free choice except with regard to emotions or drives that arise through and from our sense appetites with regard to objects or objectives that we understand to be desirable to one or more of our appetites. Thanks to the power of reason, which brings all these drives to a halt in moments of deliberation, we become free to choose in our consciousness which of these emotions will specify the action that we take as a result of our choice. There is no other way of exercising free choice for us. But choosing some emotions to act on also entails suppressing the emotions and drives in our consciousness that were in contention with the chosen ones, or at least bringing them around to allow or to support those chosen. This is what we call disciplining ourselves or learning to discipline ourselves so as to act in accordance with what we have freely chosen.

In the rational animal it is for reason and the will to regulate the sense appetites, something that nonrational animals cannot do and do not have to do since they are lacking in intelligence and free will. Regulation in nonrational animals comes from their nature as animals and from circumstances of the habitat required for their survival. But there is more to the regulation of the sense appetites in the consciousness of selves who are not only free but also called to higher forms of goodness and satisfaction than nonrational animals.

For the rational animal there is no way of exercising its spiritual powers of intelligence and free will with regard to their proper end and good as communal except with reference to our sense powers and to our sense appetites. We saw this in the twofold act of intelligence and the twofold act of the free will in our theory of selfhood with reference to sense perception and to the sense appetites. What we have to see now with regard to the practice of selfhood is the same kind of reference to sense appetites in the twofold act of the will as having to choose from a plurality of sense appetites in order to arrive at its own act of self-determination in the communal good.

Pure spirits, on the other hand, do not have to go through such complicated calculations in exercising their own intelligence and will. But as a composite of form and matter and as a substantial union of body and soul, the human self has to work and find its way to its true good through its spiritual labor of learning and discerning prudently what to do in taking action toward its second perfection in the communal good.

In doing all this, however, the human self does not find its material components as totally foreign to its spiritual and ethical constitution, nor to its spiritual components as separate from its sense appetites. The good it is concerned about is not merely pleasure in the sense appetites or utility in reshaping the world for some positive achievement of body and soul. It is the good as spiritualized in intelligence and will in communication with the sense powers and sense appetites of one and the same soul as in the animal specified as rational.

Reason is a spiritual power in the rational animal. As such it is in command of the sense appetites as well as the rational appetite. It is universal as a power encompassing all the particular powers of the rational animal that we have been referring to as particular sense appetites. It may not seem so in the early stages of a young life, when particular emotions or sense appetites seem more prevalent in regulating human conduct. But as reason and free will mature and assert themselves more in the conduct of human activity, and as the *virtues of right reasoning and justice*, not to mention *friendship*, develop in one's conscience and in one's sense of responsibility toward the communal good, we come to see the need for virtues in the sense powers and the sense appetites as part of the good for a truly ethical human life.

As right reasoning develops in the power of intelligence and in taking counsel, we begin to see the necessity of particular virtues for the particular sense powers and sense appetites of the rational composite. From the universal sense of right reasoning and justice, we go on, by analogy, to more particular virtues in the emotions themselves and in the diverse specific sense appetites that we can discern. The importance of doing so can be seen in the fact that some particular emotions or appetites in a self can be so overpowering or defused at times that they do not allow for right reasoning or for the good of justice and friendship to take shape.

We should also note that the mere fact of being ordered to the higher powers of reason and will in the rational self-consciousness adds a much broader scope to the sense powers and the sense appetites that is not found in the lower, nonrational animals, even though some of those lower animals may have much keener sense powers and sense appetites than the rational animal. This broader scope of the sense powers and appetites in the rational animal not only adds a lot more to what they can see or sense of the world in which they find themselves that lower animals do not see, smell, or sense but also entails a greater need for regulation that nature alone cannot meet and that only reasoning and willing can provide, whence comes a greater need for right reasoning and for taking counsel with other selves in justice and friendship. With the greater possibility for aberration there comes a greater necessity for responsible regulation in view of the communal good as the final end for selves.

10.3 DISTINGUISHING BETWEEN GOOD AND EVIL IN THE SENSE APPETITES

Good and evil are analogous terms relating to appetites, which are themselves analogous when we think of them as either sense appetites or the rational appetite in the rational animal. The distinction between sense appetites and the rational appetite in a reflective self-consciousness calls for some careful thinking in conceiving the good for the reflective self-consciousness. There is the good we have already spoken about in relation to the will as rational appetite, a good that is communal as well as properly personal and irreducible to any particular good relating to a particular sense appetite. Then there is the good we have touched on in relation to the sense appetites, a good that is always particular, relative to a particular sense appetite in an individual self-consciousness.

Such goods relating to particular sense appetites are real goods that sense appetites can find satisfaction in, but they are not of the same order as the *good* to which the rational appetite relates. They are good relative to a particular appetite, such as health, which is the good of a particular organ or a whole animal seeking to survive. Such goods relating to particular sense appetites might come into play in the deliberation of rational animals regarding how they will pursue their own good as personal and communal, but of themselves they are neither good nor bad ethically or morally, except as relating to the ethical good of reason and free will. They are only factors to be considered in taking counsel before choosing a course of action. They become ethically good or ethically evil in being chosen or rejected as steps to be taken toward the ethical good that is both communal and personal. They must be chosen or rejected, in whole or in part, responsibly and conscientiously, to add to the good of ethical self-consciousness. Short of that they remain merely acts of an animal intent only on survival, whether of an individual or of a species. What makes them good or evil ethically is how they affect the communal and personal good we are aiming at in the general virtues of prudence and justice.

Thus, some discernment has to take place as to what action is to be taken on the part of living things with regard to survival as a good for individuals and for the diversity of species, whatever sense appetites they might have. This discernment takes place without rational deliberation in lower animals and lesser living things. Without it there would be no survival even of the fittest. But for the rational animal the discernment takes place explicitly in its reflective self-consciousness, not just in the isolation regarding the personal good of individuals but also in the customs regarding the communal good of those same individuals in consort or in communion with one another. Hence the importance of learning from our elders what will lead to that communal good in a culture and what will not and deprive us of that good. From all of this we come to know what is good about our emotions and sense appetites and what is evil about them that can deprive us, not just of our ultimate good as rational animals, but even of pleasure and of utility for life itself.

We are not all born with the discernment we need as free agents seeking to attain the good we want as spiritual creatures, nor with a one-track sense appetite aiming at some particular good. We literally find ourselves as selves, in moments of deliberation as free agents, having to choose from a plurality of emotions so that we can proceed with one or two of them at a given time while repressing the others or even suppressing them if we find that they will deprive us of our true good as rational creatures.

We have no direct control over which emotions will move us at any given time. They come and go in our consciousness, each with a determinate object as their end. They are blind forces in our natural makeup that come into our consciousness, prior to any choice on our part, and get represented as objects to be striven for, always with many of them at the same time in one and the same consciousness and, as we have said already, in contention with one another for fulfilment. One motive alone in a rational consciousness is not a motive: it is a fixation, as Maurice Blondel says, or an addiction that obfuscates the possibility of free choice.

We are not free about having emotions or about which ones we may have or feel. Each emotion represents a determinism of its own that finds its way into our consciousness. Without a plurality of them we would not be free—that is, to choose which one or ones to which we will consent. But conversely, given a plurality of emotions to choose from, we do have to choose freely which one or ones we shall consent to and amplify with the power of our rational appetite or our free will as something original with any reflective self-consciousness, something it is responsible for as either good or evil within the communal good of any culture, presupposing always some mutual recognition among selves in any culture no matter how advanced or primitive the culture might be.

We thus are led to the question of how human emotions come to be integrated into the exercise of free will as either good or evil ethically in conjunction with the two capital virtues of right reasoning and of justice we have already singled out in relation to the two spiritual powers of intelligence and free will. How can there be ethical virtue in the sense powers and emotions, and how does such virtue come to be viewed as necessary for the personal and communal good of selves in the historical order of cultures?

10.4 THE INTEGRATION OF THE SENSE APPETITES AND REASON INTO ONE ANOTHER AS PART OF RIGHT REASONING FOR FREE AGENTS

Human emotions have long been a subject of great interest in the study of human or rational consciousness, not just with regard to how they affect human behavior but also with regard to their origin in the human composite of matter and form. How do they come to be together in human subjectivity as rational but with such a great diversity both physically and neurologically as well as psychologically? And how do they affect not just the mood of so many consciousnesses but also the very behavior human subjects? We have maintained a power of free choice for human subjects in the face of so many and such diverse emotions as a result of determinism in our soul as form of a composite. In fact, we have made it a point to say free choice itself in the will is contingent and necessary, given this plurality of motives for action of one kind or another at any moment of deliberation when we have to choose. Free choice does not depend on how strong or weak a motive might be in comparison to other motives also present in the same consciousness at the same moment of decision making. Some subjects have been known to choose to activate some weaker motive as their action just to prove to themselves and others that they were not determined by the strength of any particular motivation toward some immediate good. Determinism in the emotions is not eliminated in the exercise of free will or of the rational appetite. It is simply raised to a higher level of mediation in view of the communal as well as personal good envisaged in right reasoning. We do not choose the final good as such. We choose the way we shall take to that final good as suggested by some particular emotion or other at a moment of deliberation and taking counsel.

Emotions are not of themselves rational or irrational, good or evil, as given by nature. They are simply forces or powers in human consciousness that incline toward some object as a good that will satisfy some appetite. They are particular, with an object that is particular, one of many. Taken in isolation, each one is absolute with only a particular object at stake and originating in particular conditions that can be studied in particular sciences that are more theoretical and abstract than practical and concrete, as we have to be here in our reflection on the practice of selfhood. For in the practice of selfhood, human emotions are taken up into the realm of rationality just as reason descends into the realm of all the appetites that stir in the human spirit as influenced by both nature and external culture.

This means that in the exercise of free will, human emotions are not left in their state of pure nature, with some stronger than others at any given time and determining behavior in their favor against the weaker emotions. Emotions are elevated to a higher state of culture in the rational animal oriented toward a higher communal good, with justice and friendship as made known by right reasoning when conceived in taking counsel with other selves in mutual recognition.

It is not for us here to pursue in any detail the archaeology of how emotions and motivations come to take hold in our natural consciousness as animals. What we must examine is how the combination of our natural inclinations, given as a matter of fact and with right reasoning, takes place and how this combination entails an ethical and rational value to what would otherwise remain a matter of purely natural determinism emanating from dominant motives and inclinations, as in nonrational animals.

As subject to reasoning, emotions and passions are susceptible to becoming virtues or vices in the moral order of reasoning. To see more clearly how this integration of the sense appetites into the moral realm of reason takes place, let us reflect more carefully on what takes place rationally in the moment of deliberation and taking counsel prior to taking action of one's own. Many motives for taking action present themselves in one and the same consciousness at one and the same time. All are brought to a halt momentarily to see how and why one might be more conducive to the rational good envisioned as the final end for a person or a community. This could include taking one action rather than another or taking no action whatsoever and settling for the good already in hand, which might not be so good after all. Even settling for a good already at hand would count as taking action since it would still be a choice for a particular good at a time when we have to make a choice. It would also follow from a particular emotion out of an ardent desire or love for that good or out of a fear of losing or missing out on that goodness. Concomitant to a particular good would also be a suppression or a discipline of many other emotions, desires, or fears pressing one to take other actions or to overcome the fear of taking any action.

What the self becomes aware of in this moment of deliberation and taking counsel as the preliminary for taking action of one's own is the way in which reason and reasoning finds its way into the emotions as a regulator for taking action as a rational animal with conscience and responsibility for what it is about to do. There is no other way for the will or the rational appetite to come to the fore and exercise its power to take action, just as there is no other way for it to come to intelligence except with reference to phantasms taken from the same powers. Right reasoning in an ethical self-consciousness is not just about formal ideals of obligation in abstraction from emotions and sense appetites, as Kant and Stoics have maintained. It is about how such ideals apply for the emotions and sense appetites in matters of free choice to an ideal conceived as an end for human action and to the steps that have to be taken to attain that end, as well as to those to be avoided along the way. This is why virtue is not only a matter pertaining to intelligence and free will directly for the rational animal. It is a matter pertaining to the emotions and to the sense appetites as well.

The flip side of this interdependence between the rational appetite and the sense appetites, however, is also the possibility of undue influence and distortion in the process of right reasoning by pulling it in directions that are not in keeping with the communal good or the true good of a person. We see this in cases of addictions of all sorts, where the good is reduced to the satisfaction of only one emotion or sense appetite. We see it in cases of giving in to appetites that are not good for a person. We see it in cases of greed that do not allow for the justice and friendships that are essential to the communal good of conscientious and responsible agents in a community. In other words, it is not just reason that is taken as right in its conception of the communal and personal good but some particular emotion or sense appetite as well.

All this is an added reason for thinking of the necessity for truly moral virtue in the emotions and the sense appetites and not excluding them from the realm of morality altogether. Free choice in the rational appetite entails a power to manage our sense appetites and not to let any one of them dominate what we do, or avoid doing, in any action we take as human beings. But this power is not given by nature alone. It comes only with reasoning and taking counsel in one's self-consciousness, which is also not given by nature alone. It comes only with the practice of right reasoning as one matures in a community, in mutual recognition with other selves, in accordance with the good of that community. That is why young people are often thought of as lacking in moral sense in a community. They appear to be ruled too much by their emotions and not by reason, the supreme principle of virtue in human action. Right reasoning is not something given by nature. It is learned or acquired as a habit, as a disposition in our intelligence, to take action in view of a good to be attained as specified by reason in a community. But it is not learned or acquired without a consciousness of the necessity of another habit or disposition in our will in recognition of other selves already in communion with oneself and in collaboration toward a communal good, with the virtue of justice opening the way to the good of friendship.

It is in relation to these two virtues, prudence and justice, proper to intelligence and to free will, that the necessity of two more virtues or two more sets of virtues arises properly speaking for the emotions and the sense appetites of the rational animal, for their attunement to the good as conceived by intelligence and free will—virtues, that is—that will subordinate and regulate these lower appetites in accordance with the higher appetites of intelligence and free will. It is only with such virtues in the sense appetites that we can avoid the distortions of excess or deficiencies regarding the true good that can come from unregulated emotions and sense appetites.

It remains for us to examine how such virtues come to be in human subjectivity and what they add to the idea of a second perfection for selves in mutual recognition of one another.

10.5 THE PROBLEM OF DISCERNING WHAT IS MORALLY GOOD AND MORALLY EVIL IN ONE'S EMOTIONS RELATIVE TO A SECOND PERFECTION AS THE FINAL GOOD FOR HUMAN ACTION

We should begin by considering emotions and sense appetites for what they are as powers for taking action, as incentives to seek or to take hold of some object or other, each with its own particular satisfaction as determined by nature or by forces pressing in on them from the world at large. In the rational consciousness they have the aspect of something objective to which the self is attracted as well as something subjective in the consciousness of the one who has come to a moment of deliberation prior to taking action of one's own. As determined by nature it is neither good nor bad morally. Each is simply given in a determinate way as one of many in one and the same consciousness to be taken or to be set aside by free choice or perhaps to be held in suspense. Morality comes on the scene only with reasoning in deliberation and taking counsel in view of an end or a good that transcends any and all particular motives for action and calls for some particular action of one kind or another. Actions whose object promotes or is compatible with the true good are deemed morally good. Those actions whose object is something incompatible with the true good are deemed morally evil.

The question then is to ask in what sense can particular determinate acts be deemed morally good in relation to an end or an object that is transcendent, when there is only one transcendent end or object and there are many particular and diverse acts to be considered and to be taken toward that end. How can so many different acts emanating from so many different emotions and sense appetites all be judged as morally good or evil relative to one's final end or good without including a dimension of rationality in each of them, which makes right reasoning an *analogous* cause of all the particular and diverse virtues we find in the performance of particular emotions and sense appetites by the rational animal? Morality is not a univocal term that applies only to the rational functions of human intelligence. It is an analogous term that applies to all actions taken in the framework of prudence or right reasoning and of justice with friendship pertaining to a good that is communal and personal at the same time. There are no virtues in the emotions and sense appetites without this framework of virtues in human intelligence and the rational appetite. And conversely the framework of virtues in human intelligence and in the rational appetite does not and cannot function properly without some framework of virtues in the emotions and the sense appetites, as suggested earlier in relation to the integration of the two frameworks with one another.

This means that there has to be a development of virtues in the emotions and sense appetites concomitantly with the development of virtues in the rational appetite and vice versa. We have already seen how this development takes place in the rational appetite through deliberation and taking counsel in exercising free choice. How does it take place in the analogous realm of the sense appetites in human subjectivity?

10.6 HOW MORAL VIRTUE EMERGES IN THE EMOTIONS AND SENSE APPETITES AS A NECESSARY COMPLEMENT TO THE VIRTUES OF PRUDENCE AND JUSTICE IN INTELLIGENCE AND FREE WILL, AND HOW IT COMES TO BE DISTINGUISHED IN TWO CAPITAL VIRTUES, COURAGE AND TEMPERANCE, SUMMING UP ALL VIRTUES IN THE EMOTIONS OF SELVES IN A CULTURE

The question of virtue first comes to the fore in human consciousness at moments of deliberation and taking counsel in view of what good to pursue at such particular moments in consideration of a more universal and communal good. The idea of a universal and communal good, as mentioned earlier, might be dim at first, especially as pertaining to one's own second perfection, to be attained by our own rational initiative and our own particularly decided action. But the idea of a universal communal good comes at the origin of mutual recognition between selves, which is also the beginning of self-consciousness, and it matures gradually as one learns more about oneself and about the world of many selves.

Virtue is not something given by nature, as we have maintained already. The power to think and the power to choose are given by nature in a rational consciousness. But they have to be exercised to become conscious in our selves, and in being exercised they give rise to *habits*: good habits or virtues if they are conducive to a good for the species in nature and bad habits or vices if they deprive the animal of its specific good as an animal. Human beings develop such habits as well for their individual and specific good of surviving even as animals. These habits also come from nature for the rational animal, not to mention from *culture*, which also has its way of developing habits as if by nature but not without some intervention of reason and free choice in human action among selves.

Virtue must also be a habit, but it does not come from nature alone nor from external culture alone. It comes only from repeated acts in one's subjectivity that become dispositions to act always in view of the good as conceived in right reasoning for a rational appetite that is free. As a *virtue, right reasoning* comes to be as a disposition to reason rightly in whatever appetite or appetites may be driving a subject toward for its second perfection as a rational and sensible self. That is not given by nature. It is acquired by a repeated practice of deliberation and taking council in a community.

As a virtue, justice comes to be as a disposition to choose in view of the communal good as understood in intelligence, which alone is able to say whether an end is good for a particular self or for a community of selves. Dispositions of this kind, which are moral dispositions, do not come without repeated acts of openness to common interests with other selves. Nor do they happen in one single act, such as drawing up a constitution to be adhered to by a nation. Such a single act, though it is decisive for a community, has to be gone over repeatedly as the sociohistorical conditions change in a community, lest the society veer off into paths incompatible with the truly communal good and thereby betray their ideal of justice for all and friendship in class struggles of all kinds.

This in turn requires a development of virtues in the many emotions and sense appetites that intervene in human, action that is at once according to right reasoning and justice or friendship. Emotions and sense appetites, as they emerge from nature into individual human consciousnesses, are not ipso facto attuned to some universal or communal good as conceived by human intelligence in a framework of justice and friendship. They are purely from the nature of the individual animals that we are. There are many emotions and sense appetites that come to the fore at any given moment in the life of a rational animal, each with its own object and each with its degree of intensity in tending toward its object, all within one and the same consciousness and all contending with one another for immediate satisfaction, as we saw earlier in reflection on the moment of deliberation in the exercise of free choice.

These emotions and sense appetites are seen as predetermined for every individual self but not all equally. Some are stronger than others, and some weaker. Some may be so strong that they overpower all the others, leaving us with the impression of a one-track mind carried away by some passion or other. Some may be so weak that they disappear in the consciousness at the moment of deliberation so that if there were only one very strong overpowering emotion, the free agent would be determined to follow that one since some action has to be taken, even with the fear of taking any action whatsoever.

The condition of free choice for the free agent thus entails a plurality of emotions and sense appetites from which to choose. The rational power brings all of these emotions to a halt momentarily in order to deliberate about them and choose its own way from among them. This is where reasoning begins to emerge, first as a habit in accordance with its nature or as influenced by a culture. But then it acquires the habit or the virtue of right reasoning only by repeated acts in view of some ideal good, or else it becomes vicious by repeated acts of turning away from such ideal goods.

In all of this, reason and good will are not turning away from emotions and free will. They are working with them at every turn. When they choose to go with one emotion or a set of emotions as they must, they must choose against other emotions that are also in contention for satisfaction in the deliberative consciousness. This is the point where moral virtue is required to descend into the emotions and the natural appetites, even for the sake of right reasoning and justice or friendship.

For reasoning can be distorted by strong emotions and lose sight of the true good of the rational animal, as in the case of greed going against the communal good of justice in modern society. If we have an excessive desire for money, many other selves may be deprived of their fair share of wealth in modern society. Or if we have an excessive fear of selves different from our self, many may be marginalized from the communal good we take to be necessary for mutual recognition. There can be no right reasoning about how to get to the communal good in historical consciousness unless the emotions and sense appetites of reflective self-consciousness are brought into line with right reasoning and justice or friendship as virtues.

It remains for us to examine how this takes place in the exercise of free choice under the guidance of the more spiritual virtues of prudence and justice.

10.7 FINDING THE MEAN BETWEEN EXCESS AND DEFICIENCY IN THE FLOW OF EMOTIONS AND SENSE APPETITES AND DEVELOPING DISPOSITIONS COMPATIBLE WITH IDEALS OF JUSTICE AND FRIENDSHIP

Human emotions and sense appetites are not oriented by nature to anything like a communal good as we have found in terms of the rational appetite that follows from right reasoning. Each one is particular and ordered to some particular object that is for the good that will satisfy a particular emotion. Different sense appetites are identified by the different objects they are oriented to and desire. What is important for the rational animal is that there are always many appetites in one's consciousness, each vying with others for fulfillment, which sets up a necessity for free choice as to which must prevail for a self at a given moment of its existence.

The problem for free choice is thus to pick an emotion from a set of emotions, none of which is equal to the total good of a self. Moreover this is further complicated by the fact that the power of these emotions to come to action is never equal in all these emotions. Some can be very powerful to the point of overpowering all other emotions in one's consciousness, thus leaving little or no room for free choice. Others can be so weak that they hardly show in a consciousness or do not show at all, though they may be quite real for that consciousness. The fact is that every self has a plethora of emotions to contend with and every one of these emotions can fluctuate at different moments of one's life and has to be contended with in the exercise of deliberation and free will, no matter how weak or strong they might be at any given moment. Each one must be given its due without excess or deficiency at the service of the communal good.

Thus we come to the idea of a "happy medium" in right reasoning about the emotions. The idea is not to suppress emotions altogether or to exclude them from all moral reasoning. It is rather to find a way of including them as part of the rational or moral good for a community and of adding to the satisfaction of that good as a matter of *virtue*. For there is no communal or distributive justice in this world without individual justice where everyone in a community gets his due and some satisfaction of all one's emotional needs as a self.

Finding the happy medium in one's emotional life is not an easy task. It means acquiring virtues in the plethora of our emotions, many of which can be vicious by reason of excess or deficiency relative to the happy medium. Virtue comes only with repeated acts in the emotions, as well as in reason and free will—acts discerned in right reasoning—and in taking counsel with other selves as well as with the state of our emotions at a given time and in particular circumstances. There is no true communion of selves without some virtue of camaraderie in the emotions of its members. And that counts morally for the communal good as well as for the natural and historical good. A happy society at peace with itself is ethically better than one still struggling to find its good as a community of selves in the world.

Many distinct virtues have been identified for human emotions. Volumes have been written to list them all as ethically sound in contrast to vices of excess or of deficiency in the exercise of one's emotions. But two have been singled out on the level of emotions as cardinal virtues in addition to the two cardinal virtues of prudence and justice or friendship on the level of spirit, going all the way back to Aristotle, who was the first to propose this idea of four cardinal virtues. The reason for proposing this scheme for virtue in the emotions and sense appetites goes back to his analysis of the human emotions, where he distinguished between emotions having to do with a good that is difficult to attain and those relating to a good that is easy to attain. The good that is difficult to attain or maintain required *courage* on the part of the self. The good that is easy to attain or maintain requires only desire or love for that good, as Aristotle put it.

Emotions and sense appetites are determined for us by nature, as we have seen, and by external cultural factors. Each one has its own object as it appears in consciousness, which is the particular good for which it has an appetite. What is characteristic of human emotions is that there are always many of them that surge into human conscious at any given time and that together in one consciousness they are open to a broader, more universal good such as health and communal well-being through reason, which holds them in check in view of choosing the one or the combination that will be for the greater good of the selfhood. That is how human emotions enter into the realm of morality as good or evil or as more or less good and more or less evil, depending on how they meet the test of reason as it relates to the true good of selfhood, communal as well as personal.

No single free choice in one's life determines the true once and for all. But each one is a beginning for a new stage of life where the right emotions have to be promoted and put into practice by free choice of the rational appetite, and the wrong emotions—or those thought to be wrong—have to be disciplined or brought into line with those thought to be right. The moral self is never free of emotions, and that is why we must entertain the thought of virtue in the emotions and sense appetites for the self as rational animal, since human reason requires it in the very exercise of free will in the rational appetite for a good that is communal as well as personal.

We should note, however, that this extension of the notion of virtue and moral good into the realm of the sense appetites cannot be a simplistic application of a univocal concept, supposedly by something called pure reason, to the realm of emotions and sense appetites, much less a rejection of the entire realm of emotions as having nothing to do with reason or as contrary to reason. This would be to wipe out the entire realm of historical practices from the realm of morality. Human emotions and sense appetites include many and diverse specific differences that come into play in moments that require deliberation and free choice. Reason has to relate to all these differences as a matter of prudence in right reasoning in figuring which ones are for the true good of the self and which ones are not. This cannot happen if reason is taken as purely abstract and univocal, which would be applicable to only one specific difference of emotion and leave all the others out of consideration. Reason has to entertain a whole plurality of emotions and the differences between them relative to the true good of selfhood. In this sense it cannot be taken as a univocal cause of virtue in the sense appetites, but as Aquinas pointed out, it has to be taken as an *analogical cause* of the virtues in the appetites from the highest to the lowest, as long as they are conducive to the true communal and personal good of selfhood as seen in historical right reasoning.

The question for us then becomes: how do we proceed, in right reasoning, in determining right from wrong, good from bad, in so many and such diverse emotions and sense appetites? Concretely, this means determining not just what works and what does not work for some particular good in purely utilitarian fashion but also what is conducive to the more universal and true good of selfhood in oneself and in one's community.

Starting from the basic division we have already alluded to in the emotions, those that have to do with a good that is difficult to attain or to maintain and those that have to do with a good that one simply loves or needs, we can say that all or most are simply given by nature according to different degrees of intensity in one's consciousness and that they are all incentives or motives for action on the part of the self, possibilities that present themselves in a self's consciousness. The plurality and the diversity of such impulses makes free choice possible and necessary for every self. The practical and moral problem that presents itself then is which one, or which set, to follow in taking action, and how far to go with each chosen emotion in the light of reason and of the appetite for the true good of the self in communion with other selves, or for what we would call social justice.

Emotions as such and sense appetites as given by nature are not de facto oriented to a communal good or to the good of oneself as a whole. They are of themselves geared to some object that may or may not be good for a person or for a group as a whole, as viewed by reason. They can be classified in many different ways with respect to many objects that might or might not be truly good for a person, but it is for reason to say which are good or which are bad for the person or the community that harbors them. Moreover, the intensity with which these emotions, whether good or bad for the whole good of a self in communion with other selves, can vary immensely, not only within each individual self but even within each emotion in one and the same individual self at different times and under different circumstances. This is all part of the contention we spoke of earlier in relation to the moment of deliberation in self-consciousness that precedes free choice in the rational appetite and that makes free choice necessary as a step toward self-determination regarding the universal good of oneself and others.

The question for deliberation in the ethical sense then is to determine which of the objects presented by the sense appetites will be for the true good of the self as a whole and which will not be for that good. There is something good in every object of sense appetite that is not deceived by appearances, but even that sort of good can be bad for the good of the whole in self-determination, either absolutely, such as the good one would feel in killing another person or oneself, or relatively to the subjective conditions found in oneself when deliberating about what to do amid the plurality of emotions calling for some action in one's consciousness at one and the same time. We do not always act as deliberately as we should, but even when we give in to some emotion or other in our sense appetites, we must always repress or suppress other emotions also present in our consciousness. To choose freely, one course of action is always to discipline ourselves with regard to what other emotions in our consciousness might have called for, which is where the ethical formation of virtue begins to take place in our emotions and our sense appetites under the influence of right reasoning and communal justice.

Without right reasoning and communal justice, there could be no virtue in the sense appetites. There would be only an interplay of emotions that would settle into patterns enabling survival of different species as social wholes, each with a required habitat of its own. When reason and free will intervene in this animal interplay of emotions, they add a lot to it in scope, as we find in cultures of so many kinds. But they add also to the turmoil among them, promoting some and curbing others in ways that have to be regulated by reasoning in the process of deliberation prior to any exercise of free choice by the rational appetite in search of its own true good as rational and free.

Every emotion can have highs and lows. Some can be so high that they dominate all other emotions, as if they did not count as emotions. Some can be so low that they are left in the dark and out of consideration in any process of deliberation such that they never get attention. Some can be so strong subjectively that they affect the reasoning of a self so that the self cannot see or entertain the good or the necessity of other emotions for the good of oneself or of other selves, as when greed for money obscures or obliterates the requirements for what is due to others in justice and friendship. No one is given a perfect equilibrium of all one's emotions from the beginning by nature. That is something each self must struggle for within oneself. And that is why we need to develop virtues in our sense appetites in coordination with the virtues of right reasoning and justice in the rational appetite.

Virtues, as we have seen, are not given by nature or by any external cultural influences, even in the sense appetites. As dispositions for taking action they are developed by repeated acts taken deliberately to attain some good for oneself and for other selves that is a matter of both intention and achievement for selves as a whole. Nature and *habit* afford us some powers and dispositions for attaining goods of all kinds, but it is left to us as rational agents to choose which of these powers and dispositions to exercise and which to let go of and even resist to achieve our personal and communal good as we conceive it. We cannot simply ignore them as if they did not count for something as ethical and moral. In choosing freely what we will do or have to do, we have to choose from among our emotions or passions as well as how we shall adjust them so that they will serve the personal and communal good. We have to choose not just once but repeatedly so as to form our character in a way that is virtuous and not vicious in any way. For there is always the risk that some emotion or sense appetite will distract us or derail us either by excess or deficiency of what the rational order calls for in action. We know this in taking care of our health, and we have to learn the same discernment in taking care of our personal and communal moral good, whence the need for moral virtue in the emotions and the sense appetites.

10.8 THE CARDINAL VIRTUES OF COURAGE AND TEMPERANCE IN THE SENSE APPETITES

We could distinguish as many virtues in our sense powers as we can distinguish sense appetites or emotions in our consciousness. But we will not try to do this here. Instead we will reflect on the two cardinal virtues that have been distinguished in keeping with the two types of appetites that have long been distinguished by philosophers, ethicists, and in order to show how they become an integral part of ethical virtue as a whole by their extension of right reasoning and free willing into the sense appetites.

Two types of appetite have been distinguished on the basis of how they relate to their objective good, or the good that is their objective. First, there are the appetites that relate to their good as readily granted or as easy to obtain and to maintain and enjoy. These are the appetites that have been labeled as *concupiscible* in the many cultures that take sense appetites as desires distinct from one another as well as from the rational appetite. Then there are appetites that come into play when their objective good is difficult to attain or maintain or in danger of being lost. These are the ones that have been labeled *irascible* because they require something more aggressive to attain or maintain one's good in the face of adverse circumstances.

The point of the distinction is to indicate how some sense appetites or emotions follow spontaneously and necessarily from nature when their object or their good is presented to them in consciousness. These are the *concupiscible* appetites found in anyone who has a desire for life, for survival, for growth, and even for learning about others and about the world in which we live, all goods that are readily available to the senses and their satisfaction for the rational animal. Then there are sense appetites or emotions that come into play when a desired good is difficult to obtain or maintain once it is obtained and requires a special resolve on the part of the one desiring that good. These are called *irascible* appetites because of the element of anger (*ira* being Latin for anger) and irritation in them due to the need to struggle for attaining or maintaining what is the good for them or for the self.

It is from this sort of distinction in the sense appetites that we are led to the distinction between two capital virtues for the sense appetites: the virtue of *temperance* for the concupiscible appetites and the virtue of *courage* for the irascible appetites. But there is more to the derivation than meets the eye if we keep in mind that it takes reason to form virtue in the senses rather than just the senses without reason. The reason why this is so is that of themselves the sense appetites all have their own particular good with which they are concerned. Each one is on its own, as it were, and in contention with many others in one and the same consciousness. Some may be highly energized and others may be dormant. The energized ones may be excessive and the dormant ones may be deficient, with many in between, each and all of them representing some interest in a particular good for the self.

The purpose of reason in deliberation is not to eliminate from consideration the good of all sense appetites and emotions in self-consciousness in favor of some abstract good of pure reason in the rational appetite. It is rather to look for the goods and appetites that will advance the good of the whole and to guard against those that would deviate from that good, similar to a disease deviating from good health. This is what we call forming one's *conscience* in terms of what we do in this world with due regard for the good of other selves as well as one's own. It is also to discern as evil what would be excessive in some emotions and what would be deficient in other emotions with respect to the personal and communal good of the whole. It is to form the virtues that we need in our sense appetites to lead a good and happy life as selves in this world, by finding the happy medium between excess and deficiency in all our emotions and sense appetites in keeping with the virtues of right reasoning and justice that is friendly.

All of this development of virtues does not take place in an instant. It takes place over long periods of a lifetime as we become more and more deliberate in taking action while taking counsel with other rational selves, including lawmakers, and with the emotions and the sense appetites nature and external cultures have given us as dispositions to take certain actions and to avoid certain others. Gradually we learn what actions are good for us and for our community and what actions are not good for either one. And virtue comes to the fore by taking repeated actions of our own for the good while avoiding vicious action that can be either excessive of the happy medium or fall short of it as deficient, all of this coming after and following the exercise of right reasoning in mutual recognition with other selves, also forming virtues of their own in their self-consciousness, so that in the end we find ourselves ethically good as virtuous persons in communities or cultures that are ethically good as rational and just.

10.9 THE NECESSITY OF MANY PARTICULAR VIRTUES TO BALANCE THE SENSE APPETITES AS PART OF THE SECOND PERFECTION WE SEEK IN THE COMMUNAL GOOD OF OUR ETHICAL SELF-CONSCIOUSNESS IN THE DIVERSITY OF CULTURES

We shall not try to explore here all or any of the particular virtues necessary for selves to be able to enjoy their ethical good of selfhood. That is something for particular sciences of the practice of selfhood to do in keeping with particular emotions and sense appetites that are of special concern for different people, either because the emotions are exaggerated or lacking in temperance or because the emotions are stifled or lacking in courage. Such disorders in the emotions and sense appetites might be due to physical handicaps in individual selves, as neurologists and psychologists could say. But they also correspond to the spontaneous emergence of a great diversity of emotions and sense appetites, some very strong and others very weak. It is for right reasoning to regulate them in keeping with general justice and the communal good and to bring them into the realm of the ethical good in exercising free choice conscientiously and responsibly.

We have already seen how prudence and justice are general virtues encompassing many particular virtues, not just of prudence and justice including particular sciences but of all particular virtues, simply as virtues, whether in the self's intelligence and free will or in the emotions and sense appetites. Something similar can be said about temperance and courage. They are general virtues encompassing the two kinds of virtues called for in the emotions and sense appetites. That is why temperance and courage are listed as capital virtues along with prudence and justice. Ethical consciousness in selves does not try to take itself out of sense consciousness. It sinks itself into sense consciousness in exercising prudence and free choice by giving itself to one emotional option and enabling that emotion to shape its character. That is how rational ethical consciousness takes shape in the emotions and the sense appetites. There are many emotions to be brought in line with right reasoning and justice, some of them requiring much struggle and discipline to acquire as a particular virtue, not given by nature, while others come more easily or spontaneously for some individuals. In any case it should be understood that these particular virtues are not given by nature and must be acquired by repeated acts in the course of one's life no less than the more general virtues we call the cardinal virtues.

It should be further understood that we cannot acquire the more essential virtues of right reasoning and general justice without also acquiring certain particular virtues in the concupiscible and the irascible appetites that could derail us in our reasoning or in our sense of justice regarding the communal good. For example, in a very rich society such as ours in the United States, the desire for riches can be so great even among the richest, so excessive that it dulls the intelligence in reasoning to think only of making ever more money for oneself and for one's immediate associates and not for all those who labor for making that money. Reasoning for such people becomes greed that cuts itself off from the other section of society involved in making that money for the communal good. This is a case of distortion in reasoning lacking any concern for the majority of selves trying to make a decent living in a culture.

But there is more of this distortion that can also come from the side of the irascible appetites. It could be that one has reasoned rightly regarding the moral or ethical necessity to share the wealth accumulating in this or that culture with all who contribute to the culture but lacks the courage to do anything about changing the mode of operation and lends itself only to the greedy in control of operations. There is no inclination to broadcast the lack of right reasoning in the mode of operation that perpetuates injustice of the worst kind. Working toward a more just arrangement in the distribution of wealth in a culture is not an easy goal to attain.

But it will not happen unless we overcome the fear that keeps us from taking action, as activists are always prone to tell us.

Thus, just as we had to recognize the importance and the spiritual value of particular sciences regarding certain aspects of selfhood in human existence, both material and spiritual, at the beginning of our theory of selfhood, so also at the end of our philosophical consideration of the practice of selfhood we have to recognize the importance and the ethical value of particular virtues in the rational practice of selfhood in human historical existence. Ethical life in the historical order of cultures is not just a struggle to rise above all emotions or utilitarian aspirations to some realm of abstract so-called pure reason, as Kant would have it. It is rather a struggle to form virtues in our diverse sense appetites so that we may enjoy living within the constraints of right reasoning and of general or social justice in keeping with a second perfection of the communal good we are aiming at as selves.

This includes speculative sciences as habits or virtues of intelligence to be acquired in addition to practical sciences in the appetites, sense as well as rational, to be put into practice in whatever we undertake to make of ourselves in this world. It is something we undertake to accomplish even at a very young age, long before we explicitly realize it in our own reflective self-consciousness as we have tried to do here in our intersubjective philosophy of our human existence, something that goes on for the whole of our lives with the support of other selves, such as ourselves, who care about selfhood and selves until death.

Each living self has his or her own individual inclinations to contend with in right reasoning and in taking counsel with other selves, inclinations that must be brought into the pale of rational self-consciousness as virtuous dispositions through deliberate choice in keeping with right reasoning, inclinations that call for different kinds of adjustments, or a happy medium, at different stages of one's life in communion with other selves. It is not for a philosophy of human existence or the practice of selfhood to do this for anyone in particular. This is something for each self to do for oneself as different circumstances call for in one's culture or communal good with other selves. But it has to be done over time and in the changing circumstances of one's life if there is to be moral satisfaction or happiness in this worldly life. This is why we can say that virtue of every kind is not only part of a self's second perfection but also its own reward for acquiring the proper disposition of a rational self. To fail in acquiring virtues of all kinds in one's life is not just to be vicious in some respects but also to fail somehow as a rational spirit in its second or final perfection in this world, regardless of whether or not there is an afterlife.

CONCLUSION

This concludes our critical reflection on the theory and the practice of selfhood as selves in mutual recognition existing in both the natural order of substances and in the historical order of cultures or communities in this world and in this life. The good we find through mutual recognition in these communities may not be entirely satisfying to our intelligence and our will, but that becomes the subject for another inquiry about a transcendent good that surpasses the good of both nature and history or culture. It is a question of religion for selves in mutual recognition that calls for critical reflection of another kind, only indirectly related to the limited capacity of our intelligence and our will.

Index